Point-counterpoint

PO

Reac

Third

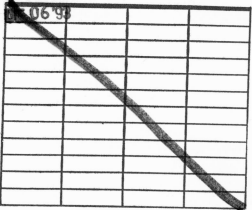

POINT-COUNTERPOINT

Readings in American Government

Third Edition

Herbert M. Levine

St. Martin's Press   New York

For Albert,
Louise, and
Philippe Boudreau

Editor: Larry Swanson
Project Editor: Beverly Hinton
Production Supervisor: Julie Toth
Text Design: Mary Beth Kilkelly/Levavi & Levavi
Cover Design: Darby Downey

Library of Congress Catalog Card Number: 88-60539

Manufactured in the United States of America.
32109
fedcba

For information, write:
St. Martin's Press, Inc.
175 Fifth Avenue
New York, NY 10010

ISBN: 0-312-00752-3

Acknowledgments

"The Constitution: Past and Present," by Thurgood Marshall. Speech at the Annual
Seminar of the San Francisco Patent and Trademark Law Association, Maui, Hawaii, May
6, 1987. Notes have been deleted.
"The Wisdom of the Framers," by William Bradford Reynolds. Speech at the Vanderbilt
University Reunion 1987 Celebration Luncheon, University Club, Nashville, Tennessee,
May 23, 1987.
"A Bicentennial Analysis of the American Political Structure," by the Committee on
the Constitutional System. *A Bicentennial Analysis of the American Political Structure:
Report and Recommendations of the Committee on the Constitutional System* (Washington, D.C.: Committee on the Constitutional System, 1987). Reprinted with the permission of the Committee. Requests for further reading should be addressed to the Committee at 1755 Massachusetts Avenue, NW, Washington, D.C. 20036 (Phone: 202/387-8787).

Acknowledgments and copyrights are continued at the back of the book on pages 371–
372, which constitute an extension of the copyright page.

Preface

The debate tradition in the United States is as old as the Republic itself. Soon after the colonists achieved independence from British rule, they debated issues as fundamental as slavery, tariffs, and the policy of the United States toward the French Revolution. Some debates in U.S. history—Lincoln-Douglas and Kennedy-Nixon—have become part of the national memory, even if misremembered or embellished.

It is with this tradition in mind that *Point-Counterpoint* has been developed. The text is a collection of readings that present contending sides of important issues in U.S. government. It is designed to contribute to a democratic tradition where vigorous controversy is regarded as both proper and desirable.

The selections deal with the basic structure of the U.S. political system, political participation, the power of government policy makers, and the direction of public policy. The format of the book encourages critical thinking. Part and chapter introductions provide important background information and a synopsis of the major points in each selection. For each debate question, one "Yes" response and one "No" response are given. "Questions for Discussion" follow each debate to help students formulate their own answers to the debate question. If both conflicting views on an issue seem convincing, students can then turn to the "Suggested Readings," which provide general background information as well as pro and con arguments.

Three cautionary points are in order. First, issues can rarely be broken down into a neat classification such as liberal or conservative. In this regard, it is often the case that some of the most meaningful controversy goes on among advocates of the same political philosophy.

Second, space limitations and the format of the book dictate that only two views—"Yes" and "No"—are given for each question. More often than not, other answers could be presented, such as "Yes, but . . . ," "No, but . . . ," or even "Maybe." In the process of debate, refinements can be developed. The yes-no approach, however, should provide a start toward understanding problems of U.S. government.

Third, the book does not present a single ideological perspective. As a whole, it does not take a side on every issue but presents, instead, many views. If there is one ideological commitment, however, it is implicit in the nature of the format: a commitment to vigorous debate as befits the democratic tradition.

I am indebted to the numerous people in the academic and publishing communities who helped me at various stages in the writing and production of this edition of *Point-Counterpoint*. The editorial consultants for the book offered superb suggestions and insights, including proposing different debate topics and making stylistic changes. Specifically, I want to acknowledge the consultants: Christopher Bosso, Northeastern University; David Burman, Arizona State University; Larry Elowitz, Georgia College; Osbin Ervin, Southern Illinois University at Carbondale; Michael Graham, San Francisco State University; Nancy Maveety, Tulane University; and Marion Tudor Moxley, El Camino College.

Four articles were written especially for this edition. The authors of these articles—Ryan J. Barilleaux, Clyde Brown, and Daniel P. Franklin—made important contributions to the book. I am appreciative of their professionalism, flexibility, attention to detail, adherence to deadlines, and good will. I thoroughly enjoyed working with each author.

I am indebted to Ann Hofstra Grogg, who copyedited the manuscript with meticulous attention to detail and with good judgment. The St. Martin's Press staff offered expert professional guidance, and I want to thank specifically Larry Swanson, the political science editor, and Beverly Hinton, the project editor.

Herbert M. Levine

Contents

Preface   v

PART I   Foundations of the United States Political System   **1**

Chapter 1   Has the Wisdom of the Framers of the Constitution in Promoting a "More Perfect Union" Been Overrated?   4

     YES   THURGOOD MARSHALL   The Constitution: Past and Present   5

     NO   WILLIAM BRADFORD REYNOLDS   The Wisdom of the Framers   9

Questions for Discussion   16
Suggested Readings   16

Chapter 2   Is the Separation of Powers Outmoded in the Twentieth Century?   17

     YES   COMMITTEE ON THE CONSTITUTIONAL SYSTEM   A Bicentennial Analysis of the American Political Structure   19

     NO   JAMES Q. WILSON   Does the Separation of Powers Still Work?   33

Questions for Discussion   48
Suggested Readings   48

Chapter 3   Should the National Government Turn Back Major Programs to the States and Localities to Strengthen Federalism?   50

     YES   ROBERT B. HAWKINS, JR.   Turnbacks: A Promising Approach   54

NO   JOSEPH P. RILEY, JR. Turnbacks: A
      Misguided Effort   58

Questions for Discussion   62
Suggested Readings   63

PART II   Popular Participation   **65**

Chapter 4   Is the United States a Racist Society?   69

YES   JUAN WILLIAMS Closed Doors: Benign
       Racism in America   70
NO   PHILIP PERLMUTTER Fallacies of Evaluation   75

Questions for Discussion   78
Suggested Readings   79

Chapter 5   Is the Feminist Movement in Decay?   80

YES   DINESH D'SOUZA, The New Feminist
       Revolt   82
NO   DOROTHY WICKENDEN, What NOW? The
       Women's Movement Looks beyond
       "Equality"   94

Questions for Discussion   103
Suggested Readings   104

Chapter 6   Do Voting and Elections Mean Anything?   105

YES   GERALD M. POMPER and SUSAN S.
       LEDERMAN, Elections and Democratic
       Politics   106
NO   HOWARD L. REITER, The Fallacy of Voting   121

Questions for Discussion   129
Suggested Readings   129

Chapter 7   Does Private Funding for Congressional
                Elections Give Undue Influence to
                Political Action Committees?   130

YES   MARK GREEN, The Case against Political
       Action Committees   132

NO JOSEPH J. FANELLI, The Case for Political
Action Committees   138

Questions for Discussion   142
Suggested Readings   143

Chapter 8 Will Political Parties Continue to Decline
in Importance?   144

YES WILLIAM CROTTY, A Concluding Note on
Political Parties and the Future   146
NO XANDRA KAYDEN and EDDIE MAYE,
JR., The Case for Resurgence   153

Questions for Discussion   158
Suggested Readings   158

Chapter 9 Do the Mass Media Have a Liberal Bias?   160

YES RICHARD A. SNYDER, Can We Trust the
Big Media?   161
NO MICHAEL MASSING, A Liberal Media Elite?   170

Questions for Discussion   173
Suggested Readings   174

PART III   Government Policy Makers   **175**

Chapter 10 Is the President Too Powerful in Foreign
Policy?   178

YES DANIEL P. FRANKLIN, Is the President
Too Powerful in Foreign Affairs?   181
NO RYAN J. BARILLEAUX, Seeing Presidential
Power Clearly   188
YES DANIEL P. FRANKLIN, Rejoinder   195
NO RYAN J. BARILLEAUX, Rejoinder   198

Questions for Discussion   199
Suggested Readings   200

Chapter 11 Should the Twenty-second Amendment
Limiting a President to Two Terms Be
Repealed?   201

YES ROBERT PREVIDI, Why Do We Limit the Democratic Process Only When It Comes to the Presidency? 202

NO WILLIAM PROXMIRE, Myth of the Day: Repeal of the Twenty-second Amendment Is a Good Idea 205

Questions for Discussion 207
Suggested Readings 207

Chapter 12 Does Congress Serve the Public Interest? 208

YES CLYDE BROWN, Congress, Politics and the Public Interest 209

NO RYAN J. BARILLEAUX, Congress and the Public Interest 216

Questions for Discussion 223
Suggested Readings 224

Chapter 13 Is the Bureaucracy Inefficient, Unnecessary, and Harmful? 225

YES MICHAEL NELSON, Bureaucracy: The Biggest Crisis of All 227

NO CHARLES T. GOODSELL, The Case for the Bureaucracy: A Brief 236

Questions for Discussion 240
Suggested Readings 240

Chapter 14 Should the Supreme Court Be Guided by a Philosophy of Judicial Activism? 242

YES LUTHER M. SWYGERT, In Defense of Judicial Activism 245

NO MALCOLM RICHARD WILKEY, Judicial Activism, Congressional Abdication, and the Need for Constitutional Reform 256

Questions for Discussion 270
Suggested Readings 270

PART IV Public Policy   **273**

Chapter 15 Should the Government Be Asked to
Solve the Social and Economic Problems
of Minorities?   275

  YES JOHN E. JACOB, The Government and
Social Problems   277
  NO GLENN C. LOURY, Internally Directed
Action for Black Community Development:
The Next Frontier for "The Movement"   285

Questions for Discussion   298
Suggested Readings   299

Chapter 16 Should the Death Penalty Be Abolished?   300

  YES COMMITTEE ON CIVIL RIGHTS OF THE
ASSOCIATION OF THE BAR OF THE CITY
OF NEW YORK, The Death Penalty   302
  NO EDWARD I. KOCH, Death and Justice   306

Questions for Discussion   311
Suggested Readings   311

Chapter 17 Should the Media Be Regulated in
Reporting Acts of Terrorism?   313

  YES EDWARD JAY EPSTEIN, Terrorism: What
Should We Do?   315
  NO BEN H. BAGDIKIAN, Terrorism and the
Media   317

Questions for Discussion   319
Suggested Readings   319

Chapter 18 Should the United States Engage in
Arms Control Negotiations with the
Soviet Union?   321

  YES MICHAEL MccGWIRE, Why the Soviets
Are Serious about Arms Control   324
  NO COLIN S. GRAY, Nuclear Delusions   334

Questions for Discussion   344
Suggested Readings   345

Chapter 19   Should U.S. Troops Withdraw from
                 Europe?   346

      YES   MELVYN KRAUSS, The U.S. and NATO:
            Should the Troops Stay?   348
      NO   JOSEF JOFFE, The U.S. and NATO: Should
            the Troops Stay?   352

Questions for Discussion   357
Suggested Readings   357

Chapter 20   Is It Wise for the United States to Use
                 Economic Sanctions Against South
                 Africa?   359

      YES   CHRISTOPHER J. DODD, The Case for
            Sanctions   361
      NO   MALCOLM WALLOP, The Case against
            Sanctions   364

Questions for Discussion   366
Suggested Readings   367

Contributors   368

Part I

Foundations of the

United States Political System

1. Has the Wisdom of the Framers of the Constitution in Promoting a "More Perfect Union" Been Overrated?

2. Is the Separation of Powers Outmoded in the Twentieth Century?

3. Should the National Government Turn Back Major Programs to the States and Localities to Strengthen Federalism?

I n 1987 the United States celebrated the two hundredth anniversary of the Constitution by drawing attention to the basic institutions and practices of the nation's political system. Political officials, leaders of private associations, and writers assessed anew the fundamental assumptions under which the U.S. political system was established; they examined how a system designed for a largely agrarian society consisting of thirteen eastern seaboard states had evolved over two centuries to meet the needs of a postindustrial society that spans a continent.

These observers often evaluated how well or how poorly the United States was living up to the ideals professed by the Framers of the Constitution. Whether positive or negative in their assessments, they focused on social, economic, and political institutions.

Those who looked favorably at the developments of the past two centuries often drew attention to a number of features: the rise in the nation's standard of living; the integration of groups from diverse ethnic, religious, and racial backgrounds into a "melting pot" in which these groups could live in peace; the resilience of the Constitution in adapting to change; the expansion of democratic practices to include ever larger numbers of people; the competition of political parties for electoral success; the freedoms accorded to U.S. citizens in expressing ideas, protesting peacefully, and responding to accusations in the criminal justice system; and the promotion of the common defense.

Those who were critical of the developments of the past two centuries pointed to different facts to justify their negative conclusions: the great disparity in income, in which less than 10 percent of the U.S. population controls 90 percent of the nation's wealth; the long history of discrimination against blacks, Hispanics, and native Americans; the use of the Constitution by the dominant economic institutions to prevent or delay social or economic change; the practical means used by government to prevent or slow down the participation of lower-income groups in the political process; the limitation of choice resulting from a two-party rather than a multiparty political system; the use by government of infiltration and disruption tactics to undermine groups holding unpopular ideas; the failure of the criminal justice system to give all defendants an equal chance regardless of income and background; and the use of military force and secret operations in influencing nations abroad, such as in Indochina in the 1960s and 1970s and in Nicaragua in the 1980s.

The views of contending sides assessing the U.S. political system raise the most fundamental issues underlying that system. This part considers three of these issues: the role of the Framers in creating a "more perfect Union"—and how perfect was and is that Union; the efficacy of the separation of powers; and the functioning of federalism.

Chapter 1

Has the Wisdom of the Framers of the Constitution in Promoting a "More Perfect Union" Been Overrated?

The Constitution establishes the ground rules governing the political system of the United States. What the Framers believed and how they acted at the Constitutional Convention at Philadelphia in 1787 raise questions about the effect these rules may have had on political behavior thereafter.

Historians disagree sharply about the Framers of the Constitution. Characterizations of delegates to the Constitutional Convention range from self-serving men of prominence seeking to promote the interests of their own economic class to pragmatic leaders encompassing profound differences of economic interest and political philosophy.

The basic facts about the Constitution, however, are generally accepted. The Articles of Confederation, presented in Congress in 1776 but not finally ratified by all the states until 1781, established a league of friendship among the states rather than a national government. The period under the Articles was marked by widespread debt, Shays' Rebellion (a revolt of poor Massachusetts farmers), economic decay, and an inability to negotiate commercial treaties. In 1786 a constitutional convention was called to revise the Articles; it met in Philadelphia from May through September 1787. Most of the delegates were young, politically experienced, financially comfortable, and afraid of the "mob." Although they shared some assumptions about government and society, they disagreed profoundly about what should and should not be included in the document they were drafting.

Despite the celebration of the Framers at many civic occasions during the Constitution's bicentennial year, some observers, like Supreme Court Justice Thurgood Marshall, think the wisdom of the Framers of the Constitution has been overrated. Marshall was the first black person appointed to the Supreme Court. Earlier in his career, he was an attorney with the National Association for the Advancement of Colored People (NAACP), and he argued major civil rights cases in the courts.

In a speech sparked by commemorations of the bicentennial, Marshall faults the Framers for producing a defective document that allowed for the perpetuation of slavery and denied black people and women the right to vote. He contends that developments *after* the writing of the Constitution created a more promising basis for justice and equality than did the accomplishments of the Framers. He emphasizes the adoption of the Fourteenth Amendment ensuring protection of life, liberty, and property of all

persons against deprivations without due process and guaranteeing the
equal protection of the laws. Credit for change, Marshall says, should go
to the people who passed amendments and laws that sought to promote
liberty for *all* the people of the United States. Marshall celebrates the
Constitution as a living document, evolving through amendments and
judicial interpretation.

Marshall's speech prompted a direct response by William Bradford
Reynolds, the assistant attorney general in the Civil Rights Division of
the Justice Department. Reynolds was a controversial figure in the Reagan administration because of his actions on civil rights matters. A number of civil rights leaders criticized him for his opposition to affirmative
action and voting rights legislation. Reynolds's supporters defended him
as a proponent of real racial equality.

In a speech delivered at Vanderbilt University, Reynolds argues that the
Framers deserve the respect accorded to them in the bicentennial celebrations. Accepting Marshall's evaluation that the original Constitution was
flawed, Reynolds still asserts that the Constitution marked "the greatest
advance for human liberty in the entire history of mankind, then or
since." Indeed, Reynolds continues, the constitutional system of divided
governmental authority and separated government power eventually allowed for blacks to secure liberty. He notes that much blame for the low
status of blacks in the United States should go not to the Framers but
rather to those justices who failed to follow the terms of the Constitution
and the laws of the land.

☑ YES

*Has the Wisdom of the Framers of the Constitution in Promoting a
"More Perfect Union" Been Overrated?*

THURGOOD MARSHALL

The Constitution: Past and Present

Nineteen-eighty-seven marks the 200th anniversary of the United States Constitution. A Commission has been established to coordinate the celebration. The
official meetings, essay contests, and festivities have begun.

The planned commemoration will span three years, and I am told 1987 is
"dedicated to the memory of the Founders and the document they drafted in
Philadelphia." We are to "recall the achievements of our Founders and the
knowledge and experience that inspired them, the nature of the government

they established, its origins, its character, and its ends, and the rights and privileges of citizenship, as well as its attendant responsibilities."

Like many anniversary celebrations, the plan for 1987 takes particular events and holds them up as the source of all the very best that has followed. Patriotic feelings will surely swell, prompting proud proclamations of the wisdom, foresight, and sense of justice shared by the Framers and reflected in a written document now yellowed with age. This is unfortunate—not the patriotism itself, but the tendency for the celebration to oversimplify, and overlook the many other events that have been instrumental to our achievements as a nation. The focus of this celebration invites a complacent belief that the vision of those who debated and compromised in Philadelphia yielded the "more perfect Union" it is said we now enjoy.

I cannot accept this invitation, for I do not believe that the meaning of the Constitution was forever "fixed" at the Philadelphia Convention. Nor do I find the wisdom, foresight, and sense of justice exhibited by the Framers particularly profound. To the contrary, the government they devised was defective from the start, requiring several amendments, a civil war, and momentous social transformation to attain the system of constitutional government, and its respect for the individual freedoms and human rights, we hold as fundamental today. When contemporary Americans cite "The Constitution," they invoke a concept that is vastly different from what the Framers barely began to construct two centuries ago.

For a sense of the evolving nature of the Constitution we need look no further than the first three words of the document's preamble: "We the People." When the Founding Fathers used this phrase in 1787, they did not have in mind the majority of America's citizens. "We the People" included, in the words of the Framers, "the whole Number of free Persons." On a matter so basic as the right to vote, for example, Negro slaves were excluded, although they were counted for representational purposes—at three-fifths each. Women did not gain the right to vote for over a hundred and thirty years.

These omissions were intentional. The record of the Framers' debates on the slave question is especially clear: The Southern States acceded to the demands of the New England States for giving Congress broad power to regulate commerce, in exchange for the right to continue the slave trade. The economic interests of the regions coalesced: New Englanders engaged in the "carrying trade" would profit from transporting slaves from Africa as well as goods produced in America by slave labor. The perpetuation of slavery ensured the primary source of wealth in the Southern States.

Despite this clear understanding of the role slavery would play in the new republic, use of the words "slaves" and "slavery" was carefully avoided in the original document. Political representation in the lower House of Congress was to be based on the population of "free Persons" in each State, plus three-fifths of all "other Persons." Moral principles against slavery, for those who had them, were compromised, with no explanation of the conflicting principles for which the American Revolutionary War had ostensibly been fought: the self-evident truths "that all men are created equal, that they are endowed by their Creator with certain unalienable Rights, that among these are Life, Liberty and the pursuit of Happiness."

It was not the first such compromise. Even these ringing phrases from the Declaration of Independence are filled with irony, for an early draft of what became that Declaration assailed the King of England for suppressing legislative attempts to end the slave trade and for encouraging slave rebellions. The final draft adopted in 1776 did not contain this criticism. And so again at the Constitutional Convention eloquent objections to the institution of slavery went unheeded, and its opponents eventually consented to a document which laid a foundation for the tragic events that were to follow.

Pennsylvania's Gouverneur Morris provides an example. He opposed slavery and the counting of slaves in determining the basis for representation in Congress. At the Convention he objected that

> the inhabitant of Georgia [or] South Carolina who goes to the coast of Africa, and in defiance of the most sacred laws of humanity tears away his fellow creatures from their dearest connections and damns them to the most cruel bondages, shall have more votes in a Government instituted for protection of the rights of mankind, than the Citizen of Pennsylvania or New Jersey who views with a laudable horror, so nefarious a practice.

And yet Gouverneur Morris eventually accepted the three-fifths accommodation. In fact, he wrote the final draft of the Constitution, the very document the bicentennial will commemorate.

As a result of compromise, the right of the Southern States to continue importing slaves was extended, officially, at least until 1808. We know that it actually lasted a good deal longer, as the Framers possessed no monopoly on the ability to trade moral principles for self-interest. But they nevertheless set an unfortunate example. Slaves could be imported, if the commercial interests of the North were protected. To make the compromise even more palatable, customs duties would be imposed at up to ten dollars per slave as a means of raising public revenues.

No doubt it will be said, when the unpleasant truth of the history of slavery in America is mentioned during this bicentennial year, that the Constitution was a product of its times, and embodied a compromise which, under other circumstances, would not have been made. But the effects of the Framers' compromise have remained for generations. They arose from the contradiction between guaranteeing liberty and justice to all, and denying both to Negroes.

The original intent of the phrase, "We the People," was far too clear for any ameliorating construction. Writing for the Supreme Court in 1857, Chief Justice Taney penned the following passage in the *Dred Scott* case, on the issue whether, in the eyes of the Framers, slaves were "constituent members of the sovereignty," and were to be included among "We the People":

We think they are not, and that they are not included, and were not intended to be included. . . . They had for more than a century before been regarded as beings of an inferior order, and altogether unfit to associate with the white race . . . ; and so far inferior, that they had no rights which the white man was bound to respect; and that the negro might justly and lawfully be reduced to slavery for his benefit. . . . [A]ccordingly, a negro of the African race was regarded . . . as an article of property, and held, and bought and sold as such. . . . [N]o one seems to have doubted the correctness of the prevailing opinion of the time.

And so, nearly seven decades after the Constitutional Convention, the Supreme Court reaffirmed the prevailing opinion of the Framers regarding the rights of Negroes in America. It took a bloody civil war before the 13th Amendment could be adopted to abolish slavery, though not the consequences slavery would have for future Americans.

While the Union survived the civil war, the Constitution did not. In its place arose a new, more promising basis for justice and equality, the 14th Amendment, ensuring protection of the life, liberty, and property of *all* persons against deprivations without due process, and guaranteeing legal protection of the laws. And yet almost another century would pass before any significant recognition was obtained of the rights of black Americans to share equally even in such basic opportunities as education, housing, and employment, and to have their votes counted, and counted equally. In the meantime, blacks joined America's military to fight its wars and invested untold hours working in its factories and on its farms, contributing to the development of this country's magnificent wealth and waiting to share in its prosperity.

What is striking is the role legal principles have played throughout America's history in determining the condition of Negroes. They were enslaved by law, emancipated by law, disenfranchised and segregated by law; and, finally, they have begun to win equality by law. Along the way, new constitutional principles have emerged to meet the challenges of a changing society. The progress has been dramatic, and it will continue.

The men who gathered in Philadelphia in 1787 could not have envisioned these changes. They could not have imagined, nor would they have accepted, that the document they were drafting would one day be construed by a Supreme Court to which had been appointed a woman and the descendent of an African slave. "We the People" no longer enslave, but the credit does not belong to the Framers. It belongs to those who refused to acquiesce in outdated notions of "liberty," "justice," and "equality," and who strived to better them.

And so we must be careful, when focusing on the events which took place in Philadelphia two centuries ago, that we not overlook the momentous events which followed, and thereby lose our proper sense of perspective. Otherwise, the odds are that for many Americans the bicentennial celebration will be little more than a blind pilgrimage to the shrine of the original document now stored in a vault in the National Archives. If we seek, instead, a sensitive understanding of the Constitution's inherent defects, and its promising evolution through 200 years of history, the celebration of the "Miracle at Philadelphia" will, in my view, be a far more meaningful and humbling experience. We will see that the true miracle was not the birth of the Constitution, but its life, a life nurtured through two turbulent centuries of our own making, and a life embodying much good fortune that was not.

Thus, in this bicentennial year, we may not all participate in the festivities with flag-waving fervor. Some may more quietly commemorate the suffering, struggle, and sacrifice that has triumphed over much of what was wrong with the original document, and observe the anniversary with hopes not realized and promises not fulfilled. I plan to celebrate the bicentennial of the Constitution as a living document, including the Bill of Rights and the other amendments protecting individual freedoms and human rights.

☑ NO

Has the Wisdom of the Framers of the Constitution in Promoting a "More Perfect Union" Been Overrated?

WILLIAM BRADFORD REYNOLDS
The Wisdom of the Framers

Let me start with the observation that I regard myself to be most privileged to be a public servant at a time when we celebrate the 200th Anniversary of the Constitution—a magnificent document that has, in my view, no equal in history and every reason to be feted. It is by now no revelation that the Framers would be aghast at the size and reach of government today; but they would also be enormously proud of how much of their legacy has endured. The vitality of the original Constitution, and its various amendments, is reflected by its ability to withstand spirited debate over its content and meaning, a process that thankfully has been taking place with more and more enthusiasm in town meetings and forums all around the country, involving students, public officials, and citizens of every variety in evaluating how well our Constitution has served us over the past two centuries. I find it remarkable—and an enormous tribute to the Constitution—that in every instance about which I have read, these gatherings have been hard-pressed to think of ways in which to improve it in any meaningful manner.

That is not to say that the original Constitution of 1787 was flawless. And in our celebration of the document, we must not overlook its flaws and our long and painful struggles to correct them.

If there was any tendency to do so, it was no doubt corrected a few weeks ago when Justice Thurgood Marshall spoke in Hawaii on the Constitution's Bicentennial celebration. Whatever degree of disagreement one might have with Justice Marshall's comments, he has invigorated the debate on the meaning and vitality of constitutional principles in a focused way that can only serve to underscore the importance of the document itself and why it is so deserving of this Bicentennial celebration.

In recounting his remarks, I will rely on Justice Marshall's own words. He began by warning against what he called the "tendency for the celebration to oversimplify" the adoption and meaning of the Constitution of 1787 and to "overlook the many other events that have been instrumental to our achievements as a nation"—events that, as he explains, included the Civil War and the amendments added to the Constitution in its wake. Thus, he rejected what he described as a complacent belief that the "vision of those who debated and compromised in Philadelphia yielded the 'more perfect Union' it is said we now enjoy." Justice Marshall remarked further that he does not believe—and I quote—that "the meaning of the Constitution was forever 'fixed' at the Philadelphia Convention"; nor does he find "the wisdom, foresight, and sense of justice exhibited by the Framers particularly profound." The government the Framers of 1787 devised, he declared, "was defective from the start, requiring several amendments, a civil war, and momentous social transformation to attain the system of constitutional government, and its respect for the individual freedoms and human rights, we hold as fundamental today."

More specifically, Justice Marshall faulted the original Constitution because, as he put it, the Framers "did not have in mind the majority of America's citizens." The Preamble's "We the People," the Justice said, included only whites. Justice Marshall observes that the Constitution tacitly addressed the slavery issue in two ways: in Article I, section 2 by counting "other Persons" as three-fifths of "free Persons" for purposes of Congressional representation; and in Article I, section 9, by protecting the authority of states to continue importing slaves until 1808. Because the original Constitution was defective in this manner, Justice Marshall holds that "while the Union survived the civil war, the Constitution did not." Taking its place, he said, was "a new, more promising basis for justice and equality, the 14th Amendment, ensuring protection of the life, liberty, and property of *all* persons against deprivations without due process, and guaranteeing equal protection of the laws." For Justice Marshall, it is this new Constitution that we should celebrate; not the old one, which contains "outdated notions of 'liberty,' 'justice,' and 'equality.'" Thus, Justice Marshall declines to participate in the festivities with "flag-waving fervor," but rather plans to celebrate the Bicentennial of the Constitution as a "living document, including the Bill of Rights and the other amendments protecting individual freedoms and human rights."

Justice Marshall chose to focus almost exclusively on the most tragic aspects of the American experience, but he is absolutely right to remind us of them. For the Constitution was intended to be the culmination of a great struggle for the natural rights of men—a philosophy whose cornerstone is the absolute guarantee of equality under the law. When the Framers sought to protect in the Constitution the fundamental rights of man but failed to guarantee explicitly those rights to every individual, they introduced a self-contradiction that preordained struggles and conflicts we continue to confront today.

I am concerned, however, that what Justice Marshall has encouraged is far more than a simple mid-course correction in our celebration of the Constitution. It is one thing to be reminded of the compromise on slavery during the making of the Constitution. It is quite another, however, to encourage the view that there are two constitutions, the one of 1787, the other consisting of the Bill of Rights and the 14th Amendment; that the old one is so thoroughly defective that it did not survive the Civil War, and that the new one alone is worthy of celebration. Certainly, we ought to understand and appreciate the original Constitution in light of its weaknesses as well as its considerable strengths. But in the process, we ought to respectfully decline the invitation to consign it to the dustbin of history. That is a judgment as wrong as any on the other side of the ledger that uncritically praises the document of 1787. We indeed need what Justice Marshall called for—a "proper sense of perspective."

Notwithstanding its very serious flaws, the Constitution in its original form constituted the greatest advance for human liberty in the entire history of mankind, then or since. Indeed, it was only by preserving our underlying *constitutional system*—one of divided governmental authority and separated government powers—that blacks could enjoy the fruits of liberty once that self-contradiction I alluded to was corrected.

Fresh from the experience of subjugation under the British crown on one hand, and the failure of the Articles of Confederation on the other, the Framers understood that there is an interdependent relationship between fundamental rights and the structure and powers of government. Thus, they crafted a government of limited powers, grounded in natural law principles and deriving its authority from the consent of the governed. They designed a system to protect individual rights through a balance and separation of governmental powers, which would forever ensure that the new national government would not exceed its enumerated powers. Not the least of these checks against governmental invasions of individual rights was the creation in Article III of an independent judiciary as a guardian of constitutional values.

Many of the Framers were not satisfied to protect individual rights merely by limiting the power of national government; they insisted upon a Bill of Rights to safeguard explicitly those rights they deemed most fundamental. Although the Bill of Rights was separately adopted, it would be [an] error to view the original Constitution apart from the first ten amendments, for the Framers agreed from the outset that the rights enumerated in the Bill of Rights were the object of government to protect. Beyond setting forth specific rights essential to a free people, the Framers established in the Ninth and Tenth Amendments a decentralized federal structure to more fully secure the free exercise of individual rights and self-government.

This was the basic structure of government the Framers deemed necessary to vindicate the principles of the American Revolution as set forth in the Declaration of Independence; and that, in my view, is the unique and remarkable achievement we celebrate today. But in celebrating the triumph of the Constitution, I am in full agreement that we must not overlook those parts of the constitutional experiment that were not noble and which, fortunately, have long since been corrected. Indeed, the experience of the Framers' compromise on the issue of "equality under law" provides us with important lessons even today.

From our historical vantage point, there is certainly no excuse for the original Constitution's failure to repudiate slavery. In making this deal with the devil—and departing from the absolute principle of "equality under law"—the Framers undermined the moral legitimacy of the Constitution.

But we ought to recognize that on this issue the Framers were faced with a Hobson's choice. The Constitution required unanimous ratification by the states, and at least two of the states refused to consent unless the slave trade was protected. James Wilson explained the dilemma: "Under the present Confederation, the states may admit the importation of slaves as long as they please; but by this article, after the year 1808, the Congress will have power to prohibit such importation. . . . I consider this as laying the foundation for banishing slavery out of this country." We know now that this hope was far too optimistic; and indeed, it would take the Civil War to rid the nation of that evil institution.

But even as the Framers were acceding to this compromise, they were sowing the seeds for the expansion of freedom to all individuals when circumstances would permit. James Wilson, for example, emphasized that "the term *slave* was not *admitted* in this *Constitution*." Instead, the term "Person" was used, suggesting that when the slaves became "free Persons," they would be entitled to all the rights appertaining to free individuals.

Indeed, many abolitionist leaders argued that the Constitution, by its omission of any mention of slavery, did not tolerate slavery. Noting that the Constitution nowhere mentions the word "slave," Frederick Douglass declared that "[i]n that instrument, I hold there is neither warrant, license, nor sanction of the hateful thing." Yet such arguments were tragically unheeded by the United States Supreme Court in the *Dred Scott* decision, which provided succor to the notion that there are justifications for exceptions to the principle of "equality under law"—a notion that despite its sordid origins has not been totally erased to this day.

Indeed, the *Dred Scott* decision illustrates that a significant part of the responsibility for our failure to make good on the principle of "equality under law" can and should be assigned less to shortcomings in the original Constitution—as Justice Marshall would have us believe—but to those who sat where Justice Marshall now sits, charged with interpreting that document.

Justice Marshall apparently believes that the original flaws in the Constitution dictated the result in *Dred Scott*. I am more inclined toward the view of my colleagues at the Department of Justice, Charles J. Cooper and Nelson Lund, who argue that Chief Justice Taney's constitutional interpretation was "loose, disingenuous, and result-oriented." Justice Curtis' dissent sounded a warning over this type of judicial interpretation unattached to constitutional moorings that is as compelling now as it was 125 years ago:

> Political reasons have not the requisite certainty to afford rules of interpretation. They are different in different men. They are different in the same men at different times. And when a strict interpretation of the Constitution, according to the fixed rules which govern the interpretation of laws, is abandoned, and the theoretical opinions of individuals are allowed to control its meaning, we no longer have a Constitution; we are under the government of individual men, who for the time being have power to declare what the Constitution is, according to their own views of what it ought to mean.

The judiciary's tragic failure to follow the terms of the Constitution did not occur in this one instance only. Indeed, the Civil War amendments and civil rights legislation passed in that era were in the next several decades emptied of meaning by the Supreme Court in decision after decision. In *Plessy* v. *Ferguson*, to cite but one example, the Court once again stepped in and, over the lone, brilliant dissent of the elder Justice Harlan, shamefully sacrificed the principle of "equality under law."

I daresay that had the Court fully honored its mandate under the original Constitution in *Dred Scott*, or under the Fourteenth Amendment in *Plessy* v. *Ferguson*, we could well have escaped much of the racial strife and social devisiveness that Justice Marshall lays at the doorstep of the Constitution itself. Indeed, the tragic legacy of those decisions—the deadening consequences that so regularly flow from a compromise (no matter how well intended) of the principle of "equality under law"—provides a sobering lesson for the present Court as it struggles with similar issues involving race and gender discrimination. These are issues that no less so than in an earlier era leave hanging in the balance the overarching question of whether the liberating promise of the Constitution, as originally understood and subsequently articulated in explicit terms by ratification of the Civil War amendments, will or will not be fulfilled for all Americans.

Justice Marshall, I would respectfully submit, too casually brushes so weighty a concern to one side in contending that the Constitution did not survive the Civil War. One would think that this assertion would at least invite from some quarter the obvious questions: Did separation of powers survive the Civil War? Did the executive branch and the Congress? Did, indeed, the institution of judicial review?

I must admit to quite a different reading of history, one that has an abiding appreciation of the fact that our Constitution did survive so cataclysmic an upheaval as the Civil War. In all too many instances of internal strife among a People, one form of subjugation is ultimately replaced by another. But the Civil War produced a far different (indeed unique) result: its consequence was to more perfectly secure and extend to all Americans—through the Thirteenth, Fourteenth, and Fifteenth Amendments—the blessings of liberty as set forth in the Declaration of Independence, blessings of liberty that had already been secured for other Americans in the original Constitution and Bill of Rights. It is revisionist history of the worst sort to suggest that the Fourteenth Amendment created a blank constitutional slate on which judges could write their own personalized definition of equality or fundamental rights. The Civil War Amendments were a logical extension of what had come before: they represented *evolutionary*, not *revolutionary* change.

To be sure, the Fourteenth Amendment does offer support for Justice Marshall's claim that the Constitution is "a living document," but only in the sense that the Constitution itself provides a mechanism—namely, the amendment process—to reflect changing social realities. Indeed, this orderly process for constitutional "evolution" is a part of the original Constitution's genius, for it provides a mechanism to correct flaws while safeguarding the essential integrity of our constitutional structure. But the existence of this mechanism—coupled with the system of checks and balances among the three branches of the federal government and the strong endorsement of federalism principles embodied in the Tenth Amendment—makes it abundantly clear that the Framers gave no license to judges (members of the Branch regarded, to borrow from Alexander Hamilton, as the "least dangerous" of the three) to construe constitutional provisions as they see fit.

There is good reason for this confluence of restraints on judicial activism. The Constitution is not a mass of fungible, abstract principles whose meaning varies with time; rather, it comprises a broad societal consensus on certain fundamental, absolute principles necessary for the protection of individual liberty. The Framers believed that these constitutional values should not be lightly disturbed or set aside. Accordingly, the Constitution was structured so as to require that any change reflect the broadest expression of societal consensus.

This does not leave the Supreme Court or lower federal courts unable to apply the Constitution to circumstances never contemplated by the Framers. But the Judges are not free to disengage from our constitutional moorings in furtherance of their own social agendas; they are not free to determine that the constitutional principles themselves are unwise or obsolete.

Indeed, the very premise on which rests the notion that the Constitution as originally framed has no relevance today is fatally flawed. For the fact remains that the core structure upon which the Constitution was based—a government of limited powers, federalism, separation of powers, protection of fundamental individual rights—has proven in the past two centuries far superior to any other governmental system in protecting human freedoms. And where proponents of change have successfully secured the broad consensus necessary to amend the Constitution, they have expanded and perfected those protections. But judicial activism as an illegitimate substitute for the amendment process can only jeopardize our fundamental freedoms by denigrating the structural underpinnings vital to their survival.

Justice Marshall's contrary thesis is gerry-built on a regrettable overstatement of perceived flaws in the Constitution without so much as a passing reference to the qualities that have endured for the past two hundred years: a governmental structure that has withstood the test of time, weathered turbulent conflicts, and proven itself to be the greatest engine for individual freedom in the history of mankind. That remarkable accomplishment is certainly worth the celebration it is receiving, and much, much more.

Let us not be content with less than a complete appreciation for this document on which our Republic stands. Let us accept Justice Marshall's invitation to explore fully the lessons of the past two centuries. But let us decline his invitation to break the Constitution into two, and to reject the document of 1787 and accept only that which followed the Civil War. We are under a Constitution; it is the original Constitution together with its twenty-six amendments that we must seek to understand and uphold. Let us never forget that the Constitution is in its entirety the Supreme Law of the Land, and all of the branches—the executive, legislative, and judicial—are subordinate to it. We must embrace the Constitution as a whole: not uncritically, but not unlovingly either. Our task, in this Bicentennial year, should be that of loving critics. For our Constitution has provided this great nation of ours with a charter for liberty and government that has enabled us to move ever closer to that "more perfect Union" the Framers envisioned.

In conclusion, it is fitting that I call on the words of former Chief Justice Warren Burger, the Chairman of the Bicentennial Commission. He said it best when he remarked that the Constitution "isn't perfect, but it's the best thing in the world." Our Constitution embodies the American spirit, the American Dream, and America's doctrinal commitment to civil rights—those fundamental rights we all hold equally as American citizens. For this reason, I respectfully part company with Justice Marshall in my view that it is indeed our Constitution as framed two centuries ago, and amended thereafter from time to time, that stands tall today as "the source of all the very best that has followed." Let us not hesitate to celebrate.

Questions for Discussion

1. How did the political system adopted by the United States in the late eighteenth century compare to the political systems in other countries during the same period in terms of ensuring individual freedom?
2. What would have been the consequences to the political development of the United States had the Framers included provisions outlawing slavery and granting political equality for blacks?
3. What were the assumptions of the Framers about the relationship between individuals and the government?
4. What effect did the constitutional prescription to divide power between a central government and the states and between the different branches of the central government have on the condition of black people?
5. What evidence can you supply to accept or reject the proposition that the Constitution did not survive the Civil War?
6. What impact should the intent of the Framers have on Supreme Court justices in deciding cases today? What are the reasons for your answer?

Suggested Readings

Beard, Charles A. *An Economic Interpretation of the Constitution of the United States.* New York: Free Press, 1986. [Reprinted, originally published New York: Macmillan, 1913.]

Berns, Walter. *Taking the Constitution Seriously.* New York: Simon & Schuster, 1987.

Currie, David P. *The Constitution in the Supreme Court: The First Hundred Years, 1789–1888.* Chicago: Univ. of Chicago Press, 1985.

Farrand, Max, ed. *The Records of the Federal Convention of 1787.* New Haven: Yale Univ. Press, 1937.

Hamilton, Alexander, James Madison, and John Jay. *The Federalist Papers,* edited by Clinton Rossiter. New York: New American Library, 1961.

Ketcham, Ralph, ed. *The Anti-Federalist Papers; and the Constitutional Convention Debates.* New York: New American Library, 1986.

Loury, Glenn C. " 'Matters of Color'—Blacks and the Constitutional Order." *Public Interest,* no. 86 (Winter 1987), 109–123.

McDonald, Forrest. *We the People: Economic Origins of the Constitution.* Chicago: Univ. of Chicago Press, 1958.

Mee, Charles L., Jr. *The Genius of the People.* New York: Harper & Row, 1987.

Morris, Richard B. *Witnesses at the Creation: Hamilton, Madison, Jay and the Constitution.* New York: New American Library, 1986.

Storing, Herbert J., with the assistance of Murray Dry, eds. *The Complete Anti-Federalist.* 7 vols. Chicago: Univ. of Chicago Press, 1981.

Chapter 2

Is the Separation of Powers Outmoded in the Twentieth Century?

It is generally accepted that without compromise the Constitutional Convention would have failed. One important conflict was between the large states, which favored representation based on population, and the small states, which wanted each state to have equal representation. This conflict was resolved by establishing a House of Representatives constituted on the basis of population and a Senate represented on the principle of state equality. Another conflict involved popular participation in the political process. This division was resolved by permitting the House of Representatives to be elected by popular vote and the Senate to be elected by the state legislatures (the Seventeenth Amendment ratified in 1913 required the direct election of senators).

The Constitution provided for a stronger central government than had existed under the Articles of Confederation. That new government was to be a republic in which the president and Congress would be elected directly or indirectly by the people. The Constitution also provided for the establishment of the basic institutions of the national government: the presidency, the Congress, and the Supreme Court. Specific provisions were made for how leaders would be chosen for these offices and how their authority would be limited.

The Framers feared the concentration of power in the hands of a few, but they also wanted to avoid "mob rule" by the majority. A fundamental feature of the new Constitution was, therefore, a system of shared power. Each branch of the federal government has primary power in one area, but that power is not total. Congress, consequently, has primary legislative power; the president, primary executive power; and the Supreme Court, primary judiciary power.

Each of these powers, however, is shared. The president exercises some judicial power (the nomination of judges to the Supreme Court) and some legislative power (the vetoing of legislation). Congress has some executive power (Senate confirmation of executive appointments) and some judicial power (impeachment by the House of Representatives). The Supreme Court, too, has some legislative power (the interpretation of laws) and some executive power (the administration of laws to ensure compliance with judicial decisions).

But this central feature of the Constitution is itself under debate. The Committee on the Constitutional System (CCS), a nonpartisan organization composed of present and past government officials and private citizens, argues that the system is outmoded. The CCS is chaired by Senator Nancy Landon Kassebaum, Republican from Kansas; C. Douglas Dillon, former secretary of the treasury and undersecretary of state; and Lloyd N. Cutler, former counsel to the president. Its purpose is to study and analyze the U.S. constitutional system.

In its *Report and Recommendations,* the CCS points to strains in the constitutional system, such as the mounting national debt, conflicts between Congress and the president over foreign policy, and malfunctions of the modern electoral system. The report places principal blame for these developments on the diffuse structure of the separation of powers and the decline in party loyalty and party cohesion at all levels of the political system. It notes the adverse effects of the system: a brief "honeymoon" between president and Congress, divided government, lack of party cohesion in Congress, loss of accountability, and lack of a mechanism for replacing failed or deadlocked government. It presents proposals adopted by the CCS and additional proposals worth considering. According to the CCS, such proposals would strengthen party cohesion, improve collaboration between the executive and legislative branches, and reduce the costs of campaigning for election.

In essence, the CCS would like the U.S. constitutional system to pattern itself after the British parliamentary system. In the British system the prime minister is a member of Parliament; the majority party or a majority coalition of parties controls the House of Commons—the chief legislative institution; and party members in the House of Commons generally vote the way the party decides. A losing vote in the House of Commons results in new elections for all members of that chamber.

James Q. Wilson, Collins Professor of Management at the University of California at Los Angeles, argues that the criticisms against the existing constitutional system are not valid. He contends that the national deficit, failures of economic policy, and conflicts between the executive and legislative branches on foreign policy matters are not caused by the separation of powers and that proposed reforms will not solve the inherent problems. He notes that there are two fundamental arguments for a constitutional system of separate institutions sharing powers: "It helps preserve liberty and it slows the pace of political change." In his view these arguments are as valid today as they were when the Constitution was written.

Both selections mention political parties, a political institution not mentioned in the Constitution because formal parties did not exist when the Constitution was drafted. Like some other institutions not mentioned or emphasized in the Constitution—the committee system in Congress and the bureaucracy, for example—political parties have evolved to meet the needs of a changing society and have come to play an important role in the U.S. political process, as we shall see in Part Two.

Is the Separation of Powers Outmoded in the Twentieth Century?

COMMITTEE ON THE CONSTITUTIONAL SYSTEM

A Bicentennial Analysis of the American Political Structure

Two hundred years ago, the founders of the American republic decided that the governmental system that had guided them safely through the War for Independence was in need of change. They became convinced that nothing short of a new constitution would meet the demands that lay ahead.

Having reached this conclusion, they did not hesitate to take the necessary action. The result was the framing and ratification of the United States Constitution.

As we approach the bicentennial of the Constitution, Americans are eager to honor the framers' work, which is truly one of the great achievements of human history.

The system designed in 1787 has proven remarkably adaptable to the changing demands of a growing nation. Political leaders have been imaginative and bold in finding ways to adapt the system to meet evolving national responsibilities and needs. Hamilton, Jefferson and Madison themselves took the lead in creating the party system, building greater cohesion and efficiency into the lawmaking process.

As the United States shifted from an agricultural to an industrial society and the regulation of commercial and financial markets became too complex for a government of separated powers, a later generation of politicians invented the independent regulatory commission, combining rule-making, administrative and adjudicatory powers in a single governmental body.

During the 1930's, new signs of strain began to appear. In response to the Great Depression, the government embarked on a vast set of programs to manage the growth of our modern industrial economy and provide a measure of social justice for those who suffered from its malfunctions. Then dangerous challenges to American security arose in Europe and the Far East and in our own national defense, and we had to assume global military and foreign policy responsibilities. These developments, domestic and foreign, required the federal government to undertake new tasks that were unprecedented in kind or scope and could hardly have been foreseen by the framers.

Thoughtful observers soon realized that the governmental structure was straining under this enormous additional load. A series of commissions chaired by Louis Brownlow, Herbert Hoover and Roy Ash made sweeping recommendations that became the basis for extensive modernization of the executive branch. Distinguished panels in the Senate and House chaired by Mike Monroney and Robert LaFollette, Jr., Richard Bolling, Adlai Stevenson III and William Brock brought about important changes in the procedures and committee structure of Congress. Groups outside the government (such as the National Academy of Public Administration, the Committee on Political Parties of the American Political Science Association and the Committee for Economic Development), as well as individual analysts and authors, offered other suggestions for reform.

Though most of these studies confined themselves to recommending adjustments within the existing framework, many recognized that the twentieth-century problems confronting our eighteenth-century American political system might require changes in the constitutional structure. Changes in statutes and party rules are of course less difficult to make and ought to be tried before changes in the Constitution itself. Changes in the Constitution should not be shunned, however, if critical modern problems cannot be solved by other means.

In the last Federalist Paper, Alexander Hamilton urged that the Constitution be ratified despite the objections that were being raised, because there would be opportunity later to make amendments as experience revealed the need. James Madison and Gouverneur Morris likewise acknowledged imperfections in the framers' brilliant work.

For example, the same document that established the Bill of Rights also countenanced the continued practice of slavery. When that contradiction became apparent over the next century, the resulting constitutional crisis produced a terrible civil war. Abraham Lincoln called a distracted nation to attention with the words, "We must disenthrall ourselves." "The dogmas of the quiet past," he added, "are inadequate to the stormy present. . . . As our case is new, so we must think anew, and act anew." And the Constitution was amended to outlaw slavery, root and branch.

Thomas Jefferson considered the amendment process one of the Constitution's most important features. "I am certainly not an advocate for frequent and untried changes in laws and constitutions," he wrote. "But I know also that laws and institutions must go hand in hand with the progress of the human mind. As that becomes more developed, more enlightened, as new discoveries are made, new truths disclosed, and manners and opinions change with the change of circumstances, institutions must advance also and keep pace with the times."

As Jefferson foresaw, we too face unprecedented challenges. If aspects of the system framed in 1787 prevent the national government from meeting its present responsibilities, we must identify the outmoded features, separate them from the good and durable parts of the system and make the necessary modifications.

To do so is not to reject the great work of our forebears. It honors their spirit in the most sincere way: by seeking to emulate it.

SIGNS OF STRAIN

As the bicentennial draws near, the signs of strain in our governing processes are unmistakable.

Perhaps the most alarming evidence is the mounting national debt, fueled anew each year by outsized and unsustainable deficits that defy the good intentions of legislators and Presidents.

Consistency in our foreign and national security policies is also frustrated by an institutional contest of wills between Presidents and shifting, cross-party coalitions within the Congress. Over forty treaties submitted to the Senate for ratification since World War II have either been rejected or have never come to a vote. Among those that have never come to a vote are SALT [Strategic Arms Limitation Treaty] II, the 1974 and 1976 treaties on underground nuclear tests and explosions, maritime boundary treaties with Mexico and Canada, several UN [United Nations] and OAS [Organization of American States] human rights conventions, and a wide variety of bilateral trade, tax and environmental treaties. Meanwhile presidential concern over "leaks" and frustration with congressionally imposed restrictions have led Presidents and their staffs to launch important diplomatic, military and covert activities in secret and without consulting Congress.

Further problems—particularly damaging in a nation dedicated to the principle of self-government—stem from malfunctions of the modern electoral system: the high cost of running for office, the corroding influence of campaign contributions from single-interest groups, the stupefying length of campaigns (for the presidency, usually several years from initiation to inauguration), and persistently low turnout rates (among the lowest in the world for nations with competitive elections).

CAUSES

Sensing the failures and weaknesses in governmental performance, people tend to blame particular politicians or the complexity of the modern world. But our public officials are no less competent, either individually or as a group, than they used to be. Nor do our problems, as complex as they are, defy rational solutions consistent with our basic constitutional liberties. The difficulty lies mainly in the diffuse structure of the executive-legislative process and in the decline of party loyalty and cohesion at all levels of the political system.

The separation of powers, as a principle of constitutional structure, has served us well in preventing tyranny and the abuse of high office, but it has done so by encouraging confrontation, indecision and deadlock, and by diffusing accountability for the results.

Ideally our two-party system should counteract the centrifugal tendencies of the separation of powers, with each party's politicians committed to a common philosophy of government and to specific program goals for which they stand accountable at the next election. In fact, throughout most of the nineteenth century and until after the end of World War II, the loyalty of most politicians to their party was deeply felt. They ran for office on a ticket selected by the party's leaders. Once in office, they recognized a common stake in the success of their party's governance and their joint accountability as candidates of the party at the next election.

In recent decades, however, political reforms and technological changes have worked together to weaken the parties and undermine their ability to draw the separated parts of the government into coherent action. Beginning in the late nineteenth century, Congress enacted a series of measures that redistributed functions previously performed by the parties. Civil service systems stripped the parties of much of their patronage.

The rise of the welfare state took away many opportunities for service by which the parties had won and held the loyalty of their followers. The secret ballot replaced the "tickets" which had previously been prepared by the parties and handed to the voters to cast into the ballot box. The 17th Amendment (ratified in 1913), which required the direct election of Senators, dealt another blow to party cohesiveness. So did the direct primary, which came to dominate the nomination of presidential candidates, particularly after 1968.

Modern technology has enabled candidates to appeal to voters directly, through television, computer-assisted mailings and telephone campaigns, and by quick visits in jet airplanes, all of which have lessened their dependence on party organizations and leaders. The key to these technologies is money, but candidates found they could raise it directly for themselves better than through the party organization. At the same time, interest groups found they could exercise more power over legislative votes by contributing directly to selected candidates rather than to a party.

The habits of voters also changed in this new environment. Party loyalty had been the rule for most of the nineteenth century, but by the last quarter of the twentieth century, one-third of all voters were registered as independents, and even among voters registering with parties, ticket-splitting became the norm.

Many of these changes resulted from laudable reforms and were, in any case, inevitable. No one wants to roll the clock back to the time when party bosses and local "machines" dominated the political process.

Nevertheless, we need to recognize that the weakening of parties in the electoral arena has contributed to the disintegration of party cohesion among the officials we elect to public office. Members of Congress who owe their election less to their party than to their own endeavors and their own sources of funds have little incentive to cooperate with party leaders in the Congress, much less their party's incumbent in the White House. And the proliferation of congressional committees and subcommittees has increased the disarray.

There are now so many that almost every member is the chairman or ranking minority member of at least one committee or subcommittee, with all the political influence, proliferating staffs, publicity and fund-raising potential needed to remain in office.

EFFECTS

Because the separation of powers encourages conflict between the branches and because the parties are weak, the capacity of the federal government to fashion, enact and administer coherent public policy has diminished and the ability of elected officials to avoid accountability for governmental failures has grown. More specifically, the problems include:

Brief Honeymoons

Only the first few months of each four-year presidential term provide an opportunity for decisive action on domestic problems. By the second year, congressional incumbents are engrossed in the mid-term election and defer difficult decisions that will offend any important interest group.

The mid-term election usually results in a setback for the President's party that weakens his leadership and increases the stalemate and deadlock in the Congress. After the mid-term election, the government comes close to immobility as the President and Congress focus their energies on the imminent presidential election.

Divided Government

We have had divided government (one party winning the White House and the other a majority in one or both houses of Congress) 60 percent of the time since 1956 and 80 percent of the time since 1968, compared to less than 25 percent of the time from the adoption of the Constitution until World War II.

This has led to inconsistency, incoherence and even stagnation in national policy. Affirmative policy decisions, as well as the nondecisions resulting from frequent deadlocks that block any action at all, are reached by shifting majorities built out of cross-party coalitions that change from one issue to the next.

Divided government in turn reflects the decline in party loyalty and the growing practice of ticket-splitting among the electorate. In 1900 only four percent of all congressional districts were carried by one party's presidential candidate and the other party's candidate for Member of the House. By 1984, because of the growth of ticket-splitting, this happened in 44 percent of all congressional districts.

One of Woodrow Wilson's themes during the campaign of 1912—a time of divided government—was that only party government (with one party success-fully bridging the separated powers by winning control of the Presidency and both houses of Congress) could carry a coherent program into effect. The voters in 1912 responded by choosing party government, and Wilson's New Freedom program was successfully legislated.

Lack of Party Cohesion in Congress

Even in times of united government, disunity persists between the branches—and between and within the two houses of Congress—because many members of both the President's party and the opposition party reject the positions taken by their leaders. Legislators today have less reason to stick with their party's position and more reason to follow the urgings of non-party political action committees, which provide more of their campaign funds than the party does. The summary rejection of President Reagan's budget in 1986, even by mem-bers of his own party in the Republican-controlled Senate, dramatically illus-trates the lack of party cohesion in the current political environment. This lack of cohesion induces Presidents and their staffs, as noted above, to conceal important foreign policy initiatives even from the leaders of their own party in Congress.

Loss of Accountability

Divided government and party disunity also lead to diffused accountability. No elected official defends the sum of all the inconsistent policy decisions made by so many shifting cross-party coalitions, and each successfully shifts the blame to others. Polls show the public is dissatisfied with the governmen-tal institutions—especially Congress and the bureaucracy—that legislate and administer this hodge-podge of policies. But the public seldom holds a party accountable for these failures, and it hardly ever holds individual legislators responsible.

Since World War II, 90 percent of each party's incumbent legislators who sought another term have been reelected, even in years when their party lost the White House. In 1986 the figure was 97 percent. Benjamin Franklin's famous maxim, "We must all hang together, or assuredly we shall all hang separately," no longer applies to the Members of Congress of either party.

Lack of a Mechanism for Replacing Failed or Deadlocked Government

Presently there is no way between our fixed election dates to resolve basic disagreements between the President and Congress by referring them to the electorate. The only way to remove a failed President is by a House impeachment and Senate trial for "treason, bribery, or other high crimes and misdemeanors." And between the fixed election dates there is no way to reorient a Congress in which one or both houses obstruct an important and popular presidential program.

REMEDIES

In seeking to adjust the constitutional system to modern conditions, we must be careful to preserve its enduring virtues. We must continue to respect the Bill of Rights, protected by an independent judiciary, and we must continue to insist that elected officials be able to monitor one another's performance and call one another to account.

Consistent with these principles, it should be possible to design improvements that would encourage party cohesion and lessen the deadlock between the executive and legislative branches without sacrificing essential checks and balances. The Committee on the Constitutional System offers the following proposals as sufficiently meritorious to warrant national consideration and debate. Some of these proposals call only for adopting new party rules or statutes, while others would require amendments to the Constitution.

PROPOSALS WHICH COMMAND MAJORITY SUPPORT AMONG OUR MEMBERSHIP

Strengthening Parties as Agents of Cohesion and Accountability

1. THE PARTY PRESIDENTIAL NOMINATING CONVENTION The parties should amend their rules for the presidential nominating conventions so as to entitle all winners of the party nominations for the House and Senate, plus the holdover Senators, to seats as uncommitted voting delegates in the presidential nominating convention. This would give the congressional candidates of the party a significant voice in selecting the presidential candidate, increase the loyalties between them in the election campaign, improve cohesion between the President and the legislative incumbents of his party and tend to make them jointly accountable to the voters in the next election.

2. OPTIONAL STRAIGHT-TICKET BALLOTING Congress should enact a statute requiring all states to include a line or lever on federal election ballots enabling voters, if they so desire, to cast a straight-line party ballot for a party's candidates for all open federal offices.

A recent survey shows that nineteen states, including Illinois, New York and Pennsylvania, already have such statutes and that ticket-splitting is less common in those states. This would encourage party loyalty at the voter level and among a party's federal candidates. To the extent that it reduced ticket-splitting, it would lessen the likelihood of divided federal government, while still leaving voters free to split their tickets if they chose.

3. PUBLIC FINANCING OF CONGRESSIONAL CAMPAIGNS Congress should amend the campaign financing laws to create a Congressional Broadcast Fund similar to the existing Presidential Campaign Fund. This fund would be available to each party under a formula similar to that used for the Presidential Campaign Fund, on condition that the party and its candidates expend no other funds on campaign broadcasts. Half of each party's share would go to the nominees themselves. The other half would go to the party's Senate and House campaign committees, which could apportion the funds among candidates so as to maximize the party's chances of winning a legislative majority.

By requiring candidates to look to the party for a substantial part of their broadcast funds, this proposal would help to build party loyalty and cohesion. It would also provide a constitutional way of limiting expenditures on the largest single component of campaign financing costs.

Improving Collaboration between the Executive and Legislative Branches

1. FOUR-YEAR TERMS FOR HOUSE MEMBERS AND EIGHT-YEAR TERMS FOR SENATORS, WITH FEDERAL ELECTIONS EVERY FOURTH YEAR The present system of staggered elections has the effect of pulling the branches apart. Members of the House, who run every two years, feel a political need to demonstrate their independence from the White House, particularly in off-year elections. So do the one-third of the Senators who face an election within two years. Every other time an incumbent in either house runs for reelection, there is no presidential campaign.

The effect is to encourage legislators to distance themselves from the President and from presidential programs that may involve a difficult, short-term adjustment on the way to a worthwhile, longer-term result.

The Constitution could be amended so that the President and Members of the House would serve concurrent, four-year terms, and one Senator from each state would be elected for an eight-year term at each presidential election. This would eliminate the present House and Senate elections in the middle of the presidential term. It would lengthen and coordinate the political horizons of all incumbents. Presidents and legislators could join to enact necessary measures with the promise of longer-run benefits, without having to worry about an imminent election before the benefits were realized.

With fewer elections, the aggregate cost of campaign financing should go down, and legislators would be less frequently or immediately in thrall to the interest groups on whom they depend for funds. The honeymoon for enacting a President's program would be longer. With a four-year life for each Congress, the legislative process for the budget and other measures could be made more orderly and deliberate.

Alternatives. If the eight-year term for Senators were deemed too long, the Senate term could be shortened to four years, concurrent with the terms of the President and the House, which would also eliminate the mid-term election. Of, if the Senate would not accept a shortened term, we could keep the present six-year term. This would retain a limited mid-term election (for one-third of the Senate), permitting a partial referendum on government policy, at the cost of shortening the political horizon of one-third of the Senate.

2. PERMITTING MEMBERS OF CONGRESS TO SERVE IN THE CABINET The Constitution now bars members of Congress from serving as heads of administrative departments or agencies or holding any other executive-branch position. This provision was intended to prevent the President from dominating Congress by offering executive positions to key legislators. But its principal effect has been to deprive the nation of administrators who would have the confidence of both the executive and legislative branches.

If the barrier were removed from the Constitution, Presidents would have the option of appointing leading legislators to cabinet positions, and legislators would have the option of accepting such offers, without being required to give up their seats in Congress. Such ties between the branches might encourage closer collaboration and help to prevent stalemates. They would broaden both the range of talent available to a President in forming his administration and the base of political leadership in the executive branch.

Under such an amendment, of course, a President would not be obliged to appoint any members of Congress to his cabinet, nor would they be obliged to accept.

Woodrow Wilson strongly favored this amendment, as a means to encourage closer collaboration between the branches. While modern legislators may have less time and incentive to join the cabinet than earlier generations, there is no longer any reason for a constitutional barrier to an experiment that has considerable promise and little risk.

3. RELAXING THE REQUIREMENTS FOR TREATY RATIFICATION The ability to enter into formal agreements with other nations is vital to effective national government in an increasingly interdependent world. The present constitutional requirement that treaties require the approval of two-thirds of the Senate has been a major barrier to the use of treaties and has led to evasion of the treaty process by way of executive agreements.

To restore an appropriate congressional role in the making of agreements with foreign powers, this provision should be amended to require that treaties can take effect with the approving vote of a constitutional majority of both houses. If the Senate does not join in proposing such an amendment, it should at least approve an amendment reducing the present requirement of approval by two-thirds of the Senate to 60 percent.

Reducing the Costs of Campaigning for Election

The lack of any legal limit on total campaign expenditures has led to a spiraling, competitive escalation in campaign costs. In the 1986 mid-term election, the legislative candidates raised and spent $342 million, up 30 percent over 1984. The cost of campaigning has put a contested seat in Congress beyond the means of everyone who is not either personally wealthy or willing to become dependent on well-heeled special interest groups. The Supreme Court's interpretation of the First Amendment seems to prohibit Congress from limiting private campaign expenditures by legislation, although the Court has authorized public financing on the condition that candidates who accept it limit their expenditures to these federal funds.

A constitutional amendment allowing Congress to set reasonable limits on campaign expenditures would not endanger the freedom of expression guaranteed by the First Amendment. If such an amendment were adopted, many able citizens who now reject the idea of standing for election might be attracted to political office, and the divisive influence of interest group contributions might be reduced to the point where more cohesive government would again become feasible.

ADDITIONAL PROPOSALS WORTH CONSIDERING

The changes recommended in the previous section command majority support among members of the Committee on the Constitutional System. A number of other ideas have found less than majority support to date, but some members believe they are important enough to deserve further discussion. They fall into four categories.

Strengthening Party Cohesion and Party Accountability

1. ENCOURAGING PRESIDENTIAL APPEARANCES BEFORE CONGRESS

Congress and the President should work out mutually agreeable voluntary arrangements for periodic presidential appearances before major congressional committees. These appearances would be used to present presidential positions and to answer congressional questions about presidential actions and proposals. Such arrangements would be consistent with the provision in Article II that the President "shall from time to time give to the Congress information on the State of the Union." They would also encourage greater cohesion between the President and the members of his party in Congress.

2. CREATING A SHADOW CABINET FOR THE LEGISLATIVE OPPOSITION

Legislators of the party losing the presidential election should organize a "shadow cabinet." The party's leaders in each house might alternate annually as leader and spokesman of the shadow cabinet, and the party's chairman or ranking member of the major committees in each house might alternate annually as shadow spokesmen in their particular fields, with their counterparts in the other house serving as deputy spokesmen. The shadow cabinet could coordinate party positions on legislative issues and act as party spokesmen before the public.

Reducing the Likelihood of Divided Government

For 20 of the last 32 years—and for 14 out of the last 18—the White House and at least one house of Congress have been controlled by opposing parties. Some of the measures suggested above should reduce the likelihood of divided government, but they may be insufficient to eliminate it. If divided government is recognized as the preeminent cause of interbranch conflict and policy stalemate and deadlock, two stronger approaches are worth considering.

1. MANDATORY STRAIGHT TICKETS The first approach is to make straight-ticket voting not merely easier, as suggested above, but compulsory. By constitutional amendment, each party's nominees for President, Vice President, Senate and House could be placed on the ballot as a single slate, with the voter required to cast his or her vote for one of the party slates in its entirety.

The drawback to this idea is that Americans are strongly committed to voting for the person rather than the party. They would not be easily convinced to sacrifice this freedom in the interest of party loyalty and cohesion.

2. SEQUENTIAL ELECTIONS The second approach is for Congress to enact a statute providing for sequential elections in presidential years, with the voting for President and Vice President to be conducted two to four weeks before the voting for members of Congress. Under such a proposal voters would already know, at the time they balloted for members of Congress, which party they have entrusted with the presidency. This would give the newly elected President an opportunity to persuade voters to elect a majority of the same party to Congress and thus give the party a better opportunity to carry out its program.

The drawbacks here are that in the congressional election Americans might still vote for the person rather than the party. Also, there would probably be a considerable fall-off in the number of voters in the congressional election.

Calling New Elections in the Event of Deadlock or Governmental Failure

If it were possible for a President to call new elections, or for Congress to do so, we would have a mechanism for resolving deadlocks over fundamental policy issues. Indeed, the very existence of such a mechanism would be an inducement to avoid a deadlock that could trigger new elections. It would also make it possible to reconstitute a government that had palpably failed for any other reason.

There are formidable obstacles to incorporating such a device in our present system. Should the President alone, or Congress alone, or both the President and Congress be empowered to call for new elections? How soon should they follow after the passage of the resolution calling for them? Are we prepared to vote in a month other than November? Should there be full new terms for the winners (perhaps adjusted to the regular January expiration dates), or should they fill just the unexpired terms?

These questions can probably be answered. The real questions are whether we need such a strong device for breaking deadlocks or for removing Presidents who have failed for reasons other than impeachable conduct, and whether it is likely that in a special election the electorate would break the deadlock or would simply reelect all the incumbents.

Most constitutional democracies employ such a device, and it deserves serious consideration. It is not inconsistent with separated powers, and it might well operate to encourage cooperation between the branches in order to forestall the ordeal of special elections.

Reexamining the Federal-State Relationship

The weaknesses of the federal government are in large part the result of overload. This overload could be lessened by a better division of responsibility among federal, state and local governments.

A special convocation could be held every ten years with delegates to be selected in equal numbers by federal, state and local governments in a manner to be determined by Congress, to make recommendations to achieve a more cooperative, equitable, efficient, accountable and responsive federal system, under procedures requiring Congress and the state legislatures to vote on each recommendation.

MINORITY PROPOSAL FOR A POSSIBLE PACKAGE

Further discussion of these measures, and others that may be advanced, may well produce a package offering total benefits greater than the sum of the individual parts.

Some of our members believe, for example, that the following measures could be combined into a desirable package.

1. Adopting four-year terms for House members and eight-year terms for Senators, with elections in presidential years.
2. Empowering the President (perhaps with the consent of a specified number of members of one or both houses) or the Congress (by a special or regular majority of both houses, or perhaps even by an absolute majority of the members of one house) to call for a prompt election to all federal offices for new, full terms.
3. Permitting the President to appoint members of Congress to the executive branch without requiring them to give up their seats.
4. Allowing Congress, by constitutional amendment, if necessary, to place reasonable limitations on the total that may be spent in a political campaign.
5. Holding a federal-state-local convocation every ten years to make recommendations for improving the federal system.

A WORD ABOUT PROCEDURES

Article V of the Constitution sets forth two procedures for amending the Constitution. The first is for Congress, by two-thirds majorities of both houses, to submit proposed amendments for ratification by the states. The second is for the legislatures of two-thirds of the states to petition Congress to call a convention for the purpose of proposing amendments. In either case, the proposed amendments do not become part of the Constitution until ratified by three-quarters of the states.

The former method has been used for each of the twenty-six amendments currently in the Constitution. It is a proven way to insure thoughtful consideration for proposed reforms.

The only time in American history when the alternative method may have served a useful purpose was in the drive for the 17th Amendment, which provided for the direct election of United States Senators. Resistance to passage in the Senate led backers to attempt the alternate route. Eventually, the Senate capitulated and helped to frame a congressional resolution that was subsequently ratified.

The Committee on the Constitutional System strongly favors the traditional congressional method for proposing constitutional amendments. We hope that Congress will soon initiate a study to determine whether the Constitution in its present form can provide effective, accountable government for a third century, whether perceived weaknesses in our political structure can be remedied by changes in party rule and statutes, or whether changes in the Constitution itself may be desirable. . . .

CONCLUSION

In presenting this analysis and list of proposals, the Committee wishes to stress its central conviction. The best way to honor the framers of the Constitution during this bicentennial era is to follow their example.

When the parlous state of affairs under the Continental Congress raised doubts about the fitness of the new nation's frame of government, George Washington and his associates took steps to meet the challenge. They adopted the changes necessary (in the words of the resolution that called the Convention of 1787 into being) to "render the federal constitution adequate to the exigencies of government and the preservation of the union."

Two hundred years later, we stand in awe of their achievement. We disserve their memory, however, if we ignore signs that our political system today faces challenges that it is not equipped to meet.

We need to face up to these shortcomings in the capacity of our two-hundred-year-old political structure to cope with a global economy and prevent a nuclear war. We may ultimately conclude that these shortcomings can be remedied without major structural changes, or that any major changes needed to correct them would create even greater problems. But we cannot be confident of having reached the right conclusions until we confront the problems, trace them to their roots and examine the alternatives.

It is in this spirit that we offer these proposals.

 NO

Is the Separation of Powers Outmoded in the Twentieth Century?

JAMES Q. WILSON
Does the Separation of Powers Still Work?

If one is asked to explain why the American government acts as it does with respect to almost any policy issue, the chances are probably eight in ten that the right answer is the separation of powers. The existence of three separate institutions with independent constitutional standing and, in two cases, distinct electoral constituencies is what distinguishes American government from parliamentary democracies. The separation of powers is the source of the enormous influence that Congress exercises over both the broad outlines and minute details of public policy, an influence that has led Daniel Patrick Moynihan to remark that the United States is the only major government with a legislative branch and that leads many European observers to doubt that this country is really governed at all. The separation of powers is also at the root of the courts' authority to declare presidential and congressional acts unconstitutional and thus is a major cause of one kind of judicial activism.

If one is asked what is wrong with American government, the odds are great—maybe not eight in ten, but better than one in two—that the reply will refer to some aspect of our politics that can be explained by the separation of powers: "The president cannot negotiate for the United States on delicate foreign policy matters." "Congress meddles in the work of bureaucratic agencies." "There are too many government leaks to the press." "The Pentagon is not under strong, unified management." "There are too many patronage (i.e., political) appointees in government agencies." "There are too few policy-oriented (i.e., political) appointees in government agencies."

If one makes a list of the most frequently proposed alterations in our constitutional arrangements, the odds are high that these proposals will call for a reduction in the separation of powers: "Let the president put some members of Congress in his cabinet." "Have the president and members of Congress who are from the president's party run as a team." "Allow the president to dissolve Congress." "Allow Congress to call for a special presidential election." "Curb the power of judicial review."

If one listens to the reflections of presidents and their aides, no matter whether they are liberals or conservatives, the most common complaint is that the president does not have enough power. Roosevelt, Truman, Eisenhower, Kennedy, Nixon, Carter, Reagan: All have remarked on how little the president can do compared to what the public expects him to do. Roosevelt, Truman, and Nixon appointed commissions (the President's Commission on Administrative Management [PCAM], the Hoover Commission, and the Ash Commission) to advise them on how best to extend their control over the bureaucracy; Nixon (like many presidents before him) tried to impound funds that Congress had ordered him to spend; Carter made a largely futile effort to weaken congressional control over the bureaucracy; Ford and Reagan have argued that the War Powers Act, which requires congressional participation in presidential decisions to commit armed forces, is unconstitutional. And on and on.

It is as if almost everybody were expressing devotion to the Constitution in general but not to the central principle on which it rests. Does anybody like the separation of powers? Can anything good be said for it?

THE SEPARATION OF POWERS IN THE COURTS

There is one group devoted to the principle: the Supreme Court. It may be activist in interpreting the Bill of Rights, but on the separation of powers it has adopted the most literal readings of the Constitution. In 1926, it held that Congress cannot deny to the president the right to remove an executive official he has appointed[1] (nine years later the Court modified that ruling to allow congressional restrictions on presidential appointments to independent regulatory commissions).[2] In 1975, it held that President Nixon could not impound (i.e., fail to spend) funds appropriated by Congress.[3] The following year it decided that Congress could not appoint members of the Federal Election Commission.[4] In 1983, it overturned the legislative veto, a procedure whereby Congress had granted discretionary authority to the president or subordinate officials subject to the right of Congress to block a proposed exercise of that authority by adopting a resolution.[5] Three years later it struck down a part of the Gramm-Rudman deficit reduction act because the across-the-board spending reductions mandated by the act were, under certain circumstances, to be executed by the Comptroller General. It seems that, because the Comptroller

General can be removed by Congress, he is subservient to Congress and so cannot exercise "executive powers."[6]

From time to time, the Court recognizes that the Founders never intended to create a government based on a strict separation of powers but rather one based, in the words of Richard E. Neustadt, on separate institutions sharing powers. But whenever the Court finds a statement specifying how those powers are to be shared, it tends to give to those words the most narrow construction. For example, its objection to the legislative veto was that such congressional resolutions have the force of law even though they are not signed by the president (never mind that the president may have signed a law creating the system of legislative vetoes); a law, to be a law, "shall be presented to the President of the United States" for his signature or veto as required by the language of Article I. And in the Gramm-Rudman case, the Court was unimpressed by the fact that the Comptroller General, since the creation of the post in 1921, has been a largely nonpartisan and neutral officer who serves a fifteen-year term and who can only be removed for cause and with the assent of both the president and Congress.

It is hard to find an area of constitutional law in which the Court has been as nonactivist as with respect to the separation of powers. The uncharitable may argue that the Court's faithfulness to text on this issue is necessary to empower it to be activist on other issues, for without strict adherence to the doctrine of separated powers the Court itself might not be able to assert the authority, nowhere mentioned in the Constitution, to declare acts of Congress unconstitutional. Perhaps; certainly *Marbury* v. *Madison* (1803), the first case to announce the Court's power to invalidate acts of Congress, was also the first case to argue that Congress had violated the separation of powers (by attempting to enlarge the original jurisdiction of the Court).

Whatever the Court's motives, its words echo hollowly in the halls of contemporary political debate. Scarcely any other voice is raised in praise of the separation of powers, except in the most abstract sense. Separated powers are a fine idea, it would seem, except when they prevent me from having my way.

Of course, it was precisely to prevent officials from having their way that powers were separated in the first place. As Chief Justice Burger said in the Court's opinion in the Gramm-Rudman case, the institutions of government were deliberately arranged to create a system that "produces conflicts, confusion, and discordance." Few presidents probably cared for that arrangement very much, but their complaints were of little moment during the century and a half or so when the national government played a minor role in public affairs (except in wartime, and then the Court, with only a few exceptions, allowed the president quite sweeping powers free of any but the most essential congressional checks). Once the national government began—or tried to begin—to play a large role, presidents, and people who looked to the president for action, visibly and audibly chafed under their constitutional restraints.

THE CASE AGAINST THE SEPARATION OF POWERS

There have always been two distinct, though often intertwined, strands in the case against the separation of powers. One is the liberal case: The federal government should play a large and active role in human affairs by supplying services, reducing economic inequality, and catering to the demands of those who find themselves at a disadvantage in the marketplace. During most of this century, presidents have been more sensitive to the urban and industrial constituencies who make these demands than has Congress. Therefore, the powers of the president should be enlarged and those of Congress (or those parts of Congress that are "obstructionist") should be reduced. From this perspective, it made sense to weaken the authority of congressional committees, or at least the committees headed by powerful conservatives (such as the House Rules Committee under the leadership of the legendary Judge Howard Smith of Virginia). It also made sense to call, as did James MacGregor Burns and E. E. Schattschneider, for strong political parties headed by the president, or presidential candidates, that would be able to command the loyalty of party members in Congress to the president's program and supplant the loyalty those members gave to committee chairmen. When Burns wrote of the "deadlock of democracy," he was writing of the political barriers to the enactment of a liberal agenda.

The other case is the rationalist one. Whether policies are liberal or conservative, they should be made decisively, efficiently, and on the basis of comprehensive principles. The public interest was not well served by simply adding up individual preferences into a "patchwork" or "crazy quilt" of inconsistent programs administered in "wasteful" ways by "duplicative" agencies. The public interest was better served by having a unitary view of what was good for the nation "as a whole." Only a single official could design and propose an internally consistent set of policies based on some overriding principle. In our system that person is the president. Therefore, the president should have more power. In this view, it made sense to give the president firmer control over the bureaucracy, equip him with sufficient staff to develop programs and oversee their administration, empower him to recognize government agencies, and strengthen his hand in dealing with Congress. In theory, a rationalized national government could serve either liberal ends (by enacting broad welfare and regulatory programs) or conservative ones (by cutting waste, reducing spending, and simplifying or minimizing regulation). The rationalist view especially emphasized the foreign policy role of the president. With Tocqueville, it noted that diplomacy is especially difficult in a democracy owing to the need for secrecy, speed, and unity of action, all hampered by the fact that the president must share power with Congress.

The existence of two arguments against checks and balances helps explain why a liberal, Harry Truman, could appoint a conservative, Herbert Hoover, to recommend ways of improving government; why presidents of all stripes have been able to make plausible cases in favor of enhancing their powers; and why movements for constitutional "reform" are able to recruit conservative business-men as well as liberal academics into their ranks.

These reform movements, though they have helped change aspects of the presidency, have not had a fundamental impact on the separation of powers. To the extent the separation of powers has been altered, it has been the result of events more than plans, events that helped liberals more than rationalists.

Liberals achieved the enactment of a large part of their agenda as a conse-quence of two windows of opportunity that opened thirty years apart. The Great Depression enabled an overwhelming Democratic majority in Congress, aided (after 1935) by a slim but solid majority on the Supreme Court, to lay the foundations for the modern welfare state. In 1965, a landslide electoral victory by Lyndon Johnson and the arrival of a liberal majority in both houses of Congress set the stage for a vast expansion of the welfare state and the enact-ment of dozens of consumer- and environmental-protection laws.

Rationalists made some gains in wartime, when the president gained en-hanced authority over the government and the economy, but most of these gains faded with the return to peace. Otherwise, rationalists have had to plug away at small, painfully won changes—the passage of the Budget and Account-ing Act in 1921 (that created the Bureau of the Budget and the General Account-ing Office), the acquisition by the president in 1935 of the power to reorganize by executive order (subject to a legislative veto), the expansion of the White House office pursuant to the recommendations of the PCAM, the passage of the Legislative Reorganization Act of 1946 that reduced the number of standing committees of Congress and laid the groundwork for the growth in congres-sional staff, and the creation in 1978 of the Senior Executive Service (SES) to permit more flexible use of high-level bureaucrats. Some of these changes, especially the creation of the Bureau of the Budget and the attendant growth of presidential control over the budget and the legislative agenda, were of great moment, but many proved to be short-lived or chimerical gains. The power to reorganize expired, and now that the legislative veto has been deemed uncon-stitutional, it probably cannot be revived. The White House staff has grown so much that it has become a bureaucratic problem in its own right. The reduction in the number of congressional committees was quickly followed by the growth in the number of subcommittees, leaving authority in Congress at least as decentralized as it had once been. The Senior Executive Service has been a disappointment: Not many top-level bureaucrats moved from one agency to another, rarely was a SES member fired, and the availability of cash bonuses did not seem to enhance performance.

Moreover, the very success of the liberals in supplying the agenda for and expanding the role of the federal government was achieved at the cost of major setbacks for the rationalist cause. The government became big before the presi-dent became institutionally (as opposed to personally) powerful. What Roosevelt and Johnson created, their successors could not easily manage. Moreover, the liberal gains in the late 1960s and early 1970s were accompanied by a radical decentralization of Congress. Liberal majorities in the House and Senate confronted the conservatives holding power as chairmen of certain key committees, such as the House Rules Committee and the House Ways and Means Committee. To move their agenda onto the floor where its passage was assured, liberals had to unseat committee chairmen they regarded as obstructionist, enhance the power of individual members at the expense of committee chairmen, modify the rules to make it harder to bottle up legislation in committee, and (in the Senate) alter, slightly, the cloture rule to reduce the threat of a filibuster. The effect of these changes, chiefly wrought by the House Democratic caucus, was to increase the power of individual congressmen and reduce the power of congressional leaders.

Politically, if not constitutionally, powers became more rather than less separated. The president now was held responsible for every imaginable domestic and foreign problem, but his capacity to make a systematic response to these problems was reduced by two changes: The growth in the size of the government had contributed to the growth in the number and variety of interest groups that sought to block presidential initiatives, and the decentralization of Congress reduced the president's ability to negotiate with a handful of congressional leaders who could help build legislative majorities.

Critics of the separation of powers could have made one of two responses to this state of affairs. The rationalist might have argued for a reduction in the size and scope of the federal government on the grounds that our policy commitments now exceeded our capacity to manage them. Or the rationalist could have reaffirmed his alliance with the liberals by arguing for more profound and sweeping changes—necessarily involving constitutional revision—in order to reduce the separation of powers sufficiently to permit the president to direct affairs in the new order. By and large, rationalists have chosen the second course, and so we have such groups as the Committee on the Constitutional System (CCS), led by Lloyd Cutler, C. Douglas Dillon, and Senator Nancy Landon Kassebaum. Thirty or forty years ago, I surmise, such a group would have been arguing for a stronger Bureau of the Budget, a bigger White House staff, a more effective civil service system, fewer congressional committees, and (perhaps) stronger political parties. Most of those things happened, but now they seem inadequate to the task of directing a vast federal government. And so the call has gone out for constitutional reform.

To the CCS and its supporters, the need for fundamental change is almost self-evident. Perhaps that is why so little of their writing is devoted to making the case for change. The most important essay, Lloyd Cutler's "To Form a Government,"[7] is almost the only systematic effort to explain why we need to modify the separation of powers. Given their premises, of course, the need for change *is* virtually self-evident. To them, the public interest is a discoverable set of principles and goals from which right actions can be inferred. The means to achieve these ends must be comprehensively and efficiently related to those ends. This is more easily done by one mind than by 535, by an official responsible to a national electorate than by one beholden to many small electorates, and by a person able to carry out his policies subject to the check of electoral defeat than by one who cannot carry out any policies at all without first overcoming countless checks by subcommittees, committees, interest groups, and houses of Congress. The rationalist position, like rationality itself, seems to require little defense.

THE INTENT OF THE FRAMERS

But of course the Framers of the Constitution were not trying to create a government that would discern national goals and serve them efficiently and with dispatch; they were trying to create a limited government that would serve only those goals that could survive a process of consultation and bargaining designed to prevent the mischief of factions and the tyranny of passionate majorities or ambitious politicians. The CCS and its allies understand this but argue that conditions have changed since 1787: Public affairs today are more complex, interdependent, and fraught with peril than they were in the nineteenth century, and so we must modify our governing arrangements in order to meet these new challenges.

It is not difficult, of course, to produce a litany of difficulties facing the nation: a large budget and trade deficit, the threat of nuclear war, a complex array of international commitments, an economy painfully adjusting to new kinds of international competition, the cancer of crime and drug abuse, and so on. But it is not clear that these "new realities" are fundamentally different from the kinds of problems faced by Washington's first administration and it is certainly far from clear that they constitute a case for constitutional change.

The first administrations had to salvage a disrupted economy, pay off or otherwise settle a crushing war debt funded by worthless paper, worry about the presence of hostile British forces in Canada and a British navy at sea, cope with French control of the Mississippi River valley and Spanish control of Florida, put down a rebellion of Pennsylvania farmers protesting the tax on whiskey, reconcile the deep ideological divisions stirred up by the French Revolution, make legitimate the government in the eyes of skeptical Anti-Federalists and Jeffersonian Democrats, do battle with Indians waging war on the periphery of the new republic, and settle the hotly contested Jefferson-Adams presidential race by going to thirty-six ballots in the House of Representatives. Hardly simple times; hardly an easy test for the new constitutional order. It survived.

Today, the case for constitutional change is being made to a nation prosperous and at peace whose political institutions enjoy unquestioned legitimacy.

Decision making is as contentious and protracted now as it was two hundred years ago, but under circumstances that are far more conducive to success and popular support than once was the case. In 1986, one can only be amused to reread the 1974 essay by Charles Hardin on why our government was then in crisis and why only major "constitutional surgery" could correct it. Watergate, the supposedly "imperial presidency," and popular distrust of government were the crisis; the cure required these changes: electing the president and Congress for coterminous four-year terms, abolishing the office of vice president, allowing Congress to remove a president by a vote of no confidence, giving the president an automatic majority in the House of Representatives, and so on. Of course, the "crisis" ended without any of these "cures." Watergate was handled by the normal constitutional procedures—congressional investigations, criminal trials, and the prospect of impeachment—and the presidency and the president are once again in high repute.

REAL AND IMAGINED PROBLEMS

But generalities cannot settle the matter. Let us look at the specific ways in which the constitutional system is allegedly defective: the deficit, economic policy, and foreign affairs.

1. The Deficit

C. Douglas Dillon has argued for a parliamentary democracy because, unlike our system, it would more effectively address the problem of the deficit. There are two things wrong with his argument. The first is that there is no evidence at all that the deficit is a consequence of the separation of powers. At the President's request, taxes were cut. At the President's request, defense spending was increased. At the President's request, the Social Security system was preserved intact, with minor adjustments in tax and benefit levels. At the President's request, budgets were submitted that were not in balance. There are important differences between what the President has requested and Congress has approved with respect to many spending bills, but all of these differences, if resolved in the president's favor, would not produce a balanced budget. The deficit would be somewhat less, but not substantially so, if all presidential requests were automatically enacted by a subservient Congress. If Mr. Dillon is worried about the deficit, he need not vote for constitutional reform; he need only have voted against Mr. Reagan.

The second difficulty with the Dillon argument is immediately apparent when we examine the budgets of parliamentary democracies. There are impor-

Table 1. Deficit Comparison Across Nations for 1984[a]

Country	Percentage of GNP
Italy	12.4
Ireland	12.3
Belgium	10.3
Greece	9.8
Denmark	6.0
Netherlands	5.9
Spain	5.7
Canada	5.3
France	3.5
Sweden	3.5
UNITED STATES	3.1
United Kingdom	2.8
Japan	2.3
Germany	1.4
Norway	−2.4

[a] *Source:* Vito Tanzi, "The Deficit Experience in Industrial Countries," in Phillip Cagan, ed., *The Economy in Deficit* (Washington, D.C.: American Enterprise Institute, 1985), pp. 94–95.

tant conceptual problems in comparing deficits across nations—consider, for example, the problem of comparing governments that do and do not own major industries, or that of comparing deficits between high- and low-inflation countries. Taking into account all these problems, Vito Tanzi of the International Monetary Fund, using data from the Organization for Economic Cooperation and Development (OECD), produces estimates for the 1984 deficit, measured in percentage of gross national product, that are arranged from high to low in Table 1.

Every nation on this list with a fiscal deficit except ours has a parliamentary democracy; that is to say, it is not governed in accordance with the separation of powers. Japan, Germany, and Norway have deficits smaller than ours; Italy, Ireland, Belgium, Greece, Denmark, the Netherlands, Spain, and Canada have much larger ones; France, Sweden, and the United Kingdom are about on a par with us. The safest conclusion that can be drawn from this list is that form of government has no effect on the size of the deficit.

A bolder inference, for which a case might be made, is that parliamentary regimes, by concentrating power in the hands of the executive, facilitate the adoption of new spending measures designed to satisfy the constituencies that brought the prime minister and his party into power. David Cameron has shown, for example, that government spending as a percentage of the gross domestic product and the rate of increase in that spending over the last twenty years or so has been higher in Belgium, France, Italy, the Netherlands, Norway, Sweden, and West Germany than in the United States. Only in Spain and

Japan did the government spend less, and the rate of increase in spending in these countries was faster than it was in this country.[8] Moreover, much (but not all) of the difference between high- and low-spending nations is associated with leftist party control of the government. In any nation, liberals can win elections; in the United States, it is harder for them (or for conservatives) thereby to win control of the government. Parliamentary democracies may have the ability to make the "hard choices" the rationalists want, but it is far from clear they have any desire to do so. What is clear is that it is easier for them to make the easy choices.

2. Economic Policy

We are constantly reminded that we live in an interdependent world undergoing rapid technological and economic change. Those who remind us of this situation claim that the United States does not respond to that change very well. We save and invest too little. We import too much. We allow jobs to be destroyed by Asian competitors. We fail to rebuild our smokestack industries. We regulate in cumbersome ways. We have too many small farmers. Our legal system imposes costly delays.

The implication of these criticisms is that there is a correct economic policy that a bold president would implement. (Among my students at UCLA [University of California at Los Angeles] there is a widespread belief that a sufficiently bold president would turn out to be either Lee Iacocca or Peter Ueberroth.) If the right president can be found, then he should be given the freedom to design and carry out his economic policy. If he fails, the voters will punish him at the next election; if he succeeds, the voters will reward him (unless, of course, constitutional reformers have succeeded in limiting him to a single six-year term).

In support of the virtues of greater decisiveness and comprehensiveness in economic policymaking, one can point to the fact that many other industrial nations have been more successful than the United States in taxing consumption (for example, the value added tax) and rewarding investment (for example, by not taxing capital gains). There is also evidence from several studies of other countries that their system of environmental regulation is less adversarial and less legalistic but just as effective as that in the United States.[9]

These are weighty arguments, but it is not clear they weigh in favor of movement toward a parliamentary regime. First, it is not obvious what economic policy is correct. Of course, advocates of a rationalist governing system will respond that, though no one knows for certain what policies will work, at least a strong, executive-centered system will permit us to try a given policy. Their view is that a yes-or-no referendum by the public is a better check on economic policymaking than a detailed scrutiny and amendment by Congress.

I am not convinced. We may make new economic policy in half-hearted steps or tolerate inconsistent economic programs, but we thereby hedge our bets and avoid the extreme swings in policy that are characteristic of some other regimes. Britain nationalized, denationalized, renationalized, and then denationalized again several of its basic industries. France appears on the verge of doing the same.

Second, it is increasingly implausible to use "deadlock" as a word to describe American policymaking in America. After many decades of increased regulation of prices and conditions of entry in such industries as domestic banking, aviation, securities trading, and telecommunications, a more or less measured and careful process of deregulation has begun that, though far from constituting a revolution, has revealed this nation's capacity for learning and self-correction. After decades during which Democrats demanded steeply progressive tax rates and Republicans went along in return for extensive deductions, the president and Congress renegotiated the terms of that old compact in favor of a system with less steep rates and fewer loopholes.

Third, the adversarial and legalistic nature of economic regulation here, while indisputable, reflects many factors in addition to the separation of powers. No doubt the separation of powers intensifies the adversarial nature of our regulatory system by empowering congressional critics of current regulatory law and enabling the courts to play a large role in reviewing and reversing regulatory decisions. But we live in an adversarial culture, the product of centuries devoted to defining politics as a struggle over rights. We are deeply imbued with a populist suspicion of the sort of behind-the-scenes negotiations that characterize regulatory policymaking in England and Sweden. The centralized nature of political and economic life abroad facilitates the settlement of issues by negotiations among peak associations, whereas here the decentralized political order and the more competitive economic one make it impossible to commit either the government or economic actors to the syndicalist pattern of decision making so often seen in Europe.

3. Foreign Policy

Lloyd Cutler makes much of President Carter's inability to get the Senate to ratify the SALT [Strategic Arms Limitation Treaty] II treaty in 1979. A president able to "form a government" would have been able to commit this country to such a treaty. Cutler points out that no prime minister is faced with the need to obtain senatorial ratification of treaties.

True enough. But one moment: The Senate rarely fails to ratify a treaty. It has approved something approaching a thousand treaties and turned down about twenty and just five in this century, of which only the Treaty of Versailles, establishing the League of Nations, was an important defeat. Of course, it can talk a treaty to death, as it almost did with SALT II (the *coup de grace* was not Senate but Soviet behavior—the USSR invaded Afghanistan before the treaty could come to a vote). But in general the Senate tends to go along.

The crucial question should not be whether the president should have more power over the Senate but whether the treaties that failed ratification were in the public interest. Just before describing Carter's problems with SALT II, Cutler speaks of the need for "making those decisions we all know must be made." Was SALT II such a decision? If so, Cutler leaves the argument unstated. Strong arguments can be and were made against it. Many thoughtful people believed that it was a bad treaty. The notion that ratification should be made easier so that the real check on the success of the president's policy is public reaction at the next election is chimerical: People rarely, if ever, vote for or against presidents because of the treaties they have signed, for the obvious reason that, barring some dramatic incident, the people have no way of knowing whether the treaty was a good or bad idea.

Foreign policy is more than treaties, of course. It is not hard to think of circumstances in which one would want the president to have a freer hand. It is not hard to think of ways of giving him a freer hand. If constitutional reformers are so keen on supplying a freer hand, it is curious that they spend so much time discussing quasi-parliamentary procedures and so little time discussing the virtues of repealing the War Powers Act, modifying congressional supervision of the Central Intelligence Agency, and eliminating the legislative veto over arms sales, none of which requires a constitutional amendment. One wonders whether the rationalists are really rationalists and not actually liberals in rationalist clothing, eager to have a president powerful enough to sign arms-control and nuclear-test-ban agreements but not strong enough to commit troops to Grenada or Lebanon or provide aid to anti-Marxist rebels in Central America or Angola.

Still, a strong case can be made that in negotiating with foreign powers, the president of the United States is in an awkward position, not simply or even mainly because he must get the Senate to ratify his treaties, but because he must publicly negotiate simultaneously with both Congress (and congressionally amplified domestic pressures) and the foreign power. When President Nixon was negotiating with the North Vietnamese to end the war in Southeast Asia, he had to make concessions to both Congress and the enemy, reducing any incentive the enemy had to make concessions in return. As President Reagan negotiates with the Soviet Union over arms control, it would be difficult for him to make credible and useful offers to constrain deployment of anti-satellite weapons or the "Star Wars" defense system if Congress, in advance of the negotiations, places, on its own initiative, constraints on these weapons. It is hard to play poker if someone on your side frequently proclaims that you will give away certain chips regardless of what your opponent may do.

But it is unlikely that any of the most frequently discussed constitutional changes would materially improve the president's bargaining position. Putting members of Congress in the cabinet, letting the president serve a six-year term, or having the president and House members run as a team would leave the president and Congress in essentially the same relationship as they are now: rivals for control over the direction of foreign policy.

THE UNWRITTEN CONSTITUTION

There are two fundamental arguments for a constitutional system of separate institutions sharing powers: It helps preserve liberty and it slows the pace of political change. Those arguments are as valid today as they were in 1787. Individual liberties are more secure when the actions of one part of the national government can be checked by, or appealed to, another. Political change is slower, and so the growth of new programs and public spending is slower, when any new proposal must survive the political obstacle course of bureaus, subcommittees, committees, and houses of Congress.

Rationalists may view the delays, confusion, and inconsistencies produced by this system as costly, as of course they are. But they should not assume that if the costs were reduced or eliminated by reducing or eliminating the separation of powers, the advantages of this system would remain. Even Lloyd Cutler recognizes that a congressional system has some advantages over a parliamentary one; for one thing, the former permits investigations of executive misconduct that the latter does not. Watergate comes quickly to mind, but there are many other examples—Teapot Dome, defense procurement scandals, civil rights abuses, and organized crime. On a smaller scale, one cannot complain to one's congressman about an injustice and have much hope of redress if the power of Congress has been reduced.

Liberal proponents of reducing the separation of powers know full well that it impedes political change and that, I believe, is the major reason they favor such a reduction. At one time they might have worried that an executive-dominated system would threaten liberty, but they have become accustomed (and with good reason) to looking to the courts for the protection of personal liberty, and so this worry no longer seems as serious. That it is a larger state they wish and not simply a more efficient one is evident from the fact that, whereas they have often been eager to curb the independence of Congress, they have never (since 1935) been eager to curb the independence of the courts. Yet judicial independence is probably as much a source of delays, confusion, and uncertainty as is congressional independence (consider how court review affects the operation of public schools, the management of prisons, or the settlement of personal injury claims). If over the last half century the courts had been under the control of conservative rather than liberal activists (or even under the control of conservatives, period), I imagine that liberal enthusiasm for constitutional reforms would not stop at the courthouse door.

Defending the principle of separation of powers is not the same as defending the practices that have developed around these constitutional principles. Don K. Price, like me, argues against constitutional change but argues in favor of changes in the "unwritten constitution," those customs and arrangements that allow a government of separate institutions to work at all.[10]

The most important provision of the unwritten constitution is the internal organization and procedures of Congress. The Constitution requires that the House and the Senate as a whole enact legislation, but it is silent on how many additional "enactments" must occur within the House and the Senate. At one time, there were virtually no congressional committees and no chairmen, at another time there were many powerful chairmen; at one time members of the House had great autonomy, at another time they yielded immense authority to the Speaker; at one time the House Rules Committee dominated the legislative process, at another time it played a smaller role; at one time seniority alone determined who should be chairman, at another time the party caucus influenced the choice of chairmen.

LEADERSHIP IN THE STATES

The variety of unwritten constitutions that can exist within a system of separate institutions is revealed by the experience of American state legislatures. No one can understand the politics of California by reading its constitution, because nowhere does it mention the extraordinary power exercised by the speaker of the assembly. Willie Brown is not elected speaker by the voters of the state, yet next to Governor George Deukmejian he is the most powerful official in that state. People accustomed to think of a lieutenant governor as a political nobody would not be prepared for the extraordinary power enjoyed by the lieutenant governor of Texas, who not only presides over the state senate but chooses the members and chairmen of its committees. If you went to Mississippi to do business with the state, you might think it important to meet the governor, but most people there will tell you that it is more important to meet with the speaker of the House. Like his counterparts in California and several other states, Speaker C. B. "Buddie" Newman of Mississippi can control the composition and leadership of key committees and determine the fate of much legislation.

The Congress of the United States, by contrast, is extremely decentralized and individualized. Speaker Sam Rayburn during the 1950s was not nearly as powerful as Speaker Thomas Reed in the 1890s, but he was far more powerful than Speaker Tip O'Neill in the 1980s. Congress, especially the House, has chosen to have weak leadership; in principle it could choose to have strong leadership. The methods are neither obscure nor unconstitutional: vest in the speaker or the majority leader the power to select and remove committee chairmen; change campaign finance laws so that the House and Senate campaign committees could raise and spend large sums of money on behalf of individual candidates and place control of these entities firmly in the hands of the speaker or majority leader; reduce the ability of individual members to create their own political action committees or to receive funds directly from the political action committees of others; and strengthen the power of the speaker or the majority leader to choose which committees shall consider bills and which bills will come to the floor for a vote. All of these things are done in state governments operating under essentially the same separation-of-powers principles as shape the national government.

It is not entirely clear why state legislatures (including such progressive ones as those in California, Massachusetts, and New York) should have resisted the tides of individualization and decentralization that have engulfed Congress. But two things are clear: First, the weakening of congressional leadership has been accomplished chiefly at the initiative of liberals who regarded strong leaders and chairmen as a barrier to liberal policies. Second, that weakening has reduced, or at least vastly complicated, the ability of the president to negotiate effectively with Congress. If one wishes to preserve the system of checks and balances but facilitate the process of bargaining and reciprocity essential to its operation, it makes more sense to enable the president to negotiate with four or five congressional leaders who can make commitments than to require him (or his legislative affairs staff) to negotiate with scores or even hundreds of individual members, none of whom can commit anyone but himself.

I am not optimistic that Congress will restore strong leadership. As I have written elsewhere,[11] there are very few examples in American history of people who possess certain powers voting to give them up or of people deciding they favored less democracy rather than more. And even if congressional leadership is strengthened, the president will certainly not be able to dominate the leaders who emerge. But it is in this area of the unwritten constitution that remedies for the defects of the separation of powers must be found. There are no constitutional remedies short of the abolition of the principle itself, and that is a price that two hundred years of successful constitutional government should have taught us is too high to pay.

NOTES

1. *Myers v. United States*, 272 U.S. 52 (1926).
2. *Humphrey's Executor v. United States*, 295 U.S. 602 (1935).
3. *Train v. City of New York*, 420 U.S. 35 (1975).
4. *Buckley v. Valeo*, 424 U.S. 1 (1976).
5. *Immigration and Naturalization Service v. Chadha*, 103 S. Ct. 2764 (1983).
6. *Bowsher v. Synar*, 106 S. Ct. 3181 (1986).
7. Lloyd N. Cutler, "To Form a Government," *Foreign Affairs*, Fall 1980, pp. 126–143.
8. David R. Cameron, "Does Government Cause Inflation? Taxes, Spending, and Deficits," in Leon N. Lindberg and Charles S. Maier, eds., *The Politics of Inflation and Economic Stagflation* (Washington, D.C.: Brookings Institution, 1985), pp. 230–232.
9. David Vogel, *National Styles of Regulation* (Ithaca, N.Y.: Cornell University Press, 1986); Steven J. Kelman, *Regulating America, Regulating Sweden* (Cambridge, Mass.: MIT Press, 1981).

10. Don K. Price, *America's Unwritten Constitution* (Baton Rouge, La.: Louisiana State University Press, 1983).

11. James Q. Wilson, "Political Parties and the Separation of Powers," in Robert A. Goldwin and Art Kaufman, eds., *Separation of Powers—Does It Still Work?* (Washington, D.C.: American Enterprise Institute, 1986), pp. 18–37.

Questions for Discussion

1. What changes would have to be made in the Constitution for the United States to adopt a British-type parliamentary system?
2. Who would be the winners and losers of such changes?
3. To what extent has the changing character of the United States from a small agrarian society to a large postindustrial society made the system of separation of powers outmoded?
4. Would the adoption of a parliamentary political system in 1787 have changed the course of U.S. history? If so, how?
5. Is a parliamentary system more accountable to the people than a system of separated powers?
6. What would be the effect of the calling of a new constitutional convention in the 1990s to remedy the alleged defects of the U.S. political system?

Suggested Readings

Bonafede, Dom. "Reform of U.S. System of Government Is on the Minds and Agendas of Many." *National Journal,* 17, no. 26 (June 29, 1985), 1521–1524.

Cutler, Lloyd N. "To Form a Government." *Foreign Affairs,* 59, no. 1 (Fall 1980), 126–143.

Fisher, Louis. *The Politics of Shared Power: Congress and the Executive.* 2nd ed. Washington, D.C.: CQ Press, 1987.

Goldwin, Robert A., and Art Kaufman, eds. *Separation of Powers—Does It Still Work?* Washington, D.C.: American Enterprise Institute for Public Policy Research, 1986.

Price, Don K. "The Parliamentary and Presidential Systems." *Public Administration Review,* 3, no. 4 (Autumn 1943), 317–334.

Robinson, Donald L., ed. *Reforming American Government: The Bicentennial Papers of the Committee on the Constitutional System.* Boulder: Westview Press, 1985.

Scarrow, Howard A. "Parliamentary and Presidential Government Compared." *Current History,* 66, no. 394 (June 1974), 264–267, 272.

Sundquist, James L. *Constitutional Reform and Effective Government.* Washington, D.C.: Brookings Institution, 1986.

U.S. Cong. *Political Economy and Constitutional Reform.* Hearings before the
    Joint Economic Committee, 97th Cong., 2nd Sess., 1982. 2 vols.
Weaver, R. Kent. "Are Parliamentary Systems Better?" *Brookings Review*, 3, no. 4
    (Summer 1985), 16–25.
See also Suggested Readings for Chapter 1.

Chapter 3

Should the National Government Turn Back Major Programs to the States and Localities to Strengthen Federalism?

An understanding of the federal system today requires an examination of what federalism is, why it was established, and how it has evolved. Federalism is a system of government under which power is distributed between central and regional authorities in a way that provides each with important power and functions. The United States is but one of many federal systems around the world. Canada, India, and the Federal Republic of Germany are examples of nations that have federal systems. In the United States the central authority is known as the federal government, and the regional authorities are the state governments.

Federalism is a structural feature not necessarily coterminous with democracy. A federal system divides power. A unitary system, in contrast, concentrates power. In a unitary system power is controlled by the central authorities, as it is, for example, in Great Britain, France, and Poland. In Great Britain, regional governing authorities are created, abolished, or rearranged by the central government at Westminster. In the federal system of the United States, however, state governments cannot be so restructured. No state boundary can be changed by the government in Washington, D.C., acting on its own authority. (An exception occurred during the Civil War when the state of West Virginia was created out of Virginia.)

A federal system was adopted in 1787 because a unitary structure would have been unacceptable to the people of the United States, who had strong loyalties to their states. In addition, the Framers of the Constitution wanted a government that would be stronger than the one existing under the Articles of Confederation, but they feared a central government that was too powerful. The federal system allowed for a compromise between those who favored a strong central government and those who supported a weak central government.

The central governnment was given some exclusive powers (e.g., to coin money and to establish tariffs). The states and federal government shared some powers (e.g., to tax and to spend money). The Tenth Amendment to the Constitution provides that "the powers not delegated to the United States by the Constitution, nor prohibited by it to the States, are reserved to the States respectively, or to the people."

The Constitution is not so clear, however, about where the powers of the central government end. Two centuries of conflict over this issue of states' rights have marked U.S. history. In general, the trend has been away from states' rights and toward national supremacy.

Those who argue for states' rights contend that the Constitution must be interpreted strictly. Congress should legislate only in those areas that are specifically delegated to it in the Constitution and should leave all those powers not mentioned to the states. Those who argue for national supremacy maintain, however, that the Constitution establishes a strong central government with vast authority. They support a broad interpretation of the federal government's powers.

National supremacy proponents have won victories, although they have always been under attack by states' rights advocates. In 1819, for example, in *McCulloch* v. *Maryland*, the Supreme Court upheld the power of the federal government to create a bank despite the fact that the Constitution does not grant an expressed power to the national government for this purpose. The Court held that Congress was granted broad scope through Article I, Section 8, Clause 18 of the Constitution, which gives Congress the power "to make all laws which shall be necessary and proper" to carry out its enumerated powers.[1]

As the character of U.S. society has changed, so, too, have the institutions of government. The relationship between the states and the national government has been influenced by these changes. With the emergence of large corporations whose activities transcend state boundaries, the role of the federal government in regulating interstate commerce has increased. Other economic problems, such as unemployment and inflation, can no longer be satisfactorily handled at the state level and require the federal government's attention.

States' rights became the slogan of groups who benefited from decentralized control—such as big business and segregationists—while national supremacy was heralded by groups that received strong support from Washington—such as labor unions and civil rights advocates. In those instances in which the states were unable or unwilling to meet the needs of a changing industrial economy and to respond to the pressures of social problems, the national government asserted its authority—often at the expense of the states. The courts have upheld the right of the federal government to move into areas previously dominated by the states—such as education, housing, commerce, and employment.

Because the issue of states' rights has become so prominent in the course of U.S. history, it would be wrong to conclude that the relationship between the federal government and the states is best categorized as a zero-sum game, that is, whatever one side gains, the other side loses. Today *cooperation* rather than *conflict* characterizes the relations between the two levels of government, as may be seen from the kinds of federal assistance given to the states.

The federal government collects taxes and disburses its revenues to state governments to be used for purposes such as housing, education, health, transportation, highways, and law enforcement. Interestingly, the states have not asserted the doctrine of states' rights to prevent the money from flowing to their own coffers, but rather they have encouraged and lobbied for more aid. There are three basic types of economic assistance: categorical grants, block grants, and revenue sharing. Each type has advantages and disadvantages that are loudly proclaimed by the groups and agencies that benefit the most.

A categorical grant is an allocation for a specific purpose, such as hospital equipment or school lunches. Under this type of grant, the state may administer a program but must comply with rigid federal guidelines dealing with policies and expenditures. Sometimes the federal grant depends on the state's providing matching funds (that is, contributing state money) in amounts ranging from 10 to 50 percent of the federal government contribution.

A block grant is an allocation for broad rather than narrow functions. Unlike the categorical grant with its rather specific designation of programs, the block grant is allocated for such general policy areas as education, transportation, and law enforcement. A block grant for education can be used for any kind of educational assistance decided upon by state authorities, although it is subject to general federal government regulations. State agencies have much more flexibility in using block grants than they have with categorical grants.

Revenue sharing, a more recent innovation in grants, was probably the Nixon administration's major achievement in domestic policy. Under revenue sharing the federal government provides a general grant to the states and localities to be used as they see fit, but with certain restrictions. In 1980 Congress removed state governments from the list of beneficiaries. Cities, however, continued to receive funds through revenue sharing until 1986, when revenue sharing was completely terminated.

The Reagan administration came to power in 1981 with a commitment to strengthen state governments. In 1982 President Ronald Reagan introduced a program called the New Federalism through which federal government programs would be shifted to the states. The program did not succeed because state governments felt they would not receive sufficient financial support to run those programs. During the Reagan years, federal grants to state and local governments have decreased steadily as a percentage of total federal outlays, dropping from 15.5 percent in fiscal year 1980 to an estimated 11.1 percent in fiscal year 1986.[2]

Since the federal government and state governments have so intertwined their activities, attention has been directed to rearranging federal government–state government relationships. Specifically, the Advisory Commission on Intergovernmental Relations (ACIR), an organization established to promote better coordination and control of powers on the federal, state, and local levels, has recommended "turnbacks"—simultaneous repeal of federal grant-in-aid programs to state and local governments and relinquishment of tax bases—as an approach to achieving increased accountability in the federal system.

In the debate that follows, Robert B. Hawkins, Jr., of ACIR, defends turnbacks. He makes the following points:

1. The federal system has become "congested, overloaded, intrusive, inefficient, and unaccountable." Turnbacks would help correct these defects.
2. It would be possible to apply turnbacks to state and local control in 177 programs.
3. Turnbacks would restore some of the benefits of a federal system, most notably by providing a way to accommodate differing social and political climates across a vast country.

Joseph P. Riley, Jr., who is mayor of Charleston, South Carolina, president of the U.S. Conference of Mayors, and a member of ACIR, regards turnbacks as a misguided effort that would be harmful to the cities. He argues:

1. The current system of grants does not congest the federal system.
2. Turnbacks would mean a dereliction of responsibilities by Washington, particularly toward the nation's cities.
3. Many of the problems of the cities are national in scope and can be solved only by an intergovernmental partnership.
4. Instead of turnbacks, the federal government ought to allow for more flexibility in existing programs.
5. Turnbacks will not produce greater governmental efficiency.

NOTES

1. *McCulloch v. Maryland*, 4 Wheat. 316 (1819).
2. Steve Blakely, "Officials Say Budget Hits States, Cities Hardest," *Congressional Quarterly Weekly Reports*, 44, no. 7 (February 15, 1986), 309.

Should the National Government Turn Back Major Programs to the States and Localities to Strengthen Federalism?

ROBERT B. HAWKINS, JR.
Turnbacks: A Promising Approach

Because a recurrent theme in American political history has been the great emphasis placed on political decentralization as an enduring value, ACIR [Advisory Commission on Intergovernmental Relations] has recommended turnbacks—simultaneous repeal of federal grant-in-aid programs to state and local governments and relinquishment of tax bases—as a promising approach to achieving increased accountability in our federal system. While some obviously localistic programs have previously been folded into block grants, there remains a plethora of categorical grants best financed and administered at the state and local levels.

Over the past 30 years, federal grants-in-aid have grown exorbitantly, both in number and in aggregate dollars. Observers of the intergovernmental system, including ACIR, repeatedly stated that the increasing fiscal and political power of the national government relative to its state and local partners brought the federal system into imbalance. Because of the intricate accumulation of program constraints and requirements, public officials' responsiveness and accountability to the citizenry frequently became impeded. This often distorted the public choices made by the various units of governments administering intergovernmental programs.

More recently, the pressure of huge federal budget deficits engendered cutbacks in grant funding, and this has led to a kind of de facto, disorganized decentralization wherein state and local governments are now financing some program responsibilities formerly funded by Washington. Turnbacks represent a path toward an orderly sorting out of responsibilities: the federal government's withdrawal from programs would be accomplished concurrent with a certainty of funding resources.

DECONGESTING THE SYSTEM

In other reports, the Commission has characterized the present federal system in such terms as "congested, overloaded, intrusive, inefficient, and unaccountable." This has led to an unmanageable national political agenda, promoted undue federal interference in the operations of state and local governments, and frequently produced incongruences between citizen preferences and the goods and services provided by their governments. The cumulative effect of financial reliance on the national government, and the many conditions and requirements attached to the federal aid, has been to erode the authority of state and local officials. Because most grant-in-aid programs lack flexibility in design and implementation, the most desirable characteristics of a federal system—innovation and diversity—have been seriously retarded.

The Commission believes that the federal government should return many responsibilities more appropriately handled by states and localities or private institutions, along with the revenue sources to pay for them. Such an initiative would provide a means to augment permanently the tax bases of state and local governments, and improve the predictability of state and local revenues. Along with economic efficiency, turnbacks also would enhance political accountability by giving citizens greater access to elected and appointed officials making public choices.

As the first step in proposing turnbacks, the Commission established a test of vital national interest—i.e., only when a program meets certain criteria is national government action justified. . . . Applying it to the more than 400 existing federal grants-in-aid, the Commission identified a "candidate list" of 177 programs that could be returned to state or local control. These were in the area of arts and humanities, community development, criminal justice, economic development, economic opportunity, elementary and secondary education, employment and training, food and nutrition, highways and public transportation, libraries, medical assistance, natural resources conservation and development, occupational safety and health, vocational education, volunteer services, and water pollution control.

THE REVENUE RETURN

The approach selected by the Commission for returning revenue sources is for the federal government to relinquish all or part of a tax base it currently uses. Chief among those that could be returned to the states (and in some cases directly to localities) are the federal excise taxes on motor fuels, cigarettes, telephones and alcohol. The Commission also noted that the personal income tax is probably the best tax to return in part to state and local governments in seeking to achieve greater political decentralization. Unfortunately, revenue returns by cutting federal income taxation—in light of the tax reform effort—is politically the most difficult to achieve.

While the Commission did not propose any specific legislation, the report accompanying the recommendation (*Devolving Federal Program Responsibilities and Revenue Sources to State and Local Governments*, A-104) includes five possible ways for the federal government to give serious consideration to turnbacks. Each package would return federal excise taxes to the states while the federal government recedes from a variety of programs. The five packages involve $10 billion, $17 billion, $18 billion, $21 billion, and $22 billion in programmatic authority, and would replace from 84% to 98% of the revenues with excise taxes. In addition, the recommendation directed the ACIR staff to develop alternative packages at the request of interested parties.

PRINCIPLES AND PRAGMATISM

The Commission further recommended that any turnback package be based on the following principles:

- The legislation should provide for an adequate transition period to allow state and local governments to adjust to the new environment of increased political decentralization.
- It should include an adequate pass-through of state funds to local governments during the transition period.
- There should be a mechanism during the transition period to facilitate any state legislative or constitutional changes necessary to adjust the political and fiscal relationship between states and their local governments.

There is an important pragmatic rationale for examining turnbacks at this time. The fiscal reality of current intergovernmental relations is that the federal grant-in-aid system has been under constant budgetary pressure since the mid-70s, and that federal grants will undoubtedly be subject to increased pressures for the foreseeable future. Since 1978, overall spending by states and localities, in constant dollars, has been stable. However, the relative importance of sources of spending has changed dramatically as state and local revenues from their own levies have increased at the same time that federal assistance has declined. In 1978, intergovernmental grants were equal to 36.7% of state and local "own-source" spending; by 1984, that figure declined to 26.9%.

To diminish deficits, it is certain that the Congress will continue to seek spending reductions from that portion of the domestic budget that finances grants-in-aid to state and local governments. Turnbacks offer a way to help meet the mandate for deficit reduction in an efficient and equitable manner.

In a sense, turnbacks might be considered a successor to revenue sharing. While that position may chagrin those who have long supported the revenue sharing concept (including ACIR), the political reality is that the program will almost surely be terminated. Because revenue sharing was originally to be the major decentralization mechanism in the federal system, its demise necessitates a replacement. Turnbacks, which involve both programmatic and tax source returns to states and localities, can act not only as a replacement for revenue sharing, but would represent a true return of authority. For as long as Washington controls the purse strings on the revenues of other units of government, states and localities can never be certain of levels of funding; nor can they be truly self-governing.

Equally as important as fiscal concerns is the restoration of sound federalism principles inherent in the turnback concept. Writing in his autobiography at the age of 77, Thomas Jefferson said: "Were not this great country already divided into states, that division must be made, that each might do for itself what concerns itself directly, and what it can so much better do than a distant authority. . . . Were we directed from Washington when to sow, and when to reap, we should soon want bread." Turnbacks endeavor to restore the Jeffersonian virtues of diversity and decentralization that have been seriously eroded over the past two or three decades.

As the number and financial magnitude of federal grants multiplied during the 1960s and 1970s, so did the federal mandates attached to them. Almost every grant became a vehicle for meeting national environmental, civil rights, handicapped access, relocation, historical preservation, citizen participation, and planning standards. In addition, the federal government mandated detailed standards for budgeting, reporting, auditing and other administrative standards. These often confrontational national policies generated massive amounts of new litigation, and because of the federal dollars involved most of the cases upheld federal dominance in these matters. The federal courts not only acceded to the judgement of the Congress in most cases, but even went beyond the vagueness of laws to supply concrete operational interpretations and direct administrative remedies.

Taken together, the activities of the national government have significantly weakened state and local governments' political and fiscal accountability to their citizens by driving a wedge between taxing and spending choices. The will of local majorities has been broadly and unjustifiably thwarted. Washington's activism also has unnecessarily burdened other units of government with intrusive requirements and onerous demands and procedures. This has had the effect of circumscribing the authority of states and localities to the point of hampering effective governance.

The Commission's turnback recommendation contemplates the return of three kinds of responsibilities to the state and local levels: the responsibility of deciding whether and in what amounts to provide certain goods and services which currently are federally supported; the responsibility of deciding how to provide them; and the responsibility for raising the revenue to finance any increase in state and local government activity necessitated by these state and local decisions. Citizens' choices on whether a given service is better assumed by the public sector, as opposed to the private sector or by volunteers, can better be articulated through the state and local political process than by Washington.

At its core, federalism concerns itself with the constitutional design of multilevel government—what James Madison called a "compound republic." Indeed, a compound society such as the United States cannot be governed without a system to accommodate diversity. While some might view decentralization as fostering disparity—a diminishing of national community—those of us who seek to return authority to states and localities see it as fostering harmony among a diverse people. Surely, we are one nation, but it is a nation of unique parts. Turnbacks offer a way to accommodate differing social and political climates across a vast land, and for a diverse people to demand those government services they want and need.

 ☑ N O

Should the National Government Turn Back Major Programs to the States and Localities to Strengthen Federalism?

JOSEPH P. RILEY, JR.
Turnbacks: A Misguided Effort

In one year [in 1987], we will celebrate the 200th anniversary of our Constitution, our commitment to a federal system and the rejection of a confederation. Ironically, the proposed use of turnbacks to achieve increased political decentralization flouts the principles we are preparing to celebrate. The revenue turnback proposal is a philosophically driven and misguided effort. If its directives were enacted by the Congress, our cities and their citizens would incur substantial harm.

This proposal personifies the sin of excess, a hallmark of the far left and the far right. Excess, or at least the fear of excess, provoked a national re-evaluation of the federal system. The rapid growth and escalation of categorical federal programs in the 1950s, 1960s and early 1970s led to allegations that the federal system was congested and had caused a loss of local autonomy. The criticism that a national response to problems might have been carried to excess in some areas was fair. The result was a re-evaluation of the system, and the pendulum began swinging back in the other direction. This swing led to a substantial decongestion in the federal system.

Two important examples illustrate measures adopted to decongest the system. The General Revenue Sharing program was in part a response to this effort. The program is the diametric opposite of a categorical grant; there is little red tape; it has complete respect for local autonomy and is allocated at the "level of government closest to the people." It is ironic that the leading proponent of the decongestion of the federal system is recommending the abolition of

General Revenue Sharing, however, much to the fiscal harm of local governments and their citizens.

The Community Development Block Grant (CDBG) program was another
response to the need to decongest the federal system. CDBG replaced many
categorical federal programs and replaced them with one block grant where,
under general federal guidelines, local governments have the autonomy to
allocate the money where the local level deems necessary. This successful
program has spirited the revitalization of hundreds of cities and communities
across this country; yet it is another program slated to be dissolved under this
proposal, causing more harm to our cities.

The growth of the federal government in relation to programs affecting
state and local governments started to reverse in the mid-1970s. By 1978,
dollars allocated to state and local governments had peaked. Since 1978,
there has been a substantial reduction of programs and funding. Federal
funds for urban-related programs have been reduced substantially. For most
cities, we have had a near-fatal dose of antihistamine. We can afford no
more decongestion.

We have a decentralized government by any reasonable standard. In my city
of Charleston, this year's budget required a property tax increase, in part because of a reduction in General Revenue Sharing funds. If General Revenue
Sharing is completely abolished next year, we will have another and far more
substantial property tax increase.

Most cities in our country, Charleston included, suffer from a relatively
insufficient tax base and very limited sources of revenue, tightly restricted by
state constitutions and state statutes. We do not feel congested by the federal
system; we pass our budgets and ordinances without supervision by federal or
state bureaucrats. At City Council meetings, the talk is not of decongestion but
of a lack of resources.

EXCESSIVE DECENTRALIZATION

If the proliferation of categorical grants-in-aid during the 1960s and 1970s
resulted in excessive centralization of government, then the sin of excessive
decentralization is likewise committed in this Commission recommendation. It
would result in a dereliction of responsibilities by Washington, particularly
toward the nation's cities.

This turnback effort is not primarily an effort to decongest; it expresses the
philosophical imperative of some to have our national government wash its
hands of any concern for local needs and problems. It is the philosophy that
"this is not our problem—it's your problem in the cities." Local governments
are viewed as not only autonomous but also just as one of the many Third
World countries. This turnback philosophy believes that public transportation

is not our problem as a nation—it's your problem in the city. The hungry and the homeless, the mentally ill, the terrible cycle of poverty and unemployment in the central cities are not problems of the United States, but localized inconveniences to be borne solely by the states and cities. To be sure, the problems of public transportation, economic development, slums, poverty and homelessness are local problems and can be solved only when there is a determined and aggressive partnership driven at the local level. But these problems can never be solved if our national government does not share its part of the responsibility of that partnership.

NATIONAL ISSUES—NATIONAL RESPONSES

There is no need to apologize for this last generation's national efforts to address issues national in scope by assisting state and local entities. This effort, in historical perspective, has made our country greater. The mid-course corrections required by such a complex undertaking are in place. Now the entire federal-city partnership is being threatened by a philosophy that would inject a fatal dose of antihistamine into a system of government where there is scant evidence that congestion even exists.

Under the turnback philosophy, one would argue that there would never have been a National Endowment for the Arts or a National Endowment for the Humanities. That would have been most unfortunate for our country, because these two agencies have given national leadership, encouragement and modest funding to thousands of artistic endeavors throughout our country that have made this a richer nation. Under the turnback philosophy, there would never have been an Urban Mass Transportation Administration that helped to develop a national consensus on the need to "decongest" our central cities and make our urban areas more livable.

Urban Development Action Grants are not pervasive; they are targeted to our most distressed central cities. Pollution control grants are not intrusive; they help preserve our national environment. Community Development Block Grants are not unmanageable; the program replaced scores of categorical programs and helped revitalize hundreds of cities across our country. General Revenue Sharing is not inefficient; it has complete respect for local autonomy and is allocated at the level of government closest to the people. And these programs—along with scores of others—are costly and unaccountable only to the extent that the Congress imposes excessive restrictions. What is needed is not a turnback, but more flexibility in existing programs.

I ask the proponents of a large-scale turnback program to climb down from their ivory towers and come to my city. I can show them how those national efforts, carried out by an autonomous, uncongested, local, closest-to-the-people government, have immeasurably improved my city and all of its people—who are, by the way, American citizens, part of this nation and part of the federal government.

They are not part of a confederation. The confederation ended almost 200 years ago. They are part of a national government and have reason to expect that their national government, as well as their state and local governments, will accept a responsibility to address their needs, whatever they are, wherever they are found.

The rationale for this ACIR [Advisory Commission on Intergovernmental Relations] turnback recommendation relies on unsubstantiated generalizations which few state and local elected officials and civil servants would endorse.

A major federal turnback effort would do substantial harm to my city and most cities of our country. It would end programs that have been good and successful and would create, at best, an uncertain future. There is little chance that most of the initiative sponsored by these programs would be kept. Certainly, the cold-hearted suggestion to give a tobacco excise tax to state governments, and the other turnback taxes, present no long-term financial hopes. Further, there are state constitutional and statutory barriers to any legitimate pass-through of this taxing authority to local governments. In terms of turning back revenue to localities, many local governmental units do not have the authority—and possibly not the capacity—to pick up the funding of turned-back programs, even though such programs are needed.

The claim that turnbacks are efficient is specious. There are many national initiatives that cannot be divided by fifty in terms of the states or by a thousand or more in terms of cities. The turnback proposal supports a theory that we would have fifty Institutes of Museum Services, or perhaps a thousand. One national Institute of Museum Services can help set some national goals and thoughtfully allocate money where it can be wisely and prudently used. A plethora of Institutes of Museum Services would consume the modest amount of available money just in terms of administrative and bureaucratic expenses. The same can be said of many federal programs that can be run far more efficiently by a small national staff than by fifty state staffs or a thousand local staffs. There are many more examples of this inconsistency in the turnback philosophy.

DEFICIT REDUCTION

Turnback proponents cite the need to reduce the federal deficit. Their implication that federal grant-in-aid programs continue to grow is erroneous. It is important to remember that in the last six years when the federal deficit has shot up from $70 billion to more than $200 billion, urban programs have been severely reduced. There was a definite peaking in 1978 of dollars allocated to state and local governments. Between 1980 and 1985, total federal expenditures increased by 23.3%, with defense increasing by 33.9% and interest on the debt increasing 86%, while federal grants to state and local governments decreased. Local governments have already taken more than their fair share of federal budget cuts. It is unrealistic and unfair, if not dishonest, to argue or even to hint that federal urban programs caused the explosion in the size of the national deficit.

The linking of turnbacks with deficit reduction carries scant cogency because our country's basic deficit problem is caused by a failure of political will to deal at the federal level with its root causes and a lack of fiscal discipline in defense spending. This has precious little to do with intergovernmental relations and turnbacks.

The recommendation fails to recognize the constraints within the Congressional process which severely limit the use of turnbacks: the overlapping jurisdiction of committees; the competing interest groups and their reluctance to see their programs changed or given to another level of government; and the reluctance of elected officials, having enacted taxes and being criticized for it, to hand the revenue over to another jurisdiction.

In my opinion, this federal turnback proposal belongs in the files of the ACIR. This proposal swings far too sharply to the right.

Our country will always seek to provide national initiatives—and we should. A given President and Congress will, as they should, look out across this great country, see problems that are important—whether they are housing, economic development, mass transit, encouragement of the arts, poverty, hunger, AIDS or cancer—and they will seek to develop a national response. Because of our experiences in the 1950s, 1960s and 1970s, our country will be less likely to develop a heavy-handed categorical approach and will be more likely to involve the states and localities to every extent possible. Washington will be far more alert to the excesses of a national response, but not oblivious to national need.

The error of this massive turnback program is that it forgets that we are a nation and we should be proud of, not apologetic for, being so. I believe that in years to come this ACIR report will be considered a benchmark—the benchmark of when the pendulum had swung too far to the right.

Questions for Discussion

1. What criteria can be used in evaluating whether a policy area properly belongs to the states or to the federal government?
2. Who would be helped and who would be hurt by the system of turnbacks advocated by the ACIR?

3. How are innovation and diversity encouraged in the existing system of federal grants? How are they impeded?
4. What effect would turnbacks have on political accountability?
5. What effect would the ACIR program on turnbacks have on (1) the level of government spending, and (2) the level of taxes?

Suggested Readings

Blakeley, Steve. "Officials Say Budget Hits States, Cities Hardest." *Congressional Quarterly Weekly Report*, 44, no. 7 (February 15, 1986), 309–311.

Bowman, Ann O'M., and Richard C. Kearney. *The Resurgence of the States*. Englewood Cliffs, N.J.: Prentice-Hall, 1986.

Caraley, Demetrios. "Changing Conceptions of Federalism." *Political Science Quarterly*, 101, no. 2 (1986), 289–306.

Commager, Henry Steele. "Tocqueville's Mistake." *Harper's*, 269, no. 1611 (August 1984), 69–74.

Derthick, Martha. "American Federalism: Madison's Middle Ground in the 1980s." *Public Administration Review*, 47, no. 1 (January–February 1987), 66–74.

Fein, Bruce. "Let the States Decide." *World & I*, 2, no. 1 (January 1987), 183–188.

Nice, David C. *Federalism: The Politics of Intergovernmental Relations*. New York: St. Martin's Press, 1987.

Ross, Michael J. *State and Local Politics and Policy: Change and Reform*. Englewood Cliffs, N.J.: Prentice-Hall, 1987.

Saikowski, Charlotte. "The States Make a Comeback." *Christian Science Monitor*, February 12, 1987, pp. 18–21.

U.S. Cong., Senate. *Comprehensive Federalism Reform*. Hearing before the Subcommittee on Intergovernmental Relations of the Committee on Governmental Affairs, 99th Cong., 2nd Sess., 1986.

Part II

Popular Participation

4. *Is the United States a Racist Society?*

5. *Is the Feminist Movement in Decay?*

6. *Do Voting and Elections Mean Anything?*

7. *Does Private Funding for Congressional Elections Give Undue Influence to Political Action Committees?*

8. *Will Political Parties Continue to Decline in Importance?*

9. *Do the Mass Media Have a Liberal Bias?*

D emocracies pride themselves on the freedom of people to participate in the political process. Such participation takes many
forms, including forming private associations known as interest
groups, getting involved in political campaigns, voting, working for political parties, and expressing ideas through speech or the mass media.

The traditional definition of an interest group is a collection of people
with common interests who work together to achieve those interests.
When a group becomes involved in the activities of government, it is
known as a political interest group.

More than a century ago, Alexis de Tocqueville observed that the
people of the United States have a propensity to form associations. This
observation has become as valid a description of the 1980s as it was of
the 1830s. The United States has a large number of political interest
groups—business, labor, professional, religious, and social reform. At the
same time, many citizens do not belong to organizations other than
religious and social groups, which in some cases have no significant
political role.

Interest groups engage in a variety of activities, including making financial contributions to candidates for public office and to political parties,
getting their viewpoints known to the general public and to other groups,
organizing demonstrations, and influencing government officials. Legitimate political behavior in a democracy allows for great freedom to participate in these ways. The First Amendment to the Constitution is often
cited as the basis for such political behavior. That amendment states:

> Congress shall make no law respecting an establishment of reli-
> gion, or prohibiting the free exercise thereof; or abridging the freedom
> of speech, or of the press; or the right of the people peaceably to
> assemble, and to petition the Government for a redress of grievances.

One form of political activity is involvement in political campaigns and
elections. In a democracy people are free to support candidates of their
choice. Such support may consist of merely voting in an election, but it
may also include organizing meetings, soliciting support for candidates,
raising and spending money for candidates, and publicizing issues.

Democracy requires that information be widely disseminated. The
same First Amendment that protects the rights of individuals and groups
to engage in political activities also safeguards the press and other media

such as television, radio, and magazines. Television, particularly, has become the chief source of news for many people.

What people do and what they think are of vital importance to government officials. In democracies (and even in many dictatorships) government makes every effort to know what public opinion is on many issues. Sometimes government leads and sometimes it follows public opinion.

Although modern dictatorships rely on political participation, that participation is generally controlled by the ruling dictatorship. Interest groups are not spontaneous organizations designed to be independent from government but are linked to government primarily through government-controlled leadership. And so, for example, trade unions are not free to strike or engage in protest activities—at least not legitimately. People are not free to form competitive political parties, and often there is only one political party that dominates elections. That party is regarded as having a special role in mobilizing the masses.

In many modern dictatorships elections do take place, but they are generally rigged. Where opposing candidates are permitted to compete, there is generally no significant difference between the candidates on issues. Protest movements and mass demonstrations are broken up, sometimes ruthlessly, unless those movements are controlled by the government. To be sure, protest movements and demonstrations do exist in some modern dictatorships, but government tries to control or suppress them.

In modern dictatorships, moreover, the media are not free to report the news in an objective manner. Instead, the media reflect the wishes of the ruling dictators. News is suppressed, opposition newspapers are closed down. There is only one truth—that of the government—disseminated through television, radio, magazines, and newspapers.

Most of the people in the world live in systems that are ruled by dictators. The degree of dictatorship varies. Some dictatorships are more ruthless than others. Communist countries have created an ideology of Marxism-Leninism that goes counter to the basic principles underlying the U.S. political system. Many noncommunist regimes are also dictatorial. In this regard Chile is ruled by a military dictatorship. South Africa denies the right to vote to its majority black population and breaks up demonstrations designed to change white minority rule. Paraguay has an abysmal record on protecting basic human rights.

Although democracies are fundamentally different from dictatorships, even democracies do not always live up to the standards of freedom which they cherish. In this regard, the political behavior of nongovernmental organizations in the United States poses problems for those interested in protecting democratic processes. Although it is relatively easy to discuss democracy in the abstract, actual practices in the U.S. political system raise thorny questions about the application of democracy to concrete situations. This part considers six current issues relating to popular participation in the democratic process: the degree of racism in U.S. society, the strength and direction of feminism, the importance and impact of voting, the ways in which contributions by special interest groups may or may not influence the democratic process, the effectiveness of political parties, and the role of the mass media in shaping public opinion.

Chapter 4

Is the United States a Racist Society?

For those committed to racial equality, the 1960s was a glorious period. Groups from nearly all sectors of U.S. society united to work for the political rights of black people. Moreover, those gains that were achieved came through the efforts of a movement committed to peaceful protest.

As barriers to political participation were removed, blacks won offices in electoral contests at national, state, and local levels. Major cities such as Atlanta, Chicago, Los Angeles, Detroit, and Philadelphia elected black mayors. Blacks were appointed to judgeships, the most notable example being Thurgood Marshall as the first black member of the U.S. Supreme Court. Cabinet posts and civil service positions were opened up to blacks as well.

Blacks also made gains in society generally. They were accepted as students into major universities; they entered corporate posts from which they had previously been excluded. Significant strides were made toward the goal of a multiracial society in such areas as housing, education, and employment.

Still, as indicated in the selections by John E. Jacob and Glenn C. Loury in Part Four, for many blacks the gains were limited. The overall figures on level of income, employment in corporate management positions, educational achievement, health, life expectancy, and punishment for criminal offenses showed that blacks fared poorly compared to whites—at least as far as percentages are concerned.

The continued disparity between the condition of whites and blacks has raised the issue of racial prejudice in the United States. That subject is considered here in the selections by Juan Williams, a national correspondent for the *Washington Post*, and writer Philip Perlmutter.

Williams describes racism in the United States as persistent. He notes that white people think that many black people are criminals even though statistics on crime show that the stereotype is wrong. Moreover, 70 percent of blacks earn less than $20,000 per year and blacks earn on average 56 cents for every dollar earned by whites. According to Williams, to be born black in the United States means to be denied many of the opportunities open to white people.

Perlmutter argues that those who see the United States as a racist society commit a number of perceptual, philosophical, logical, and historical fallacies. These fallacies are:

1. selective perception, wherein only injustices are seen or reported and improvements ignored.
2. vestigial observation, wherein present-day symptoms or charges of bigotry are confused with yesteryears' actual diseases.
3. petrified language, in which terms from the past are missapplied to the present.
4. indiscriminate comparisons, in which one group is criticized or condemned for not being like another group.
5. pseudo-egalitarianism, in which all people and groups are considered fundamentally alike and that if only everyone were treated equally, no differences would exist and intergroup harmony would prevail.
6. "doomsday" generalization, which foresees a group's eventual extinction because of historic and immutable bigotry.

☑ Y E S

Is the United States a Racist Society?

JUAN WILLIAMS

Closed Doors: Benign Racism in America

A friend of mine, a drummer, recently went to Norway with his band. He called the other day to say he isn't coming back. Charles Mana can't believe the life he lives there as a 30-year-old black man. When he walks down the street at night he doesn't have to cut a wide path around white people. He's not used to being asked by an elderly white woman on the train to help her carry her bag to a dark parking lot. His efforts to gain the attention of nightclubs do not run into the racial barriers of heavy metal (white) versus urban progressive (black) rock. He can play his sound and people listen to it for what it is. The in-crowd that runs the music industry is not averse to a black musician who isn't already a celebrity. In the United States he had to deal with the elite and nervous group of black executives at white record companies who were chary of taking a risk on an unproven talent. And in Norway, he said, doormen, store owners, and salesmen don't treat him like a potential thief, "like a nigger back home."

I'm pleased for Charlie. But his call left me raw, stripping away any pretense left in my day-to-day existence that it is possible to be more than a "black" in America. Every nation, including Norway, has its own benighted minority. But in the United States it is the current fashion to pretend that we've put all that behind us. I'm not part of that fashionable crowd. Although I've become callused to much of the indignity that goes with having dark skin in white America, racism is a constant reality for me. And when the calluses peel away, I feel anew how much of my identity is drained from me in trying not to scare whites while walking down the street; in standing on a street corner fruitlessly waving my hand for a cab; in dealing with bosses who see me as a symbol of racial progress for the company or as another disgruntled black employee; in going shopping in a store where my skin color makes me an automatic robbery suspect.

This last point was raised in a recent controversial column by *Washington Post* columnist Richard Cohen. He supported Washington store owners who often won't let young black men through the door on the grounds that they are potential thieves. If they are admitted to the store, salespeople surround them until they leave. Cohen rationally argued that the store owners' actions are justified since the statistics show that young black men commit most of the District's [District of Columbia] robberies and muggings. I found the column an outrageous offering of well-dressed bigotry, and I was dismayed to hear white friends defend it as an opinion rooted in truth.

In fact, it is a lie. A convenient, racist lie. Nationally 21 percent of all robberies and muggings are committed by black males between the ages of 18 and 29. White males between the same ages commit exactly the same percentage of the muggings and robberies. (In Washington, where 70 percent of the population is black, the police department reports that 41 percent of all robberies and attempted robberies are committed by black males age 18 to 24.) My only association with any black muggers and robbers is my skin color. Most young black men in this city can make the same prosaic claim. That truth escapes those who are quick to draw dubious links between crime and race, even those liberal, presumably fair-minded whites such as Cohen. They work with blacks; they claim they are not bigoted at all. Their adherence to the old stereotypes is thus all the more baffling and insidious.

Whites have far less to fear from a potential black mugger than a black person does. For example, according to the Department of Justice's "National Crime Victim Survey," in robberies committed by blacks, 14 percent of the victims are white and 83 percent are black. Of course, anyone seeing another person approaching on a deserted street has reason to be paranoid. In one way or another, crime periodically intrudes upon the lives of most Americans. And young black men do commit a disproportionate share of muggings in some cities. But if a black person has been beaten up or robbed by another black person, he or she doesn't leap to the conclusion that young men with black skin should be automatically suspect as muggers and/or robbers. Those victims know other black people as brothers, friends, and so on, and retain their ability to treat them as individuals.

Some whites seem not to want to bother to make this distinction between individual blacks. They may figure it costs them less to close their doors to some blacks or to make black shoppers feel uncomfortable than to be robbed by a black thief. The price paid by blacks—the loss of their individual identity and achieved self-worth—is not an issue for them. It is for me.

In truth, Cohen's column is an exposé of the first order. The revealed instinct to bigotry and the attempt to justify it in print as protecting one's self (or store) against crime offer a rare public glimpse of the subterranean pool of prejudices now judged acceptable among some whites for news columns, over the dinner table, among sophisticated friends and colleagues, and even to a black friend from whom they seek reassurance that they have good reason for their racism. The operative principle guiding most of this is not so much simple racial hate as it is indifference. I find that whites generally prefer not to think about blacks or racial issues. It is too burdensome to go through the deep waters of race relations. There are too many instances of clear-cut injustice, too much guilt. (My favorite evasion: "I've never discriminated against anyone. Why do I have to do anything for blacks?") Let's talk about arms control and the Evil Empire.

Much of the increasing ease with which some whites avoid thinking about race (not to mention some blacks who either feel weary of discussing the subject or believe they can score points with whites by not mentioning it) is due to a sense of comfort from the progress that has been made in race relations since the not-so-long-ago evil days of strict segregation. The sight of well-dressed blacks in the corridors of big corporations and lunching downtown with their American Express cards is reassurance enough that race relations in the United States aren't deteriorating after all.

But whether you are black or white, there is, finally, no pretending, as President Reagan would have it, that race doesn't matter in the United States because we are a "color-blind" society. Race remains the central domestic issue in the nation. Even if some blacks are doing better (there are more black doctors and lawyers than ever, although they still amount to less than one percent of the nation's doctors and lawyers), consider that 70 percent of blacks still earn under $20,000 a year. Black college graduates are often earning about the same as their white counterparts, but blacks still earn, on average, about 56 cents for every dollar earned by whites—a drop of about five points in the last decade. Unemployment is currently three times higher among black Americans than among white Americans.

Increasingly, those who bother to respond at all to these unpleasant truths contend that blacks need to practice more "self-help" to end their dependence on the government, to lower illegitimate birth rates, to encourage excellence in school. In policymaking and intellectual circles these days, "self-help" is the equivalent of a "Get Out of Jail Free" card in Monopoly. These people insist that blacks can solve their own problems, competing and succeeding in the American mainstream as have Asians, West Indians, Hispanics, or any other minority that has made a place for itself in the land of opportunity.

Black intellectuals such as Thomas Sowell and Glenn Loury have been among those who contend that blacks need to direct more energy into straightening their own house. Well, the argument is not without truth. There is much the black community can do to start and support its own businesses, offer clear moral guidance to children on the problems of drugs and teenage pregnancy. People need to know that some patterns of behavior hurt them and their community. But this is not a new argument. Throughout the history of this nation, blacks have practiced self-help in churches, black schools, black fraternities, and tightly knit families; and more recently through groups like the NAACP [National Association for the Advancement of Colored People] and Urban League. A far more urgent reality is this country's history of legal, government-enforced discrimination against black people.

One recent study showed that for young men graduating from high school, the best route to a job was through relatives. The absence or small number of older black workers—due to outright discrimination in the '40s, '50s, and '60s—means that young black men don't get into the job pipeline at the same rate as white youngsters. Another study found that a black person renting an apartment or house hunting in the Washington, D.C., area has about a 50 percent chance of being turned away solely on the basis of race. A black, middle-class Boston developer told the *Boston Globe* last year that he was shut out by white architects and builders when he tried to get contracts in white neighborhoods. He found the banks reluctant to deal with a new developer who was black, and the insurance companies adamant in their refusal to adjust bonding requirements for a developer who was not one of the boys among the established white developers in town.

In Washington that benign racism continues to prevail. It is not only jewelry stores that exclude black people. Blacks are not even allowed in the door for the serious business of politics unless there is a black faction to be placated with a token face. The Democratic National Committee recently held a high-powered dinner for its top fund-raisers and best known politicians and did not invite a single black politician—not Bill Gray, chairman of the House Budget Committee, and not Jesse Jackson, the presidential candidate in 1984. When Mickey Leland, chairman of the Congressional Black Caucus, protested about the all-white meeting, he was told that Jackson had not raised money for the party and Gray was not a presidential candidate. This is the black community's reward for voting overwhelmingly for Democratic candidates. And yet blacks who criticize the Democratic Party for this sort of insult are denounced as demagogues.

It has gone almost without notice that President Reagan has not met with black civil rights leaders or spoken to major black groups in over five years. He also refuses to meet with elected black politicians. The Defense Department, the State Department, and the security agencies don't have blacks (with their perspectives and ideas) in executive positions and are not interested in Americans of color unless they need the face to satisfy an affirmative action goal.

The effect of the Reagan approach has been to narrow the entire civil rights policy debate to a zero-sum game in which blacks are trying to take away jobs and opportunity from whites. In that atmosphere there is little room for a middle ground. Blacks and whites are polarized. Even conservative, middle-class blacks who favor more discipline and hard work in the black community, and who are raising questions about affirmative action goals and quotas, are uneasy about the administration's civil rights ideals. It is all too apparent that while Reagan's men speak in self-righteous tones about discrimination against hardworking whites and the need for blacks to do more to help themselves, these men have neglected violations of black voting rights to the point where Reagan resisted signing an extension of the Voting Rights Act; twisted the Civil Rights Commission into an advocacy group for the administration's position that helping blacks is reverse discrimination; and tried to restore tax breaks to segregationist schools.

But perhaps the most damaging of all the race-conscious trends in America is a presumption I find common among whites. The presumption is that if a black person were skilled he would perform just like a white person—play office politics as a white would, get the same encouragement and the same measure of respect from his peers as a white would, be invited to the right dinner parties—in other words, earn the right to be treated white. This is what whites are saying when they confide to friends, some black, that they can't find black professionals able to handle the job or able to meet the standards of the other workers. We'd love to have a black, they say, but we can't sacrifice standards.

A bright black person still needs added support in a white work environment simply because to be black in most white corporate settings is to be an outsider, and outsiders don't do well in any corporation. They are not in on the gossip, they don't have the mentors or the contacts. Blacks are not party to the support system of corporate networks and old school ties that provide the boosts neces-sary to even the brightest white people. I've been in a job where I've worked hard, displayed loyalty to the company, and yet management never displays the trust in me that they place in my white colleagues. Contrary to popular belief, even today this nation is far from a meritocracy. Morris Abram, a white man on Reagan's reconstituted Civil Rights Commission and a firm believer in America as a color-blind meritocracy, obtained a job at the commission for a friend of his son. Self-help indeed.

Why should whites be asked to disregard race when discussing crime, but urged to take it into account when dealing with blacks in the workplace? When is discrimination racist, and when is it both legitimate and necessary? It is no secret that distinctions between black and white behavior have been used throughout this country's history to exclude blacks from the fundamental rights and privileges of American citizenship. Surely the right to enter a jewelry store without being harassed because of one's age, sex, or skin color is one of them. The purpose of the civil rights movement was not to abolish the differences among races, but to ensure that blacks (and women and other minorities) are granted the rights they have been systematically denied. Affirmative action in the workplace has played a critical role in that process. When can whites legitimately say they've redressed the sins of a racist past? I don't know. I do know that there must be better proof than there is today that the practice of discrimination through exclusion has been relinquished.

To be born black in this country today still means that you will likely go to a second-rate big-city public school. Even if you get through high school and into college, you will find a declining number of black students in colleges, and those who are left are often bitterly alienated by the absence of any concession to the difficulty of being black in an overwhelmingly white environment. Ed Meese and Ronald Reagan seem to be joined by increasing numbers of Americans who object to special treatment. Their anthem is equality for all. For Charlie Mana, that anthem wasn't enough.

$\boxed{\checkmark}$ *NO*

Is the United States a Racist Society?

PHILIP PERLMUTTER
Fallacies of Evaluation

In any discussion of prejudice and discrimination, two questions inevitably arise over facts and values. One is whether or not America was or is democratic or undemocratic, racist or free, and, as if to gain a more reasoned answer, the adverbs "really" or "truly" are added. Qualified or not, the question attempts to assess the facts as they were or are.

The second question attempts to evaluate the situation over a period of time. Have conditions been improving or getting worse since the writing of the Bill of Rights, the 14th Amendment, the 1954 Supreme Court desegregation decision, Martin Luther King Jr.'s 1963 March on Washington, the War on Poverty, or any president's term of office. Here, too, for added emphasis, "really" or "truly" is inserted to affirm or challenge the evaluation. While only a foolish few would try to deny the existence of intergroup hostility, an equally foolish few would argue an absence of improvement.

The justification for a positive or negative assessment is usually laden with passion, ideology, politics—and, at times, historical ignorance. Nevertheless, the questions are appropriate, for they reflect a profound concern about basic values, beliefs and ideals.

All too often in recent years, the answers have been in the negative, regardless of who was President, with intergroup relations projected as bad or never worse, and as if any admission of societal well-being or progress was tantamount to being uncaring or callous to existing social ills. Such assessments are not only inaccurate, but work against solving the very problems deplored. They fail to recognize that over the years intergroup relations have been changing for the better, and that positive changes have been accumulating, with little backsliding.

Such meliorism is usually scorned, particularly by those who believe America a racist or a well-intentioned nation heading towards two separate and unequal societies. Such people—whether reformers or revolutionaries—commit a number of perceptual, philosophical, logical and historical fallacies:

First is that of selective perception, wherein only injustices are seen or reported and improvements ignored. Thus, it is commonplace for many minority leaders to espouse solutions to bigotry, which can vary with what most members of their group believe. For example, while increasing numbers of "minority" leaders have called for "quotas," polls have consistently shown minority group members opposing them.

For example, as far back as 1977, at least 80 percent of women and 55 percent of Blacks preferred "ability" to "preferential treatment." Five years later, a broad range of ethnic groups believed that ability based on test scores should be the main consideration for jobs and college entrances: Poles by 81.5 percent; Italians, 80 percent; Irish, 77.5 percent; Jews, 76 percent; and Hispanics, 60.5 percent. In 1983, 77.7 percent of whites and 52.2 percent of non-whites polled believed companies should hire "the most qualified person," while only 15.3 percent of whites and 40.7 percent of non-whites believed companies should be legally required to hire a certain percentage of minority group members, even if not the most qualified. Similarly, an early 1984 Gallup Poll revealed that women, too, chose "ability" over "preferential treatment" in "getting jobs and places in college" by 84 percent to 11 percent—and non-whites did so by 64 percent to 27 percent.

Similarly, though outright racists have opposed school busing (forced or voluntary), so have a majority of people of both races:

- A 1976 Harris poll showed that 51 percent of the Blacks and 81 percent of the whites did so, and in another poll, 52 percent of the Blacks and 75 percent of the whites believed "busing school children across district lines makes relations between the races worse."
- A 1981 Newsweek poll of black opinion revealed half of the respondents agreeing that school busing "caused more difficulties than it is worth." Similarly, a New York Times/CBS News Poll found that 45 percent of the Blacks polled opposed school busing for racial integration, while only 37 percent favored it. Even in some cities where busing had been introduced, Black opposition increased. For example, before busing began in 1977 in Wilmington, Delaware, 40 percent of the Black parents opposed it, but a year later, the percentage rose to 50 percent, though there had been no violence or picketing by whites. Some Black leaders, like Derrick A. Bell, Jr., who had represented the

NAACP in over 300 school desegregation cases, now claimed that the equating of "racially balanced schools with the right to an equal education opportunity is a certain formula for losing both" and that integrated schools did not bring about "either interracial understanding or academic improvement for poor black children."

- In 1982, polls revealed broad ethnic opposition to busing for improving school racial balance: Irish, 79.5 percent; Italian, 79 percent; Polish, 74 percent; Jewish, 68 percent; and Hispanic, 50.5 percent.

A second fallacy is that of vestigial observation, wherein present-day symptoms or charges of bigotry are confused with yesteryear's actual diseases. Any college or industry which does not admit or hire a particular minority group member or set percentage is vulnerable to vilification for bigotry, though the greater truth is that more minorities than ever before are entering schools and obtaining jobs. Gone are the virulent anti-Japanese, anti-Chinese, anti-Catholic or anti-Semitic behaviors of past decades and centuries. The reality of the day is that groups once excluded are now included, and that with increasing frequency, it is done on a preferential basis.

Another fallacy is that of petrified language. Though the deplored situation may have changed or disappeared, the language description remains and is applied to a different situation. Thus, any unequal pay for women is referred to as "sexism," or any brutality against a minority member is labelled "genocide," or any criticism of a minority is rejected as "anti-Semitism," or "racism." Simply put, every example or alleged example of inequality, brutality or criticism is not group oppression, genocide or racism. Ironically, rather than "discrimination" being defined as invidious treatment because of race, sex, religion or national origin, it has come to mean absence of favorable treatment because of such factors.

Fourth is the fallacy of indiscriminate comparisons, where a group is criticized or condemned for not being like "our" group—or "our" group is hailed because it is not like *that* one. No or little thought is given to the sociological factors which contributed to differences between "we" and "they," nor is there any historical recognition that today's non-discriminated against groups were once so targeted. History shows that nothing said about today's Black, Asian or Hispanic groups was not said about yesteryear's Irish, Italian, Greek, Polish, Jewish, or Scotch-Irish immigrants.

Pseudo-egalitarianism is a fifth fallacy, wherein all people and groups are considered fundamentally alike and that if only everyone were treated equally, no differences would exist and intergroup harmony would prevail. Existing differences in learning, income, educational achievement, or social behavior are credited, or blamed, on living in privileged circumstances or a hostile environment. Such reasoning invariably ignores that within and between groups some people work harder or do not want to work harder than others, save or spend more, have larger or smaller families, prefer certain games and pastimes, and are not equally motivated by nature or nurture to obtain the same goals in life.

Prejudice and discrimination alone can never explain why some groups succeed in rising to higher socio-economic and educational levels than other groups, as in the cases of Jews, Chinese, Japanese, Irish, Armenians, Huguenots, and Mormons—or why some groups have more family members working or not working. Also at work are differential age levels in high-level jobs, which are usually reached at the age of 40 or 50. For example, the Mexican American and Puerto Rican average age is below twenty, that of Irish American and Italian Americans is over thirty, and that of Jews is over forty. Thus, gaining experience and obtaining good jobs is intricately related to getting older, so that minority group representation in high level jobs cannot be compared to representation in a population that includes many five-year-olds—yet it is.

In education, too, some minorities have higher percentages of young people. While nearly one-third of all white Americans are 19 years old or under, it is 40 percent for all Blacks and Hispanics, who represent close to 30 percent of the nation's high school student body, though comprising 20 percent of the total population. In 1983, approximately 50 percent of all Black and 60 percent of all Hispanic households had children of school age—in contrast to less than 40 percent of white households.

The last fallacy is that of "doomsday" generalization, which foresees a group's eventual extinction because of historic and immutable bigotry. Thus, the Jewish Defense League and the early Black Panthers saw another holocaust or genocide in the making because of latent or blatant examples of anti-Semitism or racism, though both were at their lowest levels—attitudinally and behaviorally. Similarly, there are millennialists—religious and political—who await an imminent "end of days" or world revolution, which, as of this writing, has not occurred.

How shall groups be evaluated? Certainly not as above—and certainly not in absolute or politically partisan concepts, which distort the potentiality and actuality of group existence and progress.

Questions for Discussion

1. What criteria should be used in evaluating whether a country is racist?
2. How would you compare racism in the United States with racism in other countries?
3. How would you evaluate the degree of racism against racial minorities other than blacks in the United States?
4. To what do you attribute the small percentage of blacks in key positions of government and business?

5. How would you evaluate the behavior of a shop owner who will not allow young black men through the door of the shop on the grounds that they are potential thieves or muggers?

Suggested Readings

Dunbar, Leslie W., ed. *Minority Report: What Has Happened to Blacks, Hispanics, American Indians, and Other Minorities in the Eighties?* New York: Pantheon Books, 1984.

Friedman, Murray. "America Is Not a Racist Society." *Wall Street Journal,* February 20, 1987, p. 20.

Friedrich, Otto. "Racism on the Rise." *Time,* 129, no. 5 (February 2, 1987), 18–21.

"Moving Up at Last?" [forum with Juan Williams, Glenn C. Loury, Julian Bond, Frank Mingo, and Paula Giddings]. *Harper's,* 274, no. 1641 (February 1987), 35–39, 42–46.

New York National Urban League. *The State of Black America 1987.* New York: New York National Urban League, 1987.

Pettigrew, Thomas F. "New Patterns of Racism: The Different Worlds of 1984 and 1964." *Rutgers Law Review,* 37, no. 4 (Summer 1985), 673–706.

Sobran, Joseph. "Howard Beach: The Uses and Abuses of Race." *National Review,* 39, no. 5 (March 27, 1987), 28–30, 33, 36, 38.

Wattenberg, Ben J. *The Good News Is the Bad News Is Wrong.* New York: Simon & Schuster, 1984.

Wilhelm, Sidney M. "The Economic Demise of Blacks in America: A Prelude to Genocide?" *Journal of Black Studies,* 17, no. 2 (December 1986), 201–254.

See also Suggested Readings for Chapter 15.

Is the Feminist Movement in Decay?

The twentieth century has witnessed steady changes in the status of women. At the beginning of the century, in most states women were not permitted to vote. The Nineteenth Amendment to the Constitution, ratified in 1920, declared that the right of United States citizens to vote "shall not be denied or abridged by the United States or by any States on account of sex." Although granted voting power, women still faced laws and practices that were discriminatory.

In the decades immediately after the adoption of the Nineteenth Amendment, few women served in the Congress or in leadership positions in the executive branch of government. Women were generally denied the opportunity to reach top-level positions in the corporate world. Many professional schools, such as those in law and medicine, restricted the number of women admitted as students. To the extent that women were encouraged to pursue professional careers, those careers were in such areas as nursing and elementary-school teaching. In some areas, such as fire fighting and law enforcement, laws specifically excluded women from jobs. The pay for women was much lower than the pay for men even when they performed the same jobs.

World War II marked one turning point in the status of women. Since men were drafted into the armed forces, women were asked to perform jobs from which they were previously excluded, such as working in heavy industry. When the war ended, however, women were called upon to give up their jobs so that the male veterans who had fought in the war could be employed.

The 1960s, with the rise of the feminist movement, marked another turning point in the status of women. The National Organization for Women (NOW) was created in 1966, largely through the inspiration of writer Betty Friedan, author of the landmark *Feminine Mystique* (1963), and through the efforts of other feminist activists. NOW was committed to eliminating the legal, social, political, and economic impediments to women's equality in society. From its beginning until the present, NOW has been a liberal organization, and not all women have been in agreement with its agenda—particularly on the issue of the right to abortion, which NOW endorses. Phyllis Schlafly, a conservative leader of the Eagle Forum, for example, has opposed NOW's commitments to such matters as abortion, sexual freedom, gay rights, and an emphasis on government programs to strengthen the welfare state.

Much of the efforts of NOW were directed to the ratification of the Equal Rights Amendment (ERA), which would have prohibited discrimination on the basis of sex. The amendment, which was approved by Congress in 1972, failed to achieve the necessary ratification of three-fourths of the state legislatures and, consequently, did not become the law of the land. Supporters of the proposed amendment argued that its adoption would end the many discriminatory laws against women and that it was needed to promote genuine equality. Critics of the ERA contended that its adoption would be harmful to women in that legal protections for women would be at risk.

NOW and other women's organizations helped to bring about many improvements in the status of women. Women were elected to local, state, and national office and appointed to key posts previously held by men alone. The barriers for female admission to professional schools have been removed. Today, it is not uncommon for law schools and medical schools to have one-third to one-half of their students composed of women.

With the defeat of the ERA and acknowledged shifts in the thinking of early feminist leaders, however, some observers have argued that the feminist movement is now in decay. Dinesh D'Souza, a former managing editor of the conservative journal *Policy Review*, argues that it is. As evidence he cites the failure of the ERA, the defeat in 1984 of a Democratic party slate whose vice-presidential candidate was Geraldine Ferraro, and some Supreme Court decisions that have been unfavorable to NOW. D'Souza contends, however, that the main problem for feminists is the massive erosion of support among women for feminist views on child rearing and on the family and the strong feminist identification with lesbianism. Many women, he adds, have found laws enacted largely through the efforts of the feminist movement to be harmful to women.

Dorothy Wickenden, managing editor of the *New Republic*, is more optimistic about the future of the feminist movement. She identifies the feminist difficulty as arising out of conflicts between the equal rights feminists and the social feminists. The equal rights feminists favor promoting equal rights in defiance of gender differences. The social feminists are dubious about aspiring to standards of public and private life established by and for men. Wickenden argues that the feminist movement has been remarkably successful in securing individual freedom. It should start now to launch a major offensive for a series of concrete social reforms and changes in the workplace.

Is the Feminist Movement in Decay?

DINESH D'SOUZA
The New Feminist Revolt

While women in America are doing better than ever, the women's movement is in decay and despair. The reason is that feminism, which once helped open many windows of opportunity for women, has now turned against itself. Many of feminism's pioneers and its most brilliant advocates are now protesting the very social developments they cheered and accelerated only a couple of decades ago—developments that have proved harmful to the interests of most women.

American women have made remarkable professional advances in the last 15 years. Now there are 104,000 female lawyers, up from 13,000 in 1970; 130,000 female bankers, up from 43,000; 101,000 female engineers, up from 21,000; and 83,000 female doctors, up from 29,000. Even the physically strenuous and hazardous fields are now open to women. Today there are 96,000 women who are truck drivers, compared with 42,000 in 1970; 78,000 woman construction workers, compared with 61,000 in 1970; and 72,000 policewomen, compared with 22,000 in 1970. Indeed the representation of women in every part of the work force has increased: women continue to dominate traditionally female occupations such as nursing and secretarial work, but they have also penetrated the computer industry, stockbroking, wholesale and retail products, university teaching and administration, real estate, and the media.

Women are scaling higher and higher rungs on the political ladder. According to the Center for the American Woman at Rutgers University, more than 15,000 women now hold elective office, up from around 5,500 in 1975, a 300 percent increase. There are more women in the Senate and the House of Representatives than ever before. In the home, men and women share cooking, laundry, and other responsibilities in a way they never did. Female sexuality is considered just as legitimate as male sexuality: some of the old double standards have been repealed. Finally, abuses to which women have always been subject are receiving the attention they deserve. Rape and wife abuse both inspire a public horror and bring stern penalties in court; previously, though not exactly vaunted social customs, they were downplayed in the absence of totally unambiguous evidence. The feminist movement catalyzed and, in some cases, initiated these social developments, for which the vast majority of American women owe it a great debt.

Yet the feminist movement enters [1986] anxious and demoralized. Its problems are acknowledged by many of the prime movers of women's liberation. Betty Friedan writes about a "profound paralysis" in feminism. Judy Goldsmith says this is an "extremely difficult period" in which the women's movement finds it "nearly impossible to make advances." Andrea Dworkin observes that "The women's movement is in decay and is not likely to recover very soon." Susan Brownmiller admits that "The steam has run out of feminism." This is lugubrious rhetoric coming from women who once displayed extraordinary vitality and optimism. Predicting nothing less than a transformation of Western society, they propelled their feminist ideology to the center of public and private discourse. They challenged the conventions of language, of social protocol, of religious practice, of raising children. Only two decades later, with only a fraction of their expansive agenda met, these women are all suffering post-feminist depression.

Partly they are responding to a series of political defeats. Despite an energetic, multi-million dollar campaign, enormous encouragement from the media, and the endorsement of countless public officials, feminists were unable to get the Equal Rights Amendment (E.R.A.) ratified. Nor, despite their extravagant promises, were they able to prevent the President's re-election with Geraldine Ferraro on the Democratic ticket. The Reagan Administration, feminists complain, has diminished the trend of female political appointments, balked at affirmative action for women, proposed regulations to limit abortion and birth control for minors, and scaled back federal handouts such as Aid to Families with Dependent Children (A.F.D.C.) which primarily benefit women. Of late the Supreme Court has not been cooperative either: its *Grove City* ruling narrowed the interpretation of Title IX to ban sex discrimination only in specific educational programs that receive federal funding; it has permitted Congress to cut off Medicaid funds for the purpose of abortion; it may soon reconsider the constitutionality of *Roe v. Wade*.

EROSION OF SUPPORT

But the main problem for feminism is not ephemeral political reversals. It is the massive erosion of support among American women. Not just women, but also young career women who owe most to the feminist crusades of an earlier era and ought to be the movement's fiercest defenders and ripest recruits. Jean Bethke Elshtain, a feminist professor at the University of Massachusetts at Amherst, writes that the women's movement is perceived by young women as harboring "contempt for the female body, for pregnancy, for childbirth, and child-rearing." Also as an outlet for "mean-spirited denunciation of all relations between men and women." In 1981, the *New York Times Magazine* published a lead article by a feminist noting with dismay that most females in their 20s view feminists as "bored," "unhappy," "bitter," "tired," and "lacking in humor." Moreover, "feminism has come to be strongly identified with lesbianism."

It's not simply a matter of skewed perceptions, which, after all, could be triumphantly ascribed to the patriarchal press. The most intelligent and influential feminists of the 1960s and 1970s are now recanting important aspects of their previous thought and, in the process, turning against the most ingrained assumptions of the women's movement. Betty Friedan's 1963 classic, *The Feminine Mystique,* helped launch the feminist movement by identifying the family as an oppressive institution in which women's needs were systematically denied. Recently, in *The Second Stage,* Friedan worries about "feminist denial of the importance of family, of women's own needs to give and get love and nurture." She calls for a revival of the American family, and feminist relationships with men based on mutual love and cooperation, not hostility.

In 1970, Germaine Greer wrote *The Female Eunuch,* which condemned motherhood as a handicap and pregnancy as an illness. "If women are to effect a significant amelioration in their condition," Greer wrote, "it seems obvious that they must refuse to marry." Instead, they should be "deliberately promiscuous" but not conceive babies. In 1984, Greer published *Sex and Destiny,* a self-avowed "attack upon the ideology of sexual freedom," in which she blames artificial birth control for the decline of fertility in the West, laments family breakup and autotelic sex, decries the 600,000 annual sterilizations in this country, and says the export of contraceptive technology to the Third World is "evil."

Susan Brownmiller, whose *Against Our Will* alerted an entire generation of feminists to rape and sexual politics, now scarcely misses an opportunity to excoriate the women's movement. It ignores "profound biological and psychological differences" between men and women, she says, and is fixated on issues such as comparable worth, which she finds "dumb" and "dopey." In apparent opposition to such feminist causes as affirmative action and maternity leave with pay, Brownmiller remarks, "I don't see why men should have to step aside and wait for women to catch up after they've taken time off to have children. That's very difficult truth for a lot of feminists, who don't want to believe that there are these differences or that there could be a handicap." Brownmiller's point is that if women choose to have children, an option not open to men, they should "accept the consequences of that choice."

"DAYS OF OUTRAGE"

Recently, Eleanor Smeal was elected president of the National Organization for Women (NOW) on a pledge to break the apostasy and bewilderment in the movement and revive the catatonic troopers. She has announced a 200,000 person rally in support of abortion on demand in the spring of 1986. Other planned NOW events include an "emergency campaign" to revive the Civil Rights Restoration Act of 1984, the reintroduction of E.R.A. in state legislatures, a "stepped up fight" to legitimate homosexual and lesbian lifestyles, a drive for comparable worth legislation, the sponsorship of Vatican embassy "days of outrage" to oppose Catholic teaching on sexuality, and the cementing of a "strong alliance" with the disarmament movement.

Smeal's adrenalin-charged approach stirred up many NOW delegates, yet there are grave doubts within the organization over whether the real problems of feminism can be addressed merely through pungent talk and indignant marches. "Futile nostalgia for the radical marching tunes of another day will not enlist a new generation in different circumstances," warns Betty Friedan, the founder of NOW. Indeed Friedan argues that one reason NOW's membership has been plummeting, from 200,000 a few years ago to 130,000 today, is that feminists have failed to confront the empirical results of programs they backed in the past.

An increasing number of thoughtful feminists, though, are beginning to take on these issues. After helping to remedy social evils that existed, they are now turning their attention to social ills that they helped to cause. They are coming to terms with the negative fallout of the women's movement, debating these in candid and undogmatic terms, and sometimes arriving at solutions which fall outside the parameters of feminist orthodoxy or perhaps even repudiate the earlier tenets of feminism.

The best example of such an issue is no-fault divorce. There are now such easy, egalitarian divorce laws in 48 states, passed largely in response to pressure from the women's movement. But in a recent book that is drawing a great deal of perspiration in feminist quarters, *The Divorce Revolution,* Lenore Weitzman points out that men have benefited from no-fault divorce laws and women have been harmed. Her study of 3,000 cases shows that, as a result of these laws, divorced women and their children suffered a 73 percent drop in their standard of living, while their ex-husbands enjoyed a 42 percent rise in theirs.

This happened partly because of married women's relative lack of job training resulting in lesser earnings in the marketplace. Also because equal sharing of property under no-fault laws usually means the forced sale of the family home, which previously used to be awarded to the wife and children. Child support payments by the father almost always end when the kids turn 18, just about the time that college expenses begin and the mother must pay exorbitant bills. Easy, no-fault divorce laws may also have contributed to the larger number of divorces in the United States, spreading their economic consequences to more and more women. The number of divorces has risen from 479,000 in 1965 to over a million last year [in 1985].

The deleterious consequences for women of no-fault divorce laws are not merely economic. Feminist author Barbara Ehrenreich points out that divorced women are much less likely to get married again, and the likelihood of marriage for women falls off sharply with age. Thus women are often deprived of intimate companionship in the later, more difficult years of life. In the 45–54 age group, for example, more than 60 percent of divorced men remarry, compared with only 38 percent of women. Part of the reason is that older men have a much easier time finding considerably younger women to wed. "Men can reasonably expect to have two marriages," Ehrenreich says. "Women can expect to grow old without a partner." Feminists have roundly condemned the social reality that women depreciate faster than men, but they have no idea what to do about it.

A few feminists have begun to reconsider no-fault divorce. Judy Goldsmith, former president of NOW, who was recently ousted from the position by Smeal, says the laws need "careful re-evaluation" and recommends tighter restrictions on divorce and more lucrative settlements for women. Gloria Steinem, editor of *Ms.*, says the forced relocation of women and children after the family house is sold "poses enormous hardship." But she, like most feminists, does not advocate greater legal restrictions on divorce, such as a mandatory waiting period, because this is what anti-feminists want. Some women's advocates have simply reconciled themselves to the consequences of no-fault laws. Barbara Ehrenreich's only advice is that women alter their expectations to include loneliness and financial hardship. Karen DeCrow, NOW president from 1974–1977, believes "Women should no longer look on marriage as a source of income and stability, only as a source of companionship and sexual pleasure. They should stop assuming that because their marriages are ending, they should be supported for life."

WOMEN IN POVERTY

Feminists are becoming increasingly aware of the role of divorce and out-of-wedlock births in generating poverty for women in the United States. Previously it was thought that poverty was simply a function of omnipresent sexual discrimination. But the feminization of poverty in this country has come about precisely as sexual discrimination has decreased—thanks to social and legal prohibition. Divorced and unmarried women with children frequently do not marry; as a result, their children are raised in single-parent households. There are now 10 million female-headed households in the U.S.; 35 percent of them live below the poverty line. In 1959, only 25 percent of poor whites and 29 percent of poor blacks lived in female-headed households; in 1984, 42 percent of poor whites and 68 percent of poor blacks did. Few of these women were poor when they lived with their husbands or their parents. It is when the pregnant teenager leaves her home and lives alone with her child that she is most likely to be hungry and homeless; the poverty rate for such women is 70 percent. Similarly, it is when a divorced woman tries to raise her children on her own that the economic condition of her household tends to deteriorate.

It is ironic, given this, that virtually all the early feminist literature inveighed against the traditional family and against having children within marriage. Marriage was equated with subjugation, with incarceration, with slavery; husbands were "predators" (Susan Brownmiller), "oppressors" (Kate Millett), and "cannibalists" (Ti-Grace Atkinson). Pregnancy was "a temporary deformation of the woman's body for the sake of the species" (Shulamith Firestone). Children were instruments of the confinement of women in the home. At the same time, feminists showed no animus whatsoever against teenage pregnancy and births out of wedlock; these were treated as socially inevitable and a sign of the erosion of suffocating norms. Feminists protested all societal attitudes that discouraged divorce and unmarried births, portraying them as antiquated and cruel.

The only feminist solution for female-headed households, increased government aid to unwed mothers to ameliorate their condition, was tried during the 1960s and 1970s; the evidence now shows that it failed miserably, and may have added to the problem it was designed to solve. For example, the number of female-headed black households has more than doubled since 1965, as increased welfare payments reduced women's incentives to stay with their husbands, as well as providing men with excuses to leave their wives and children. "What middle class white feminists construed as oppressive, the family, has been the main source of economic stability of poor black women," comments Jean Elshtain. In fact, she says, "Many feminist ideas and proposals have deepened the inequities between men and women. Some of the results we should have predicted. But it's time to admit that the feminist vision was limited. We can't keep blaming everything on sexism and backlash."

"DOPEY" COMPARABLE WORTH

A few feminists are even taking on the recent drive of the women's movement for comparable worth on the grounds that it is an implicit rejection of what feminists fought for during the last 20 years. The initial goal of feminism was to pry open erstwhile male professions. The assumption was that women were just as good as men in the marketplace; if jobs were equally open to them, they would be able to compete with men, and pay equity would soon be achieved. As Sally Ride became an astronaut, Geraldine Ferraro a vice-presidential candidate, and thousands of other women ascended to top positions in corporations and government, this objective seemed to be realizable.

But then it became clear to feminists that not many women immediately qualified for the most attractive of these jobs, that several competent women who struggled hard for their promotions then quit because of their inexplicable desire to have children, and that the majority of women showed no particular desire to enter well-paying but physically demanding areas such as construction work. Feminist theorists who cogitated over this problem came up with a panacea: if women don't want the lucrative male jobs, they reasoned, female salaries should be elevated by legislative mandate to masculine levels.

The market mechanism is usually used to set wages, but feminists have never been unduly enthusiastic about the market. The market is "racist and sexist," says Jennifer Brown, president of the New York chapter of NOW. "I don't trust the market. Frankly, I detest it." Feminists have called for consulting firms to set prices for jobs based on credentials and skills, and courts to instruct employers to raise women's pay based on these evaluations. To see how this works, consider the following assessment from the court case of *American Federation of State, County, and Municipal Employees v. State of Washington:*

	Nurse	Typist	Truck Driver
Knowledge and Skill	280	106	61
Mental Demands	122	23	10
Accountability	160	23	13
Working Conditions	11	0	13
TOTAL VALUE	573	152	97

Confronted with this table, Jean Elshtain says, "This is arbitrary. Absurd. Almost nightmarish. All I can imagine is thousands of bureaucrats sitting around trying to figure out what jobs are worth." The calculus obviously overvalues credentials and undervalues unpleasant working conditions and temporary and irregular hours, she points out. Karen DeCrow adds, "In the market system, we don't pay people on the basis of training alone." By most comparable worth criteria, she says, "Bruce Springsteen would probably get minimum wage." DeCrow views the feminist drive on this issue mainly as a "consciousness-raising device." Susan Brownmiller alleges that comparable worth "makes a mockery out of work" by pretending it can be objectively assessed for monetary value. So far the courts have sided with these two feminists against the majority of their colleagues, ruling that actual discrimination has to be proven before women's wages are elevated by fiat.

THE OBLIGING PORNOGRAPHER

In the social arena, the most significant development that feminists initially accepted as a sign of sexual liberation but are now gravely regretting is pornography. Most feminists were never for pornography, but certainly did not mind the way it undermined traditional values and marital fidelity. Many criticized pornography for only depicting trashy and dumb-looking women, but *Playboy* promptly accommodated them with special features on "Women of the Ivy League" and "Women of Mensa." Some feminists berated the double standards by which men could view pornography with immunity while women were supposed to be uninterested in it; again, the pornographers obliged with *Playgirl* and male striptease shows.

Many feminists drew distinctions between pornography and erotica but others were quick to expose these as jesuitical and legally irrelevant. Karen DeCrow now publishes articles in *Penthouse* savagely critical of her feminist friends who work to outlaw smut. Conceding that most pornography caters to men, DeCrow maintains that this is because "Women have not had the freedom to express an interest in sex. They have been taught to reject the erotic." The most dangerous thing feminists can have in this country is censorship, DeCrow argues. "Our social movement is radical and often unpopular. Any mechanism for banning material will hurt us." Among the feminists who continue to oppose antiporn activism are Ellen Willis of the *Village Voice*, who says that "in rejecting sexual repression and hypocrisy, pornography expresses a radical impulse" that should attract feminists, and Betty Friedan, who worries that pornography protests are "giving the impression on college campuses that to be a feminist is to be against sex."

But these rationalizations for legalized pornography are becoming more and more scarce in the feminist movement. The reason is the incredible proliferation of pornography in the last decade. Today's market brings an estimated $7 billion in annual revenues, an average of $30 for each man, woman and child in the United States. The menu has expanded beyond spontaneous heterosexual liaisons into a smorgasbord of homosexuality, bestiality, sex with inanimate objects, gang rape, necrophilia, and sex murders. Even children are not exempt from the cast of characters.

None of this was predicted by the early feminists, most of whom believed that as constricting social norms were set aside, sex could be freer and less perverted and consequently the demand for pornography would evaporate. In fact, it greatly multiplied and, in a perverse application of Gresham's Law, bad sex began to drive out good sex. Feminist opposition to pornorgraphy has become increasingly belligerent. Many groups are casting their civil libertarian rhetoric aside to argue for the legal prohibition of materials that portray women being raped, slashed, beaten, and humiliated—and loving it.

Feminists who have resisted the impulse to censor pornography find themselves having to condemn another feminist enterprise: attempts to sanitize allegedly sexist works of literature and religion. Take the case of the National Council of Churches responding to feminist pressure and rewriting the Bible to expunge patriarchal images. Judy Goldsmith objects, "To take the sexism out of the Bible as though it wasn't there is basically a lie." There is both sex and sexism in that document, she says, and both should be left in. Karen DeCrow concurs. "The Judeo-Christian religion has been very woman hating," she says.

"I don't know if sanitizing it is such a good idea. Women should know where the real tradition comes from."

In the other camp, feminists who have come to recognize the dangers of pornography and the harm done to women by it are now conceding that, on the issue, they were wrong and the anti-feminists were right. "Phyllis Schlafly had been making trenchant comments about pornography long before us," admits Twiss Butler, a NOW member who works on the issue. "When Jerry Falwell starts saying that there is real harm in pornography, then that is valuable to me," says Andrea Dworkin, founder of Women Against Pornography (W.A.P.). Dworkin views pornography as nocturnal holocaust, "Dachau in the bedroom," but she has reason for her apoplexy: when she was married to a Dutch freethinker, she says, she was regularly battered by him. "Both of us read pornography," Dworkin recalls. It gave them "the wrong idea" of what constitutes fulfilling relationships. Now Dworkin blames not just the porn triumvirate—Hugh Hefner, Al Goldstein, and Larry Flynt—but the values of liberalism, feminism, and the sexual revolution itself for the social abuse that women suffer.

"Women who have lived through the sexual revolution have a lot of remorse," Dworkin says. "They got hurt badly. Sexual liberation only made life harder for women. They got used. They got abused. They got beaten. They got raped." The multiplication of sexual partners for women, Dworkin maintains, meant more instances of abuse simply by the "mathematics of the issue." But many feminists cling to the rhetoric of sexual liberation, Dworkin says, because "they aren't really consistent advocates of women's rights. They are concerned with the values of liberalism first and the values of women second." NOW leaders are "incredibly cowardly and timid" on the porn issue, Dworkin charges, "because they don't want to alienate their liberal supporters." Eleanor Smeal has said there is a "fascist undertone" to the antipornography movement.

Dworkin is not the only feminist to disavow most of the offshoots of the sexual revolution. Feminist activist Rachel McNair says, "The sexual revolution has become an excuse for sexual exploitation. The idea of sex as totally recreational has turned women into objects of recreation, into playthings." Germaine Greer laments, "People are now blaming me for the sexual revolution" but in fact it was "not done by me, but by Hugh Hefner." These are unusual complaints coming from someone who publicized her spontaneous affairs, advocated the abolition of panties, and gave rousing speeches on "the great vaginal odor problem."

A similar epiphany came to Dierdre English, former executive editor of *Mother Jones,* who recently wrote an article wondering whether the feminists who heralded sexual liberation had in fact played into the hands of men. "Men have reaped more than their share of benefits from women's liberation." English wrote. "If a woman gets pregnant," for example, "the man who 20 years ago might have married her may today feel that he is gallant if he splits the cost of abortion."

ABORTION CHIC

A pro-choice position on abortion remains a central doctrine of the feminist creed. Some feminists even go so far as to deliberately get pregnant so they can have abortions in order to show their fertility and commitment to feminist principles, as the *Village Voice* reported in its February 4, 1981 article "Abortion Chic." One of the books recommended in a NOW catalog is *Abortion Is a Blessing*. Even on this issue, though, there are fissures in the movement. A few of them concern the fetus. Kathleen McDonnell's recent book *Not an Easy Choice: A Feminist Reexamines Abortion,* argues that even pro-choice advocates (such as herself) cannot avert their gaze from the mounting scientific evidence that the fetus is a human being. Some feminists have expressed dismay over the prospect of female fetuses being disproportionately destroyed with the development of gender-identifying technology. As it is, 15 million fetuses, 51 percent of them female, have not seen life because of the painful prerogatives exercised by American women.

Most feminist concern about abortion, however, focuses on arguments that not just the unborn but also pregnant women suffer enormously as a result of abortion. Women Exploited by Abortion (WEBA), a newly formed group, has provoked great writhing in the feminist camp by documenting the physical harm and psychological devastation of hundreds of women who were led to believe they were simply "controlling their bodies." Feminists for Life, another recently launched organization, distributes materials arguing that the risk and the trauma of abortion falls entirely on women; men experience the relief without the internal convulsions. It has always surprised feminists that more men than women support abortion on demand; they predicted that this issue would align male and female on opposite sides of the political trench. Now feminists are beginning to see why the majority of their oppressors are with them on the abortion question.

The whole notion of the right to control one's body has, in some cases, taken on a peculiar connotation. The New York chapter of NOW opposes city regulations that require bars and restaurants to display signs saying, "Warning: Drinking alcoholic beverages during pregnancy can cause birth defects." Similar to smoking warnings, this is intended to protect pregnant women who have already elected to have their babies. But, New York NOW declares, "We are most uneasy about the step this legislation takes toward protecting the unborn at the expense of women's freedom." Many feminists realize that the rhetoric of abortion rights, thus applied, hardly serves the interests of women. Led by Margery Shaw, a genetics and health law professor at the University of Texas at Houston, a number of feminists who support *Roe v. Wade* have condemned the NOW stance toward the New York regulation.

Germaine Greer's book *Sex and Destiny* has provoked most of the contro-

versy surrounding birth control practices in Third World nations. She is challenging a feminist movement that is united in opposition to conservative groups
which seek to deny foreign aid to countries using tax policy or outright coercion to influence the number of children that are born each year. Ominous
population explosion figures have made American feminists understandably
eager to stem the tide of brown and yellow babies. But to brown and yellow
mothers it makes all the difference whether they choose to have children or
whether the government decides for them. At international conferences of
feminists, they have pointed out the irony that while Western feminists demand
the right to control their bodies, they are perfectly willing to let Third World
states regulate the pregnancies of their women.

Germaine Greer sides with the Asian and African women on this question. In
fact, she argues that for all their cultural habits, Third World women remain
more connected than Western women to their bodies, to their fertility. Thus
they are, in this crucial respect, more feminine than their European and American counterparts. In industrialized countries, Greer says, sex has been virtually
severed from fertility, and most female behavior is not catered to children (who
are generally viewed as nuisances) but to the libido of the male. Greer gives the
example of the female breast, in the underdeveloped world used primarily to
provide milk to the baby, in the West often denied to the infant and used mostly
for male "fetishistic delectation."

Betty Friedan got a glimpse of the Third World liberated point of view at a
U.N. [United Nations] Conference on Women in Copenhagen where, she
says, Asian and Middle Eastern feminists ardently defended the chador and the
veil, arguing, "It gives us more freedom." "We don't have to take so much time
to dress up," etc. Further, some Iranian women maintained that Western feminists who lamented sexual role-playing nevertheless spent a great deal of their
time accentuating their female contours and prettying themselves up for male
attention. Greer argues that in underdeveloped countries female behavior and
female sexuality are not primarily aimed at short-term male satisfaction but at
giving birth to children and lifelong security in an immediate or extended
family.

LESBIAN LABELS

Homosexuality is another issue where we find feminism repudiating ideas and
events that it once hailed as liberating. Susan Brownmiller remarks that when
feminists adopted the lesbian cause they didn't see the slippery slope. "We
tried to make people proud of who they were," she says. "That wasn't so bad
when the gays and lesbians felt a sense of self-worth. But then the sadomaso-
chists came out of the closet and became proud of themselves." Many of the
bizarre sex practices of homosexuals have contributed to the degradation of sex

and disrupted relations between men and women in society, Brownmiller says. Conceding that the lesbian label has become "a burden," Brownmiller insists, "We must protect the rights of lesbians while distancing ourselves from the label."

NOW has been battered with allegations of lesbianism by such groups as Phyllis Schlafly's Eagle Forum, so its leadership is now cagey on the issue. The group has stopped distributing its brochure on lesbianism where it asserts, "We must be willing to risk the loss of heterosexual privileges if we are to build a truly feminist society." NOW admits that 20 percent of its members are lesbians, a figure that Sonia Johnson—the excommunicated Mormon housewife who almost became head of NOW in 1982—says is probably higher. The NOW leadership, Johnson alleges, is unwilling to admit the lesbian character of the organization. "NOW is always telling lesbians to hide and disguise their sexuality. I don't see why they should do this." Johnson believes that perhaps all women "have to choose women sexually for a while if only to understand what a women's world would be like." Asked how many lesbians she worked with during her years in the NOW leadership, Johnson estimated, "a quarter to a half" of the NOW activists.

Finally, feminism is also at odds with itself when women who do not espouse the entire feminist agenda rise to top positions in business and government. It is extremely galling to feminist groups that most prominent women in American political life seem to be conservative. While NOW is firmly wedded to the Democratic Party, Jeane Kirkpatrick, Elizabeth Dole, Sandra Day O'Connor, Paula Hawkins, and Nancy Kassebaum are all Republicans. All of these women are committed to women's equality, and some explicitly identify themselves as feminists. But even as feminist groups declare that their mission is to help women rise to higher and higher posts in politics, they ridicule and denounce conservative women who represent, in some sense, the greatest triumph of feminist aspirations. Sonia Johnson calls Kirkpatrick and Margaret Thatcher "female impersonators" who "look like women, but are inculturated as men."

When Sandra Day O'Connor recently got an award from a bar association in New York, over 60 female lawyers and law professors signed a petition calling the choice "an affront to women," even though O'Connor consistently votes right on feminist issues. The implication here is that if a woman doesn't agree with the feminist agenda in its entirety, she is, at best, opposed to the interests of women, and, at worst, a man in disguise. Even Betty Friedan was described as "falling into the old male pattern" by Gloria Steinem when she advised feminists to cast aside some of their excesses.

All this should suggest the degree to which feminists have turned against their fellow activists and their political and social agenda of the 1960s and 1970s. The new feminist agenda is closer to the hearts of the majority of American women. But it is a road paved over the corpse of the contemporary women's movement.

Is the Feminist Movement in Decay?

DOROTHY WICKENDEN

What NOW? The Women's Movement Looks beyond "Equality"

Nobody seems to have a kind word for the women's movement these days. Its leaders are suffering from "post-feminist depression." It has reached a state of "profound paralysis." Its largest and strongest proponent, the National Organization for Women, has shown itself to be nothing more than a "colorless liberal organization." American women "have less economic security than their mothers did, and are considerably worse off than women in other advanced countries." Only the first of these assessments is from a conservative ideologue—Dinesh D'Souza, in an article called "The New Feminist Revolt: This Time It's against Feminism." The second is from NOW's founder, Betty Friedan, whose advice on "How to Get the Women's Movement Moving Again" was prefaced by a stern critique of its current strategies; the third is from a radical feminist, Brett Harvey; and the fourth is from an economist, Sylvia Ann Hewlett, whose new book, *A Lesser Life: The Myth of Women's Liberation in America,* is a withering examination of the failures of contemporary feminism.

Meanwhile, there have been cries of betrayal within NOW. Last July [in 1985] the press relished a ruthless battle for NOW's presidency between the incumbent, Judy Goldsmith, and her predecessor, Eleanor Smeal. Behind the personal feud was a significant disagreement over tactics. The "moderate" Goldsmith charged Smeal with "character assassination" and "a ward boss mentality." She called Smeal's relentless pursuit of the Equal Rights Amendment "an exercise in futility." She pleaded for coalition-building and expanding NOW's agenda. The "militant" Smeal accused Goldsmith of abandoning the ERA [Equal Rights Amendment], losing NOW members, and becoming a mere "arm of the Democratic Party." She talked of revolution. "We don't take our right-wing fascist opponents seriously enough," she scolded the delegates at the convention in New Orleans. "We must recognize bigotry when it raises its ugly head. We must wrap it around the neck of the right wing." Smeal defeated Goldsmith. And, as promised, she took women back to the streets with a rousing national march for abortion rights and birth control. Eighty thousand people showed up for the March 9 [1986] demonstration in Washington, representing groups ranging from Baby Boomers for Choice to Lesbian and Gay Quakers.

Fractiousness among feminists and dour predictions of the movement's imminent collapse are nothing new. Ten years ago, when the radical revolt against liberal feminism was at its peak, Veronica Geng wrote off NOW in an article for

94

Harper's called "Requiem for the Women's Movement." NOW, she said, "tried to refute a male fantasy with another male fantasy: see Betty's wholesome family, see Gloria's beauty, see Marlene's fulfilling job, see our docile masses, who all think the same reasonable thoughts. As it turned out, this strategy played a large part in creating the worst possible image: that of an unwelcoming movement, closed to dissent." Over half a century ago—when traditionalists were claiming that expanding women's lives beyond the domestic realm would lead to effeminacy among men and insanity among women—suffragists were divided among themselves over strategy. And while suffragists proclaimed that the women's vote would usher in an era of enlightened social reform, other feminists warned that it would do nothing to improve the lot of women who needed it most: the working class and poor. The current debate is only the latest expression of a century-old split among feminist forces about how to revolutionize the role of women in American society.

Much of this dissension has grown out of a flaw at the heart of mainstream feminist theory, which has both exaggerated the potential for political unity among women and slighted the significance of biological distinctions between the sexes. The premise of "equal rights" feminism is that social, legal, and economic equality must be pursued in defiance of gender differences. By contrast, social feminists, radical feminists, and others have always been dubious about the wisdom of aspiring to standards of public and private life established by and for men. At the turn of the century Charlotte Perkins Gilman argued not only that women had the right to employment, but that society would have to find a way to make it possible to balance the demands of child-rearing and work. Today even women who fought most vigorously for equal rights are finding the approach increasingly problematic. Yet the voices of dissent are not urging a recantation of feminism. They urge a new definition of equal opportunity—one that will be almost as unsettling to NOW as to Reaganites. As Betty Friedan put it in *The Second Stage* (1981): "The equality we fought for isn't livable, isn't workable, isn't comfortable in the terms that structured our battle."

That battle was largely shaped, of course, by Friedan herself and the National Organization for Women. She and a dozen or so other activists established NOW in 1966 after concluding that the 1964 Civil Rights Act, which banned job discrimination on the grounds of sex as well as race, religion, and national origin, would not be enough to prod government agencies to act on complaints of sex discrimination. NOW's intention never was to subvert male bastions of power, but to work through the legislatures, Congress, courts, and grass-roots organizations to enable women to work alongside men in education, employment, and politics.

The successes of the egalitarian tradition of feminism—from the 19th Amendment in 1920 to *Roe v. Wade* in 1973—have been considerable. The women's movement has knocked down sex discrimination in higher education and Olympic sports, in credit applications and the English language. It has shaped policy in the professions and politics, reconstituted relations between the sexes, and dramatically altered the terms of debate within the Catholic Church. Nevertheless, its limitations are clearer than ever. The issues that feminists historically have rallied around—the Equal Rights Amendment and reproductive freedom—arguably have helped to marshal reactionary forces as much as to mobilize women. The reason is obvious. Women bear children, a fact that cannot be transformed by legislation or swept away with rhetoric. A politics built upon the right to control childbearing and the denial of sexual differences is dangerously vulnerable when it comes to one of the most fiercely guarded institutions of American society: the family.

This weakness has been exposed in two critical political battles over the ERA. In 1923, when the ERA was first proposed by Alice Paul's National Woman's Party, it aroused deep disagreements among women over promised public freedoms and existing private responsibilities. Many feminists, including Eleanor Roosevelt and groups such as the National League of Women Voters, the Women's Trade Union League, and the Council of Jewish Women, actively opposed the ERA, arguing that women's needs are different from men's, and that it would deprive women of the few social supports they had. Far from uniting women along the lines of gender, the ERA divided them along the lines of class. In *Women and Equality* (1977), William H. Chafe describes the strategy of the National Woman's Party. He could almost be describing NOW's strategy in the 1970s:

> . . . the NWP devoted its entire energies to the fight for an ERA, eschewing identification with other questions such as birth control or maternal and infant care. . . . In the process . . . the NWP, already a small elitist organization, alienated most working women (the ERA prior to 1941 would have brought invalidation of protective legislation for working women such as minimum-wage laws), spent an excessive amount of energy battling over women's organizations, and tended to ignore the extent to which the roots of sex inequality went beyond the reach of even the most powerful constitutional amendment.

In the 1970s the ERA became a cause not only for women demanding their full legal rights as American citizens, but also for the conservatives' "profamily" agenda. The final ratification drive gave Phyllis Schlafly and the burgeoning Moral Majority (not to mention the John Birch Society) a platform from which to blame feminism for robbing women of their livelihood, releasing dangerous male sexual urges, destroying the family, and murdering the unborn. This hysterical response caught feminists off guard. Schlafly's STOP ERA campaign was largely a reaction to the counterculture, yet the ERA campaign was in part an effort by the moderate women's movement to shake off the vague revolutionism of radical feminism. Smeal and Goldsmith say that in the end it wasn't Schlafly that killed the ERA, but the obstructionist tactics of a handful of legislators and lobbyists in a few conservative states. There are, though, less visible lessons of the ERA's defeat, which NOW still refuses to recognize. The first is the political delicacy (and the unintended consequences) of any move to amend the Constitution. The second is that even many supporters of the ERA were skeptical about its potential for bringing about a more egalitarian society. The third is that investing too heavily in a single approach to women's rights can be foolhardy.

Today Eleanor Smeal stubbornly insists that the best way to revive the women's movement is to renew the ERA campaign and undercut the right on the issues of birth control, abortion, and pay equity. "There is no liberty for women," she told me, "if they can't control their own fertility." In a recent speech to Catholic University students, she took up this theme with fervor, stressing the urgency of retaining women's right to birth control in this country, and pressing for it in Africa. After her talk, when a Hispanic woman rose to ask why minorities had the impression that NOW sometimes seems oblivious to their concerns, Smeal replied indignantly, "The opposition is primarily male. That's a fact. . . . You should be proud of the fight women have waged."

To be sure, it is thanks to the organized women's movement that a majority of American women now take for granted the right to control their own fertility. And professional women are reaping the rewards of the efforts of NOW, the Women's Equity Action League, the National Women's Political Caucus, and numerous other groups. College graduates are routinely postponing marriage and pursuing careers in fields that used to be virtually closed to women: law, medicine, engineering, banking. And women are getting elected to political office in unprecedented numbers. Fourteen years ago there were 362 female state legislators; today there are 1,103. So far 19 women have announced plans to run for governor in 1986. Yet NOW and its sister organizations have been unable to shake the charge of elitism. In particular, they are accused of benignly neglecting what has become the most intractable "women's issue": the worsening economic plight of millions of American women and their children.

Thus while Smeal continues to warn her audiences of creeping fundamentalism, women from outside the NOW camp are warning of the pitfalls of egalitarian feminism. Some (who emphasize that they fully support the pro-choice cause) complain that in effect the most powerful groups have been pursuing a kind of trickle-down feminism: open up opportunities in mayoralties and state legislatures and the U.S. Congress, in higher education and the professions, and eventually all women will benefit. Julia Scott at the Children's Defense Fund says that in the long fight for the ERA, "the fight to help support the working class and poor was dropped." Eleanor Guggenheimer, at the Child Care Action Campaign, says that the ERA proved to be such a tremendous fund-raising success that NOW lost sight of the immediate worries of many women: how to care for their children while meeting the demands of their jobs. "You ask women how they feel about the family, and the floodgates open. They will tell you it's unbelievably difficult to find day care. Divorced women will tell you their fears of taking another day off when their child is sick—they're scared to death of being fired. They worry about keeping food on the table."

The fact is that millions of American women aren't doing well at all. There is still a large discrepancy between male and female wages. (According to the U.S. Census Bureau, women who work full-time still earn on average only 61 cents to every dollar paid to men.) Working women still cluster in low-paying, sex-segregated jobs in the "pink-collar ghetto." And female poverty gets worse all the time. Three out of five adults officially designated as below the poverty line are women, and close to half of the poor families in America are headed by women. Minority women and their children are the most disadvantaged group in America: two-thirds of the children in black and Hispanic female-headed households are poor. All of these trends have been exacerbated by the Reagan counterrevolution. While talking about the sanctity of family life, the right has whittled away social programs that serve primarily the families of poor and working women: AFDC, child nutrition, food stamps, day care.

The biggest challenge for women's organizations is no longer simply to expand equal opportunities, or even to fight the Reagan administration on affirmative action and social issues. The most critical and difficult work lies in finding ways to help women maintain a decent standard of living without neglecting their children. The traditional approach to equality has proved inadequate here. Women, like minority groups, have discovered that discrimination is not the only significant barrier to economic advancement, and that equal rights and even ostensibly equal treatment do not necessarily lead to true equality.

In some cases the sex-blind pursuit of equal rights has even exacerbated social and economic injustices. The reforms in divorce law, for example, which set out to ensure equal treatment for men and women, have instead helped men at women's expense, as Lenore Weitzman shows in *The Divorce Revolution*. (See "Cruel Contracts" by Maggie Scarf, *New Republic,* April 21, [1986]). Although Smeal says that she and other feminists had reservations about the equitable divorce laws all along, the principle behind them is precisely that principle of equality supported by NOW. "No-fault attempts to treat men and women equally—*or as if they were equal*—at the point of divorce," Weitzman says. "However, it ignores the *structural* inequality between men and women in the larger society." Under the new system, judges rarely acknowledge the economic vulnerability of women who have spent years raising their children. Instead, they assume that the real barrier to self-sufficiency is the woman's reluctance to go out and get a job. Permanent alimony—which was always rare (in 1968, for example, under 20 percent of divorced wives in California were awarded alimony)—is now virtually nonexistent, and by 1978 only 13 percent of mothers with children under six were awarded even temporary alimony. What's more, although the vast majority of divorced women continue to care for their children, child support is grossly inadequate, and between 60 and 80 percent of fathers refuse to comply with court-ordered payments. Not surprisingly, within the first year of divorce, women and their children experience a 73 percent drop in their standard of living, and men a 42 percent rise.

In the workplace, too, a doctrinaire adherence to the ideal of equality has proved troublesome. The women's movement, along with numerous civil rights and labor groups and the Democratic Party, believes that the way to correct the disparities between men's and women's work and wages is through comparable worth, or "pay equity," as it is now called. The proponents of pay equity have made Americans aware of the dismal facts about job segregation and its threat to women's economic well-being, and by now most states either have introduced or are considering pay-equity plans. They have been less successful in analyzing and attacking the underlying sources of the wage gap.

Pay-equity enthusiasts assume that long-standing patterns of sexual discrimination are the principal reason that women continue to be underpaid and segregated in "women's work." They tend to downplay women's other handicaps, such as less education and job training and fewer years in the work force. They largely overlook sweeping socioeconomic changes of the last decade— such as deindustrialization and the rise of service industries—which also shape employment patterns. And they often fail to take account of women's continuing responsibilities at home.

The dangers of a single-minded focus on discrimination as the cause of women's low status and low pay on the job suddenly became evident when the long discrimination case against Sears Roebuck & Company was lost. In 1979 the Equal Employment Opportunity Commission filed suit, charging Sears with sex discrimination in hiring, promotion, and pay. But the court found that not only had Sears met reasonable standards for hiring women; its record on affirmative action was commendable. It was the first big retail chain in the country to adopt an affirmative action plan. Moreover, the EEOC never came forth with a witness who could convincingly testify to discrimination. The judge criticized the statistical evidence presented by the EEOC showing the paucity of women in commission sales jobs, and said that women had proved to be both less interested in and less qualified for those jobs. NOW and other women's groups, which had championed the case, greeted the decision with dismay. It is all the more difficult to argue for proportional representation if women don't clamor as eagerly as men to sell automotive parts and aluminum siding.

Barnard history professor Rosalind Rosenberg, who testified on behalf of Sears in the suit, points out that feminists' preoccupation with discrimination "threatens to cripple the cause of working women, not advance it." Perpetually worried about potential encroachment upon equal opportunities, NOW doesn't fully concede the more obvious restrictions on women's time and ambitions: the presence of small children, the absence of affordable day care, and the difficulty of taking on jobs that require extra training, overtime, and travel. Pay equity may result at last in higher wages for women in underpaid jobs. But it will not necessarily ensure an equal distribution of labor.

Another source of controversy among feminists is the issue of benefits for pregnant workers. NOW is currently airing the same debate that divided feminists in the 1920s. Does protective legislation, granting women different benefits from those of their male co-workers, necessarily discriminate unfairly against women? Does an insistence on sex-neutral policies necessarily work in women's best interest? One of NOW's achievements, in Smeal's first term as president, was passage of the 1978 Pregnancy Discrimination Act, which prohibits employers from firing a woman solely because she is pregnant. Today NOW, the ACLU [American Civil Liberties Union], and the League of Women Voters, along with conservative business groups and the Reagan Justice Department, are challenging a California law requiring employers to grant special benefits to pregnant employees (up to four months' leave, and a guarantee to reinstate them afterward). NOW believes that the disability benefits should be extended to all workers; the Justice Department wants to eliminate them. Both argue that the law discriminates against workers who are not pregnant. The case has gone to the Supreme Court.

Smeal says: "Our worry is protective labor legislation. In the past it was used not to hire women. . . . Our fear is that what appears to be a benefit will be used against us. If a person is disabled—male or female—she should be able to take a four-month leave without pay, and not be fired." This stand is clearly sensible, and NOW was an early supporter of Representative Pat Schroeder's Parental and Medical Leave Bill, currently before Congress, which would require employers to provide up to 26 weeks of unpaid leave for all employees with medical disabilities, including pregnancy, and would enable either parent to take up to 18 weeks of leave after the birth or adoption of a baby, or to care for a sick child. The worker would also be guaranteed the same or a similar job upon return.

Others, though, insist that women will never be able to compete fairly in public life if they aren't granted compensation for their work as mothers. Sylvia Hewlett charges in A Lesser Life that one result of the movement's reluctance to publicize women's continuing responsibilities at home is that the United States is the only industrial country in the world with no statutory maternity leave, and one of the few without subsidized day care. Hewlett argues that the social feminists in Western Europe have achieved more for working women by demanding special privileges than the equal-rights feminists in America have by taking an uncompromising stand on sex-blind laws and social policy. In France, Sweden, West Germany, Denmark, Italy, and England—all of which provide some form of subsidized day care, job protection, and paid maternity leave—the difference between male and female wages has been narrowing. The wage gap in America is the same as it was in 1939.

The tactics of mainstream feminists have been harshly scrutinized lately in politics as well. While saying that women in the workplace are driven by the same motivations as men, NOW has consistently argued that the sexes think and behave differently in politics. In 1984 Smeal wrote a book called *Why and How Women Will Elect the Next President,* which predicted that a woman would strengthen the presidential ticket and widen the gender gap, and that abortion and the ERA would be major election issues. Both Smeal and Goldsmith resent the labeling of NOW as a special-interest group. But NOW treats women as a critical voting bloc sharing distinctive concerns, and uses this presumption to wield its considerable influence in pressuring politicians. This is the role of any lobbying group. The problem in the 1984 election was that NOW's highly publicized demand that Walter Mondale choose a female running mate was seen by Mondale supporters (and exploited by Reagan supporters) as conclusive evidence that he was indeed the malleable captive of special interests. Liberal columnists came down particularly hard on NOW. During its July convention in Miami, where Mondale was welcomed with the chant, "Win with a woman, run with a woman," Richard Cohen wrote that the Democratic candidate was being "henpecked." "It will seem to many Americans that the choice of a woman . . . will result not from Mondale's sincere commitment to feminism . . . or even the stellar qualifications of a particular woman, but from the hectoring and—yes— threats of the organized women's movement."

In the end, the gender gap proved to be far less decisive in the 1984 presidential campaign than the Democrats had hoped and the Republicans had feared. And the pressure to choose a female running mate caused Mondale to select a woman with liabilities and a lack of qualifications that would have ruled out a male candidate. The vanishing promise of the gender gap may be largely attributed to Mondale's overwhelming weaknesses and Reagan's unassailable strengths. But far from helping to overcome those failings, NOW helped to expose them.

Betty Friedan, for one, has long been imploring her followers to accept the limits of legal remedies and divisive political tactics. In *The Second Stage* she replaced her explosive talk of "the comfortable concentration camp" of the suburban housewife with heady visions of "the new frontier where the issues of the second stage will be joined": the family. But this change of tack has elicited mutters of annoyance from the movement's current leaders, one of whom calls her criticisms "cavalier and galling." It was *The Feminine Mystique,* after all, which first emboldened a generation of women to shake off the constraints of traditional motherhood and marriage.

Friedan self-righteously blames her radical sisters for the movement's vulnerability on the family issue. "For us, with our roots in the middle American mainstream and our own fifties' families," Friedan wrote in *The Second Stage,* "equality and the personhood of women never meant destruction of the family, repudiation of marriage and motherhood, or implacable sexual war against men." That "pseudo-radical cop-out" was perpetrated by young extremists, "scarred early by the feminine mystique, and without firm roots in family or career, [who] gave vent to their rage in a rhetoric of sexual politics based on a serious ideological mistake." Perhaps. The radical feminists were certainly more uncompromising in their desire to overthrow what Kate Millett described as "patriarchy's chief institution." Yet in the 1960s and 1970s the liberal feminists showed scant concern for that institution themselves, except where it impinged on their independence. It is only in recent years that the family has become politically fashionable again.

Today the weaknesses of the old tactics are clear, yet the solutions seem to be as elusive as ever. Like the civil rights movement it sprang from, the women's movement is having trouble reconciling the old politics of separatism with the new politics of accommodation. *The Second Stage* ends with a peroration on the need for "*human* liberation," and Friedan's recent article on resuscitating feminism talks lyrically of "international networking" with Third World women under a baobab tree in Nairobi at the U.N. Conference for Women. Her list of priorities includes: "a new round of consciousness-raising," "get off the pornography kick," "confront the illusion of equality in divorce," "affirm the differences between men and women," and so on. Nothing objectionable there, but not much to rally around either.

On the other hand, feminists won't get the better of fundamentalists in an overwrought debate over the rights of the unborn vs. the rights of women. Smeal has it wrong when she blames "the opposition" for all that ails feminism. This is just a more sophisticated strain of the paranoia that has long run through the rhetoric of the movement. Generic man is no longer the enemy (except in the eyes of antipornography fanatics like Andrea Dworkin). Today the oppressor that NOW denounces is embodied in "the male Catholic hierarchy," fundamentalists like Jerry Falwell, and ideologues like Ronald Reagan. In fact the women's movement has been remarkably successful in securing individual rights. What's needed is a new, generous, workable ideal of social justice. NOW, like the Democratic Party, hasn't yet convinced the public that it has more to offer than ineffectual reaction to Reaganism.

The sanctimony and hypocrisy behind the conservative talk about the family is obvious, and feminists should be the first to do something about it. As Goldsmith says, "We need to comfortably and affirmatively take back that ground that is legitimately ours. We are the people who really care about the family." This means vigorously endorsing progressive programs that work. The Child Care Action Campaign, working with other national child-care agencies and an insurance agent, recently succeeded in obtaining liability insurance for day-care centers, family day-care homes, and Head Start programs across the country that had been on the verge of closing. The Children's Defense Fund, long before Bill Moyers, has discussed the crisis in teenage pregnancy and tirelessly reported the effects of Reagan budget cuts on children. The House Select Committee on Children, Youth, and Families has been a forceful advocate of Schroeder's parental leave policy, and of tax reforms that would aid families. And it has drafted a bill that would improve and expand day-care facilities through public-private partnerships, and would restore federal funding to programs serving poor families.

Kathy Wilson, the former head of the National Women's Political Caucus, rightly points out that NOW serves an invaluable function as "the two-by-four used to get the attention of the mule." Pat Reuss, the legal director at the Women's Equity Action League, says that the moderate women's movement "has to have a group on the cutting edge. We pray they won't embarrass us, but we're glad they're out there." NOW's energetic lobbying in recent months on behalf of the Civil Rights Restoration Act (which would overturn the Supreme Court's *Grove City* decision limiting the government's ability to enforce civil rights laws at federally funded institutions) has been commended by feminists from many camps.

Few would question that the victories won by the equal rights advocates have formed the foundations of contemporary feminism. But the time has come for a radical departure. Instead of simply fighting off the "pro-family" and anti-civil rights crusaders, NOW could use its political power to launch a major offensive for a series of concrete social reforms and changes in the workplace—beginning with affordable, widely available, licensed day care. That may sound more pragmatic than principled. But it could enable women, and men, to meet the demands of both their public and private lives. And it would address the fundamental family issue of the 1980s, which is the economic one.

Back in 1938, in an editorial in the *New Republic* expressing strong reservations about the ERA, Felix Frankfurter was quoted as saying: "The legal position of woman cannot be stated in a single, simple formula, because her life cannot be expressed in a single, simple relation. Woman's legal status necessarily involves complicated formulations, because a woman occupies many relations. The law must have regard for woman in her manifold relations as an individual, as a wage-earner, as a wife, as a mother, as a citizen." It is this expansive vision that feminists need to recapture. NOW's problem these days, for all Smeal's rhetoric, is that is isn't militant enough.

Questions for Discussion

1. What is feminism? Has feminism been a success or failure?
2. What is the relationship between liberalism and feminism?
3. How should (or should not) the family be evaluated as an oppressive institution?
4. What should be the consequences of the biological and psychological differences between men and women to laws and government policies?
5. What are the unanticipated consequences of the laws and judicial decisions that have been gained in large part because of the demands of feminists?
6. Why do women earn an average 61 cents for every dollar earned by men?

Suggested Readings

Astrachan, Anthony. *How Men Feel: Their Response to Women's Demand for Equality and Power.* Garden City, N.Y.: Anchor Press/Doubleday, 1986.

Bonafede, Dom. "Still a Long Way to Go." *National Journal,* 18, no. 37, (September 13, 1986), 2175–2179.

Cott, Nancy. *The Grounding of Feminism.* New Haven: Yale Univ. Press, 1987.

Donovan, Josephine. *Feminist Theory: The Intellectual Traditions of American Feminism.* New York: F. Ungar, 1985.

Friedan, Betty. *The Second Stage.* Rev. ed. New York: Summit Books, 1986.

Hacker, Andrew. "Women at Work." *New York Review of Books,* 33, no. 13 (August 14, 1986), 26–32.

Levin, Michael E. *Feminism and Freedom.* New Brunswick, N.J.: Transaction Books, 1987.

MacKinnon, Catharine A. *Feminism Unmodified: Discourses on Life and Law.* Cambridge, Mass.: Harvard Univ. Press, 1987.

Mainland, Mary. "Feminist Myths Reconsidered," *America,* 151, no. 19 (December 15, 1984), 396–399.

Podhoretz, Norman. "The Different Natures and Needs of Women." *Human Events,* 46, no. 35 (August 1986), 5–6.

Chapter 6

Do Voting and Elections Mean Anything?

A central feature of political democracy is universal suffrage. The United States today has a voting system based on universal suffrage. With the exception of people under the age of eighteen, felons, or the insane, every U.S. citizen has the right to vote. Restrictions based on registration and residence impose the only limits on this right.

Restrictions on the right to vote have existed throughout most of U.S. history. Under Article I, Section 4 of the Constitution, the states can determine the "times, places, and manner" for holding elections, but Congress is permitted to alter such regulations except as to the places in choosing senators. (Until 1913, senators were chosen by state legislatures.) In the early years of the Republic only male property owners were allowed to vote in most states. The trend has been to expand the franchise to include groups previously excluded. At first property ownership as a voting requirement was eliminated. The Fifteenth Amendment to the Constitution, adopted in 1870, forbade any state to deny or abridge the right to vote "on account of race, color, or previous condition of servitude."

States, however, found ways to prevent blacks from voting. In effect, blacks were excluded from exercising their votes in the South through such devices as literacy tests, the white primary, and the poll tax, which required the payment of a fee to vote. Intimidation by some whites made it unlikely that blacks would organize for the purpose of exercising the right to vote. Primaries were considered to be "private organizations" and, consequently, not subject to the Fifteenth Amendment. Some of these restrictions also effectively disfranchised some whites. The poll tax kept poor whites from voting, and literacy tests were used to keep immigrants from voting.

The twentieth century brought major changes. The Nineteenth Amendment allowed women to vote. The Twenty-fourth Amendment, adopted in 1964, made the payment of a poll tax or any tax illegal in federal elections, both primaries and elections. The Voting Rights Act of 1965 assured that black people could vote in every state. The Twenty-sixth Amendment, adopted in 1971, established eighteen as the minimum age for voting. Supreme Court decisions and state legislation eliminated literacy tests. As a result of all these measures, the right to vote is virtually universal in the United States.

Yet many U.S. citizens do not exercise that right. In the 1984 general election, for example, the turnout rate of voters was 53.3 percent, compared to 54.4 percent in 1976 and the post–World War II high of 62.8 percent in 1960. In state and local elections the turnout is generally lower than in national elections.

Nonvoting has been attributed to many causes. Some observers comment that registration rules are a major reason that people do not vote. Many people move each year, and newcomers often cannot vote because of residence requirements. But many people do not vote because they decide not to or have no inclination to.

The failure of many U.S. citizens to vote has raised the issue of whether voting and elections mean anything. Political scientists Gerald M. Pomper and Susan S. Lederman argue that they do and summarize their findings in a selection from their study. Specifically, they contend:

1. On the basis of empirical evidence, there appears to be a linkage between the appeals of parties and the demands of the electorate. Politicians do redeem most of their promises.
2. The effect of elections is indirect.

Elections constitute endorsements or rejections of a politician's policies. Voting serves to influence rather than to control the actions of politicians.

Howard L. Reiter, a political scientist at the University of Connecticut, argues that voting is not effective in translating the beliefs of the people of the United States into public policy. He contends:

1. It is difficult to determine the meaning of a candidate's victory or defeat because different people vote for the same candidate for different reasons.
2. Most of the major issues of U.S. history have been resolved not by elections but by other historical forces.
3. Voting is not cost efficient.

YES

Do Voting and Elections Mean Anything?

GERALD M. POMPER AND SUSAN S. LEDERMAN
Elections and Democratic Politics

Political theorists have emphasized the dangers of direct voter control, while finding benefits in indirect influence. Our examination has revealed little evidence of the former process, but we have uncovered many indications of the latter. American institutions serve to limit the electorate's command over government actions, but they do provide many opportunities for the expression of voters' demands. The character of the electorate is consistent with these expectations. The voters are not prepared to exercise a sovereign control over policy, but they are ready and able to press their personal interests.

Empirical studies confirm these generalizations. In presidential elections, the voters' principal role has been to maintain or displace the party in power. Programs have followed from the actions of the governing coalition, retrospectively judged by the electorate, not from explicit popular directives. In gubernatorial contests as well, the voters have not consistently demanded either low state taxes or high spending, but have responded differently to the varying initiatives of politicians.

These initiatives, as expressed in national party platforms, have been relatively specific and related to the apparent interests of the citizenry. Despite the apparent lack of direct control, therefore, there seems to be a linkage between the appeals of parties and the demands of the electorate. The existence of such a linkage is confirmed by actions on platform promises. Politicians do redeem most of their promises, and the parties reveal considerable internal unity and interparty difference in their actions. Another indication of linkage between official policies and voter interests is provided by the history of southern blacks. Despite their generally depressed state, blacks have found better protection of their natural rights when they have had the vote as a means of defense.

The policy effects of elections are not their only functions. Many other results may follow from popular selection. For example, the choice of rulers by ballot promotes the recruitment of officials with characteristics distinct from those designated through inheritance, lot, or force.[1] Suffrage may also affect the personal characteristics of the citizens. Mill believed that individuals developed more competence, awareness, and ambition when they participated in government.[2] In the struggle for civil rights as well, demands for voting rights have been the stimulus to broad mobilization of the black community.[3]

A major function attributed to elections is the promotion of political stability.[4] Through its votes, the populace is seen as expressing its allegiance to the existing constitution. Whether elections are only ritualistic as in the Soviet Union, or involve some real choice, their common effect is to bolster the legitimacy of the holders of power. "Elections commit the people to a sense of responsibility for their own betterment. . . . It seems clear that they are essential to us as props of the sentiment of legitimacy and the sentiment of participation."[5]

Our stress has not been on these important intangible effects of elections, but on their policy consequences. It remains now to draw our varied findings together in a general conception of the effects of popular intervention on the action of government. We first examine the theory of elections as mandates. Subsequently, we analyze the process of indirect electoral influence and its implications for American politics.

ELECTIONS AS MANDATES

A mandate would be the most general form of direct voter control. In this theory, political contests are seen as debates over future governmental policies, and the ballot as the means of resolving the debates. Consequently, voting is presumed to result in a relatively specific set of instructions by the electors to officials. Voters are principally concerned with issues, and candidates elected on the party ticket and platform are bound to implement the policies prescribed by the electorate. This theory has been particularly associated with the Labour party of Great Britain, although it is supported in other nations as well.

Under the mandate principle, issue conflicts or broad policy innovations are decided by "going to the country" for a final decision. According to this rule, even a party's legislative majority "does not necessarily entitle it to introduce a major change of policy, of a kind likely to arouse intense public controversy, if the electors have not had the chance to express their view on the subject."[6]

For example, the British Liberal party in 1906 successfully campaigned on behalf of a low-tariff policy. Finding the results a mandate, the Commons subsequently resolved: "That this House, recognizing that in the recent general election the people of the United Kingdom have demonstrated their unqualified fidelity to the principle and practice of the Free Trade, deems it right to record its determination to resist any proposal . . . to create in this country a system of Protection."[7] Similarly, in the United States, many persons interpreted the successive presidential elections of 1964, 1968, and 1972 as mandates to limit American involvement in Vietnam.

For elections to serve as mandates, three conditions would need to be fulfilled: (1) governmental institutions would facilitate the implementation of popular verdicts in official policy; (2) voters would be concerned primarily with future policy questions; (3) majority preferences on these questions as expressed in elections could be ascertained. However, in the United States at least, none of these three conditions is substantially satisfied.

It would be difficult to implement a mandate in America. A popular program must overcome the multiple cracks of federalism; the decentralized party system; the independent powers of bureaucracies, courts, and public authorities; and manifold checks and balances. Critical areas of policy affecting the public are outside the normal work of government, and are determined by "private" corporations. If public support for a given proposal is strong and definitive, these barriers are not insurmountable. In most instances, the electorate's wishes are not that clear.

Moreover, voters are not necessarily activated by policy considerations, at least not in the coherent and prospective fashion suggested by the mandate theory. Traditional partisanship and candidate evaluations account for much of the balloting. While many voters are concerned with their particular interests, only a minority are aware of or interested in the entire range of policies or general ideological postures. The relevant "issues" of a campaign therefore differ from one individual or group to another, and a common interpretation of the mandate of an election would be difficult to secure. Furthermore, voters are more conscious of past than future policies. They make retrospective judgments on the record of the incumbent party, more often than prospective choices between alternative programs.

Even if voters were primarily motivated by future policy questions, the popular mandate would be difficult to define. Victory for a given party does not necessarily mean that a majority supports each of its programs. Voters are not always consistent in their policy or partisan preferences. In the postwar period the electorate has generally favored the Democrats on domestic welfare issues, but has been more favorable to the Republicans on questions of foreign policy.[8] In state politics, as seen in the controversy over California's Proposition 13, voters may support both lower taxes and high levels of government spending.[9]

To the extent that voters are concerned with policy questions, their involvement normally extends only to a limited number of issues. On any given matter of public policy, the party's voters will include not only advocates of its position but also many who are indifferent to or ignorant of this stand, and some who oppose the party but still vote for it because of other considerations. In fact, by combining "passionate minorities" it is theoretically possible for a party to win a majority vote, even though each of its individual policies is supported only by a fraction of the electorate.[10]

A total popular majority is composed of many policy minorities. Rarely, if ever, is this minority united on all particular issues. The victory of a party thus cannot be interpreted as endorsement of its total platform. Presidents often attempt to claim popular mandates for their preferred policies, but their efforts should be regarded as tactical assertions in their legislative struggles, not as demonstrable arguments.[11] Jimmy Carter's victory in the 1976 presidential race cannot be taken as popular support for his energy policy or any other "moral equivalent of war." Even less can a 1976 decision of the electorate be seen as endorsing his actions in the unforeseen Iranian crisis of 1979 and 1980.

Furthermore, even a majority of voters would not include a majority of the total adult population. Nearly half of American adults now do not participate in presidential balloting. It is possible that the nonvoters, concentrated among persons of low social and economic status, may have sharply different policy views from those of the active citizenry. While current research does not indicate such a discrepancy of views, we cannot fully predict the future behavior of any newly mobilized voters.[12]

For a mandate to be valid, it should be based on an informed choice of the electorate. If a party's voters support its policies without thought and simply because of their partisanship, this loyalty clearly does not impose any restraints on the government. Nor is a mandate discernible if no alternatives to the winning party's program are available. In order for the voters to make a decision on public policy, they must have a defined choice. On most issues,

American parties do not offer clearly different policies. This similarity is often due to the fact that both parties support a program of proven popularity. In other cases, however, the absence of a choice makes it dubious that the voters clearly supported the policy in question.

Mandates are difficult to achieve, determine, and implement. The difficulties were made evident in the presidential election of 1920, which Woodrow Wilson had hoped would be a "great and solemn referendum" on American participation in the League of Nations. His hopes were disappointed. National institutions did not provide for a referendum or any other direct test. In the presidential campaign the issue was clouded by other questions, by vagueness, and by the personalities of the candidates. Interpretation of the results was difficult. "The Republicans and Harding, however, victors by a seven million vote majority and hence free to interpret the election results as they saw fit, declared that the American people had, once and for all, rejected the notion of the League of Nations."[13] If a mandate could not be clearly obtained on this issue, policy decisions in elections must be unlikely in general.

The Vietnam war issue, significant in three different presidential elections, provides further illustration of the complexities of popular mandates. In each of the three races from 1964 to 1972, many observers, and particularly critics of American involvement, read the returns as a popular call for restraint on U.S. military action. Examination of voter opinion, detailed in Table 1, does not support this view. In the earliest stages of the American intervention, President Johnson received support from advocates of both quick withdrawal and an escalated use of force, with fullest endorsement from those taking the moderate position, to "keep our soldiers in Vietnam, but try to end the fighting."

By 1968, with American involvement and casualties at their height, overall opinion had begun to turn against the war, but the election results did not show a sharp polarization. Hubert Humphrey did receive more support from "doves" than "hawks," but the differences were not extreme. Not until the third election, that of 1972, was there a distinct alignment of policy preference and voting choice. Democrat George McGovern drew exceptional support from those favoring immediate withdrawal. His defeat, then, could be accurately interpreted as a rejection of that policy and an apparent endorsement of the Nixon administration's alternative position of gradual disengagement.[14]

Even this agonizing case shows the limitations of particular mandates. It was not until after a decade of substantial American involvement in Vietnam—and fifty thousand casualties—that the electorate was presented with distinct alternatives and was prepared to choose. Furthermore, it still was not provided with full and honest information, as the Nixon administration engaged in deception, subversion, and secret bombings while claiming to be negotiating for a rapid truce. In the end, American policy did change, but the actions of war protestors and the growing doubts of experts may be credited with the result as much as the electorate at large.[15]

The general absence of mandates is consistent with our specific findings on

Table 1 Opinion on Vietnam and Democratic Presidential Vote, 1964–1972

		Policy Position	
Democratic Vote	Withdrawal	Moderate	Use All Force
1964	63[a]	82	52
1968	50	44	33
1972	57	26	14

[a] *Entries are the percentage voting Democratic of those holding the stated opinion in each year.*

direct voter control. We have found few programmatic directives by the citizenry in presidential elections, gubernatorial contests, or southern history. In these instances, as in the debate on Vietnam, "the vocabulary of the voice of the people consists mainly of the words 'yes' and 'no'; and at times one cannot be certain which word is being uttered."[16]

POWER AND INFLUENCE

The effect of elections must be indirect. Initiatives in a democratic system lie not with the voters but with politicians. A realistic theory of elections would define mandates, when they exist, not as programmatic but as personal. As British Conservatives and Liberals have argued, "the party which wins an election has 'a mandate to govern,' it being understood that unless the election happens to have been dominated by a single issue (which is exceptional), the government should be free to pursue whatever policies it finds appropriate."[17]

An electoral victory does not commit the politician to the voters' program, but rather serves as popular endorsement of his policies; the politician offers a proposal, and the electorate approves, condemns, or fails to respond. A proper analogy might be an auction, with the candidates and parties offering their wares, and waiting hopefully for a response from the audience. It is this sort of endorsement that Lyndon Johnson requested and received in 1964, when he declared, "I ask the American people for a mandate, not to preside over a finished program, not just to keep things going. I ask the American people for a mandate to begin."[18] The voters granted the mandate, but the President and his party largely determined its content.

Politicians in a democracy enjoy wide discretion. "The leading statesmen in a free country have great momentary power. They settle the conversation of mankind. . . . It is they who, by a great speech or two, determine what shall be said and what shall be written for long after. . . . In excited states of the public mind they have scarcely any discretion at all. The tendency of the public perturbation determines what shall and what shall not be dealt with. But, upon the other hand, in quiet times statesmen have great power; where there is no fire lighted they can settle what fire shall be lit."[19]

Elections are important as limits on these initiatives. In a theoretical sense, elections are significant not as *power in* government, but as an *influence on* government. Power "manifests itself by the behavior of a person or group when it conforms to the preferences, whether expressed or implied, of another person or group." If mandates controlled official behavior, then voters would be exercising power, but the absence of mandates also implies the absence of power. What the voters do exercise is influence, an effect rather than a control, on the conduct of officials. Influence "rests upon the capacity of human beings to imagine and thus to anticipate the reactions of those who are affected by their actions. Influence flows into the human relation whenever the influencer's *reaction* might spell disadvantage and even disaster for the actor, who foresees the effect the action might have and alters it more or less in accordance with this foresight."[20] Because politicians might be affected by the voters in the next election, they regulate their conduct appropriately.

To exert their influence, voters have the most obvious and vital sanction: they control the politician's job. They can quickly and bloodlessly dismiss an offensive official and thereby end his power, prestige, and profit. No explanations need be given by the electorate, and no appeal can be taken from its decisions, however arbitrary and capricious. The voters are not informed or interested enough to decide specific policy, but their final control over the politician means that he must make great efforts to satisfy popular needs and notions, wants and whims.

The existence of the vote does not make politicians better as individuals; it simply forces them to give greater consideration to demands of enfranchised and sizable groups, who hold a weapon of potentially great force. As Tocqueville wrote: "The men who are entrusted with the direction of public affairs in the United States are frequently inferior, in both capacity and morality . . . but they will never systematically adopt a line of conduct hostile to the majority; and they cannot give a dangerous or exclusive tendency to the government."[21]

There are other means of influence than the pressures of elections. Money, status, and skill can be used by groups devoid of any significant number of votes, as demonstrated by the political strength of such diverse interests as physicians and criminals. The influence of elections is still unique because votes provide a vital sanction. The ability to punish politicians is probably the most important weapon available to citizens. It is direct, authoritative, and free from official control. Other pressures on politicians gain in potency when supported by votes, whereas the lack of votes diminishes the impact of alternative methods. "It is because there are elections from time to time that the precise demands made on the people's behalf are always listened to. Elections are important not only for what happens at them but for what happens because of them."[22]

An extensive study of American local communities illustrates the point.

Agreement between leaders and followers on the relative importance of issues was found to be higher in communities of high voting participation. Leaders gave more attention to mass concerns where voting rates were high. Moreover, voting increased the impact of other forms of political participation. Where turnout was high, citizens engaged in such activities as campaigning, community organizations, or personal contacting were also more likely to have their preferences reflected by public officials. "Elections themselves may not be capable of dealing with the vast array of specific problems faced by citizens and groups, but the general pressure of the vote appears to enforce the effectiveness of the other, more specific modes of participation."[23]

The voters usually employ their powerful sanction retrospectively. They judge the politician after he has acted, finding personal satisfactions or discontents with the results of these actions. Such judgment is within the competence of the electors. They need not be experts, able to judge the technicalities of law or the merits of contrasting proposals for the future. They need only be able to perceive improvement or deterioration in their personal situation. An uneducated South Carolina Negro in 1877 perfectly expressed the workings of retrospective control. Explaining his rejection of the Redeemers' promises, he explained, "Den say dem *will* do dis and dat. I ain't ax no man what him *will* do—I ax him what him *hab* done."[24]

The fact of retrospective judgment affects the politician's initiatives as well. Knowing that a day of reckoning is fixed by the calendar, he must strive to make that day pleasant for the voters. Knowing the voters' past attitudes, the parties must plan their future behavior accordingly. Having made promises for which they will be called to account, they must seek to fulfill these pledges. Politicians are free from popular dictation, but not from popular responsibility. "By virtue of the combination of the electorate's retrospective judgment and the custom of party accountability the electorate can exert a prospective influence if not control. Governments must worry, not about the meaning of past elections, but about their fate at future elections."[25]

The issue of Vietnam is again illustrative. The war in Southeast Asia became politically important in 1968, when the effect of the Johnson administration's actions had been brought home to the voters, not in the pre-escalation year of 1964. The electorate responded to the reality of that policy, not because it violated a presumed mandate.

By 1968 public disillusionment with the American intervention was widespread, and the Democratic incumbents were subject to criticism within and outside their own party. The decline in public support of the war brought all major candidates to promise its end. The Republicans, and particularly Richard Nixon, joined in the pledge, but provided no specific program, instead seeking the support of all critical voters. Within the Democratic party, discontent with the administration found expression in the nominating campaigns of Senators Eugene McCarthy and Robert Kennedy. Ultimately the party convention, and its nominee, Hubert Humphrey, joined in pledging a peace effort.

No specific mandate came from the voters. Nevertheless, their expression of dissatisfaction led all parties to repudiate past policy and brought a new administration to power. Even though reluctant and slow, the new Nixon government had no political option open but eventually to remove American troops from Vietnam. It then used its record of gradual withdrawal from the war to win resounding approval of its actions in the 1972 race.

The ambiguous mandate of 1964 became a major issue for the citizenry in 1968, and a record for judgment in 1972. Incumbent and prospective Presidents heard, solicited, and responded to the retrospective judgment of the electorate. The political process provided an outlet for criticism, an opportunity for choice, and a means of change. Moreover, the voters' judgment also had a prospective effect. The war was clearly an electoral liability, and this political fact conditioned presidential actions throughout the 1970s. Whether for good or ill, American military power was restricted in Angola, Cambodia, Sinai, and other areas, most notably Iran. The political consequences of Vietnam made new American initiatives unlikely. The governors were shown ultimately dependent on the consent of the governed.

LINKING GOVERNED AND GOVERNORS

Decisions at the ballot box are intermittent and generalized. An election for any particular office occurs only once every two or four years, and the judgment made is of a total record, not individual actions. The significance of elections extends beyond these limited occasions. Their influence is considerably magnified by politicians' anticipations of the reactions of the voters. These anticipated reactions are the vital link between the interests of the voters and the actions of government. They affect politicians continuously and on all issues. In most cases, the politician "is free to act as he thinks best because the ordinary citizen is not pounding on his door with demands for action." Nevertheless, the politician remains responsive, for "his freedom to act is limited by the fact that he believes there *will* be pounding on his door if he does not act in ways that are responsive."[26]

In looking ahead to the next election, politicians cannot take comfort in the ignorance or apathy of the majority of voters on any particular problem. We have seen . . . that voters are aware of their particular interests, even though they are not typically concerned with the broad range of issues. Winning politicians therefore believe that their policy positions are important and act accordingly.[27] Victory may depend on marginal votes, and the politician must therefore be sensitive to any group which can provide that crucial margin. "Public spokesmen, be they congressmen or others, have a sharp ear attuned to complaints that foreshadow discontent. They react, not to actual opinion, but to their image of what opinion could become if not forestalled by action on their part. And often they are right. The very lack of concern for small grievances might well crystallize a genuinely hostile community sentiment."[28] The electoral threat feared by politicians may not actually materialize, but "because of its *possible* occurrence, the person or persons under the influence of another will anticipate the reaction of him who exercises the influence."[29]

Anticipation of voter reactions is manifested in the policies that politicians reject, adopt, and propose. One important, though elusive, manifestation is the exclusion of certain issues from political debate. "Leaders respond to many elements of public opinion that *could* affect an electoral decision, even though these opinions may not have influenced the public's choice in any actual election. In gauging popular attitudes, political leaders develop a strong sense of what the permissible bounds of policy are."[30]

Illustratively, while the level of governmental support for schools is still debated, the more fundamental question of the desirability of free public education is so fully accepted that it never becomes an election issue. The consensus of the society is maintained by the parties' foresight of the electoral consequences of denying that consensus. By contrast, the massive Goldwater defeat in 1964 followed the apparent Republican denial of the settled principle of governmental responsibility for social welfare.[31] . . . We also found protection for blacks associated with suffrage. Oppressive actions were less likely to be taken when the oppressed might retaliate at the polls.[32]

Anticipated reactions help to account for the actions politicians take as well as those they forego. Parties and officials follow policies they believe the voters want, even though there is no demonstrable mandate. . . . The advent of a national majority party usually results in new public policies to meet the presumed interests of the party's voting coalition. Judging past performance, the voters continue the existing majority party in office, in a Maintaining or Converting election, or install its opposition in a Deviating or Realigning contest. In state politics, governors raise and lower taxes and expenditures in anticipation of popular demands. These actions follow more from the governors' commitments than from decisions at the polls. The case of the New Jersey income tax . . . is illustrative. Intervention by the voters does not dictate, but legitimizes, party control and programs.

Similar behavior is evident in Congress. The representative must rely on his own perceptions of the voters' present and future demands, rather than awaiting an electoral mandate. "A Congressman has a very wide range of choices on any given issue, as far as his constituency is concerned. There is no district viewpoint as such to be represented on the overwhelming majority of issues. A few will care one way, and a few the other, but the issue will be insignificant or unknown to the great majority."[33] In his actions, the representative must guess the uncertain reactions of the electorate. Congressmen are apt to vote as they believe their constituents desire. In fact, these perceptions are more strongly related to the congressman's roll-call votes than either his personal attitudes or even the district's surveyed opinion.[34]

Anticipated reactions explain both common and unusual behavior of these legislators. On most votes, representatives see no conflict between the demands of their constituency, their party, and their own views. When such differences are perceived, their vote is for the constituency interest, leading oil-state Democrats to oppose taxes on energy producers and New England Republicans to seek to control the prices "free enterprise" can charge consumers. Much of the legislators' efforts are directed toward the voters at home—advertising their efforts, claiming credit for the benefits received, taking positions for recognition among the voters, and explaining their actions in speeches or in personal appearances.[35]

In seeking to satisfy the voters, politicians also deal with emerging questions. Many of their initiatives are attempts to arouse a favorable response from the electorate, so as to maintain and increase their own popular support. Candidates are advanced who may catch the public fancy. Promises are made in the hope that the voters will be attracted to a new program. Governmental benefits are provided for the citizenry and then stressed in the incumbents' campaign for reelection. These actions are not necessarily demanded by the voters. They are trade goods offered by politicians in the speculative hope that constituents will purchase them with the currency of their votes.

We have seen . . . how the parties anticipate the desires of the voters, making specific pledges of future action in their platforms, particularly on issues involving tangible and divisible benefits. Having made a large number of such pledges, the winning party honors most of its commitments, thereby mitigating opposition attacks, and then seeks reelection on its achievements. Relative party cohesion on disputatious pledges and the concentration of platforms on the incumbents' performance allow the voters to render a retrospective judgment on these initiatives.

Similar behavior has been evident in the South. . . . Afro-Americans have rarely had control over state governments, but the existence of a black electorate has been associated with the protection of vital rights. To appeal to blacks, white officials have protected life, limited segregation, and promoted education. Anticipated reactions have brought politicians to favor a degree of racial equality in their initiatives.

Elected governments are not unique. Anticipated reactions may influence all regimes, and a sensitivity to public opinion is expedient even in primitive or authoritarian societies. When faced with electoral sanctions, however, the government not only may, but must, anticipate these reactions. Recent history indicates the efficacy of the ballot. No freely elected leader has made the disastrous decisions of a Hitler to conduct a suicidal war or of a Stalin virtually to destroy his nation's defense or of an Idi Amin to engage in the genocide of his own people. Leaders in democracies have not necessarily been personally wise or moral, but they apparently have been restrained by the need to win public favor in an election. Elections can provide the protection envisioned by theorists favorable to democracy.

Without elections, some protections are still available, but they are extraordinary and uncertain. A tribal chief who is especially unfit may be killed or abandoned.[36] Assassinations, revolutions, and foreign intervention are available to remove officials who are particularly onerous. Government may have the good sense to restrain itself. Nevertheless, without the ballot, as Mill recognized, rulers "can with impunity disregard" the citizens' desires, but they "are under a necessity of considering the interests of those who have the suffrage."[37]

The ballot does not guarantee full responsiveness on the part of rulers. They may misperceive or disregard citizen needs. As the history of blacks in both South and North has demonstrated, other resources are useful, and even necessary, for the full protection of individuals. The limitations of elections can be particularly serious for such socially deprived groups. They are unlikely to have other resources, and their reliance on the ballot must be correspondingly greater. Failure to achieve their goals may cause bitter despair and even rejection of the electoral process, as exemplified by the extreme advocates of "black power."

Elections still remain the primary way of achieving popular goals. Deprived groups with few resources other than their numbers must be aware particularly of the uses of politics. Their vital resource must be employed where it is most effective—at the polls. The ballot does not guarantee improvement, but it does create opportunities for the amelioration of social conditions by bringing officials to consider the interests of any significant group. Elections in democracies allow a change of rule in ordinary ways and without awaiting extraordinary occasions. In such systems, therefore, officials avoid not only the extremely unpopular action but even the uncomfortable. A greater sensitivity by politicians to the anticipated reactions of the public is necessitated. No better means of protection has been devised. Security has not been provided by depending on the good will of rulers, on the presumed identity of interests between governed or governors, or on institutional controls, such as a federal structure, or supervision by a monopolistic political party. To the ancient question "Who will guard the guardians?" there is only one answer: those who choose the guardians.

CONCLUSION: THE MEANINGFUL BALLOT

To provide guardianship, elections must be well designed. There is no protection from the ballot unless each of the links in the chain between governed and governors is tempered and strong. To forge these links, however, is difficult. The initiatives of politicians may be irrelevant or appropriate. Their anticipations of voter reactions may be erroneous or accurate. The voters may be ready or unprepared to express their interests and to exercise a retrospective judgment. Meaningful elections require more than the casting of ballots. Other important conditions must be met.

Implicit in this study has been the assumption of an appropriate election structure. Without attempting an elaborate analysis in this conclusion, we can suggest some of the elements of this structure.[38] The first necessity for meaningful elections is an organized party system. . . . We have noted the vital role of political parties. They provide the means through which voter needs and discontents are heard and resolved. Without a choice between at least two competing parties, the electorate is powerless to exert its influence.

A related vital requirement is for free competition between the parties. The voters must be able to hear diverse opinions and be able to make an uncoerced choice. To provide this opportunity, the parties must be allowed significant opportunities to make their appeals. Nomination and campaigning must be available to the full range of candidates, and the means provided for transmitting their appeals to the electorate. A legitimate democratic election also requires that all of the adult population be enfranchised, that the ballot be intelligible to the voters, and that the winning party have some claim to explicit or tacit support by an electoral majority. It is also obviously necessary that the votes be honestly cast and counted.

Elections in the United States do largely meet the standards of meaningful popular decisions; true voter influence exists. The two parties compete freely with one another, and the extent of their competition is spreading to virtually all states. Access to the voters is open to diverse candidates, and no party or administration can control the means of communication. Suffrage is virtually universal, and voters have fairly simple choices to make for regular offices. In the overwhelming number of cases, voting is conducted honestly.

To fully effectuate popular influence, however, improvements are required in the American electoral system. Most critically needed are measures to strengthen the political parties, the vehicles for effective voter choice. Throughout the past two decades, the parties have deteriorated. They have lost campaigning functions to the mass media and political consultants. Waves of "reform" have limited their ability to nominate candidates and organize effectively. Electoral financing has been taken over by interest groups, government, and individual contributors. Legislative leaders have lost their few powers of party discipline within national and state legislatures. With the decline of parties have also come decreasing participation in elections but increasing levels of public cynicism and political alienation.[39] Party revival is necessary if these trends are to be reversed.

Party—and democratic—renewal in the United States will require a detailed and sustained program. It will necessarily involve providing funding for political parties as well as candidates, limiting the open and exhausting primaries in presidential nominations, and rebuilding a local base for popular participation in the parties. Without such changes, and even without parties, elections in America will certainly remain. Yet, to be meaningful, they must also be organized by the parties, our long-standing agencies with a collective responsibility to the public. Without parties, elections will be only plebiscites or rituals.

Whatever the future may hold, present conditions in the United States do enable the voters to influence, but not control, the government. The evidence of this study does not confirm the most extravagant expectations of popular sovereignty. Neither are elections demonstrably dangerous or meaningless. Most basically, we have found the ballot to be an effective means for the protection of citizen interests. Elections in America ultimately provide only one, but the most vital, mandate. Echoing the words but not the despair of Linda Loman, of *Death of a Salesman*, the voters authoritatively command: "Attention must be paid."

NOTES

1. Change in the character of public officials on the advent of universal suffrage is illustrated in Robert A. Dahl, *Who Governs?* (New Haven: Yale University Press, 1961), chaps. 2–5.

2. John Stuart Mill, *Considerations on Representative Government* (New York: Liberal Arts Press, 1958), chap. 3.

3. William R. Keech, *The Impact of Negro Voting* (Chicago: Rand McNally, 1968), chap. 1.

4. The "allegiance-maintaining" function of voting and the choice of leadership through elections is stressed in the thorough survey of Richard Rose and Harve Mossawir, "Voting and Elections: A Functional Analysis," *Political Studies* 15 (June 1967): 173–201.

5. W. J. M. MacKenzie, "The Export of Electoral Systems," *Political Studies* 5 (October 1957): 256. Cf. R. S. Milne, "Elections in Developing Countries," *Parliamentary Affairs* 18 (Winter 1964–65): 53–60.

6. A. H. Birch, *Representative and Responsible Government* (London: Allen & Unwin, 1964), p. 117.

7. Cecil S. Emden, *The People and the Constitution* (2nd ed.; London: Oxford University Press, 1956), p. 225. The discussion of mandates, in both normative and empirical terms, is related to the debate over "responsible party government." This issue is ably discussed by Allan P. Sindler, *Political Parties in the United States* (New York: St. Martin's, 1966), chap. 5.

8. Donald E. Stokes, "Some Dynamic Elements of Contests for the Presidency," *American Political Science Review* 60 (March 1966): 20–21; and Gerald M. Pomper, *Voters' Choice* (New York: Harper & Row, 1975), pp. 151–58.

9. Everett Carl Ladd et al., "The Polls: Taxing and Spending," *Public Opinion Quarterly* 43 (Spring 1979): 126–35. See also Robert Axelrod, "The Structure of Public Opinion on Policy Issues," *Public Opinion Quarterly* 31 (Spring 1967): 51–60.

10. See Anthony Downs, *An Economic Theory of Democracy* (New York: Harper & Row, 1957), pp. 55–60. . . .

11. Richard Pious, *The American Presidency* (New York: Basic, 1979), pp. 107–11.

12. Steven J. Rosenstone and Raymond E. Wolfinger, "The Effect of Registration Laws on Voter Turnout," *American Political Science Review* 72 (March 1978): 39–41. See also E. E. Schattschneider, *The Semi-Sovereign People* (New York: Holt, Rinehart & Winston, 1960), chap. 6.

13. Richard L. Merritt, "Woodrow Wilson and the Great and Solemn Referendum, 1920," *Review of Politics* 27 (January 1965): 78–104. The quotation is from p. 103. The Republican platform was ambiguous, the party pledging no more than "such agreements with other nations as shall meet the full duty of America to civilization and humanity" (Donald B. Johnson, *National Party Platforms* [Urbana: University of Illinois Press, 1978], 1:231).

14. See Sidney Verba et al., "Public Opinion and the War in Vietnam," *American Political Science Review* 61 (June 1967): 319–25, for the early period; and Warren E. Miller and Teresa E. Levitan, *Leadership and Change* (Cambridge, Mass.: Winthrop, 1976), pp. 133–36, for the later elections.

15. Among the more useful books in a burgeoning literature on this period, see Townsend Hoopes, *The Limits of Intervention* (New York: Longman, 1973); and William Shawcross, *Sideshow* (New York: Pocket Books, 1979).

16. V. O. Key, Jr., *Politics, Parties and Pressure Groups* (5th ed.; New York: Crowell, 1964), p. 544.

17. Birch, *Representative and Responsible Government*, pp. 116–17.

18. In accepting the Democratic nomination; *The New York Times,* August 28, 1964, p. 12.

19. Walter Bagehot, *The English Constitution* (Garden City, N.Y.: Doubleday Dolphin Books, n.d.), pp. 18–19.

20. Carl J. Friedrich, *Man and His Government* (New York: McGraw-Hill, 1963), pp. 199, 201.

21. Alexis de Tocqueville, *Democracy in America,* ed. Phillips Bradley (New York: Vintage, 1954), 1:248.

22. John Plamenatz, "Electoral Studies and Democratic Theory: A British View," *Political Studies* 6 (February 1958): 9.

23. Sidney Verba and Norman Nie, *Participation in America* (New York: Harper & Row, 1972), pp. 322–27.

24. George B. Tindall, *South Carolina Negroes, 1877–1900* (Columbia: University of South Carolina Press, 1952), p. 13.

25. V. O. Key, Jr., with the assistance of Milton C. Cummings, Jr., *The Responsible Electorate* (Cambridge, Mass.: Harvard University Press, 1966), pp. 76–77.

26. Gabriel A. Almond and Sidney Verba, *The Civic Culture* (Boston: Little, Brown, 1965), p. 352.

27. John W. Kingdon, "Politicians' Beliefs about Voters," *American Political Science Review* 61 (March 1967): 137–45.

28. Raymond A. Bauer, Ithiel deSola Pool, and Louis A. Dexter, *American Business and Public Policy* (New York: Atherton, 1963), p. 315.

29. Friedrich, *Man and Government,* p. 204.

30. Angus Campbell et al., *The American Voter* New York: Wiley, 1960, p. 547.

31. See Philip Converse et al., "Electoral Myth and Reality: The 1964 Election," *American Political Science Review* 59 (June 1965): 321–36.

32. Another example is provided by the former leader of Tammany Hall. He finds that electoral tickets "balanced" among ethnic groups are required to avoid potential protest, rather than to satisfy any explicit demand. See Edward N. Costikyan, *Behind Closed Doors* (New York: Harcourt Brace Jovanovich, 1966), pp. 181–82.

33. Lewis A. Dexter, "The Representative and His District," *Human Organization* 16 (Spring 1957–58): 4.

34. Warren E. Miller and Donald E. Stokes, "Constituency Influence in Congress," in Angus Campbell et al., *Elections and the Political Order* (New York: Wiley, 1966), pp. 362–66. See also Charles F. Cnudde and Donald J. McCrone, "The Linkage Between Constituency Attitudes and Congressional Voting Behavior: A Causal Model," *American Political Science Review* 60 (March 1966): 66–72.

35. The constant concern for voter reaction is a unifying theme in three recent and excellent works on Congress: John Kingdom, *Congressmen's Voting Decisions* (New York: Harper & Row, 1973); David Mayhew, *Congress: The Electoral Connection* (New Haven: Yale University Press, 1974); and Richard Fenno, *Home Style* (Boston: Little, Brown, 1978).

36. See I. Schapera, *Government and Politics in Tribal Societies* (London: Watts, 1956).

37. Mill, *Considerations,* p. 131.

38. For a fuller discussion, see Henry B. Mayo, *An Introduction to Democratic Theory* (New York: Oxford University Press, 1960), chaps. 5–8.

39. For analysis of the problems, see Austin Ranney, *Curing the Mischiefs of Faction* (Berkeley: University of California Press, 1975); David Broder, *The Party's Over* (New York: Harper & Row, 1972); and Everett Carll Ladd, *Where Have All the Voters Gone?* (New York: Norton, 1978).

Do Voting and Elections Mean Anything?

HOWARD L. REITER
The Fallacy of Voting

On November 6, 1984, ninety-three million Americans trooped to the polls and cast their votes for president and numerous other offices. It was really a remarkable exercise—ninety-three million people, each convinced that going to a polling place and marking a ballot was a sensible thing to do. Indeed, most Americans consider voting to be the most important single element of American democracy; in the words of the man who won the American presidency that day, voting is "the crown jewel of American liberties."[1] The right to vote is considered so central that it is cited as the reason that Americans die in wars. Voting is the least controversial of the demands that oppressed groups make, and the right that Americans expect foreign nations like South Vietnam and El Salvador to guarantee if they expect our support.

Why has voting always been so venerated by Americans? The answer we usually think of is that voting is the way in which the political beliefs of the American people are translated into government policy. By being given a choice of leaders, we supposedly can select the one whose views are closest to our own and therefore get those views carried out; of course, the stipulation is that a majority of the voters agree with us. In this way, the majority rules in our political system. It is a pleasant view of how American democracy works, but it is one with a number of problems.

ISSUES AND VOTING

Let us imagine, for example, several voters faced, on that November day in 1984, with a choice for president among Ronald Reagan, Walter Mondale, and several other candidates. (No doubt there really were voters who had the following thoughts.)

Joan: "I'd really like to vote for someone I agree with, but the problem is that the candidates are so vague about their views. And they say different things to different audiences. How can a voter decide? I'll just have to make a guess as to who will do what I want."

Bill: "I don't like any of them. Why do we always have to choose the lesser evil, instead of the greater good?"

Mary: "I guess I like Reagan more than Mondale on several issues, like

121

cutting Federal spending, abortion, and stopping the Russians; but I like Mondale more on the Equal Rights Amendment, peace, and gun control. No matter who I vote for, I'm only going to get some of the policies I want."

Bob: "I like practically all of Reagan's policies, but I'm afraid he'll get us into a nuclear war. I may have to vote for Mondale for that reason alone, but I'd hate for anyone to think that I like his record."

Laura: "To me, there is no more important issue than national health insurance. Yet neither of the candidates wants it."

Sam: "I prefer Mondale's policies to Reagan's, but he has been such an inept candidate that I am going to vote for Reagan anyway. We need a strong leader in the White House."

Leslie: "I don't have a lot of time to devote to reading about the campaign or watching it on TV, but I know that Republicans generally favor the issues I like, so I guess I'll vote for Reagan for that reason."

Notice how each of these intelligent, issue-oriented voters makes it hard for us to interpret the presidential vote in 1984 as an expression of public opinion. Joan has a hard time telling where the candidates stand, and whatever choice she ends up making will hardly be an expression of which one represents her views best. Bill's vote for the "lesser evil" is hardly an endorsement of his chosen candidate's views. Mary's vote is only an endorsement of *some* of her candidate's positions, and a rejection of others. Bob's vote for Mondale is only an expression of his fear of Reagan, not a ratification of Mondale's views. Whoever gets Laura's vote does not express her view on the most important issue to her. Reagan does not express Sam's views on issues; he only got Sam's vote because of his personal qualities. And Reagan only represents Leslie's views if he fits Leslie's notion of a typical Republican candidate.

What all this means is that to interpret the fact that the millions of people who voted for Reagan were actually endorsing his policy views is seriously to misinterpret their motives, if indeed there were many Joans, Bills, Marys, Bobs, Lauras, Sams, and Leslies in his coalition. The same goes for Mondale or any other candidate. This realization makes a mockery of a winning candidate's claim that he or she has a "mandate" from the voters, having received instructions as to how to behave in office. Only those voters who know all of a candidate's major positions and agree with all of them can be said to have contributed to such a mandate. Even then, the winner has no mandate for carrying out less-publicized positions.

Indeed, it is possible for a candidate to win a majority of the vote while the voters reject most of his or her stands on issues. Imagine that Reagan and Mondale are running against each other in a three-person electorate; we'll call those voters John, Cathy and Lee. There are five issues important to the voters: ERA [Equal Rights Amendment], budget cuts, disarmament, abortion, and busing. In the following table, we can see which candidate each voter agrees with on each issue:

	John	Cathy	Lee
ERA	Reagan	Reagan	Mondale
Budget cuts	Reagan	Mondale	Mondale
Disarmament	Mondale	Reagan	Mondale
Abortion	Reagan	Mondale	Mondale
Busing	Mondale	Reagan	Mondale

If you read *across* each issue in the table, you will see that two out of three voters agreed with Mondale on every issue except ERA. If you read *down* each voter's column, you will see that John and Cathy voted for Reagan—assuming that each voter chose the candidate whom he or she agreed with the most—and Lee voted for Mondale. Therefore Reagan won two-thirds of the voters, who agreed with him on only one out of five issues! I'm not suggesting that this kind of outcome ordinarily happens, but it is a good illustration of the problems of expecting elections to serve as an expression of public opinion.

Another variation of this problem is the possibility that a candidate may win by amassing a coalition of small groups of voters, each of which favors a policy that is highly unpopular with all other voters. By making selective appeals, a candidate can win the votes of people who want to bring back slavery, people who want to outlaw the eating of meat, people who want to expel New England from the union, and so forth, until that candidate has a majority—but on a platform that nobody supports.

In fact, most of the major issues in American history have been resolved not by elections but by other historical forces. Take slavery, for example. The American people never elected a president who promised to abolish slavery. Abraham Lincoln was elected in 1860 on a platform not of abolition, but of simply limiting slavery to the states in which it was then located. When a civil war ensued and Lincoln saw abolition as a useful military tactic, he signed the Emancipation Proclamation, which limited emancipation only to the areas still controlled by the Confederacy. In other words it was the war, and not the vote of the American people, that abolished slavery. Similarly, the New Deal's program of social welfare in the 1930s was not brought to power by popular mandate. Franklin D. Roosevelt was elected in 1932 promising to balance the budget, and the New Deal was only a slogan. The only mandate Roosevelt received was one to experiment, and it was over the next several years that his program took shape. Indeed, the only issue referred to in the headline in the *New York Times* the morning after he was elected was the repeal of Prohibition—one of the few issues on which Roosevelt took a clear stand.

The electoral politics of the Vietnam War is especially enlightening as an illustration of how limited the electorate's influence is on policy. In 1964, Lyndon Johnson overwhelmingly defeated the hawkish Barry Goldwater, who had talked of using nuclear weapons to defoliate trees in Vietnam. Many who voted for Johnson did so expecting him to avoid military adventures, and were dismayed when, soon after the election, our involvement in Vietnam swiftly escalated. By 1968 there was widespread dissatisfaction with the war, and yet the electoral choice that year was between Johnson's vice president, Hubert Humphrey, who loyally supported the conduct of the war, and Richard Nixon, who was vague about his intentions. The millions of voters who wanted an end to the war had no choice in November 1968. For the next four years, Nixon continued and in certain respects expanded the war, while reducing the number of American troops. By 1972, advocates of American withdrawal had their champion in Democratic nominee George McGovern, who lost in a landslide to Nixon. Yet within weeks of the election, American forces were withdrawn from Vietnam. So the Vietnam era produced an electoral rejection of a hawk, followed by escalation; little choice in 1968; and an electoral rejection of a dove, followed by American withdrawal!

Even in 1984, public opinion surveys show that there was hardly a "mandate" for many of the policies of the man who won the presidential election by such a resounding margin. One reputable academic poll found no more than a quarter of the voters favoring such Reagan policies as greater involvement in Central America, greater spending on the military, and cuts in spending on the environment, education, jobs for the unemployed, science and technology, and programs to benefit blacks.[2]

Of course, everything that I have argued up to this point is aimed at suggesting that elections are not very good ways of expressing the policy views of the people who actually vote. Elections are even less effective as a means of carrying out the policy views of all citizens. At a time when nearly half the population over age eighteen doesn't even bother to vote in presidential elections, the victorious candidate is likely to win the votes of only slightly more than a quarter of the eligible voters. In 1984, for example, Reagan won about 59 percent of the votes of the 55 percent of the electorate who showed up at the polls—which means that he received the support of the 31 percent of the electorate, in an election commonly referred to as a landslide.

Some people argue that all these problems would be eliminated if citizens voted directly on issues, in referenda and initiatives. But given the low voter turnout, and the fact that the way the question is drafted can influence the outcome, it is unlikely that such practices will ever give a complete picture of public opinion on a particular subject. Furthermore, referendum and initiative elections share some of the same shortcomings as elections for candidates, and the rest of this chapter will enumerate them.

VOTING AS COST-INEFFICIENT

Economists suggest that much of human behavior can be explained by means of a cost-benefit analysis. We weigh the costs of our actions against the possible benefits, and if the benefits seem to outweigh the costs, we take the action. Why are you reading this book? The costs are the price of the book, and the fact that there are more exciting books to read, or even more exciting things to do than reading—seeing a movie, playing ball, making love, or whatever. On the other hand, the benefits include gaining knowledge (we both hope), satisfying course requirements, increasing your chances for a high grade, receiving parental approval. Implicitly, you regard these benefits as greater than those costs, and so here you are.

Economists also try to put a value on these costs and benefits, usually expressed in monetary terms. The price of this book is easy to put such a value on. The value of raising your academic average might be thought of in terms of how much more money you will earn by admission to graduate school or qualifying for another job. Even values of things like playing ball or winning parental approval can be expressed as how much you would be willing to pay for them. Economists acknowledge that people don't actually cost out all of their choices, but they do believe that people implicitly make rough cost-benefit determinations all the time. If the value of the benefits is greater than the value of the costs, then people will take the action.

What about voting? What are its costs? Well, it costs money for you to go to the polls—gasoline, car depreciation, taxi or bus fare. Let's say that you pay two dollars for transportation. Voting takes time, too, and time is valuable. Maybe you could have earned five dollars in that time. And don't forget the transportation and time costs of registering to vote—also two plus five dollars. There is also the cost of obtaining information about the campaign, such as newspapers or magazines bought for the main purpose of deciding your vote, or television or radio programs turned on? (Electricity costs money; but we should only count the print and electronic media that would not have been used if a campaign were not going on.) And there is also the time it took to read, watch or listen. Let's call those costs fifteen dollars.

Have we forgotten anything? Babysitters? (We won't count friendships lost during the campaign; arguments over candidates are not a necessary part of voting.) Let's throw in another ten dollars for miscellaneous expenses. This adds up to thirty-nine dollars as the cost of voting.

Now let's look at the benefits. There are two kinds: those that are contingent on your candidate's winning, and those that are not. In the first category are the benefits that you expect to derive from your candidate's victory. Maybe you think that your presidential candidate will be a much better manager of the economy than his or her opponent, which will enable you to earn ten thousand dollars more in four years than you otherwise would have. Or, in some cases, maybe you expect the winner to appoint you to a government job, and in four years you can earn fifty thousand dollars more than on the job you will have to take if your candidate loses. (If you're not sure you'll get the government job, you have to multiply that salary by the probability of your landing the job.)

There are also non-economic benefits that may be of value to you, such as your candidate's foreign policy, social policies, and so forth. All of these can be assigned a value.

So far, voting looks like a great bargain: thirty-nine dollars for costs, thousands of dollars for benefits. But wait a moment. Your chances of getting all those benefits do not depend on *your* vote, but on the votes of everyone. In other words, you can stay home, pocket the thirty-nine dollars, and let everyone else's votes determine whether the candidate of your choice wins. Because if he or she does win, you will get those marvelous benefits whether or not you voted (unless you are only eligible for your government job if you can prove that you voted that day). Indeed, given the fact that your lone vote is extremely unlikely to affect the outcome, especially when the electorate is large, you would be foolish to spend that thirty-nine dollars. And if we are talking about a presidential election, your single vote must make the difference as to which candidate carries your state's electoral votes, and your state's electoral votes must make the difference in the electoral college. This is exceedingly improbable.

You are probably thinking, But what if everybody thought that way? Then nobody would vote, and the system would collapse! My answer is whether or not *you* vote will not affect how most other people vote. You can pocket your thirty-nine dollars and practically nobody else will know about it one way or the other. Or, you might respond by asking, Won't my vote help to increase my candidate's showing and make a statement about the popularity of his or her views? First, recall my earlier arguments that elections are a very ineffective way of representing voters' views. But more to the point here, your one vote will not significantly affect the showing of a candidate in a major race; in a presidential contest, it will only affect whether your favorite gets 45,196,547 votes rather than 45,196,548—not enough to affect anybody's interpretation of the election.

This may strike you as very cynical or unpatriotic. I am not urging you not to vote, but only suggesting that voting is a cost-inefficient act, aside from its other shortcomings. Indeed, the only rationale for voting is the benefit to be derived whether or not your candidate wins. This can be thought of as civic pride—the satisfaction you get in voting, regardless of the outcome. You can put a value on this by thinking of how much it would cost someone to pay you not to vote. For some people, a dollar or two would be enough. For others, it would be hundreds of dollars, or even millions. And some people would never sell their participation in the electoral process. All of the people whose "price" is more than thirty-nine dollars (or whatever it costs them individually) will vote—and that is a bare majority of the eligible population.

So we conclude that if people behave the way economists think they do, then the only motive they have for voting is sentimental—we are taught that it is the patriotic, public-spirited thing to do. Otherwise it would not be worth the effort.

THE LESSONS OF VOTING

If voting is not all that it's cracked up to be, then why do we Americans depend on it so heavily to select important public officials? Perhaps part of the answer lies in the latent lessons it teaches us.

Many social activities really perform a complex set of functions.[3] Take schooling. It has an ostensible goal, the education of young people, which it more or less achieves. But public schools also teach people other things—obedience to authority, segregation of college-bound middle-class children from vocation-bound working-class and poor children, a competitive reward structure. Authority, social segregation, and competition are all features that we confront in American society all our lives. These and other concepts are the "hidden lessons" of American education.

What about voting? It has an overt purpose, the selection of candidates to hold public office, and except in the rare case of deadlocks this purpose is met. But elections have hidden lessons, too. Elections tell people that politics is most appropriately conducted in certain ways, such as:

Politics Is Individualistic

At various times and places in history, people have conducted politics by bringing the community together in one place to determine the outcome of political issues collectively. The best-known examples include the ancient Greek city-states, Israeli kibbutzim, New England town meetings, and communes of various kinds. This is a concept that is based on the argument that if politics is a society's way of deciding its collective future, then what better way is there of doing so than to have people resolve the issues through face-to-face argumentation and brainstorming? In contrast, voting is an isolated, individualized act. People do not share their ideas or persuade each other. Each person is like an unconnected atom; it is in this manner that Americans tend to see social life in general. And yet we know that some of the most important social changes have been fostered by collective movements—by abolitionists, labor organizers, civil rights workers, and antiwar protesters. Indeed, we might well ask ourselves which nation underwent more profound political change in 1980—the United States, which chose a new administration through the ballot, or Poland, which without free elections established a mass movement that brought a new era in politics. Despite the crackdown in 1981, Solidarity has redefined the parameters of Polish life.

Politics Is Private

Which question is a greater invasion of privacy, What deodorant do you use, or Whom did you vote for in the last election? There is no obvious answer. People whose only political activity is voting are left to infer that politics is intensely personal and private, almost shameful. We vote not only individually, but often in booths with curtains, like Roman Catholics confiding their sins in the confessional. Again, instead of treating politics as the most *public* of activities, because it is concerned with the future of all of us, we treat it as something to be hidden. This is not to suggest that there is no virtue in the secret ballot, only that a nation whose most important political act is conducted in private is one that does not take politics seriously as the highest endeavor of the community.

Politics Is Episodic

Politics, we are encouraged to believe, occurs once a year in November, and for most adults it occurs only once every four years. We are able to discharge our highest civic function by taking a few minutes to go into a booth and flip a few levers once every four years. Although we are all free to engage in other political activities, such as collective action, writing to officials or working on campaigns, most adults are quite content to limit their political activity to that once-in-a-quadrennium lever flip. And if we think of voting as the crown jewel of our liberties, we will not think that citizenship requires anything else.

All in all, the message that elections sends us is to be passive about politics. Don't take action that involves any effort, don't unite with other citizens to achieve political goals, just respond to the choice that the ballot box gives us. In a strange way, then, elections condition us *away* from politics. A nation which defines its precious heritage in terms of political rights discourages its citizens from all but the *least* social, *least* public, and *least* political form of activity. This should raise the most profound questions for us. Why should we as a society discourage political activism? What is the real role that voting plays in our politics?

NOTES

1. "Voting Rights Act Signed by Reagan," New York Times, 30 June, 1982, p. A16.
2. National survey of the Center for Political Studies of the University of Michigan, distributed by the Inter-University Consortium for Political Research.
3. The distinction between manifest and latent functions is developed in Robert K. Merton, Social Theory and Social Structure (Glencoe, Ill.: Free Press, 1949), 21–82.

Questions for Discussion

1. Do elections matter?
2. What should elections determine?
3. What would be the political consequences of a major expansion in the voting turnout?
4. What effect has the enfranchisement of blacks in the United States had on their political power?
5. What effect does voting have on an individual's participation in other forms of political activity?
6. What kinds of voter registration requirements should there be?
7. What effect would the existence of a multiparty system in the United States have on voter turnout?

Suggested Readings

Behn, Robert D., and James W. Vaupel. "The Wasted Vote Fallacy." *Journal of Policy Analysis and Management*, 3, no. 4 (Summer 1984), pp. 607–612.

Bennett, Stephen E. *Apathy in America, 1960–1984: Causes and Consequences of Citizen Political Indifference*. New York: Dobbs Ferry, 1986.

Burnham, Walter Dean. *The Current Crisis in American Politics*. New York: Oxford Univ. Press, 1982.

Conway, M. Margaret. *Political Participation in the United States*. Washington, D.C.: CQ Press, 1985.

Flanagan, William H., and Nancy H. Zingale. *Political Behavior of the American Electorate*. 6th ed. Boston: Allyn and Bacon, 1987.

Gans, Curtis B. "Apathy Stands In As American Condition." *Los Angeles Times*, March 12, 1986, sec. II, p. 5.

Ginsberg, Benjamin, and Alan Stone, eds. *Do Elections Matter?* Armonk, N.Y.: M.E. Sharpe, 1986.

Petrocik, John R. "Voter Turnout and Electoral Preference: The Anomalous Reagan Elections." In *Thomas P. O'Neill, Jr. Symposium on American Politics*, edited by Kay Lehman Schlozman, pp. 239–259, Boston: Allen & Unwin, 1987.

U.S. Cong., House of Representatives. *Voter Registration*. Hearing before the Committee on House Administration, Task Force on Elections, 98th Cong., 2nd Sess., 1984.

Zimmerman, Joseph F. *Participatory Democracy: Populism Revived*. New York: Praeger, 1986.

Chapter 7

Does Private Funding for Congressional Elections Give Undue Influence to Political Action Committees?

For most of U.S. history the funding of political campaigns was left entirely to private sources. Unlike the practice in countries where the government underwrites the expense of campaigning, in the United States political parties and candidates have had to attract donations from individuals and groups.

In the twentieth century, campaign contributions have come under greater government regulation. In 1907 Congress passed a law prohibiting corporations from using their own funds in federal election campaigns. A similar prohibition was enacted for labor unions in 1943. Between 1947 and 1962 the law governing campaign expenditures forbade both corporate and union contributions and expenditures in federal primaries, general elections, and nominating conventions.

A number of laws were passed in the 1970s to deal with campaign finance. Many resulted from the revelations of illegal corporate contributions to the Committee to Reelect the President, the campaign organization for the reelection of President Richard Nixon. Successful challenges to some provisions in these laws resulted in Supreme Court decisions invalidating some restrictions on campaign finance in federal elections.

Today, campaign finance laws require that all federal candidates must disclose their campaign contributions. For presidential contests, a system of matching grants and public financing was established, and expenditure limits were set. No limits were placed on how much a congressional candidate's campaign committee could spend on the candidate's campaign.

One of the consequences of the campaign reform legislation was the growth of political action committees (PACs). A PAC is a private organization concerned with promoting economic, social, or ideological goals in public policy through electoral and other forms of political activity. PACs contribute money to candidates for public office. In addition, some of them help with getting out the vote and with voter registration.

PACs originated with trade unions in the 1930s. Their real development occurred in the 1970s and thereafter as a result of campaign finance reform. The Federal Election Commission (FEC), the government unit charged with enforcing federal election laws, classifies PACs under six categories: corporate PACs, labor PACs, trade/membership/health PACs, nonconnected PACs, cooperative PACs, and corporation without stock PACs.

According to the FEC, there were 608 PACs at the end of 1974. By the end of 1986 the number of PACs had increased to 4,157.[1] Not only has the number of PACs increased, but so, too, have PAC expenditures. FEC figures show the increase. For the election cycle of 1977–1978, PACs contributed $77.4 million to candidates. In the 1985–1986 election cycle, PACs contributed $338.3 million.[2]

Bills have been introduced into each chamber of Congress to replace private funding of congressional campaigns with a system of public funding. In the debate that follows, Mark Green and Joseph J. Fanelli express differing views on congressional campaign finance reform. Both selections are statements submitted to the Senate Committee on Rules and Administration, which was considering reform legislation on campaign finance in 1986.

Green, president of the Democracy Project on Campaign Reform and in 1986 an unsuccessful candidate for the U.S. Senate from New York on the Democratic party ticket, argues against the current system of campaign finance. Specifically, he contends:

1. Money buys influence, access, and even votes themselves.
2. Special interest money can paralyze Congress.
3. Special interest PACs discriminate against the groups that do not have PACs.
4. The PAC process is an incumbent-protection process.

He then refutes the arguments that have been made to defend PACs.

Joseph J. Fanelli, president of the Business-Industry Political Action Committee, makes the case for PACs. Specifically, he denies the assertions of the PAC critics and argues:

1. The political system of the United States is based on individual involvement in political campaigns. Restrictions against PACs would harm a fundamental principle of that system.
2. It is fundamentally wrong to use tax revenues for political candidates taxpayers might oppose.
3. In a period of high federal government deficits, it is wrong to add a new government program requiring additional revenues.
4. The FEC would not be able to administer public finance.
5. Public finance would encourage incompetent candidates to run for office.
6. The public is opposed to public funding in congressional campaigns.
7. It would be impossible to produce a fair system of disbursing funds to campaigns in different regions of the country.

NOTES

1. Federal Election Commission News Release, "FEC Releases New PAC Count," January 12, 1987.

2. Federal Election Commission News Release, "FEC Releases First Complete PAC Figures for 1985–86," May 21, 1987.

Does Private Funding for Congressional Elections Give Undue
Influence to Political Action Committees?

MARK GREEN

The Case against Political Action Committees

This is the eighth time I have testified before Congress on the subject of campaign finance reform. The first time was in 1974, two years after my book *Who
Runs Congress?* was first published. That year, campaign spending for congressional elections was $72 million, and political action committees spent $12
million. In the last election, congressional campaign spending rose to $377
million. And PACs gave a staggering $100 million—almost a thousand percent
increase over 1974.

It is evident that such unrelenting growth in campaign spending in general
and PAC [Political Action Committee] spending in particular affects how the
legislature works—and doesn't. First, money buys influence, access, or even
votes themselves. When I testify at these hearings and imply that people "give
to get"—that there is legislatively interested money—I sometimes encounter
angry public denials. Yet privately, we all acknowledge the truth of Rep. Barney Frank's observation that "We are the only human beings in the world who
are expected to take thousands of dollars from perfect strangers on important
matters and not be affected by it."

Second, special interest money can paralyze Congress. In an institution that
has more than 300 committees and subcommittees, it is not hard for monied
interests to find a beachhead in one or more committees in order to stop
legislation from going forward. Those of us who lobbied Congress or state
legislatures know how hard it is to get legislation enacted—and how easy it is to
get legislation stymied. A vivid example is the extraordinary volume of spending (and lobbying) prompted by the merest whiff of tax reform.

Third, special interest PACs discriminate against the PAC-less. Who has
access to PACs? Is it the Hispanic child on the lower east side of Manhattan
who has a PAC? Is it an unemployed teenager in Buffalo, a small farmer going
under, a consumer paying more for goods because of an antitrust exemption?
And who has access to PAC money? It is not the first-time women or minority
candidates, who might not have gone to school with the men who dominate
PAC spending decisions. This is not a partisan point. For it was Majority Leader
Robert Dole who noted "There's no Poor PAC."

And finally, the PAC process is a true incumbent-protection system, for the
money goes predominantly to one party, the incumbency party, as Common
Cause president Fred Wertheimer calls it. According to *What Price PACs?*, a

Twentieth Century Fund study conducted by political scientist Frank Sorauf, in House elections in 1982, 67 percent of all PAC money went to incumbents; in the Senate, 64 percent went to incumbents. "Most PACs have parent organizations, and most of those organizations have legislative interests and Washington representatives," observes Sorauf. "Supporting incumbents is thus a strategy of risk avoidance, of consolidating and protecting influence already won; it is the strategy of the already influential."

THE AVALANCHE OF EVIDENCE

Today, the Senate is seriously considering campaign finance reform for the first time since 1977. At this hearing and at prior sessions in the Fall, you have heard testimony about the rising costs of campaigns and the increasing role of political action committees. But the most persuasive testimony has come from Senators and Representatives themselves.

In response to a challenge from Bernadette Budde, the director of Business-Industry PAC (BIPAC), to "show me the bodies" of members of Congress who were influenced by campaign contributions, I interviewed twenty-nine Representatives and Senators in 1982. Not surprisingly, the laws of human nature have not been repealed. Here is the avalanche of evidence:

Republican Representative Claudine Schneider of Rhode Island in 1982 tried to persuade a Republican colleague to oppose more funding for the Clinch River Breeder Reactor. He declined, explaining, "Westinghouse is a big contributor of mine."

Another Republican Representative, Jim Leach of Iowa, tells how he once suggested to an urban Democrat with no dairy constituency that it might be politically wisest for him to oppose a dairy price support measure, and was told, "Yeah, but their PAC gave me money. I have to support them."

A New York Democrat admitted that he voted for the Alaska Gas Pipeline, even though he opposed it on the merits, because "I didn't want the construction unions contributing to my opponent."

In the mid-1970s, a labor union that gave Rep. Leon Panetta (D-CA) a $1500 contribution asked for support of pending "cargo preference legislation." When Panetta asked about the substance of the bill, he was told, "I don't have to tell you anything substantively—we gave you money. We support the bill, and we expect you to." Panetta kicked the lobbyist out of his office, and voted no.

According to one PAC manager, a certain liberal Democratic Representative, unsure how to vote on the recent Reagan tax increase, was told by a business PAC that if he supported the bill, "the slate would be wiped clean" between them. The Democrat voted for the bill, for reasons having nothing to do with the business lobby. Yet when the PAC sent him a $500 check, he angrily returned it, telling the PAC manager, "It was like leaving a 20 cent tip." The PAC then doubled the contribution, which the Congressman accepted.

When Representative Dan Glickman of Kansas asked a colleague several years ago to join him in opposing a measure that would stop the Federal Trade Commission from regulating auto dealers, he was told, "I'm committed. I got a $10,000 check from the National Automobile Dealers Association. I can't change my vote now." (In a separate incident, the Iowa Beef PAC began a letter asking for Glickman's support on a bill by noting, "As we trust you will recall, the Political Action Committee of Iowa Beef Processors, Inc., has heretofore supported your candidacy. . . ." Glickman sent back their $250, and then voted for the measure, as he originally intended to.)

A drug industry lobbyist told an aide to Representative Barney Frank of Massachusetts that if Frank could co-sponsor an industry-sponsored Drug Patent Act, the lobbyist would come to Frank's first fund-raiser in Washington, D.C. Frank told the lobbyist, "Go to hell."

Former Representative Millicent Fenwick recalled, "I wasn't down here but two months [in 1974], at a dinner for Alvin Toffler, when I sat down next to a reformer in Congress and asked if he'd be overriding a President Ford veto. He said, 'Are you kidding? I took $58,000 from labor, and they want it.' "

Representative Mike Synar, Democrat of Oklahoma, says, "I go out on the floor and say to a member, 'I need your help on this bill,' and often he will say, 'I can't do that, I got $5,000 from a special interest.' So I no longer lobby Congressmen. I lobby the lobbyists to lobby the Congressmen."

We are all familiar with the correlation studies conducted by Common Cause and Public Citizen's Congress Watch. These studies have found that when specific economic interests invest substantial amounts in a large number of legislators before key votes, the dividends roll in.

And the past few years have seen numerous journalistic accounts, all persuasively documenting the impact that campaign money has on our democracy and our legislature. You are undoubtedly familiar with them: Elizabeth Drew's *Politics and Money: The New Road to Corruption;* sociologist Amitai Etzioni's *Capital Corruption;* and perhaps most impressively, the previously mentioned study conducted for the 20th Century Fund by political scientist Frank Sorauf, *What Price PACs?* These exposés usually appear as the election cycle reaches its apogee, so we can expect further documentation soon to come. And with every article, every book, public confidence in our democratic institutions diminishes.

We err if we look for a "smoking gun"—a Watergate tape of [a] Dita Beard memo that will sensationally convince even the most self-interested skeptic that the system needs to change. *For the system itself is the smoking gun.*

THE CASE FOR PACS

Despite this damning and irrefutable empirical case, some beneficiaries of the PAC process cast about for rationales for the current system. In recent years, their arguments have been widely heard. Despite all appearances, they argue, PACs actually *increase* participation and democracy. Their arguments deserve scrutiny lest they become accepted by default. Like popcorn, they contain a kernel of truth puffed up beyond recognition.

Let me walk through some of them with you.

PACs are merely exercising the right of free speech. This assertion has been made by, among others, Eugene McCarthy, the American Civil Liberties Union and that well-known champion of the Bill of Rights, Mobil Oil. "When you cut through all the anti-PAC rhetoric," stated a Mobil advertisement, "it becomes obvious that PAC opponents don't really want the voices of average citizens to be amplified."

Are PAC contributions free speech? Although money talks in American politics, that has always been the *problem*, not the goal. Money isn't speech; speech is speech.

And if money were speech, would bribery be constitutionally protected? If so, large contributors could effectively overturn the Supreme Court's reapportionment decisions; instead of one person, one vote, the standards would be many dollars, many votes. If a contribution can buy a legislative result and drown out the voices of thousands of citizens, free speech has been stifled, not encouraged.

PACs account for only a small part of all political contributions. As Richard Armstrong, head of the Public Affairs Council, a pro-business group, wrote in *Newsweek* a few years ago, "The truth is that all PACs combined, including those of labor, contribute less than one-fourth of the aggregate amount spent on election campaigns."

But a PAC need not bankroll an entire campaign to be remembered by a politician after the votes are counted. Furthermore, aggregate statistics are misleading because the inclusion of candidates who get almost no PAC money pulls down the average. In any event, PACs have supplied over 40 percent of the campaign treasuries of winning House candidates in recent elections.

Finally, PAC money, like snow in the mountains, gathers at the peaks. A large portion of it goes to committee chairs and party leaders who are most able to return favors. In 1984 the House minority leader, Robert Michel, received 58 percent of his campaign funds from PACs; House Ways and Means Committee chairman Dan Rostenkowski filled 63 percent of his coffers with PAC money.

If you take inflation into account, campaign spending has increased only 20 percent or so in the last five· years." So wrote Robert Samuelson in a review panning Elizabeth Drew's book in the *New Republic*.

Actually campaign spending has skyrocketed. Between 1972 and 1982, while the Consumer Price Index doubled, spending for House races increased 450 percent and for Senate races, 500 percent. In 1972 the average first-term representative spent less than $100,000; in 1982, about $300,000.

Consider the cases of John Culver and Peter Kostmayer. In the 1974 Iowa contest for the Senate between Culver and David Stanley, the opponents' combined expenditure was $807,037; when Culver ran for re-election against Charles Grassley in 1980, it was $3.9 million—a 487 percent increase in just one term. Kostmayer spent $58,000 to win his House seat in 1976, lost in 1980 and then spent $600,000 to win again in 1982—more than a 1,000 percent increase.

Business isn't monolithic, so business contributions have a diffuse impact. "Business rarely takes a uniform position on *any* political issue," wrote Armstrong. PAC critics, he added, "forget the many conflicts within the business community itself—big business versus small business, industry versus industry, free trade versus protectionism, and so on."

It's true that divisions can occur within an industry on specific issues—such as airline deregulation, for example. More frequently, however, business does present a united front. Is any chemical company lobbying for a stronger Superfund? Did any commodities traders' group oppose the bill that gave a tax break to commodities traders? And as the securities industry and the banks fight it out to shape the future of our financial system, where is the PAC that fights for depositors and small investors?

PAC gifts aren't inducements for future votes; they're rewards for a prior record. According to Representative Beryl Anthony, when he gets $5,000 from a PAC it "means somebody has approved of my prior service in Congress" and nothing more. If a legislator's support for the special interest group's position preceded the contribution, how could it have *resulted from* the contribution?

Then why do so many PACs cross-examine candidates in questionnaires and in person about their positions on pending matters? As Amitai Etzioni points out, "Unlike rocks, people can anticipate; they can act now in anticipation of payoff to follow." And according to Jay Angoff, when he was an attorney at Public Citizen's Congress Watch: "Whether a member votes for legislation because he has received money from a certain group or receives money because he has voted for legislation sought by the group, it makes no difference to the consumer. Either way, people who vote to further the interests of the business lobbies that contribute to their campaign continue to get ahead."

The average PAC gift is too small to make a difference. Since PAC gifts to candidates average around $600, even a lawmaker eager to sell out would be unmoved by a typical gift. Political scientist Michael Malbin observes that while several banking PACs gave Senator John Tower a total of $90,000 when he ran for re-election in 1978, his campaign spent $4 million; so banking PACs accounted for 2.5 percent of the total. Malbin asks, "Can anyone seriously argue that Tower's positions were influenced by his greed for that bit of money?"

Even in Senate races, which are far more expensive than House races, $90,000 is still $90,000. And for a House candidate, $10,000 out of total costs of $300,000, say, is surely memorable, especially if it comes early in the campaign, when a candidate needs to show credibility—or late, for that crucial media buy. Six years after I ran for the House in Manhattan, I still remember

everyone who gave me $1,000 contributions and at what stage in the campaign. How many members of Congress can't?

Even a $5,000 gift isn't enough to buy a member of Congress. According to a Mobil advertisement, "That's hardly enough to corrupt a legislator, even if he or she were disposed to be corrupted."

To that Representative Tom Downey (D-NY) quipped, "You can't buy a Congressman for $5,000, but you can buy his vote." No PAC gift would sway Senator Proxmire (D-WI) in his support of the Genocide Treaty or Representative Henry Hyde (R-IL) in his opposition to abortion, but most of the 600-odd votes a year in Congress do not involve such deep moral or philosophical commitments. As a Democratic lawmaker told *Newsday*'s Judith Bender, "If you're on the fence and it doesn't matter to you or your constituents which way you vote, but it matters to some of your biggest contributors, your mind is going to be made up very easily, because the vast majority of issues are not war and peace, equity and justice. They are really very different shades of gray."

PACs are public. They are at least an improvement over Watergate-era practices like passing cash-filled shopping bags and making secret infusions from corporate treasuries. "The signal virtue of the 1974 election law was that it required full disclosure of who is giving how much to whom," editorialized *The New Republic* in 1984. Critics should "concentrate on looking through the campaign finance and Congressional voting records to see who is in bed with whom."

No one is advocating a return to the days of Bobby Baker and Maurice Stans, but disclosure, however necessary, is not a sufficient step toward cleaning up the campaign financing process, for several reasons.

PAC men in bed with legislators do not receive the same media attention as, say, cohabiting movie stars. And disclosure isn't good enough if *both* candidates in a race are equally in hock to interest groups—a not uncommon occurrence, since almost all candidates accept PAC gifts. Finally, a Democracy Project study found that 20 percent of contributions to Republicans in close House races in the 1980 election came from business PACs that gave after the October 15 filing deadline. While legal, such quiet gifts evade the intent of campaign finance laws, for they avoid public scrutiny until after the election.

PACs increase political participation. According to a survey by Herbert Alexander, the political scientist and campaign finance expert, 100,000 people gave to business PACs between 1979 and 1980. An advertisement sponsored by United Technologies calls this phenomenon "a welcome shift toward the grassroots."

Individual PAC donors, however, participate in the least participatory way. PACs take small contributions from donors, but the donors have little if any say over how the money is disbursed. Representative Leach worries that since "groups seldom reflect the same collective judgment as their members, [the views of PAC managers], not the small contributors to their associations, become the views that carry influence."

And the way PACs raise money is frequently coercive. Consider how Dart-

Pac dunned Dart Company executives with "donation guidelines," follow-up letters pointing out that contributions were being compared with salary, group sessions and finally one-on-one grillings. In 1978, according to Nicholas Goldberg in the *Washington Monthly,* 83 percent of Dart executives contributed, giving an average of $1,030, as opposed to 0.06 percent of the company's stockholders, who averaged $27.45 each.

PAC defenders are trying to perform the political equivalent of making water run uphill. Despite the best efforts of cloistered academics and corporate public relations aides, it is impossible to deny that the swelling volume of PAC money is distorting if not corrupting the legislative process. It is my impression that after hearing these counter-arguments, the public and Congress itself have concluded that the case for PACs falls short.

 ☑ *NO*

Does Private Funding for Congressional Elections Give Undue Influence to Political Action Committees?

JOSEPH J. FANELLI

The Case for Political Action Committees

FICTIONAL PROBLEMS IN OUR PRESENT SYSTEM

It is charged that congressional votes are bought and sold with PAC [Political Action Committee] contributions as the medium of exchange. Where is the proof? Where have specific allegations been made, let alone verified?

There is that special brand of false syllogism which proceeds in this manner; first, several members of a House or Senate Committee voted for certain legislation; second, a PAC that was interested in that legislation made contributions to several of those members; third, therefore (as though it were proven beyond a doubt) their votes had been "bought" by campaign contributions.

It is charged that PAC contributions have caused the inflation of campaign costs. Rather, the elements that go into a campaign these days cost considerably more than ever: media, printing, postage, travel, salaries, telephones, computers, the need to engage the professional services of campaign consultants, lawyers and accountants in order not to run afoul of the Federal Election Committee. Then there are the wealthy candidates who are willing to spend millions and millions of dollars of their personal fortune in their own campaigns.

Another misconception is that PACs give very large sums of money to candidates. First, there is the legal limit of $5,000 per candidate, per race. But very few PACs have the resources to give the maximum in very many races. Based on our 1985 survey of business employee PACs contributing in the 1983–84 election cycle, of those responding, the average business employee PAC gave a total of $47,194 to congressional candidates. Eighty-seven percent of the business employee PACs contributed under $100,000.

Our survey also showed the average business employee PAC's contribution to House candidates was $295; the average to Senate candidates was $1,103. Are such modest amounts going to "buy" influence with candidates whose campaigns cost many, many times those amounts? And even if the average were considerably higher, where is the justification to presume that members of the House and Senate could be "bought?" Is it accurate or fair to imply that every member has his or her "price"?

It also has been charged that the contributions of PACs are responsible for keeping incumbents in office and insulating them from the voters. For several decades over 90 percent of House incumbents have been getting reelected. So this phenomenon began long before the proliferation of PACs came about. The record for Senate incumbents contrasts with that of the House; there is much more turnover. As recently as 1980 on 56 percent of the Senators seeking reelection were successful.

Contributors to PACs are said to be coerced into giving. Again, where is the proof? The participation rate of employees in most business-related PACs according to our survey is only about 31 percent, which would indicate a purely voluntary process.

PACs are said to dominate the elections for Congress. Is that possible when the total contributions of all PACs still amount to less than 30 percent of the money spent in congressional campaigns? This includes all PACs—business, labor, membership, ideological, non-connected, trade and professional associations, etc. They serve many different purposes, many conflicting purposes. Their force is diffused; their voice is muted.

Still the critics continue to talk as if all of the varieties of PACs had just one purpose and one clearly defined course of action.

That is patently false.

To continue to lump all PACs together can only be done for purposes of propaganda; it cannot be excused on grounds of ignorance.

Mr. Chairman, I repeat all of this with some degree of frustration. These facts have been told many times before. But the drumbeat of allegations continues, and it seems there are so many whose minds are made up and who refuse to be bothered about the facts. . . .

We at BIPAC [Business-Industry Political Action Committee] are opposed to public, or taxpayer, financing of election campaigns on both theoretical and practical grounds and we have testified several times before House and Senate Committees expressing our opposition.

We believe that our political system is predicated on the personal involvement of individuals, and anything that would weaken the prerogatives or incentives for individual voter participation would in turn weaken our democratic system.

We believe all citizens have the right to devote time, talent and/or resources to help elect candidates of their choice. Some may choose to do this by going door-to-door distributing information about favorite candidates or by the time-honored "stuffing of envelopes" at campaign headquarters. Others may devote special talents writing speeches and press releases, designing campaign litera-ture, or speaking; still others may offer their accounting or computer skills and many others, whose time and talents are directed otherwise, may wish to provide financial resources to help support those candidates whose views they share.

This is a basic, fundamental right in our participatory democracy.

So is the right to join with other like-minded citizens to support certain candidates or groups of candidates, whether in a political party, a club or organization, a political action committee or an ad hoc group.

We are always mystified that some people purport to see this basic American exercise—which is essential to our system—as somehow undermining our elec-toral process.

To deny citizens this right, or to supplant it with federal funds taken from taxpayers, violates the electoral system on which this Nation was founded.

We also believe it is fundamentally wrong to take tax revenues derived in part from "Citizen Jones" to give financial support to "Candidate Smith," whom Jones would never support of his own volition.

We further believe that public (taxpayer) financing, even "partial" financing, would tend to decrease individual participation in the political process. Sur-veys taken among PAC contributors, for instance, have reported repeatedly that persons are drawn into political involvement, in part, by means of participation in political action committees. The PACs help to educate voters, about candi-dates, issues and forthcoming elections; they stimulate their interest. Similarly, the ability of individuals to make a financial contribution directly to the candi-dates of their choice fosters their interest in participating further in the electoral process.

There also are practical problems concerned with taxpayer financing of elections. Faced with the present federal deficit, and the cutbacks taking place in many segments in government, this is hardly the time to adopt a new area of public expenditures. The private sector can and is providing campaign financing.

The Federal Election Commission, still virtually overwhelmed with the ad-ministrative burden imposed by the presidential and congressional finance laws, would be completely overwhelmed if it were also given responsibility for funding and monitoring congressional races, in which thousands of candidates would be seeking nomination and election to office.

We also believe the availability of public funds would encourage some candidates to run for office whose qualifications are so meager that they would never run if they had to rely on voluntary contributions. Candidates who never could hope to attract sufficient support to compete because of their lack of qualifications and/or extreme views, surely would be tempted if they could get publicly-funded support in the primary or in the general election.

Moreover, public opinion surveys have shown general opposition to tax-payer financing of congressional campaigns, but proponents apparently refuse to accept these results with which they do not agree.

It also has been pointed out that the economic, demographic and geographical makeup of congressional districts and states differ greatly; the financial needs for effective campaigning vary greatly, for instance, from a rural district with few media outlets and an urban district in the midst of a high-priced media market. No one has produced a formula for allocating funds from the Federal Treasury which would remotely approach fairness on this score.

Notwithstanding all these facts, taxpayer financing is still offered by some as a panacea for problems in the current congressional campaign financing system, some of which are real and many of which are totally fictional. . . .

PROBLEMS IN THE U.S. ELECTION SYSTEM

Mr. Chairman, there are several areas of legitimate concern with regard to our electoral system in addition to the cost of campaigns and the proper role of political action committees.

Here are some areas that I believe need to be studied:

1. Poor voter turnout.
2. The substantial advantage incumbents have over challengers; i.e. the franking privilege, newsletters, staff, etc.
3. The setting up of PACs by Senators and Members of the House for the purpose of distributing funds to colleagues.
4. The setting up of PACs by Presidential candidates for the ostensible purpose of contributing to Senatorial and Congressional campaigns but which actually are used in support of their own presidential candidacies.
5. The "privilege" of Members of the House who were elected before the 1980 election to convert left-over campaign funds to personal use.

ELECTION PRACTICES SHOULD BE REVIEWED IN TOTO

From the above list of problem areas, which certainly is not exhaustive, it would seem a thorough review of the way in which our Congress is elected would be desirable. Preferably it should be done by a mix of persons who are not themselves directly part of the process and by those in the process; it should be a truly objective, impartial assessment of current practices and what might be done to remedy shortcomings.

Studies by appointed commissions, even so-called "blue ribbon" groups, tend to be downgraded by the cynical. Too often they conclude with reports of the obvious and with recommendations that are impractical or unachievable.

In this case, a commission might do much to clear the air. I believe an objective study of campaign finance would conclude, as many have, that PACs are a positive force in the electoral system—the means by which millions of Americans have been brought into the political process and whose awareness and commitment have been enhanced. I think the supposed corrupting influence of PACs would be shown to be non-existent.

The report of such a Commission would likely conclude that the present reporting and disclosure requirements of the Federal Election Commission have produced a system where campaign giving and spending are better known than ever before, and that any proposed changes should be weighed carefully to be sure they will not do more harm than good.

Of course the possibility of public or taxpayer financing of Congressional elections also should be reviewed. Public opinion surveys continue to show that the voters reject this alternative by better than 60 percent. It has had its "never-say-die" advocates for a decade, but they have failed to rally public support for the idea. And the Congress has rejected it whenever it has been presented for a vote.

Taxpayer funding has serious flaws and should bear the most careful study.

Picking on PACs is a favorite sport for some critics, but it does not address the real problems in our system. I urge the Senate Rules Committee to look at the total picture, and not tinker with just one element that is working well.

Questions for Discussion

1. Why does Green worry about PACs?
2. How would you determine whether PACs unduly influence members of Congress?
3. How would you determine whether members of Congress unduly influence PACs?
4. Who are the principal beneficiaries of the current system of campaign finance for members of Congress? Why?
5. Who would be the principal beneficiaries of public financing for congressional campaigns? Why?

6. What effect would public financing of congressional campaigns have on freedom of speech?
7. What is the impact of PACs on the level of campaign spending?

Suggested Readings

Alexander, Herbert E., and Brian A. Haggerty. *PACs and Parties: Relationships and Interrelationships.* Los Angeles: Citizens' Research Foundation, Univ. of Southern California, 1984.

Bennett, James T., and Thomas J. DiLorenzo. *Destroying Democracy: How Government Funds Partisan Politics.* Washington, D.C.: Cato Institute, 1985.

Conway, M. Margaret. "PACs and Congressional Elections in the 1980s." In *Interest Group Politics,* edited by Allan J. Cigler and Burdett A. Loomis, pp. 70–90. 2nd ed. Washington, D.C.: CQ Press, 1986.

Dockser, Amy. "Nice PAC You've Got Here . . . A Pity If Anything Should Happen to It." *Washington Monthly,* 18, no. 12 (January 1987), 21–22, 24–25.

Drew, Elizabeth. *Politics and Money: The New Road to Corruption.* New York: Macmillan, 1983.

Etzioni, Amitai. *Capital Corruption: The New Attack on American Democracy.* San Diego: Harcourt Brace Jovanovich, 1984.

Glen, Maxwell. "Wooing Business Money." *National Journal,* 18, no. 33/34 (August 16, 1986), 2008–2011.

"Limiting Political Action Committees: Pro & Con." *Congressional Digest,* 66, no. 2 (February 1987), 33–64.

Sabato, Larry. *PAC Power: Inside the World of Political Action Committees.* New York: Norton, 1985.

Sorauf, Frank J. *What Price PACs? Report of the Twentieth Century Fund Task Force on Political Action Committees.* New York: The Fund, 1984.

U.S. Cong., Senate. *Proposed Amendments to the Federal Election Campaign Act of 1971.* Hearings before the Committee on Rules and Administration, 99th Cong., 2nd Sess., 1986.

Chapter 8

Will Political Parties Continue to Decline in Importance?

Political parties were formed after the Constitution was drafted and, consequently, are not mentioned in that document. Unlike most political democracies, the United States has a two-party system—today the Democratic party and the Republican party. The Democratic party was formed by Thomas Jefferson at the beginning of the nineteenth century. The Republican party was formed in 1854 and won its first presidential election in 1860 with Abraham Lincoln as the standard-bearer.

From time to time, third parties have appeared, and they have occasionally succeeded in winning elections in state and local as well as congressional contests. Sometimes the third parties have influenced the major parties. For example, the Populist party, composed largely of farmers and labor, was formed in 1892. Its presidential candidate won 8.5 percent of the popular vote in the election that year, and some Populist party candidates won office in state and congressional contests. In 1896, the Democratic party adopted the Populist platform, resulting in a realignment of political parties in which large numbers of voters changed their party identification. The Populist party soon ceased to exist as an independent party.

The history of political democracies and the history of political parties seem to go hand in hand. Political parties perform a variety of functions necessary for democratic rule. These include the mobilization of people to cast their ballots in elections, the recruitment of candidates for public office, the presentation of a program, the joining of diverse groups for the purpose of winning elections, and the running of government that comes from electoral victories.

The political system of Great Britain is the model of strong party government. When a general election is held in Britain, the voter casts a ballot only for a candidate in his or her political constituency, with the name of that candidate listed by party affiliation. The candidate who wins a plurality of the votes in that constituency is elected to the House of Commons, the principal legislative institution. By tradition the party that has the largest number of elected members of Parliament (if there is a majority party rather than a coalition of parties constituting the majority) forms a government. The leader of that party becomes the chief executive or prime minister and appoints a cabinet from members of Parliament who are in the winning party.

As indicated in Chapter Two, the British system allows for clear accountability. The party puts up a platform in elections and has the legislative and executive power allowing it to rule. By contrast, the U.S. party system has always been weak, largely because of the constitutional system of separation of powers and federalism.

Nevertheless, political parties, although decentralized, were strong in the nineteenth century, but their power has declined in the twentieth century. The ability of parties to select candidates has been diminished by political primaries allowing individuals and groups to put forward candidates without party approval. Candidates now obtain their finances largely on their own through campaign committees rather than through party organizations. The Civil Service, which now encompasses more than 90 percent of federal government employees, has eliminated the patronage system, whereby party workers whose party won at the federal level were rewarded with government jobs. The rise of the mass media, moreover, has meant that those who report the news play a greater influence than political parties in setting the issues before the people of the United States.

Is it likely that political parties will continue to decline in importance? Political scientist William Crotty thinks that they will. He cites the decline in the relevance of political parties in the electorate, the undercutting of campaign functions of political parties by PACs, the new technologies, and the increasing costs of politics. He notes that parties in Congress have been losing discipline and that voting along party lines has declined. He sees new political arrangements emerging, with a likely reduction in the significance of parties.

Political consultants Xandra Kayden and Eddie Maye, Jr., see a resurgence of political parties. They note improvements in the professionalism of party staffs, the increasing financial resources collected by the parties, and the tendency of political parties to counterorganize.

Will Political Parties Continue to Decline in Importance?

WILLIAM CROTTY

A Concluding Note on Political Parties and the Future

THE DECLINE

Concerning the Electorate

The number of voters participating in elections continues to decline to levels low enough for us to begin to question the relevance, and should the trend continue, the stability and representativeness of American political institutions. The picture is bleak. The electorate has become polarized between the higher socioeconomic-status adults who remain in the 30 to 50 percent of the eligible population that continues to participate in elections and the lower socioeconomic-status groups who have dropped out. How representative is a governing system that does not include in its decision making in any meaningful way those most in need of effective political representation? You will have to answer this question for yourself.

Within the evolving electorate, political parties are becoming less relevant. The number of people identifying with the major parties is decreasing, to the point where the proportion of independents equal those identifying with the larger of the two parties, the Democrats. As the number of independents increases—as it will with the entry of new voters into the electorate, a group for whom the parties have the least appeal—independents will become the dominant group in the electorate. Within the American political system an independent identification has been associated with a lack of political interest and involvement. There is evidence that this depiction is no longer totally accurate—independents are a disparate group—but the development of such a large pool of unattached voters is not a hopeful sign for a party system that has depended on a continual stream of new adherents to replenish its ranks.

The weakening of party ties has led to a volatile electorate, one capable of swinging from overwhelming majorities in favor of one party to, in the space of one election to the next, competitive outcomes or equally decisive margins in favor of the other party. The stability, predictability, and, if you will, mooring mechanisms of the American electorate have been seriously undermined. The future suggests the evolution of a basically partyless electorate, with little of the placidity of, say, the 1950s. The normal ties of identification with the parties continue to be eroded.

To make matters worse, the voters' perceptions of the political parties and of the government continues to be negative. The turnaround in indicators of public trust, efficacy, and faith in government in less than two decades has been remarkable. However one defines it, Americans are alienated from their own government and its leaders. It is unlikely that anything that has happened in recent years has renewed the voters' faith in the government.

As the electoral impact of the parties has declined, issues have increased in significance as an influence on voter decision making. Without party identification to provide a powerful (and simplifying) cue to the voter, issues decisions demand more of a voter's time and mental energy than most are willing to give. An issue-oriented electorate is one likely to increase the dominance of the better-educated and upper-income groups over electoral decisions. Lower socioeconomic groups face enormous difficulties in reincorporating themselves into the electorate without the political parties to encourage, organize, and guide their efforts. One of the strengths of the two-party system has been its ability to include large elements of the less well-off in their coalitions. The weaknesses of the parties in the electorate have already indicated that there will be future difficulties in mobilizing and attracting this vote. Specific candidates may be able to appeal enough on occasion to nonidentified, nonvoting adults to stimulate them to turn out and vote. Whether this will move, as the parties have done in the past, to incorporate these lower socioeconomic groups into the electorate in any meaningful, long-term manner and to allow them a vehicle through which to exercise a consequential influence on political decision making is doubtful. There is no evidence that the trends depicted in this book in regard to these concerns will change to any significant degree in the foreseeable future.

Concerning Campaigns, the Rise of PACs, the New Technologies, and the Increasing Costs of Politics

The campaign functions of the parties have been seriously undercut. Parties are no longer the principal funders of campaigns, PACs [Political Action Committees] are. Television has replaced the party as the dominant communicator of political information and, as a consequence, the preeminent influence on voter attitudes. Parties are no longer the major organizers of campaigns. Media consultants, public relations and professional experts can create "instant" parties for candidates with the funds to pay for them. As the campaign function of parties has decreased, the role of money—and hence of those who can supply it—has increased dramatically. The new politics is an expensive one.

The response of the parties to these developments has been uneven. The movement for party reform was an effort to produce a more participant-oriented party structure responsive to, and in line with, contemporary political concerns. The movement has experienced a varied success. The presidential nominating system has been remodeled. More voters are involved, and the decision over the nomination is now in the hands of those who take the trouble to participate in the process. This is a pronounced change from the closed, elitist nominating politics of the old (pre-1972) party system.

The reform movement may have many commendable qualities, but it has created problems. It could be argued with justification that reform resulted from the inability of the parties, and especially the larger of the two, the Democrats, to adequately represent the major concerns of the parties' constituencies. Nevertheless, in many respects, reform has also contributed to the continued erosion of the party system by weakening the parties' control over their most vital function, the nominating process.

Reformers and party regulars both recognize the problem. Many states, in order to meet the reform guidelines and (not incidentally) to benefit from the exposure television can provide, adopted primaries. In a dozen years the number of primaries has better than doubled (from sixteen to thirty-five), and the number of delegates selected through primary elections has increased from an average of less than 40 percent for the two parties to over 70 percent. Since primaries neutralize the role and influence of the party, they have contributed to its demise. The void has been filled by the media (particularly television) and by the groups with the financial resources needed to mount serious candidacies in a media-oriented age.

Reform has had little impact, good or bad, in other areas. The national party structures have shown little evidence of change. The parties also have failed to take command of the new technologies of politics and to use these to their own advantage. In this regard, Republican efforts have been more substantial and impressive than those of the Democrats.

The leaders of both parties pay lip-service to the problems the parties face. Given the chance to rebuild party coalitions and strengthen party services, they do little. From Richard Nixon to Jimmy Carter and Ronald Reagan, the chief concern of those most in a position to help revitalize the party system has been their own political survival. If the leadership of the two parties fails to recognize the fundamental seriousness of the problems confronting the parties, it is unlikely that anyone else can be of much assistance. Party regeneration will have to begin from within. At present there is no sign that party leaders truly appreciate the extent of the parties' malaise and are willing to extend themselves to do something about it. The future in these regards is bleak.

Concerning the Party in Congress and in Policy Making

The party in Congress has been subjected to an increasing dissolution of discipline and a decline in party line voting. The congressional leadership in recent years has on several occasions lined up against the president of its own party on policy issues. There has been a continuing split between the electorate of the presidential party and that of the congressional party. At the same time, the advantages of incumbency in seeking reelection have been magnified; the congressman's relation to his constituency has become more service-oriented; and PAC funds have increasingly supplied the capital needed for campaigning.

There have been reforms within the party and within the institutions of Congress. Some have helped to strengthen the party; most, however, have weakened it. Generational differences within the congressional membership have become more pronounced, with the newer members less amenable to party and presidential direction. Congressional electoral politics, the demands of legislative performance, party needs, and the will and priorities of a president, for the most part, all appear to pull in opposing directions. As a consequence, the factionalization evident in other aspects of American politics has adversely affected the national-level policy formulation and implementation and the parties' role in, and control over, them.

These changes have been in progress for at least the last several decades. To compound the difficulties and accentuate the trends, in recent years the nation has been led by presidents with weak ties to the national and congressional party and a poor understanding of party needs (at any level) or legislative demands. It may be that the worst manifestations of the debilitating forces assessed in this book have yet to be seen. If this is the case, future years will witness the continuing decline in party performance and relevance. The question remains, then, as to the consequence of these developments. What does it all mean? What will American politics be like with a progressively more ineffectual party system, one characterized by weak leadership, an increasing lack of coherence, an inability to control its own activities or members, and undue responsiveness to special interest funds and influences?

THE FUTURE

Again, we can only speculate at this point, but it would seem that a partyless politics contains both risks and opportunities. The biggest difficulty will be in the absence of the bonds that held party coalitions together and that allowed for some coherence among different levels of party concerns (the president, Congress, and the voter). These bonds—which were largely internal, personal, and attitudinal—allowed for a sense of order to prevail in American politics. Democrats, usually, stood for something; the voter did not need to know the details on every issue to reasonably assume that his party was different from the Republicans' and that it served different group needs. These are no longer safe assumptions.

A president, regardless of how liberal or conservative his program might be in contrast to that espoused by the congressional party, could count on his legislative party leaders to support his major recommendations, and therefore those of the party nationally, and to exercise their influence to have these enacted. Again, this is no longer the case. Likewise, party leaders within Congress had the tools— in consultation with the baronial committee chairpersons—to force a degree of loyalty to party-endorsed programs and therefore to deliver in some manner on policy commitments. The results were often a cautious, conservative muddle of programs; Congress was run by its most conservative interests (southerners; committee chairpersons from noncompetitive areas; interest groups with a personal stake in supporting or opposing legislation). Bold programs were hard to come by, and it took, normally, a national crisis in order to force Congress to move (Birmingham on civil rights; the Watts rioting on urban decay; Vietnam on the war powers of the president; and so on). It was not a happy situation, and it is often forgotten. A major reason for the rise of the imperial presidency, beginning with Franklin Roosevelt and the New Deal and extending through John Kennedy, Lyndon Johnson, and Richard Nixon, was the inability of Congress and the political parties to give adequate attention to the nation's needs. More and more, voters looked to the presidency for leadership with results that in the long run (Watergate) may have been predictable.

A Congress factionalized and divided to the point that it cannot act on policy questions is an unpleasant prospect. One less under the control of the president and its own more repressive elements has some positive elements. The congressional party may be in decline, but a congressional membership more in tune with and responsive (in a service-oriented way) to its constituents may allow for a more flexible approach to policy issues and one more immediately responsive to the ongoing concerns of the nation. This may be a best case example, but it is a possibility.

Toward securing the end of a Congress more in tune with its electorate, one must check the advantages of incumbency. A limitation on PAC contributions to negate their presently overwhelming influence on elections would be welcome. Also, and more generally, the public funding of congressional (and other level) elections, with spending quotas set sufficiently high to allow challengers to compete effectively with incumbents, would be a step in the right direction.

The dissolution of the party in the electorate raises other questions. To date, political parties have been the most effective vehicle found for mobilizing an electorate and, in its highly imperfect way, representing the views and serving the needs of the outgroups. Without political parties, the less well-off have no effective, consistent representational outlet. Coupled with the decline in all forms of political participation by lower socioeconomic groups, these are disturbing developments. A discontented group—and any coalition of groups not serviced by the government and its policy rewards would increase its distance from the political system—is not a happy prospect for a democracy. It has been argued that neglected lower socioeconomic groups of this type provide fertile recruiting grounds for demagogues, from the Huey Longs and Father Coughlins to the George Wallaces of the future. The threat is real enough. Political parties incorporated these groups into the government, gave them a stake in its decision making, and educated them to the nature of their own role in the political process as well as to the limits that could reasonably be expected from government activity. The parties also acted as a restraint on the prospective candidate. To win, he had to satisfy the needs of a broad coalition. To accomplish his goal, he had to be (normally) an experienced politician (thus ensuring some skill in governing) sensitive to the wishes of a diverse, but interconnected, constituency. The party provided the coherence to this coalition, and it placed limitations on what a leader could or could not do. The checks generally worked well. The system was not foolproof—the Nixon Administration's Watergate crisis is hard to explain in this context—but it did serve the ends of responsible, reasonable government managed by experienced professionals and representative of the interests of most of the groups in the nation's electorate. These functions are unlikely to be performed by any other agency. The loss to the system in these regards is incalculable.

This is not to suggest that responsible and moderate government is less likely to occur in the future. What it does argue is that the restraining influence of the political parties on candidates, campaigns, and governmental excesses will not operate as it has in the past. Similarly, the representative qualities of parties competing in a broader and more inclusive electorate are also likely to decrease.

There is no immediate or obvious solution to these dilemmas. It may be that a higher order of electorate is evolving, one with a direct concern for policy outcomes, blinded less by habitual party loyalties and more demanding of a responsive government on the contemporary issues it considers important. In such a scenario, the decline in participation—at least as worrisome as the decline in performance of its traditional functions by the party—may be a short-term phenomenon, indicative of an electorate in flux. If so, and under the right conditions, involvement in American politics could increase over the coming decades, as the governing system becomes more directly responsive to its citizenry and their concerns.

In this last regard the role of the media, especially television, could be extremely important. The failure of television to fulfill its potential as an information-distribution and educational outlet has concerned everyone from social commentators to television critics. . . . There is enormous power inherent in television to reach, educate, and involve the American citizenry more knowledgeably in its political affairs. If the concept of television constituting a public service enterprise and the belief that the airways actually do belong to the people ever gains currency, and both are heard often from representatives of the television industry and from government officials, changes of consequence could occur. The debate over the role of television and its contribution to American society is not new. The very fact that it has continued so long with little to be shown for the effort expended indicates that, realistically, little change can be anticipated.

CONCLUSION

The structure of American politics has changed in fundamental ways. These changes are likely to continue over the next several decades. A new political order is emerging with consequences yet unclear. One thing is certain. The role of the political parties within this new political arrangement will be different. More than likely, their impact will be reduced and their contributions to the governing system and the society nowhere near as substantial as they have been in the past.

It is possible to anticipate many of the changes that will come, to debate their consequences, and to move to alleviate some of the worst of the potential problems that are likely to arise. The United States has been an experiment in democratic governance, and quite clearly this experimentation will continue. Part of the debate over the emerging political order should concern the proper role and functioning a revitalized party system could play.

We end on a somber note. E. E. Schattschneider, one of the more eminent students of political parties, has claimed, "the political parties created democracy and . . . modern democracy is unthinkable save in terms of the parties."[1] Maybe so. Schattschneider was writing well over a generation ago. The contemporary era may be forced to adjust to a democratic system in which political parties no longer play a dominant role. The transformation is in progress. Future decades may see the trends developed in this book accentuated. If so, a partyless era, with implications still uncertain, may be settling on us.

NOTE

1. E. E. Schattschneider, *Party Government* (New York: Holt, Rinehart and Winston, 1942), p. 1.

Will Political Parties Continue to Decline in Importance?

XANDRA KAYDEN AND EDDIE MAYE, JR.
The Case for Resurgence

THE ACTIVISTS

The active membership of both parties has changed in the past two decades. There is a new generation of actors, tuned to the values and expectations of today's political society. There will always be a need for generational change in the parties, and in politics, if the system is to remain healthy, but the characteristic that most distinguishes this generation from its predecessors is its interest in organization. Individuals within it have been touched from time to time with the passions of the years past and committed themselves to charismatic candidates and controversial issues, but they have been tempered by the disappointments of our time, and today, they tend to be more distant, more task-oriented, more professional. How much they represent the voters within their parties remains to be seen—in all probability they are (as always) more conservative or more liberal than their respective Republican and Democratic constituents—but their ideology is usually subordinate to their desire to win.

Both party staffs are better educated and more professional than those who used to fill party positions. The Republican staffs at both the national and the state levels are much larger than their Democratic counterparts, but the most important difference is not the quantitative but the qualitative difference between who is there now and who was there before.

One reason the Democratic staff appears much smaller is because it contracts out much of the work the Republicans do in-house, such as its direct mail campaigning. It is not a surprising difference given the traditional reliance Democrats have put on campaigns compared to Republican reliance on their party for campaign support. Nonetheless, the field of campaign consulting, which has grown dramatically in recent years, is just another reflection of the need of politicians to run for office with professional help. A good number of the consultants received their training in the party and then moved on to set up their own firms, helped along by party contacts and, in many cases, party urging that the candidate hire a consultant to oversee the campaign. Recently, however, the party has begun helping candidates avoid overcharging by consultants, by providing information about rates and so on.

Professionalization usually means that standards of behavior have been inculcated in the practitioner, that he or she is judged by peers, and that there is some formal process of accreditation to which the practitioner must submit himself. For our purposes, the professionalization of politics means that campaigns will become more homogenized, perhaps more nationalized. They will employ the same techniques, they will focus on those aspects of technical development which will advance the field: for example, new approaches to selling the candidate. Political scientist Larry Sabato cited former presidential candidate Milton Schapp's comment that he was "not trying to buy the election; I'm trying to sell myself!"[1] The selling will become more sophisticated, which may not be a bad thing. In itself that does not mean the candidates sold will be better or worse, but we would argue that the more candidates are selected by the professionals, the more likely they are to be worth selling because another standard by which the professionals will judge each other is the quality of the candidate and whether or not they win. This is particularly true of the professionals within the parties, as opposed to the private consultants, because they have a longer-range perspective and a closer body of supervisors.

The professionalization of the parties, and of politics in general, is a cause and effect of a different system of rewards. What distinguishes the professionals from their forebears in party politics is a different set of rules of behavior, a different expectation of the spoils of victory. What distinguishes the professionals from the nonprofessionals is an understanding of the modern technology of campaigning and the intricacies of the law which affect the way money is raised and the distribution of campaign resources. What has not changed is the fact each election is a choice that the voters must make based on the information the campaigns provide. Who provides the information (whether amateur or professional) is not as critical as the substance of what is said.

There is something of a cultural gulf existing between the professionals in both parties and many of the volunteers at the local level. One party worker described it as drawn between the wool vested and the polyester crowd. The fact that young people come out from Washington carrying the certainty that they know the answers, along with the fact that those they have come to counsel have often participated in politics for many years, adds up to resistance about turf, more than about questions of winning. It is the conflict of class and generation. It is the kind of conflict that has characterized the change in all organizations as they move from one era to another.

THE RESOURCES

In the two years preceding the 1984 election, the Republican party raised $225.4 million, almost four times the $57.3 raised by the Democrats in the same time period. The balance was an improvement for the Democrats, who had been out-financed by five or six times in previous elections.[2] The Republicans continued to raise more money from individuals (five and a half times the Democratic proportion of individual contributions), but the Democrats raised four times the proportion of PAC funds, which are still a small, albeit growing proportion of party funding.[3]

The amount of money is phenomenal in its own right, especially if one considers that national party funds used to come entirely from the states in the form of assessments on the state committees. The amount of money is probably phenomenal for many reasons, but at the very least it is a measure of the financial strength of both parties at the national level. Money is not all that matters, even with that oft-quoted comment of California politician Jess Unruh that "Money is the mother's milk of politics." It is an indication of well-being, and it is a first step toward the resurgence of party organizations.

The fact that the Republicans have raised so much money has been widely noted for several years. For many political observers, the big question was whether or not the Democrats could ever catch up. David Adamany, President of Wayne State University, for instance, has argued that the base of the Democratic party will never yield the same financial results the Republic base has. According to Adamany:

> Contributing to politics is disproportionately an activity of the well educated, higher-income groups and of those who engage in other political activities as well. These groups are primarily Republican. . . . A further complication for the Democrats is the ideological division within the party. Givers . . . [are] much more liberal than the Democratic electorate. Since mass-mail appeals appear to be most successful when pitched to ideological groups, the Democrats may find responses to their mass-mail fund raising largely limited to the party's liberal wing, the smallest ideological group in population. . . . The Democrats draw the support of a vast majority of the nation's liberal activists, but the party is so diverse that it includes important groups of moderates and conservatives as well. It would therefore risk alienating important constituencies if it pitched its financial appeals to one ideological group within the party coalition.[4]

Only time will tell, but it should be noted that both parties have traditionally directed their fund raising to their more ideological wings: Republicans appealing to the more conservative; Democrats relying on the liberals. Even if liberals are the smallest ideological segment of the population, they are still large enough to fund a national party. As it happens, however, the party began expanding its contribution base to the rest of the Democratic constituency in 1981, reaching out to older voters on social security and prospecting many younger voters on a variety of nonideological issues with the sophisticated technology now available. The Democrats expect to catch up by 1988; certainly the potential base is there in the population among party identifiers.

The balance of party fund raising in the 1984 election does not make our case, but it does suggest the possibility that the Democrats will catch up. The rate of financial growth within the Democratic party is tied to three factors: the kind of fund raising it relies upon; the politics of the day; and the balance of power between the parties in the elective branches of government.

The Democrats began a serious shift to direct mail fund raising only after the 1980 election. The GOP began more than a decade before that, but began to see returns only several elections later. The large donors on whom the Democrats have relied since the Kennedy administration have been seriously circumscribed by the laws, and to some extent, by the loss of powerful incumbents in the White House and Senate. The shift to small donors is probably a necessity but a process which takes time and is not dependent on holding office. The argument could be made that the party out of power does better at direct mail solicitation because it has a more identifiable need to raise money. The fact that the GOP continued to out raise the Democrats once it regained the presidency is probably due more to the greater strength and sophistication of its list than to the fact of incumbency. It will take several elections for the Democrats to refine their lists and to train their donors to give to the party instead of the campaigns. Much of the perceived imbalance, after all, is due to the Democratic tendency to give to candidates rather than to the party, which does make the elections, if not the party organizations, at least, more equitable.

HISTORICAL INEVITABILITY

Cornelius Cotter and John Bibby wrote an interesting article several years ago entitled "Institutional Development of Parties and the Thesis of Party Decline."[5] Their thesis was that American political parties tend to counterorganize, a thesis originally developed by V. O. Key, but applied in this instance to the national parties and their organizational structure. The theory is that if one party in a state is strong, the other will be strong; if one party dominates, it will be broken into factions, with the minor party behaving as another faction. One of the best examples of a strong party state is Indiana, in which both parties operate with a high degree of sophistication and skill, due in large part to the 2 percent kickback to the party permitted by those receiving patronage. On the lower end of the scale, the dominance of the Democratic party in the South has usually been described as a system of factions, in which the Republican party (until recently) participates as another faction. The new organizational strength of the GOP in the South has forced Democratic state parties to make changes, to offer more to their candidates, and to try to emulate in many instances what the opponents are doing.

At the national level, Cotter and Bibby point to the history of the development of national party committees and to the support structure behind them. Typically, it is the Republicans who take the lead in organizational development, with a lag of eight to twelve years (depending on when the Democrats lose the White House) before the Democrats catch up. If these political scientists are correct, the current imbalance between the Republicans and Democrats is characteristic of the lag time.

Perhaps the most important element in party balance is the nature of a two-party system. Whether the organizations are strong or weak, sophisticated or primitive, if the party out of power has a chance of replacing the party in power, it will never fall too far behind. It is the balance of power that assures equity in the equation, not the balance of structure, or even the balance of assets.

But the assets have grown, and the structure has changed accordingly. In the long run, the resurgence of the parties depends on their ability to capture the functions parties ideally possess: control of nominations; control of party resources in elections; influencing public policy; and as a vehicle for drawing individuals in the political culture.

The resources the national party can amass and distribute today cannot be matched by any other actor in the political process because of the restrictions the campaign finance law imposes, if for no other reason. It would be difficult for anyone to run for statewide or federal office as a Republican today without the support of [his or her] party. It would be surprising if the same thing would not be equally true of Democrats in a few years' time. Even today, Democratic candidates for federal office are more apt to first make a trip to Washington to see party leaders about the support they can expect from the party directly and from the network of PACs [Political Action Committees] the party is capable of sending their way. In the old days, the first contact might have been more likely to go to the local party chairperson if not a private campaign consultant.

Party strength may come and go in American politics, just as the generations of political activists change and reflect the needs and values of their time, but the parties have demonstrated an endurance that challenges any institution in American history. The key to their success is their linkage to power. It may be that as power shifts the parties shift, that as interest in public power waxes and wanes, parties wax and wane.

It is unlikely the parties will disappear: too much is structured around them legally and culturally. Legislatures are organized by party representation. Voters may not see their political preferences as part of their sense of identity, but they do see political actors in terms of their parties and will vote on their estimation of how those politicians/parties behave. Morton Kondracke, a political journalist, has argued that the decline in partisan identification has encouraged the parties to work harder; like the brokerage house, they are now forced to win the old-fashioned way: "They have to earn it."

This has made elections more competitive across the country, which has made candidates more dependent on their party organizations. No longer can a politician in the South, for example, assume victory because he is a Democrat. He now has to run a more sophisticated campaign, and for assistance he must turn to the party organization, rather than, as before, simply taking advantage of the party name. On all levels, party aid to candidates—financial and strategic—has been growing incredibly.[6]

The changes in both parties in the past two decades have been enormous. The structures, the active participants, and the world around them have been altered. The increased financial resources at the national level in both parties (and the reversal of the flow of those resources from national to state instead of the other way around) have made many things possible. It may not be sufficient in itself to change the status of the parties in the public mind—it may not be necessary to change the status—but it is the necessary first step.

NOTES

1. Larry Sabato, *The Rise of Political Consultants: New Ways of Winning Elections* (New York: Basic Books, 1981), pp. 330–331.
2. FEC Report, cited in *The Sunday Globe*, 4 November 1984.
3. Ibid.
4. David Adamany, "Political Parties in the 1980 Election," in *Money and Politics in the United States: Financing Elections in the 1980s,* ed. Michael S. Malbin (Chatham, N.J.: Chatham Press and the American Enterprise Institute, 1984).
5. Cornelius P. Cotter and John F. Bibby, "Institutional Development of Parties and the Thesis of Party Decline," *Political Science Quarterly* 95 (Spring, 1980).
6. Morton Kondracke, "CPR for Political Parties," *The Washington Times*, 22 October 1984.

Questions for Discussion

---

1. Why have political parties declined?
2. What steps can be taken to strengthen political parties?
3. Should political parties be strengthened? Why?
4. What effect has the decline of political parties had on campaign finance?
5. What effect has the decline of political parties had on the quality of candidates?

Suggested Readings

Aronowitz, Stanley. "The Party's Over." *Progressive,* 50, no. 2 (February 1986), 19–21.

Bogdanor, Vernon, ed. *Parties and Democracy in Britain and America.* New York: Praeger, 1984.

Cutler, Lloyd, and Donald Robinson. "Breaking Our Political Gridlock." *Washington Post,* February 1, 1987, p. D2.

Epstein, Leon D. *Political Parties in the American Mold.* Madison: Univ. of Wisconsin Press, 1986.

Greenstein, Fred I., and Frank B. Feigert. *The American Party System and the American People.* 3rd ed. Englewood Cliffs, N.J.: Prentice-Hall, 1985.

Hernson, Paul S. "Do Parties Make a Difference? The Role of Party Organizations." *Journal of Politics,* 48, no. 3 (August 1986), 589–615.

Kolbe, Richard L. *American Political Parties: An Uncertain Future.* New York: Harper & Row, 1985.

McCormick, Richard L., ed. *Political Parties and the Modern State.* New Brunswick, N.J.: Rutgers Univ. Press, 1984.

Price, David E. *Bringing Back the Parties.* Washington, D.C.: CQ Press, 1984.

Wattenberg, Martin P. *The Decline of American Political Parties, 1952–1984.* Cambridge, Mass.: Harvard Univ. Press, 1986.

Chapter 9

Do the Mass Media Have a Liberal Bias?

By most accounts the mass media—television, newspapers, magazines, and the radio—play a central role in the U.S. political system. Some observers believe the media's influence is so powerful that they function as the fourth branch of government. The media's perception of political leaders and events affects what people believe, so that political leaders neglect the media at their peril. In May 1987, for example, reporters for the *Miami Herald* staked out the Washington townhouse of then Democratic presidential frontrunner Gary Hart, after the newspaper received information that a woman was staying with Hart while his wife was in Colorado. Media attention to that event was strong enough to make Hart withdraw from the campaign. Although he subsequently returned to the campaign, his organization suffered setbacks in support and funding.

Whether allegations made against Hart on the subject of sexual morality in this and other instances were accurate or not, the reporting of such a matter had a profound impact on this candidate and the entire presidential campaign as well. In previous years newspapers had adhered to a professional code that forbade reporting on certain aspects of the private lives of public figures.

The media's influence is based not only on the stories presented but on the prominence given them. An analysis of the media's reporting on a single day will show a diversity of emphases. News, or the importance of particular items of news, is not so self-evident that everyone in the journalistic profession agrees on what is, and what is not, significant. Some critics of the media have noted the importance of emphasis in coverage of the Vietnam War, coverage they claim was detrimental to U.S. foreign policy interests. Stories—particularly those filed on television that highlighted the killing of Vietnamese civilians or the use of drugs by GI's—brought the war home to viewers in a manner unfair to U.S. policy makers. These critics argue that U.S. journalists were biased, for they were not able to expose the enemy's actions and problems for balanced coverage, and in addition they were much less sensitive to U.S. government needs than had been their counterparts covering World War II.

Supporters of the media counter that these critics simply do not like the news and so are "killing the messenger." All the reporters are doing, media supporters contend, is reflecting what is happening. They add that political leaders try to dominate the news and resent when reporters get the true stories.

Media critics often contend that the media have a liberal bias, an assertion that is argued in the debate that follows by Richard A. Snyder and Michael Massing. Snyder, a former Pennsylvania state senator, argues that the media do have a liberal bias. He shows the techniques that the media use to express their biases reported as objective news. As examples, he cites reporting in the Vietnam War and the attempted assassination of Pope John Paul II.

Michael Massing, a contributing editor of *Columbia Journalism Review*, defends the media for their objectivity. He takes to task a report by Robert Lichter and Stanley Rothman that surveyed the attitudes of people in the media and found them to be liberal. Lichter and Rothman concluded that the reporters used their liberal biases in reporting the news. Massing argues that reporters are best judged by their reporting and not according to their private views and that an impartial analysis would show that the reporting is objective. In Massing's view the press is doing a better job of reporting than ever before. He also points out that newspapers and magazines are increasingly coming under the ownership of giant corporations, and that such corporations are making budgetary decisions that reduce opportunities for investigative journalism so much denounced by critics of the liberal media. Finally, he notes that political leaders are often successful in manipulating the media.

 YES

Do the Mass Media Have a Liberal Bias?

RICHARD A. SNYDER
Can We Trust the Big Media?

Some years ago when the late and great Nelson Rockefeller was campaigning for re-election as Governor of New York, he took his appeal to the street corners. David Brinkley, then of NBC, having decided on first-hand coverage, went to the same intersection and ended up standing across the street from the Governor.

But then a strange thing happened: True, a group gathered around the Governor to listen to his speech. But an even *larger* crowd clustered around Brinkley. You see, Brinkley had a following because he was seen nightly on television in millions of homes.

The incident demonstrates that even a rich and famous public official is no match for a media celebrity.

To me and perhaps to you, this raises deep concerns when we ask ourselves: Are we getting our news free of bias? Who sets our national agenda? And where does our leadership reside?

First, a word about bias. Is there bias?

Edith Efron, a free lance writer, analyzed how the networks reported a presidential campaign some years ago. Her analysis may interest you. She found the reporting loaded 3-to-1 in favor of one candidate; 2-to-1 in favor of the Left; and overwhelmingly against "the white middle class."

When she counted up the number of *words* of opinion offered from all sources, she found that ABC got as much as 48% of its opinion from reporters. As Solzhenitsyn once asked: "Who elected them?" If we do not like what a public official says, we can vote him out. Not so the newsmen.

But that is not all Miss Efron found.

Of even greater fascination were the devices cleverly used to *twist* the news. She identified upwards of 20 devices, but let me mention just a few.

False labels. Those who might be said to be in sympathy with the Left, described rioters as "demonstrators"—which I think you will agree carries with it an implication that even if you burn automobiles, loot liquor stores, or perform whatever mischief, you do so in the name of some worthy cause. Another example of the employment of euphemisms: Current liberal writers will identify Senators Weiker and Mathias as "moderates" although their voting records are every bit as liberal as Teddy Kennedy's.

Another item of bias is:

Estimate the crowds. If you favor a candidate, you tell of the unexpected size of the crowd; if you oppose a candidate, you say it was disappointing compared with the estimates. If the size was really big and you don't like the candidate, ignore the crowd altogether. Mention the apple core that someone threw at the candidate; they did that to George Wallace once.

Another method of bias:

Fake neutrality. The reporter pays a limited compliment to the political figure, and thus disarms you, the audience, and then comes right back with a thorough contradiction of the compliment, or extensive praise of the opponent. In either case, the opening compliment is a camouflage; a device to make the reporter seem objective, but used as a peg to help his opponent.

And how about *the poison sandwich?* We all have seen the equivalent of this in private life—as when a woman says of another: "She is wearing a pretty dress—it's a pity her slip is showing—but otherwise she wears it well." Ask yourself what you remember out of that ostensible compliment.

In addition to Miss Efron's bias list, let me add several warnings of my own:

Beware of "selective indignation." When a commentator or an editorial writer becomes greatly exercised about "death squads" by one side but little worried about the atrocities of the other side, ask yourself: Is he really worried about the atrocities? Or is he just using them to further his point of view?

Beware of forensic jiujitsu. Henry Kissinger told this well. When Nixon ordered a bombing there was an uproar from the *Times*, Eric Severeid, and most liberals generally; they foresaw war. However, the bombing tactic worked; the other side returned to the bargaining table. It understood hard ball. Did liberals give the Administration credit for success? No. They praised the Soviets for their "restraint."

Be suspicious of anniversaries. An anniversary is something you observe only if it serves a purpose. TMI [Three Mile Island] is five years old, hold a vigil; lighted candles and all that. Several years ago, the Monroe Doctrine was 150 years old; that might be worth observing but no one bothered; it served no special purpose.

Beware of "media events"—held solely for the cameras. When the TV people leave, the protesters go home. They are not news in the true sense. They prove only that a handful of people hold a given opinion.

One can philosophize that media favoritism of one candidate over another does no great harm in the long run, and that the republic will survive. "All life is unfair" as John Kennedy accurately reflected.

But turn to another survey, made in the '70's by the Institute of American Strategy of CBS news—which it regarded as typical of NBC and ABC as well. This was during the Vietnam conflict. It found that the themes broke down this way: Critical of the United States: 80% of the time. Critical of the South Vietnamese, our ally: 83% of the time. *Supportive* of the North Vietnamese, which we now know was communist even then: 57% of the time.

What is more sinister is the failure of the networks to report Soviet build-up in that period, even though the *Times* reported no less than 23 military developments over that same period of time, including the successful testing of a Soviet submarine which fired a missile with a 4,500 mile range. During those two years, CBS devoted a total of only one minute explicitly to a comparison of U.S. and Soviet strength.

Does this kind of bias by omission matter? It certainly does.

If the Soviets advance their territorial controls, enslave more people, increase their offensive capability, improve their bargaining position, violate the rules by using poison gas—all the time keeping their iron control by police state terrorism, the Gulag, torture, and all the rest—is it not in our interest to be informed of this? I say it is. Further, if the networks pretend to have a public obligation—in return for their free use of the airwaves and the defenses we hand them against libel actions—they at least owe us honest, unbiased, complete and consistent coverage.

As we sit here [November 5, 1984], General Westmoreland is in a courtroom pursuing his million dollar libel suit against CBS over its portrayal of his troop estimates in "60 Minutes."

If CBS is allowed to call itself a news medium instead of an entertainment, one suspects the General has an uphill fight. But even it it wins, CBS has lost something in the exposure of its crude in-house mechanics.

It is the General's contention that the Vietnam War was the only war this nation lost "on the pages of the *New York Times*." Why? Because Home Front morale is essential to victory. That sagged as media ding-donged day after day about the corruption of the South Vietnam regime, the unreliability of its troops, and our problems with drugs.

Some would date our decline from the time of the erroneous reporting of the Tet offensive—which unhappily occurred while Walter Cronkite visited Saigon. Walter felt disaster impended, and worse still, said so. Like birds flying off a telephone wire, so did other commentators. The assumption became that we would lose, and the only question was: How long can the Marines hold out?

Now what were the facts? As Peter Braestrop points out in a two volume history of Tet, we WON. The Viet Cong were heavily battered. Our Marines held out as long as we wanted them to. Yet you never would have known it from the networks. They were stuck with their story of inevitable defeat and were not about to let mere facts get in the way.

It is incredible that two of the biggest news stories of this century were ignored by major news media for several years.

Example 1. The horrible death of one million Cambodians: driven from their homes, massacred, starved, some chased into the sea; a genocide of a gentle population, a whole culture wiped out.

What treatment did this horror get? There were brief mentions of this over a period but there were dissembling excuses; news sources were uncertain (it was said), there were no reliable eyewitnesses. It was only after *Reader's Digest* exposed the situation, and the facts could no longer be denied that the press told the story and then without emotion.

Example 2. The attempted assassination of the Pope was news when it occurred. An attempt on the spiritual leader of a half billion humans, a crime unprecedented in modern times, it would seem that the background of the assassin deserved digging into—especially because the Pope had a temporal following as well as a spiritual one, and because Poland's relationship with the Soviet Union was a matter of world concern.

Surprising as it may seem, this remained hot news only briefly. Thanks to a nun who grabbed one assassin by the coat, his identity was known and he was jailed. But *who* was he? And *why* did he do it? The networks, with their millions in salaries for Brokaw, Rather, Barbara Walters, Mike Wallace, and the rest, apparently set aside no funds for this story, and the *Washington Post*, which put great effort into the Watergate job, had no extra kitty to dig into for this.

Again, the true facts surfaced because one journalist, funded by the *Reader's Digest*, went from Rome to Cairo, to Bucharest, to Ankara, to Sofia, to Switzerland, and back to Rome several times, and despite language difficulties and dissembling by police, built a most convincing case that the assassin was hired by Bulgarian secret police, for the specific job, and few doubt that the KGB instructs the Bulgarians in such matters.

"Why?" you ask, did other media ignore these exciting stories—almost to the point that they seemed to be covering them up?

The most plausible reasons seem to be:

In the case of Cambodia, the genocide was being committed with connivance of the North Vietnamese—the same people which the media told us earlier wanted only freedom and peace, and if we would only stop sending arms to the South Vietnamese all would be tranquil in Indo-China. They were not anxious to show what their policies had done to innocent Cambodians.

Did disinterest in the Pope's assassin arise from the fact that the assassin came from the Left and not the Right? Suppose the gunman had come from Chile, or South Africa, or a right-wing entity? I am going to suspect that the press would have been a bit more zealous in pursuit.

In brief, big media have a bias for pursuing facts which pillory right-wing causes, people and governments, but they have a decided blind spot for left-wing crimes, even of the highest degree. Why? Like the story of the Lady and the Tiger, I will not try to supply the answer.

Remember: No right-wing government threatens the United States. On the contrary, our arms build-up is to keep us in a negotiating position with the huge left-wing, the Soviet Union and its satellites. If we look at matters from the standpoint of our own survival, we should alert ourselves to the misdeeds of the Left and to corral support from whatever nations remain in the center and the Right.

How does Public TV come off in all this?

We admire Masterpiece Theatre, Boston Pops, MacNeil-Lehrer, Wall Street Week, Buckley's "Firing Line," Sesame Street and much else. But some criticism is in order too.

"Documentaries" on foreign matters, for instance, are leftish leaning, generally favorable to revolutionaries whose purposes would generally fit Soviet purposes. Ed Asner narrated one on Central America which Karl Myer of the *Times,* in his critique afterwards, said was "from a left-wing perspective." Another, entitled "Blood and Sand: War in the Sahara," glorified those seeking to upset Morocco's control of what was formerly Spanish Sahara. If successful, this would have given Russia a most useful foothold on the Atlantic coast.

"Independent producers," free lance people of unknown backgrounds, put such shows together, selling them to stations which, I am told, sometimes put them on the air without first watching them.

In response to criticism, Public TV has increased its effort to be balanced. Pro-Con programs were one result. But let me point out something with regard to all this:

Public TV has presented programs, interpreting past history—the Alger Hiss conviction, the Rosenberg spy case, Sacco-Vanzetti, revoking security clearance of Dr. Oppenheimer, and others. Such programs made a point of even-handed treatment, giving weight to the accusations and to the defense. So one ended saying to one's self: Were they really guilty?

However, when Public TV told of Vietnam or Watergate, it was more a reaffirmation of accepted history.

The net result is that on the issues which were decided adversely to the liberals at the time—Hiss, the Rosenbergs, etc., liberals came off with a 50–50 score. On those which liberals won in the first instance, Vietnam and Watergate, they continued to score 100–0. So on average, liberals win, 75–25.

I might feel reassured if the Vietnam program had pointed out that the liberals got us into that mess, as Patrick Moynihan said in one of his books. With the Watergate program, it should have begun with the Hiss case, which would explain why the liberals never forgave Nixon for being right, and hounded him forever thereafter.

Let me raise wider and larger questions:

We have been through two tumultuous decades: The '60's and the '70's, in which the liberals dominated the media and the trends. What happened—

- *Education lagged badly.* Look at the SAT [Scholastic Aptitude Test] scores. Look at illiteracy, absenteeism, crime in city schools. How do you study with the TV turned on? Higher education is currently under fire for mushy curricula and poor scholarship. Compare us to foreigners. We suffer.
- *Family life came apart* in many ways. Employed wives are part of the explanation, but it is difficult not to associate the trends with TV viewing. TV cannot tell us that its commercials have big appeal to consumers and at the same time disavow any connection between violent programs and the wife abuse, child abuse, shootings, stabbings, batteries, and the overall upsurge in crime.

To my mind, there is an even deeper indictment to be made in the matter of *religion.*

There would appear to be an almost unbroken conspiracy to suppress, ignore, or dissemble in the news media whenever matters of faith in a deity appear.

Several years ago Christian fundamentalists resolved to show their strength where advocates of other causes do it: In the national capital. They assembled, 500,000 strong—one of the largest groups ever to gather. For readers of the *Washington Post,* almost nothing happened. It is said the editors "did not know how to treat the story"—so unprecedented was the reporting of conventional worship. The *Post* did have space, on the same day, for news of one thousand Lesbians who were meeting in the city.

If anyone from Mars were to visit the earth and look at the list of best-sellers listed in the *New York Times'* book section, he would assume that religion was a non-existent force. Even though some of the books marketed in the religious bookstores outsell the listed "best-sellers" several times over, they are never mentioned. Why? The *Times* has responded by saying that specialty books are not included. Yet if this were true, cookbooks and Jane Fonda's exercise book would not be there either.

It would seem that the National Council of Churches, rather than funding some dubious revolutionary causes—which end up helping the Soviets—would be wiser to use its energies to ask why there is a cultural shut-out of religion in the trendy media. Has religion disappeared as a vibrant part of the American scene? Or is it just made to *appear* to be non-existent?

Religion has been demoted by the networks to almost a non-entity status. Father Mulcahey is on M*A*S*H mainly for the one-liners. When else have you seen a priest or a protestant clergyman portrayed as a spiritual helper to anyone? No longer the Barry Fitzgeralds or Bing Crosbys of the cloth. The Pope is in the news, yes, but mainly for the depiction of political conflict.

Ben Stein, son of the economist Herbert Stein, wrote a book about the Hollywood producers and writers of TV *entertainment:* people such as Norman Lear, creator of Archie Bunker. Stein found that their plots put businessmen, the military, small towns and people of wealth in a bad light. The Media Institute looked at this too. It found that two out of three businessmen were portrayed as criminal, evil, greedy or foolish.

Why? America's abundance of comforts is due to its free enterprise and the incredible resourcefulness of its industrialists, commercial people, advertising and marketing experts. Why then should a group of writers, themselves enjoying six figure incomes in some cases, be constantly depreciating what made this possible—for them, as well as the rest of us.

Stein theorizes that these writers and producers may have some hold-over of radicalism from their youth, and all of us are nostalgic about our youth. But he concludes that the dominant motive is the desire for power and influence. If TV can be used to discredit business, the military, the voting influence of the small towns—who is left to decide the national agenda and the trends of the future? You guessed it: the Hollywood people by the big swimming pool. The so-called "creative" part of the media.

What of our national agenda?

It should be responsibly compiled. Yet how much of it is not set in the Oval office, or in the Speaker's office, or in corporate board rooms? There is good reason to believe it is set by whatever editor makes up page one of the *New York Times*. Is this surprising?

Imagine you are president of the United States and James Baker, or his equivalent, walks in and says: "We have three appointments scheduled for you this morning, Mr. President, but I notice the *Times* has a big environmental story on page one. You will be asked for reaction. Shall I ask the Secretary of the Interior to send people over to brief you?" I would predict that to stay on top of a developing situation, the President would re-shuffle his appointments. Who decided his agenda? The *Times* editorial board.

Expand this situation and you will see that to a limited degree the elected officials can call *some* shots, but the media will more likely write the final program.

But, again, as Solzhenitsyn said "Who elected them?"

Is there a pat explanation for the liberal leftish slant so evident in the news, and particularly the network news?

Two researchers interviewed 250 key journalists in press and networks. The findings disclose how oddly unrepresentative journalists are of America as a whole. By a margin of four to one, they voted for McGovern in his election and tilt consistently to the Left in politics. Less than 10% attend church with regularity. Most of them are avowedly lenient in matters of fidelity, promiscuity, and pornography.

Those people are entitled to believe what they wish, of course, but when it spills over into their professional work—we should be prepared to discount their news if we do not share their views.

What can be done about the bias in media?

For starters, I suggest that you do what a patient does when he believes his doctor may be making a mistake:

Get a second opinion. Where? Howard K. Smith, one of the truly respected commentators, says that he reads the New York Times for its comprehensive coverage, but that for the editorial opinion he turns to the Wall Street Journal. Good advice. The Journal's editorials have never fallen into the liberal trap.

We are all warned about what we put in our stomachs. No poisonous additives. Not too many calories. Let us be equally careful what goes into that part of our brains which forms opinions. There are no labels "This is left-wing propaganda" on our books, news magazines, or broadcasts. We must discern it ourselves.

What else can you do?

You can "heckle the sponsors." When a biased program is put on the airwaves, sometimes with inflammatory effect, make note of the sponsors. Write them a letter. Express disapproval. If you are normally a purchaser of their products, mention that. Accuracy in Media, a zesty little flier put out weekly by Reed Irvine, will keep you abreast of what's wrong with Big Media for $15 a year. It is worth that for the spirited writing alone. But after you have enjoyed Mr. Irvine's artful taking apart of Mike Wallace, Ben Bradlee, Sam Donaldson, or whomever, he gives the names and addresses of firms which paid for the broadcast.

Mr. Irvine carries this heckling to the annual meetings of the network corporations as well as the Washington Post and the Times, in all of which he owns a share of stock. Nor is this mere troublemaking. He asks them why they lied in print or on the air, and why no retractions were made. By being accurate himself, he has earned a credibility among journalists and is quoted with increasing respect. I suggest we all get on this bandwagon. It seems headed somewhere.

Khrushchev said of America, "We will bury you."

We need not wait for the Soviets since we are doing a pretty good job of burying ourselves—at least if the major purveyors of news have their way.

- They glamourize our opponents.
- They undercut elected leadership.
- They seem always to "blame America first."
- They give us biased views of our defense.

It is time we leveled at them the same criticism they have lavished upon society as a whole.

[Here] I include . . . my interpretation of how Lincoln's Gettysburg address would have been reported if the networks had been in operation in 1863. It was designed to show how the networks impose their values on what a public figure wants to say, and how (under the guise of "fairness") networks manage to get the adversary viewpoint across, especially if it fits their ideology.

I necessarily take the part of President Lincoln and also of a mythical reporter, "Dan Gather":

Dan Gather: We're here at Gettysburg where President Lincoln will deliver an address. His press secretaries admit it will contain no news of the war . . . and little else, we expect. The President is being introduced and is putting his hat aside his chair. The next voice will be the President . . .

Lincoln: Four score and seven years ago our forefathers brought forth . . .

Gather (breaking in): As we said, it looks as though the President is giving us a run-of-the-mill backgrounder . . . nothing new up to now.

Lincoln: . . . we cannot hallow this ground. The brave men, living and dead, who struggled here . . .

Gather (breaking in): (camera pans the graveyard nearby) The President has been getting criticism because of the casualties, and many of the people here are sober and unsympathetic.

Lincoln: . . . it is for us to be dedicated to the great task remaining before us . . .

Gather (breaking in): I've been talking to some of the other correspondents. We are all convinced that the President may be laying the foundation for his re-election campaign next year. Pennsylvania is a pivotal state and coming to Gettysburg was a political decision.

Lincoln: . . . we take increased devotion to that cause for which they gave that last full measure of devotion . . .

Gather: Well, as I said, there is nothing sensational in the President's remarks and as soon as he finishes . . . yes, he's sitting down and there is polite applause. I would say very moderate applause. If President Lincoln expected to make any history here today, I would say he has drawn a blank. Now we switch you to Richmond, Virginia, to get Jeff Davis's response in line with network policy to give both sides. We switch you now to the South . . . Come in, Roger Mudd.

With such coverage as the above, Lincoln could not have won the war, freed the slaves and saved the union.

When President Reagan visited China he made several broadcasts for use over the Chinese television. Some parts of his message were deleted before it was shown. Chris Wallace, one of the young network reporters who accompanied the President, asked him how he liked having his material censored.

"It didn't bother me a bit," Reagan replied. "You people do it all the time."

☑ *NO*

Do the Mass Media Have a Liberal Bias?

MICHAEL MASSING
A Liberal Media Elite?

As long as there has been news, there has been the concept of killing the messenger. When the news is unpopular or disturbing, one remedy is to do away with those who have brought it.

In some countries, unfortunately, killing the messenger is taken quite literally. Here, we have developed a more civilized approach, which consists not of killing the messenger, but of inviting him to a panel, sitting him down, and lecturing him, telling him that he is too liberal.

Now, if someone is told that often enough, he will begin to believe it. Therefore, I am glad to have a chance to look at this question and see just how much truth there is in the assumption.

The Lichter-Rothman studies have already been nicely handled by Mr. Bradlee, and I don't want to spend too much more time on that. Several facts have eluded us in these studies, however, that I would like to bring out.

When I read the studies, I am reminded a little of the old science of phrenology, which consisted of taking the brain and trying to measure it and thereby getting some insight into the human psyche. Basically, Lichter and Rothman take journalists' minds and try to find out what opinions and attitudes lurk therein. Then somehow they come up with an idea from that of how the profession operates.

The problem is that, if we look at the survey data closely, we find that we can prove almost anything we want. We went through some numbers earlier, very quickly, but they don't seem to prove what they are supposed to prove, or not to me.

We were told that 80 percent of the so-called media elite believe that there is nothing wrong with homosexuality. That is not a shocking notion to me. Fifty-four percent find there is nothing wrong with adultery; 84 percent, four out of five, oppose state control of sexual activities. This is all from the study.

Now, if these standards are compared with those of the Moral Majority, the press is indeed a permissive lot, maybe even promiscuous. But if you compared them with other professional groups—lawyers, doctors, and even businessmen—I venture to say we will find that the media are no more tolerant of gays and philanderers than these other groups.

The same applies to political issues. If we look at the data, we find that a majority of journalists believe that the free enterprise system gives workers a fair shake and that deregulation of business is a good thing. And most believe strongly in the notion of welfare capitalism.

Again, these do not seem like particularly radical ideas to me. In fact, they seem to be quite within the American mainstream.

But enough about these statistics has been pointed out. They seem somewhat irrelevant to the matter of how the media operate. Does it really matter if Dan Rather voted for Jimmy Carter or for Ronald Reagan in 1980? Does it matter if Tom Brokaw thinks that adultery is a sin? Or does it matter where David Broder stands on the homosexuality issue?

If the real issue is the coverage, then to judge the press we have to look at what appears in newspapers and on television. Let's take the voting statistics. How the journalists voted is less important then what they actually wrote about the election.

Eighty-one percent voted for George McGovern, we are told. That is not surprising, given who he was running against, not a great friend of the media. But I wonder what Mr. McGovern would say if we asked him about the press coverage he got. If we think back to it, it was not exactly kind to him. Mr. McGovern would probably not say that he found the press to be particularly liberal.

Eighty percent also voted for Jimmy Carter. If we look at how Carter did with regard to the press, I think that he would probably start cursing them as a lot who really did not give him a chance at all and who were just out to get him.

With the current [1984 presidential] campaign, if we ask Jesse Jackson the same thing, we would get a similar response.

The issue, however, is not a matter of partisanship, whether or not the president is a Democrat or a Republican, liberal or conservative. What we are really talking about—and I am surprised to find that I agree with Mr. Murdoch here, but maybe I shouldn't be surprised—is the particular role of the press as watchdog.

This term "watchdog" has become a little unpopular these days, which is the sign of the times we are living in. But the press should cast an eye on those in power and hold officials accountable.

To me, journalism really is in the tradition of Edward R. Murrow and Lincoln

Steffens, exposing corruption in city hall and describing the plight of migrant farm workers and that of the homeless and the unemployed.

In the last ten to fifteen years the press has done a better job of this than ever before in its history, and I think Vietnam and Watergate are two of our finest chapters. What really concerns me is that this tradition might be fading, and what I fear is not that the press is too liberal, but that it is becoming less aggressive, and less a watchdog.

What is the basis of my fear? I think that the media—rather than becoming more antibusiness, more critical of business, as claimed in the studies—are becoming more similar to business. We are becoming wealthy and powerful, with a vested interest in the status quo.

Mr. Bradlee described the antecedents of *Washington Post* reporters, and I think he made quite a good point. But a lot of those *Washington Post* reporters and editors frequent the salons of Washington, go to parties, and drink cocktails with senators, members of Congress, and cabinet members.

We now have journalists who prepare presidential candidates for debates, who are put forward as vice-presidential candidates themselves, and earn about as much as the secretary of state does on the lecture circuit. Journalists, who have traditionally been outsiders looking in, are now insiders themselves. And this has to affect the way that we cover Washington and the news in general.

Media organizations themselves have become bigger, more powerful, more like other corporations. Television networks are owned, of course, by three of the biggest corporations in the country. We are seeing what bottom-line considerations they have as they cut back on documentaries and become more and more cautious about the type of documentaries they will do.

"American Parade" on CBS offered an insight into the current state of the American documentary. Newspapers are now becoming monopolies: as they too are becoming very conscious of the bottom lines, they are cutting back on investigative reporting. Many people in the profession now believe that investigative reporting is not worth the money or human investment. I disagree with them.

Arguments about the liberal press also fail to take into account the hundreds of ways in which the president and the government in general can set the news agenda. It seems especially true of the Reagan administration, and here I do differ with Mr. Murdoch. The Reagan administration has shown just how skillfully an administration can manipulate the news.

On the beaches of Normandy we had scores of journalists reporting every move; on the beaches of Grenada we had not one to report on what was going on. It was quite amazing how the administration pulled it off.

Recently at a meeting of journalists discussion centered on happenings in Central America and the press coverage there. In the end the discussion turned to a free-for-all over how this administration has intimidated journalists. Although I do not know how many people feel that intimidation, I sense that with this administration many are afraid to exercise their normal role as watchdog.

Finally, I fear the growing tide of criticism that we are getting. Most people in the profession will admit that the criticism is necessary. After so many years without it, we had become fat and, perhaps, complacent. My real concern, however, is that the criticism we get all comes from one side. We get it from Mobil Oil—and its op-ed page pieces. We get it from the Media Institute; we get it from Accuracy in Media. These are all groups with a lot of money and the expertise and savvy to get their message out. That message is generally uniform: the press is too critical, it is too antibusiness, and it is too liberal. I, for once, would like to hear some other groups speak and to have them get op-ed page pieces and hold panels like this.

For instance, what if unions were to hold panels? What would we hear from them? We would not hear that the press is too liberal. We would hear that the press is antiunion, antilabor and that papers and television are quite ready to blame unions for many of our economic ills.

And what would criticism be from blacks and Hispanics? I don't think that we would hear that the media are too critical; I think we would hear that the media have become too trendy.

More generally, if we listen to people on the street, we would find that our news organizations, which traditionally had been the champions of the underdog, have become too distant, too remote, and too out of touch.

As I see it, then, the press is at a crossroads today, with two paths before us. One is to become more passive, more deferential, and less compassionate. The other is the aggressive path, siding with the underdog and giving voice to those without one.

It is probably obvious that I advocate the second path. I believe that we should follow the old dictum: the role of the press is to comfort the afflicted and to afflict the comfortable. And if that makes us liberal, I say let's have more of it.

Questions for Discussion

1. What criteria should be used in determining whether a particular newspaper or television program is biased in presenting the news?
2. What impact does the presentation of the news have on the receiver of the information?
3. If there is a media bias, what is it?
4. How do political leaders attempt to shape the news?
5. What ethical considerations should govern the media in their reporting of the private lives of politicians?

Suggested Readings

Barnes, Fred. "Yes, Journalists Are Different." *Washingtonian*, 22, no. 1 (October 1986), 89–90.

Berkman, Ronald, and Laura W. Kitch. *Politics in the Media Age*. New York: McGraw-Hill, 1986.

Brokaw, Tom. "In Defense of TV News." *U.S. News & World Report*, 100, no. 1 *(January 13, 1986)*, 79.

"Does Television News Tilt to Left?" [interview with Rep. Phil Crane and Don Hewitt]. 98, *U.S. News & World Report*, no. 18 (May 13, 1985), 64–65.

D'Souza, Dinesh. "Mr. Donaldson Goes to Washington: Politics and Social Climbing in the TV Newsroom." *Policy Review*, no. 37 (Summer 1986), 24–31.

Graber, Doris A. *Mass Media and American Politics*. 2nd ed. Washington, D.C.: CQ Press, 1984.

Hess, Stephen. *The Government/Press Connection: Press Offices and Their Offices*. Washington, D.C.: Brookings Institution, 1984.

———. *The Washington Reporters: Newswork*. Washington, D.C.: Brookings Institution, 1981.

Kramer, Joe. "The Objectivity Meltdown." *Quill*, 75 no. 3 (March 1987), 12–17.

Lichter, S. Robert, Stanley Rothman, and Linda S. Lichter. *The Media Elite*. Bethesda, Md.: Adler & Adler, 1986.

Schneider, William, and I. A. Lewis. "Views on the News." *Public Opinion*, 8, no. 4 (August–September 1985), 6–11.

Spiegelman, Robert. "Media Manipulation of the Movement." *Social Policy*, 13, no. 1 (Summer 1982), 9–16.

Government Policy Makers

10. *Is the President Too Powerful in Foreign Policy?*

11. *Should the Twenty-second Amendment Limiting a President to Two Terms Be Repealed?*

12. *Does Congress Serve the Public Interest?*

13. *Is the Bureaucracy Inefficient, Unnecessary, and Harmful?*

14. *Should the Supreme Court Be Guided by a Philosophy of Judicial Activism?*

A s indicated in Part I, the Framers of the Constitution established a system of separation of powers and checks and balances constituted in three branches of government—legislative, executive, and judicial. The Framers feared that the concentration of powers in the hands of one branch would be a danger to liberty.

The Constitution, as has so often been said, is a living document, and it has changed over time through formal constitutional amendment, statutes, political practices, and customs. In part because of the ambiguities in some provisions of the Constitution and in part because of historical developments, power has shifted in different eras from one branch to another.

Constitutional amendments have modified the major branches of government. For example, the Seventeenth Amendment, adopted in 1913, changed the method of choosing U.S. senators from election by the state legislatures, as provided in Article I of the Constitution, to direct popular election in each state. Statutes have also changed the Constitution. Congress has passed numerous laws in the nineteenth and twentieth centuries establishing new departments and government agencies. When the Constitution was adopted, the role of government in society was minimal, but through statutes passed, particularly in this century, Congress has given executive agencies—the bureaucracy—vast powers in both domestic and foreign policy.

The formal constitutional actors in the U.S. political system have had their own impact on constitutional development. The Constitution says nothing about the power of judicial review, but the Supreme Court, under John Marshall, asserted that power in *Marbury* v. *Madison* in 1803.[1] Today the power of judicial review is an accepted principle of the U.S. political system. The Constitution, moreover, says nothing about the organization of Congress into committees, but congressional committees today play important roles in the enactment of legislation.

Custom, too, influences the Constitution. George Washington left office at the end of his second term, and a two-term tradition was widely accepted over time until Franklin D. Roosevelt was elected to a third term in 1940 and a fourth term in 1944. Adopted in 1951, however, the Twenty-second Amendment limited presidential terms to two, thus giving formal constitutional sanction to what had become a custom until Roosevelt's third term.

176

The power of the principal institutions of government depends, then, on a variety of factors. The Constitution and laws provide the basic structure and define the formal powers of the major actors in the political system. The relationship of policy makers over time, however, depends on the personalities of the policy makers, the ties between the president and influential members of Congress, the character of judicial decisions, the astuteness of top bureaucrats, and historical developments.

Part III deals with some of the important issues about the power, role, and behavior of policy makers in the national government today. Two debates are over the power of the presidency, one over the effectiveness of Congress, one over the effectiveness of the bureaucracy, and one over the role of the Supreme Court.

NOTE

1. *Marbury* v. *Madison*, 1 Cranch 137 (1803).

Chapter 10

Is the President Too Powerful in Foreign Policy?

In May 1987 a special committee of members of both the Senate and the House of Representatives opened hearings to investigate the actions of President Ronald Reagan, other members of the executive branch, and private citizens in secretly selling arms to Iran and in using the profits illegally to aid the Contras, a group of anticommunist fighters at war against the Sandinista government in Nicaragua. With massive media coverge, the committee investigated the most detailed activities of the principal actors in what has come to be called the Iran-Contra Affair.

Congressional investigations such as these into the conduct of foreign policy derive from specific authority granted in the Constitution as well as historical developments involving war and peace. The Constitution gives roles in foreign policy to *both* the president and the Congress. Article I of the Constitution grants Congress the powers to declare war; raise and support armies; provide and maintain a navy; make rules for the government and regulation of the land and naval forces; provide for calling forth the militia to execute the laws of the Union; and provide for organizing, arming, and disciplining the militia. Other provisions add to Congress's constitutional role. Such provisions include the Necessary and Proper Clause of Article I, Section 8, allowing Congress broad scope to carry out the powers specifically enumerated in the Constitution, and its general constitutional powers of taxation and appropriation.

The Senate is given specific foreign policy powers. The ratification of a treaty requires approval by two-thirds of the senators present and voting. The Senate also has the power to confirm most presidential appointments.

The president's constitutional powers are set forth in Article II. That article gives the president executive power and designates the holder of that office as commander in chief of the armed forces. In addition, the president is given power to make appointments and to make treaties, "with the Advice and Consent of the Senate." The president's oath of office includes a statement that the president agrees to "preserve, protect, and defend the Constitution."

Inherent in the Constitution itself are conflicts between the legislative and executive branches of government. Some of the principal issues that have developed over time have involved the president's right to send military forces in combat situations without the consent of Congress, the use of executive agreements instead of treaties, and the reliance on covert operations by the president and members of the agencies involved in the conduct of foreign policy.

One of the most important reasons for the growth of executive power anywhere is the existence, or the imminent prospect, of war among nations or war within a nation. Executive power tends to increase during wartime, sometimes because the legislature grants the president emergency powers and sometimes because the executive takes action without asking for the approval of Congress.

At the outbreak of the Civil War, President Abraham Lincoln took steps that, according to the Constitution, were illegal. These included spending money that had not been appropriated by Congress and blockading southern ports. Lincoln expanded the powers of the president as commander in chief beyond the intent of the Framers of the Constitution. In 1940, President Franklin Roosevelt transferred fifty ships to Great Britain in return for the leasing of some British bases in the Atlantic—without congressional authorization to take such actions. He also ordered U.S. ships to "shoot on sight" any foreign submarine in waters that he regarded were essential for the nation's defense. In giving such an order, he was making war between the United States and Germany more likely.

Since the end of World War II, the United States has become a principal actor in world politics—a status in the international community that will be discussed at greater length in Part Four. Here it is only essential to state that as a major world power, the United States has had to concern itself with global security issues in a manner unprecedented in its history.

The permanent emphasis of foreign and national security considerations has plagued executive-legislative relations since 1945. President Harry Truman sent U.S. troops to Korea without a formal declaration of war. President Dwight Eisenhower approved actions by the Central Intelligence Agency (CIA) to help bring down one government in Guatemala and put the shah in power in Iran. John Kennedy authorized the CIA to assist a military operation planned by Cuban exiles against a communist regime in Cuba—an operation that turned out to be a foreign policy disaster for the young president. He also increased the number of military advisers to Vietnam from several hundred to about seventeen thousand.

The actions of Presidents Lyndon Johnson and Richard Nixon in the war in Indochina sparked an increasing involvement by Congress in the conduct of foreign policy. Johnson raised the number of U.S. troops to five hundred thousand. Nixon engaged in a "secret" air war in Cambodia in 1969 and sent U.S. troops into that country in 1970.

The 1970s were marked by massive congressional involvement in the conduct of foreign policy. In 1971 Congress adopted legislation forbidding the expenditures of funds to carry on the war in Cambodia. Overriding a veto by President Nixon, it passed a War Powers Act (1973) sharply limiting the president's ability to send troops. Under the act the president has the power on his own authority to send U.S. armed forces into an area for a period of sixty days but then must get the approval of Congress or else terminate the use of armed forces. The president is also required to consult with Congress, if possible, before military intervention is ordered. Every president since Nixon has taken the position that the War Powers Act is unconstitutional because a statute cannot take away powers that are traditionally the preserve of presidents in the conduct of foreign policy. But every president has complied with its provisions. If and when a time comes in which a president refuses to comply with the law, the Supreme Court will decide on the constitutionality of the act.

Throughout the 1970s Congress continued to impose restrictions on executive actions in the conduct of foreign policy. To restrict some arms transfers, Congress used the legislative veto, which under certain conditions allowed either one or both chambers to cancel a proposed executive action. (The legislative veto, which had originated under Herbert Hoover in 1932 and had been applied to both domestic and foreign policy matters, was struck down as unconstitutional by the Supreme Court in 1983.)

Congress took steps to limit the actions of the president in areas other than arms transfers. In 1973 and 1974 it linked improved trade status of the Soviet Union in its dealings with the United States to a liberalization of Soviet emigration practices. The Senate failed to approve the Strategic Arms Limitation Treaty, known as SALT II, in 1979 and 1980, so President Jimmy Carter withdrew the treaty from the Senate's consideration. In an attempt to undermine President Reagan's policy in Nicaragua, Congress adopted the Boland Amendments restricting aid to the Contras in a variety of ways from 1983 to 1985. In 1986, however, Congress authorized a resumption of aid to the Contras, but stipulated that it could not be used to purchase weapons or other military equipment. In 1987, Congress approved assistance to the Contras with few restrictions, and, consequently, the U.S. government was permitted to supply the Contras with weapons and other military equipment. But the Boland Amendments had been directly responsible for the most important crisis of the Reagan administration's second term—the Iran-Contra Affair—an intensive investigation of the executive branch by both Congress and the media.

Is the president too powerful in foreign policy? Political scientist Daniel P. Franklin argues the affirmative. He contends:

1. The president exercises too much power in foreign affairs without having to account to Congress or other actors, such as the press, outside of the White House.
2. There is a temptation and tendency in the Executive Office for the president and his foreign policy advisers to conduct foreign policy through illegal means.

3. Congress can and should be brought into consultation on most foreign policy matters while decisions are being made instead of after the fact.

Political scientist Ryan J. Barilleaux argues the negative. He advances seven propositions designed to clarify the nature of presidential power in foreign affairs:

1. The United States needs a strong president for foreign affairs.
2. Presidential prerogative power, while substantial, is constrained by the Constitution, law, and public opinion.
3. Abuses of presidential power in foreign affairs are doomed to fail.
4. There is very little that a president can do in foreign affairs without congressional acquiescence or approval.
5. Attempts to inhibit presidential power through mechanical "solutions" are self-defeating.
6. The current level of presidential power in foreign affairs, however imperfect, is about the best that can reasonably be expected.
7. Realistic reforms that would not upset the basic structure of the U.S. government could help improve the situation.

Professors Franklin and Barilleaux comment on each other's selection in rejoinders.

 YES

Is the President Too Powerful in Foreign Policy?

DANIEL P. FRANKLIN

Is the President Too Powerful in Foreign Affairs?

In the nuclear age, presiding over the government of a superpower state, the president is in the position to determine not only the fate of our nation but, in some ways, the fate of the rest of the world. That sort of responsibility is much too important to be left to the haphazard, incoherent system that has become common in foreign policy decision making in the presidency since the end of World War II. Specifically, the presidency in its conduct of foreign affairs suffers from the absence of democratic control. Democratic control is essential in this instance not only because it is "right" in the philosophical sense, but because it is more efficient.

The assertion that a president has too much power in foreign policy making involves two separate but related arguments. First, in the liberal democratic sense, the president is too powerful. This means that the president exercises too much responsibility in foreign affairs without having to account to Congress or other actors (such as the press) outside the White House. In this sense, presidents become too powerful to the extent that their foreign policy authority violates the separation of powers doctrine.[1]

Second, because presidents often operate beyond the control of the other branches of government, there is a temptation and tendency in the executive office for presidents and their foreign policy advisers to conduct foreign policy through illegal means. The Iran-Contra Affair is simply one in a succession of scandals in the modern presidency that involve violations of the law in the pursuit of national security goals.[2]

To be fair, this lack of democratic control in foreign policy making is not merely the consequence of the exercise of unrestrained ambitions by unscrupulous presidents. Rather, at least three general factors account for this lack of control. First, the nature of modern warfare, airpower, and nuclear weapons, dictates that the president be able to act quickly and without restraint in emergencies. Second, because of its parochial orientation, Congress does not always display a great deal of initiative or oversight in the conduct of foreign affairs. After all, there is generally little electoral benefit to be gained for the member of Congress who is actively involved in foreign policy issues. Finally, a tradition has developed, based on precedent, that defines an expanded role for the modern presidency in foreign affairs. The courts, for their part, have either declined to intervene in preventing the expansion of presidential power in foreign policy or actively supported presidential claims in this regard. Thus, the loss of democratic control has been a gradual process in which the ambitions of individual presidents have played only a partial role.

THE PROBLEM OF DEMOCRATIC CONTROL

Most analysts agree that a democracy is a system of government characterized by the "rule of the people." Beyond that simple definition there is tremendous disagreement about the other requisites of democratic government. In fact, there is a broad variation in the structures of democratic regimes, but certain unifying characteristics seem to be common to all democracies. These basic conditions are: popular consent, popular control, and freedom of speech and of the press. Furthermore, it is essential that all of these characteristics be present at the same time for a democracy to maintain its viability. In its conduct of foreign policy, however, the presidency does not always satisfy these conditions necessary for democratic control.

Popular consent in a democracy is facilitated through uncoerced participation. To the extent that the president is popularly, freely elected, the presidency is subject to popular consent. In the realm of foreign policy, however, where much of the decision making in the postwar era is carried out by the president's staff who are subject neither to the will of Congress nor to the restraints of the professional bureaucracy, popular consent is limited.[3] Activist, experienced presidents (most notably Dwight Eisenhower) are able to control rather than be controlled by their own foreign policy staffs. However, since there is no prior experience quite like the presidency, individuals chosen to serve as president are often neither greatly interested in foreign policy nor experienced in foreign policy, or both. As a consequence, in the administration of a president who is relatively inexperienced in the presidential conduct of foreign affairs (as was John Kennedy in the Bay of Pigs invasion, Jimmy Carter in the case of the Iran hostages, and Ronald Reagan in the Iran-Contra Affair), foreign policy decision-making authority, by default, falls on the shoulders of the president's unelected staff. This situation is not only a violation of the notion of popular consent; it is a dangerous way to make policy.

For presidents, there are very real problems associated with depending too heavily on their own staffs for foreign policy expertise. Specifically, a president may become isolated in the White House from the rest of the policy-making community.[4] In that sense, while Lyndon Johnson was a very active manager of his own Vietnam policy, he was also isolated from dissenting views by staffers who were either deferent to the president, in agreement with the president, or excluded because of their dissenting views.[5] This kind of situation calls into question the wisdom of making foreign policy in the White House without requiring that the president consult with officials from outside the Executive Office.

"Popular control" means that there must be some relationship between what the public wants and what the government does. For the most part, popular control is maintained through periodic elections. Politicians will try to anticipate the desires of voters in the quest for reelection. In that sense, the president is subject to popular control. This control has, however, been eroded. For one thing, under the Twenty-second Amendment, the president cannot run for a third term and therefore is a "lame duck" throughout the second term.

There is, in addition, a more subtle violation of the principle of popular control associated with foreign policy making. The public is generally poorly informed and uninvolved in foreign affairs. There are, of course, exceptions to this rule. Certain ethnic and interest groups do have an intense interest; Jews, for instance, are often very concerned about U.S. policy toward Israel. But in the main, elected officials have very little popular guidance in these matters. In fact, the flow of influence tends to be in the other direction; public officials, and particularly the president, have a tremendous impact on public opinion. This influence over public opinion gives the president a great deal of leeway in foreign policy making. However, just because the public may have no *opinion* on foreign affairs does not mean that the public has no *stake* in foreign affairs. It is incumbent upon public officials in this instance to seek out the public interest rather than to strike out on their own. Freedom of action is not an unrestricted license for a public official in a democracy. Since there is really no such thing as a unified public interest, but only an amalgam of many points of view, representation of the public interest entails the inclusion of actors from outside the presidency in the decision-making process (including members of Congress). This is often not the pattern, however. Foreign policy decision making in the Executive Office can be, and often is, carried out largely by fiat, even including those decisions that do not involve any time constraints. This situation results in an overall derogation of popular control over foreign policy decision making.

Finally, freedom of speech and of the press is an essential component of any democratic system. After all, public participation from a position of ignorance cannot really be considered democratic participation at all. In this country we have freedom of the press, and that coverage includes the presidency. However, behind the twin veils of "executive privilege"[6] and "national security," the president has managed to arrogate the flow of information regarding national security affairs. It is not that the press cannot print or the Congress cannot investigate foreign policy activities of the presidency; the problem is that in dealing with the obstacle of governmental secrecy, Congress and the press may not know the questions to ask or what information to request. "Congress has repeatedly experienced difficulty in getting sufficient, accurate, and timely information. This was demonstrated in the Dominican Republic intervention in 1965, the Mayaguez incident in 1975, and the Iranian hostage rescue attempt in 1980, to name only a few examples. Having little information beyond that available in the media, Members of Congress enter discussions with executive branch officials on an unequal footing."[7] Ostensibly, this barrier of secrecy is designed to protect the nation's security—to keep our enemies from sharing our most sensitive intelligence. While it is true that certain information must be protected, the classification of information for security purposes may have gone well beyond the limits of what is acceptable and necessary in a viable democracy. As one frustrated (anonymous) member of Congress stated, "The actions of the United States are not secret to other nations, only to Congress and the American people."[8] As this comment implies, much of what passes for classified information is labeled secret not because it should not or is not known by our adversaries, but because that information is embarrassing to the administration and is not and should not be known (from the administration's perspective) by the people of the United States. If this were not the case, why would the executive be so reluctant to share sensitive information, even with Congress, when it is required to do so by law?

White House officials will argue that Congress is incapable of keeping a secret. However, in the aftermath of a series of revelations concerning misconduct by the Central Intelligence Agency (CIA) in the 1970s, Congress set up an intelligence review structure that is designed specifically to prevent leaks. Intelligence committee staffs are screened, committee meeting rooms are "bug-proofed," and access to sensitive information is restricted. Besides, members of Congress have plenty of options other than leaking information to the press when they object to a particular presidential action. Members can use their leverage with the president, who has, after all, an entire program to pass on the Hill. It is probably the case that most leaks originate in the bureaucracy or in the Executive Office itself. Even Nixon's White House "plumbers" instinctively knew this when they chose to wiretap the offices and telephones of the president's own National Security Council staff.[9] In the absence of at least a congressional review, the executive's penchant for secrecy violates the third minimum standard for democratic control. How can the voters, or their representatives, pass judgment on presidential actions they know nothing about?

CONSEQUENCES OF THE LOSS OF CONTROL

This disregard for the necessity of democratic control has very real consequences for the viability of policy execution. The strength of a democracy is in the public sense of involvement created by popular participation. A true democratic government is not only representative of the public, it *is* the public. Therefore, when a democratic regime makes a ruling or imposes a restriction, that policy is representative of the "general will" and is, for the public, a self-imposed restraint. In the absence of meaningful participation, society degenerates into the "lawless state." In the lawless state the government acts independently of the general will, and the public feels no obligation (nor is it morally bound) to obey the law. Furthermore, the government in a "lawless state" feels no obligation to consult the public in decision making. The degeneration of democratic control over foreign policy making in the presidency has led to a lawless state of affairs in the Executive Office.[10]

For one thing, if the public and its representatives do not get a sense that they are being consulted in matters of foreign affairs, support for administration policies will be very "shallow." Pollsters have identified the so-called rally-around-the-flag effect, or the tendency of the public to support the bold foreign policy moves of a president in the short term and not in the long term.[11] Political commentators have interpreted this effect to mean that the public does not have the "stomach" (anymore) for foreign involvement.[12] But what if this obvious distaste for interventionism is more a function of the feeling the public gets in a nondemocratic state that it has no investment (except for tax dollars, of course) in decisions made: no public involvement, no public support? If this is the case, this lack of public commitment robs us, as a democracy, of one of our primary sources of power—popular mobilization. The leader of a democratic state can count on popular support of a kind that can tap a nation's strength in no other, comparable way. With public support we fought the Second World War, rebuilt Western Europe, defended South Korea, and sustained a war effort in Vietnam for many years. These examples are evidence of a tremendous public tolerance for the sacrifice associated with interventionism. The recent decline in support for an activist foreign policy only shows that there is a limit to that tolerance. The people of the United States had, and have, "what it takes" to support a superpower policy.

At the same time, the administration that operates beyond democratic control will often behave with a certain "arrogance of power." This "arrogance of power" is the tendency of unrestrained leaders "to equate power with virtue and major responsibilities with a universal mission."[13] In other words, the presidency that is beyond democratic control not only has the latitude to go beyond constitutional restraints; it has a mistaken sense of virtue in doing so. The citizens of the lawless state are viewed contemptuously by their leaders as "subjects" rather than as equals and participants. The administration that trades in arms in direct contravention to the law, as did the Reagan administration, is an administration that holds the public and its representatives in contempt. Only a president who agrees to and is, indeed, obliged to consult with the public's representatives from outside the Executive Office will overcome the arrogance of power.

This weakness of our democratic system has not escaped the notice of our adversaries. In fact, our adversaries exploit this weakness for their own purposes. No amount of military spending (which cannot be sustained, anyhow, given the current climate of skepticism) is going to counter most Soviet threats in the absence of the support and involvement of the people of the United States. Our nuclear weapons may deter Soviet attack, but only our ideals can counter the communist threat. The Reagan administration's malfeasance in funding the Contras has created a propaganda "bonanza" for the Soviets (and for the Sandinistas). How can we argue that the Contras are a force for democracy when they are supported by undemocratic means?

IMPLEMENTATION

To say that we need to impose a democratic structure on foreign policy decision making is not to say that we should run our foreign policy by plebiscite. The vast majority of voters are neither interested nor qualified to be involved with governmental decision making on a day-to-day basis. Rather, through our representatives, we can have a participatory foreign policy without having a plebiscitary one. In a representative democracy, voters designate elected officials who, as part of their job responsibility, develop an expertise in public affairs. So, while it is probably impractical to involve the general public in foreign policy making, there are plenty of foreign policy specialists on Capitol Hill who can be tapped by the Executive Office. It would be difficult to argue that, by virtue of being governor of California, Ronald Reagan has more foreign policy expertise than Claiborne Pell (chair of the Senate Foreign Relations Committee) or Dante Fascell (chair of the House Foreign Affairs Committee) who have served in

Congress and specialized in foreign affairs for a combined total of sixty-two years! In addition, not only does the president sacrifice policy expertise when members of Congress are excluded; the president also loses political expertise and the opinions of actors who are not presidential sycophants. Even members of Congress from the president's own party would have "flagged" President Reagan's decision to approve an arms for hostage trade with Iran.

No one is going to argue that the president should be required to consult Congress (or other outsiders) in every situation. Sometimes there are physical barriers (the principals may be out of town) or time constraints. After all, the president may have as little as ten or fifteen minutes to respond to a "bolt-out-of-the-blue" Soviet attack. No one expects the president confronted with this situation to convene and consult Congress or even to call congressional leaders. However, these situations are so rare as to be virtually nonexistent. The "time constraint" argument is more often used as an excuse to avoid congressional involvement or "meaningful" consultation. Congress is thoroughly capable of acting quickly when the need arises. Congressional leaders can be summoned to the White House at a moment's notice. Meaningful consultation in this case refers to the involvement of congressional leaders *while* the decision is being made rather than after the fact. Congressional leaders were "consulted" regarding President Reagan's decision to launch a retaliatory raid against Libya, but only after the bombers were in the air.

Finally, no reform nor any amount of democratic involvement in foreign policy decision making is going to guarantee success. Mistakes will be made, the difference being that the responsibility for mistakes in a democracy is shared. In 1983, when President Reagan (under duress) negotiated an agreement with Congress to authorize the deployment of peace-keeping troops in Lebanon, the president took one of the most fateful steps of his administration. The subsequent deaths of the Marines in their Beirut barracks led not only to a shared sense of national grief, but a shared sense of responsibility among decision makers in Washington. A democratic government is a responsible government. No political leader in a democracy should have the right to control, or bear the sole responsibility of controlling, the fate of a nation.

NOTES

1. The separation of powers doctrine was the Framers' way of preventing tyranny by separating the different branches of government. The Framers recognized that the delay and conflict associated with the separation of powers was the necessary price for preventing one interest from dominating government.

2. Other obvious examples include the secret bombing of Cambodia and White House–authorized covert activities of the Central Intelligence Agency (CIA) both inside and outside the United States, including CIA participation in the break-in at Daniel Ellsberg's psychiatrist's office. Ellsberg was a Department of Defense official who leaked the contents of a secret report about the Vietnam War to the *Washington Post* and *New York Times.*

3. Thomas Cronin argues, "Perhaps the most disturbing aspect of the expansion of the presidential establishment is that it has become a powerful inner sanctum of government, isolated from

traditional, constitutional checks and balances." "The Swelling of the Presidency," in *Classic Readings in American Politics,* ed. Pietro S. Nivola and David H. Rosenbloom (New York: St. Martin's Press, 1986), p. 415.

4. For a discussion of the detrimental consequences of presidential isolation see, Irving L. Janis, *Groupthink,* 2nd ed. (Boston: Houghton Mifflin, 1982).

5. For an excellent discussion of Vietnam policy making in the Johnson administration, see James G. Thompson, "How Could Vietnam Happen? An Autopsy," *Atlantic Monthly,* 221, no. 4 (April 1968), 47–53.

6. Executive privilege is the principle, upheld by the courts, that permits presidents and their staff to withhold certain information regarding national security matters from Congress or the courts. The limits of executive privilege are not well defined, and presidents tend to be very broad in their definition of what sort of information can be withheld.

7. U.S. Cong., House of Representatives, Foreign Affairs Committee, *Strengthening Executive-Legislative Consultation on Foreign Policy,* Congress and Foreign Policy Series, no. 8 (October 1983), 65.

8. Quoted in *Congressional Quarterly Weekly Report,* 34, no. 46 (November 13, 1976) and in Charles W. Kegley and Eugene R. Wittkopf, *American Foreign Policy: Pattern and Process,* 2nd ed. (New York: St Martin's Press, 1982) p. 412.

9. The "plumbers" were White House operatives charged by Nixon to find out who leaked sensitive national security information to the press.

10. For a classic discussion of this justification of democracy, see Jean-Jacques Rousseau, *The Social Contract,* trans. Richard W. Crosby (Brunswick, Ohio: King's Court Press, 1978). Rousseau ultimately came to the conclusion that a direct democracy was the appropriate structure for a democratic state. The French Revolution and its aftermath ultimately discredited Rousseau's view of democratic structure but did not necessarily discredit his overall moral and practical justification for democracy in some form.

11. Jong R. Lee, "Rallying around the Flag: Foreign Policy Events and Presidential Popularity," *Presidential Studies Quarterly 7,* no. 4 (Fall 1977), 252–256.

12. Charles Krauthammer, "Divided Superpower: Can a Democracy Do What It Takes?" *New Republic,* 195, no. 25 (December 22, 1986), 14–17.

13. The statement from which this definition is adapted is J. William Fulbright's: "the tendency of *great nations* to equate power with virtue." *The Arrogance of Power* (New York: Random House, 1966), p. 9.

 NO

Is the President Too Powerful in Foreign Policy?

RYAN J. BARILLEAUX
Seeing Presidential Power Clearly

The presidency has long been plagued by the question of whether it endows a single official with too much power. Before the office was created, many of the nation's political leaders feared the rule of a king and wanted to ensure that the chief executive of the United States could never become one. Their descendants criticized presidential power, from "King" Andrew Jackson to the "imperial" presidencies of Lyndon Johnson and Richard Nixon. Today, in an age of nuclear weapons and guerrilla war, there is even more concern about the possible excesses of executive power.

Is the president too powerful? The question is not merely a rhetorical one, because it reflects a long-standing fear of tyrants. The people of the United States want a government that is strong, but not one so strong as to threaten liberties and the lives of citizens.

With regard to the presidency, the question essentially comes down to the issue of the president's powers in foreign affairs. Scholars have noted a distinction between presidential power in foreign affairs and in domestic matters, with the former considerably outweighing the latter in its impact on the U.S. political system. As Aaron Wildavsky put the formulation, "The United States has one President, but it has two presidencies. . . . Presidents have had much greater success in controlling the nation's defense and foreign policies than in dominating its domestic policies."[1] In domestic policy, presidential power is understood to be "the power to persuade," because presidents must convince Congress, the public, interest groups, and others to accept their policies. The president's actual ability to command is limited.

In foreign policy, however, the situation is different. The president has much greater ability to shape policy: as commander in chief of the armed forces, controller of all diplomacy, keeper of nuclear weapons, and leader of the Free World. The president decides when and on what terms the United States will negotiate with foreign nations, and controls the military might of the nation, even to the use of force in emergency situations. The president can recognize foreign governments or refuse to do so, speaking alone for the nation in world affairs and often on behalf of all democracies. The president's prerogative power in foreign affairs—that is, the power to chart a certain path—is extensive.

But is it too great? Many critics contend that it is. They argue that presidents are far too powerful for their own or the nation's good, because they can, on their own, launch an invasion or start World War III. Consequently, the nation finds itself caught in an endless series of military encounters, such as U.S. involvement in wars in Indochina in the 1960s and early 1970s, the toppling of a Marxist regime in Grenada in 1983, and the bombing of Libya in 1986. The nation, moreover, finds that its leaders have engaged in embarrassing political intrigues, such as was revealed by what has come to be known as the Iran-Contra Affair—the events in 1985 and 1986 involving selling U.S. armaments to Iran in exchange for the release of U.S. citizens held captive in Lebanon and the illegal U.S. government funding of Nicaraguan rebel forces, known as Contras, who were resisting the Marxist Sandinista government in Nicaragua. All of these events, critics contend, add up to a presidency out of control.

These charges about excessive presidential power are wrong. Of course, there are legitimate grounds for criticism of presidential foreign policy conduct; there have been excesses committed by presidents; and room for reasonable reforms certainly exists. But it is too much to say that the president is too powerful in foreign affairs. What happens is that critics see certain problems and generalize them into flaws in the basic nature of the presidency. In doing so, they fail to see presidential power clearly.

A clear view of presidential power is exactly what we need. With such a view, the problems to which critics point can be seen in context and better understood. Therefore, this essay advances seven propositions designed to clarify the nature of presidential power in foreign affairs.

1. THE UNITED STATES NEEDS A STRONG PRESIDENT FOR FOREIGN AFFAIRS

Alexander Hamilton noted government's need for a strong executive, particularly for the conduct of foreign policy. He pointed to the virtues of "unity, secrecy, and dispatch" that executives embody, all of which are necessary in the international arena.[2] The speed with which international events move, in a world of nearly two hundred nations and a growing list of nuclear powers, demands decisiveness and action such as is beyond the reach of a legislative body. Without a strong president, the United States would soon be forced to try to isolate itself from the world or sit by while events overwhelmed the nation.

To that extent, the president's foreign policy power cannot be measured against some ideal of an unaggressive and "tame" executive. Rather, the charge of too much presidential power can be made only if the powers far exceed the rather great strength that the president needs to act at all in the world arena.

2. PRESIDENTIAL PREROGATIVE POWER, WHILE SUBSTANTIAL, IS CONSTRAINED BY THE CONSTITUTION, LAW, AND PUBLIC OPINION

Even as great as it must be, the president's foreign policy power is not unlimited. Chief executives are always mindful of the limits on their powers. Indeed, President Lyndon Johnson once complained that he had only one real power (i.e., to launch a nuclear attack), and it was one that he could not use.

How is the president limited? First, the Constitution sets a number of conditions under which a president can conduct foreign affairs. Presidential appointments, whether to the position of secretary of defense or ambassadorships, require Senate confirmation. Thus the Senate is able to impose limits, albeit broad ones, on the kinds of individuals it will accept for office. President Jimmy Carter was forced to withdraw his first nominee for the position of director of the Central Intelligence Agency, Theodore Sorensen, because many senators considered Sorensen unacceptable. All treaties require Senate approval, and all money spent by the president, whether on weapons or foreign aid, must be appropriated by Congress. Congress also regulates the size of the armed forces. In short, the president must play by the rules, and the rules include congressional participation in the foreign policy process.

Second, Congress has created a number of laws that further restrict the president. The Case Act (1974), for example, requires the president to inform Congress of all agreements other than treaties that are made with foreign nations.[3] Congress can and does limit the purposes for which money may be spent, as when it prohibited the president from using federal funds to conduct a war in Southeast Asia.[4] According to the War Powers Act (1973), the president must notify Congress of any use of U.S. forces in hostile situations and receive congressional approval for maintaining them in conflict for more than sixty days.[5] The president has extensive power of initiative in international affairs, but limited power of fulfillment.

Third, a further constraint on the president is public opinion. Even when presidents have unilateral power and the approval of Congress, public disapproval may cause them to reconsider their actions. Sensing a strong public antipathy to Vietnam-type conflicts, chief executives since the mid-1970s have been reluctant to engage the nation in any military actions that cannot be resolved quickly and with few U.S. lives lost. Despite strong words about the nature of the threat that Nicaragua's Sandinista government poses to both its Central American neighbors and United States security, President Ronald Reagan has been careful not to call for the highly unpopular U.S. military involvement that his argument implies.

What this all means is that in reality presidential power in foreign affairs is more limited than it appears to be. It is not the unrestrained power that critics often suggest, but is an extension of the "power to persuade" that is recognized in domestic matters. The difference between foreign and domestic policy is that Congress and the people of the United States are willing to grant the president more latitude abroad than they do at home.

3. ABUSES OF PRESIDENTIAL POWER IN FOREIGN AFFAIRS ARE DOOMED TO FAIL

Critics of presidential power usually focus their attention on various real or alleged abuses of power by chief executives: Vietnam, the Iran-Contra Affair, and so forth. Their argument is that abuses prove the disproportionate power of the president and warrant greater restraints on the chief executive. In other words, what these critics are saying is that it is better to have a president who is too weak than to risk abuses of power.

The problem with this argument is that it is both unrealistic and incorrect. It is unrealistic because there is no way to design political institutions that cannot be abused, and efforts to do so will probably only make things worse. Restraining presidential power to the degree necessary to prevent any abuse will yield an executive incapable of the kind of "unity, secrecy, and dispatch" that the nation needs. The nation must live with the risk of abuse and be vigilant against it.

Moreover, the argument is incorrect. Abuses of presidential foreign policy power are ultimately doomed to fail. Because the government of the United States is one of separate institutions sharing power, Congress can investigate abuses such as the Iran-Contra Affair. Because the government historically has been unable to keep most things secret, problems such as Iran-Contra do not survive for long. The only "abuses" of presidential power that continue for any length of time are those, like the Vietnam War, in which Congress allows the president to act unilaterally.

There is no way to make the government foolproof against abuses and still maintain effective government. Perhaps that means that the United States will swing back and forth between too much presidential autonomy in foreign affairs and too little, but the alternative is a consistently weak executive.

4. THERE IS VERY LITTLE THAT A PRESIDENT CAN DO IN FOREIGN AFFAIRS WITHOUT CONGRESSIONAL ACQUIESCENCE OR APPROVAL

This point is even more important than the last for seeing presidential power clearly. In truth, the president's power in foreign affairs is that of initiation and persuasion: the president initiates actions, negotiations, diplomacy, policy changes, and commitments; then the president attempts to persuade Congress to go along with presidential policy. Extended presidential war making, as in Vietnam and Korea, depends on congressional acquiescence. So do treaties, national commitments, defense expenditures, foreign aid, and all other significant foreign policy decisions.

This point does not mean that the president is weak, but that many of the so-called abuses of presidential power in foreign affairs occurred with the full knowledge of Congress. For example, for six years the United States observed the nuclear arms limitation provisions it had concluded with the Soviet Union in a proposed Strategic Arms Limitation Treaty (SALT II) of 1979. It took action despite the absence of Senate approval of the agreement and in apparent violation of U.S. law, because Congress was tacitly willing to let the president do so.[6] Moreover, although the president can commit U.S. forces to hostile situations for a short time, as in bombing Libya or invading Grenada, the president must inform Congress of what is initiated and obtain its approval of any extended actions. Thus, presidents are careful about the kinds of situations in which they place themselves, for they will need Congress's support and the public's as well.

So, while the president has the upper hand in foreign policy making, the president does not have absolute power. If Congress acquiesces in presidential actions or commitments, then the problem does not lie in the executive alone.

5. ATTEMPTS TO INHIBIT PRESIDENTIAL POWER THROUGH MECHANICAL "SOLUTIONS" ARE SELF-DEFEATING

Despite the fact that many presidential "abuses" of power occur with the acquiescence or even the approval of Congress, the legislature occasionally objects to such actions and tries to prevent future problems by creating mechanical "solutions." The best example of this approach is the War Powers Act which creates a set of deadlines and requirements for the president to follow. The purpose of the act is to prevent a long-term, Vietnam-type commitment of U.S. forces without Congress's approval. But the War Powers Act has not solved the problem as intended. It has made presidents more careful about the use of force, but it has not produced a situation of legislative control over executive assertiveness in the use of force.[7]

The point here is that Congress, if it wants to restrain presidential power in foreign affairs, cannot do so by developing these mechanical "solutions." When it relies on such devices, it becomes complacent about controlling executive power or impairs the president's ability to act effectively. If Congress wants to maintain an active role in foreign policy, it can do so only by actively pursuing its traditional rights, powers, and responsibilities in that area.

6. THE CURRENT LEVEL OF PRESIDENTIAL POWER IN FOREIGN AFFAIRS, HOWEVER IMPERFECT, IS ABOUT THE BEST THAT CAN REASONABLY BE EXPECTED

The United States could do much worse than having the current system for controlling foreign policy. It could have a system of weak executive power, which might prevent presidential abuses but cost the nation its ability to cope with a dangerous world. It could have a more powerful president, checked only by personal conscience and the persuasiveness of advisers, but that situation would surely mean tyranny.

What the nation does have is a system with a strong, but restrained, executive who exercises power within a system of checks and balances upholding accountability. The United States Constitution establishes a government of three branches, each checking and balancing the wielding of power by the other two. The president has great power, but it is not absolute power. This situation is not perfect, but is workable and reasonable. It allows the president to exercise the leadership and decisiveness needed by the United States, but obligates the president to pay attention to Congress and the public. It does not create perfect equilibrium, with presidential power waxing and waning over time as circumstances and congressional and public attitudes change, but in politics equilibrium often means paralysis. Attempts to alter the system significantly, as in removing the president's power to conclude executive agreements or to employ U.S. forces abroad without congressional authorization, would not be worth whatever benefits they might bring.

7. REALISTIC REFORMS THAT WOULD NOT UPSET THE BASIC STRUCTURE OF THE U.S. GOVERNMENT COULD HELP IMPROVE THE SITUATION

For all that a clear view of presidential power reminds us of the excessiveness of critics, it also is true that the current situation is not perfect. There are realistic reforms that could make things better without damaging needed presidential powers. For example, the Case Act could be amended to require presidents to report to Congress on all significant agreements they conclude with other nations, even informal ones. Without hampering a president, this action would give Congress better information about U.S. foreign policy. Similarly, Congress could enhance its ability to play an active and responsible role in foreign affairs by coordinating its oversight of executive actions and decisions in that area: it could create a Joint Intelligence Committee, or even a Joint National Security Committee, to simplify and thus improve executive-legislative consultation on foreign policy. At present, foreign affairs and intelligence matters in Congress are divided between the House and the Senate, and within each chamber among committees on foreign affairs, armed services, and intelligence. The result is a situation of confusion that inhibits Congress's ability to oversee and respond to executive actions and decisions in foreign affairs. The president could also make a concerted effort to increase consultation with congressional leaders, even if only with members of the same party. In these ways, the chief executive could head off many potential problems.

CONCLUSION

In the final analysis, the president will consult with Congress and restrain executive power only to the extent that the president feels it necessary to do so. Therefore, critics of presidential power ought to look to Congress as well as to the executive, because the legislature's interest in and involvement with foreign policy is largely determined on Capitol Hill and not in the White House. The president does not have too much power in foreign affairs, but neither does Congress have too little. What counts is what is done with power. Perhaps Congress needs to do more.

NOTES

1. Aaron Wildavsky, "The Two Presidencies," in *The Presidency*, ed. Aaron Wildavsky (Boston: Little, Brown, 1969), p. 230.
2. Alexander Hamilton, "Federalist 70," in *The Federalist Papers*, ed. Clinton Rossiter (New York: New American Library, 1961), p. 424.
3. PL 92–403; 86 Stat. 619, August 22, 1972; 1 U.S.C. 112.
4. See Thomas M. Franck and Edward Weisband, *Foreign Policy by Congress* (New York: Oxford Univ. Press, 1979), pp. 13–57.
5. PL 93–148; 87 Stat. 555, October 24, 1973; 50 U.S.C. 1542, 1543.
6. Ryan J. Barilleaux, "Executive Non-Agreements and the Presidential-Congressional Struggle in Foreign Affairs," *World Affairs*, 148, no. 4 (Spring 1986), 217.
7. Daniel P. Franklin, "War Powers in the Modern Context," *Congress and the Presidency*, 14, no. 1 (Spring 1987), 77–92.

 YES

Is the President Too Powerful in Foreign Policy?

DANIEL P. FRANKLIN
Rejoinder

There is much about which Professor Barilleaux and I agree on the issue of presidential power in foreign policy making. I agree that presidential abuses of power are doomed to failure. That is why I would like to see those abuses prevented before they take place. I agree that superficial, mechanical "solutions" are probably inadequate and possibly even counterproductive. Mere mechanical solutions are probably not going to be a sufficient remedy for the systematic problems of the foreign affairs presidency that have become particularly acute since World War II. I even agree that the United States needs a strong president in foreign affairs. It is over this last point, however, that our two positions begin to diverge. Both Professor Barilleaux and I agree that the United States should be a strong, flexible, and influential actor on the world scene; we simply do not agree on the best way to achieve these goals.

Power, loosely defined, is the ability to make some individual, group, or nation do something that it would not ordinarily do. One major problem with this concept of power is that it is not entirely clear what a society needs to do to enhance its own national power. It is too simple to say that all a nation needs is more weapons or more troops to maximize its strength. If that were the case, the United States would have won the Vietnam War, Israel would have long since disappeared, and the shah of Iran would still be on the Peacock throne. In each of these instances, there was a distinct imbalance in military power; the United States had nuclear weapons, the North Vietnamese did not; the combined strength of the Arab nations' military forces did and does outnumber Israeli military forces by a large factor; the shah had a strong, modernized military that was, in the end, easily defeated by the largely unarmed mobs in the street. Thus, the concept of national power is much more complex than it seems to be. All kinds of factors, beside military strength, go into the calculation of national power, including natural resources, location, climate, culture, and, of course, national "will." I argued in my essay that democracy, as a political system, enhances national power. Professor Barilleaux, while he clearly does not discount the need for democratic control, sees democratic participation as much more a constraint than an opportunity. Therein lies the major difference between our two positions: we disagree on how to maximize national power.

Professor Barilleaux assumes that the presidency, because of its advantages in speed, secrecy, and expertise, is more suited as an institution for the conduct of foreign policy. With this I agree. What I disagree with is Barilleaux's tendency to assume that "making" foreign policy and "conducting" foreign policy are the same thing. Making foreign policy, as with making any other kind of national policy, is a legislative function. To the extent that Congress is invested with the legislative power, it is the responsibility of Congress to help determine foreign policy goals. As a practical matter (and constitutional by-product), the president has a tremendous input into the legislative process. Also, as a practical matter, it is not always going to be possible for the president to consult with Congress in emergency situations under severe time constraints. Nevertheless, this is not to say that Congress should be excluded from the process to the extent that it is.

Congress has a varying degree of input into the foreign policy decision-making process. On foreign trade or foreign aid issues, or even the expenditure side of military operations, Congress is an active participant. In matters of military policy outside the budget (the so-called War Powers) and intelligence concerns, Congress has much less of an impact. And, yet, it is precisely this kind of decision—the decision to commit U.S. armed forces or to embark on some kind of covert adventure—that determines long-term U.S. commitments, military and otherwise. Professor Barilleaux argues that the War Powers Act ensures congressional involvement in these decisions, but little evidence can be presented to support such a conclusion. The section of the War Powers Act that requires the president to consult with Congress before committing U.S. troops to combat abroad is merely optional. The Case Act has experienced all kinds of problems of implementation, not the least of which is the reluctance of administrations to report executive agreements to Congress pursuant to the law.[1] The Senate does have the power to confirm presidential bureaucratic appointments, but not those appointments to the president's personal staff. In other words, in these and other areas (intelligence oversight, arms control negotiations, and foreign military sales) congressional oversight is more form than substance. If this is, indeed, the case, we again return to the question of the value of congressional involvement. Should we be disturbed that congressional participation in some areas of foreign policy decision making is mostly veneer?

The answer to this question is yes. To exclude Congress from some of the most sensitive areas of foreign policy decision making, either through secrecy or by ensuring that Congress does not get involved until after the fact (until, for example, troops are already committed) is to weaken our national power. First, to bypass Congress is to lose an important independent perspective on the issue. Members of Congress represent a constituency different from that of the president. Members of Congress have a different point of view, different levels of expertise (sometimes superior to that of the president's staff), and even, at times, greater experience—all of which is lost when Congress is excluded. Professor Barilleaux does seem to acknowledge this problem when he makes some limited suggestions for facilitating congressional participation, which are, it seems, a step in the right direction. Second, excluding Congress from what are policy and, therefore, legislative decisions is a violation of the separation of powers. If this is the case, we will experience the kinds of problems the Framers were trying to prevent by applying this structure to our government. Specifically, a branch of government unrestrained by the separation of powers may become dominated by, to use James Madison's term, a "faction," and that faction will be tempted, if it is beyond control, to violate individual rights and the Constitution. Illegality is a consequence of the violation of the separation of powers. Finally, in the absence of democratic inclusion, we lose one of the most important sources of power in a democracy— sustained popular mobilization for foreign policy goals. Paradoxically, therefore, because the president is too powerful in foreign affairs, the foreign policy of the United States is weak.

NOTE

1. "In September 1975, Congress requested information from the Executive that might be pertinent to the Sinai Peace Accord wherein 200 American technicians would be sent to an area between opposing Israeli and Egyptian troops. The State Department was forced by a series of leaks to the press to acknowledge that understandings in the form of assurances regarding the 'long standing U.S. commitment to Israel' had been given to the Israelis. . . . A year later it was revealed that more than thirty 'agreements' between the American and South Korean intelligence establishments had not been reported to either Congress or the State Department." James A. Nathan and James K. Oliver, Foreign Policy Making and the American Political System, 2nd ed. (Boston: Little, Brown, 1987), p. 131.

Is the President Too Powerful in Foreign Policy?

RYAN J. BARILLEAUX
Rejoinder

The United States system of government is far from perfect, but it was created by a group of leaders who understood that perfect political institutions are unachievable. That is why the only fair way to judge the performance of U.S. political institutions is to compare them to realistic alternatives, not against visions of political perfection.

In his essay, Professor Franklin brushes dangerously close to an unrealistic criticism of presidential power in foreign affairs. He tries to develop a set of criteria for evaluating the power of the presidency, but ends up comparing existing politics to a vision of how he would wish government to be. Unfortunately, the best of all imaginable worlds is beyond our grasp: politics is the art of the possible.

Nevertheless, Professor Franklin presents a serious critique of the presidency and one that deserves some serious answers. His argument is that presidential conduct of foreign affairs is beyond democratic control because it violates all three requirements for democratic government: popular consent, popular control, and freedom of speech and of the press. Consequently, the nation does not get the foreign policy it deserves, and U.S. citizens are too vulnerable to the decisions and actions of a single officeholder.

Does the United States really have a presidency that is out of control? The evidence for that view is not convincing. Yes, there are many problems, and there have been excesses, but one cannot conclude from events such as the Vietnam War, the Iran-Contra Affair, and the bombing of Libya that there are structural flaws in the nation's leadership that threaten it with ruin. After all, time and again, events have demonstrated the power of Congress and the courts to restrain or punish the presidency. A few examples will make this point:

- During the Korean War, an attempt by President Harry Truman to force U.S. steel mills to remain open during a strike was stopped by the Supreme Court. Truman, commander in chief of a large military establishment, gave in to a court of nine elderly judges who possess no police force.
- When Congress decided that it wanted to end the Vietnam War in 1975, it voted to do so. As a result, the war ended. President Gerald Ford had no discretion regarding how or when to end the war: it ended.
- In 1975, Congress prevented President Ford from intervening in a civil

war in the African nation of Angola. Despite the very real threat of a communist victory there—a victory that ultimately occurred—the United States did not intervene.

- In the 1970s, Congress investigated and restrained the power of the Central Intelligence Agency, cutting through layers of secrecy and diminishing the power of this presidential agency to conduct intelligence and espionage activities without congressional knowledge.
- In 1979 and 1980, congressional resistance to President Jimmy Carter's Strategic Arms Limitation Treaty (SALT II) with the Soviet Union stopped the president from winning acceptance of his most-desired foreign policy initiative. Although Congress later tacitly accepted observance of the treaty without ratification, it handed the president a serious defeat as leader of foreign affairs.
- In 1986 and 1987, Congress investigated the Iran-Contra Affair, moving right to the heart of presidential conduct of foreign affairs, uncovering a number of closely held secrets, and holding accountable the government officials and private individuals involved.

These examples belie Professor Franklin's points about the presidency being out of control. Popular consent and popular control certainly exist, because Congress and public opinion can and do restrain presidents. Moreover, for all the illusion of impenetrable secrecy in the White House, there have been too many investigations of executive activities for that illusion to survive.

As my original seven propositions demonstrated, we must see presidential power clearly if we are to truly understand our government. The criticisms of Professor Franklin remind us of the problems that we face in trying to make our system work and the limitations of the system, but they do not prove that we have a presidency that thwarts the purposes of democracy.

Consequently, it is inaccurate to portray the presidency as out of control. If that were indeed the case, then the events listed above would never have occurred. But they did because the U.S. system is one of checks and balances. It is not perfect, but it works. As long as each of the three branches of government vigilantly guards against abuses of power by the others, the system will continue to function effectively into the future.

Questions for Discussion

1. What are the constitutional powers of Congress in foreign policy?
2. How should the United States go about requiring and implementing "meaningful consultation" between president and Congress, particularly in emergency situations?

3. What effect would the adoption by the United States of a parliamentary-type government have on legislative power in foreign policy?
4. How does the war against international terrorism affect the debate over presidential powers?
5. How would the Framers of the Constitution have viewed presidential power in foreign policy since the administration of Franklin Roosevelt?

Suggested Readings

Allison, Graham. *Essence of Decision*. Boston: Little, Brown, 1971.

Buchanan, Bruce. *The Presidential Experience: What the Office Does to the Man*. Englewood Cliffs, N.J.: Prentice-Hall, 1978.

Crabb, Cecil, and Pat M. Holt. *Invitation To Struggle: Congress, the President, and Foreign Policy*. 2nd ed. Washington, D.C.: CQ Press, 1984.

Destler, I. M. "The Rise of the National Security Assistant, 1961–1981." In *Perspectives on American Foreign Policy*, edited by Charles W. Kegley and Eugene R. Wittkopf, pp. 260–281, New York: St. Martin's Press, 1983.

Fisher, Louis. *The Politics of Shared Power: Congress and the Executive*. 2nd ed. Washington, D.C.: CQ Press, 1987.

George, Alexander L. "The Case of Multiple Advocacy in Making Foreign Policy." *American Political Science Review*, 66, no. 3 (September 1972), 751–785.

————. *Presidential Decisionmaking in Foreign Policy: The Effective Use of Information and Advice*. Boulder: Westview Press, 1980.

Hamilton, Alexander, James Madison, and John Jay. *The Federalist Papers*, edited by Clinton Rossiter. New York: New American Library, 1961.

Janis, Irving L. *Groupthink*. 2nd ed. Boston: Houghton Mifflin, 1982.

Krauthammer, Charles. "Divided Superpower: Can a Democracy Do What It Takes?" *New Republic*, 195, no. 25 (December 22, 1986), 14–17.

Morris, Bernard S. "Presidential Accountability in Foreign Policy: Some Recurring Problems." *Congress & the Presidency*, 13, no. 2 (Autumn 1986), 157–176.

Rousseau, Jean-Jacques. *The Social Contract*, translated by Richard W. Crosby. Brunswick, Ohio: King's Court Press, 1978.

Schlesinger, Arthur M., Jr. *The Imperial Presidency*. Boston: Houghton Mifflin, 1973.

Wormuth, Francis D., and Edwin B. Firmage, with Francis P. Butler. *To Chain the Dog of War: The War Power of Congress in History and Law*. Dallas: Southern Methodist Univ. Press, 1986.

Should the Twenty-second Amendment Limiting a President to Two Terms Be Repealed?

The Twenty-second Amendment to the Constitution limits to two the number of terms a person can hold the office of president. The adoption of the amendment was a reaction against Franklin Roosevelt, the only president to breach the *customary* limit of two terms.

. Since so many Republicans favored the two-term limit at the time the amendment was proposed, it is ironic that the two presidents who stood the greatest chance of winning a third term were Republicans—Dwight Eisenhower and Ronald Reagan. Some Republicans have, consequently, regretted the adoption of the Twenty-second Amendment. Particularly early in Reagan's second term, efforts were made by Reagan partisans, although never formally sanctioned by the president, to adopt a constitutional amendment rescinding the Twenty-second Amendment. The efforts came to naught, however, and most political observers agreed that the amendment would remain in force at least in the near future.

Still, a consideration of repeal is appropriate. Of the principal figures in the national government, only the president is limited by the number of terms that he or she may serve. Members of Congress serve for many years. Indeed, Congress rewards longevity in office through the seniority system in which one's ranking as a member of a congressional committee is based principally on how long one has been on that committee. Members of the Supreme Court serve for life.

Should the Twenty-second Amendment be repealed? Robert Previdi, a banker, argues that it should. He contends:

1. A two-term limit is undemocratic since it does not allow the people to choose to retain a president if they prefer to do so.
2. The Twenty-second Amendment weakens the effectiveness of the president, particularly in directing and administering the bureaucracy.
3. The system of checks and balances already prevents any abuses by the president.
4. The Twenty-second Amendment is in opposition to the intent of the Framers.
5. That amendment tilts power away from the president and to Congress and the courts.

Sen. William Proxmire, Democrat from Wisconsin, says that the amendment should remain in force. He argues:

1. Prohibiting a president from serving a third term allows him to be a more vigorous and forceful leader.
2. A president should not have the extra burden of running a sustained political campaign and governing the nation at the same time.
3. Permitting an individual to stay too long in the presidency stifles the growth of alternative leadership.
4. Repeal of the amendment would make dictatorship more likely.
5. A third term in office would violate U.S. tradition and custom.
6. People might follow a president who has been elected for more than two terms not with their intellects but with their emotions.
7. No one is indispensable for government leadership.
8. The infusion of new leadership in government is the essence of democracy.
9. Presidential longevity in office would result in adverse consequences for the bureaucracy and the judiciary.
10. Repeal of the amendment would threaten the system of separation of powers and checks and balances.

 YES

Should the Twenty-second Amendment Limiting a President to Two Terms Be Repealed?

ROBERT PREVIDI

Why Do We Limit the Democratic Process Only When It Comes to the Presidency?

We should not have a law to prevent freedom. The 22nd Amendment to the Constitution does this by limiting the people's ability to elect whom they want for President.

There is nothing more important in a democracy than to be able to elect to office the person "we the people" choose and for as long as we want. In the final analysis, the ability to elect freely is the crucial element of freedom.

If they were alive today, George Washington, Thomas Jefferson, Dwight D. Eisenhower and even Franklin D. Roosevelt could not be elected President no matter what the people wanted. This does not make sense. Either we believe in our system of checks and balances or we don't.

Interestingly enough, anybody, including ex-presidents, can be elected and re-elected without limit to the Senate and House of Representatives and even be appointed to the Supreme Court for life. However, the people are now forbidden by law to re-elect their President more than once—no matter what threat faces the country or how well the job is being done.

The unsoundness and illogic of the 22nd Amendment is shown by the fact that when the people would have reelected President Eisenhower in 1960, he was prevented from running—not because of his record—but because of a law. As he said to General Lyman Lemnitzer at the time, "Think of it, I'm the only person in the country who can't be elected President."

How can we let this situation continue? At a time when good leaders are rare, our current narrow-minded approach makes no sense.

If this is truly a free country, then we should abolish the Twenty-second Amendment to the Constitution, which limits the President to two terms. Repeal of the Twenty-second Amendment would enable the people—not a law— to elect and re-elect to the Presidency the person they want. If this is done, we would again be a true democracy. We can do this with full confidence, because we know the system of checks and balances works so well.

Not only is the two-term limit undemocratic, it is also dangerous and inefficient. For example, there are enormous consequences resulting from the fact that a President elected for a second term immediately becomes a lame duck on the day of his or her election.

In the give and take of politics there is nothing worse than being a lame duck. The Presidency is primarily a political job. And a lame duck President cannot be effective in dealing with Congress and the bureaucracy. Think of the consequences of this simple fact: The leader of the executive branch of the government and the one person elected to speak for all the people cannot be a strong leader because the people in the bureaucracy know they will be around when he's gone.

A related problem is that senior officials in the Executive Branch average only 20 months in office. This lack of continuity, partially caused by the term limitation, further limits the effectiveness of the President, particularly in directing and administering the bureaucracy.

What the current situation means is that in the United States we can only have a strong President for four years. And this is why we have so many stops, starts and inconsistencies in our national policy. In addition, as most good managers know, four years is a very short time to achieve truly lasting progress.

The same logic goes for foreign affairs. Both our enemies and our allies know when they deal with a second term President that he or she will not be around for long. This limitation is illogical, dangerous, and must be ended.

The concept that in a free democracy the people cannot be trusted to elect their leader is incomprehensible. How can this be justified? Are the people just not smart enough? When it comes to the Presidency, is limited freedom better than total freedom? Why did Congress pass the Twenty-second Amendment? And why was it ratified by the states? When the Amendment was proposed, shortly after the administration of Franklin D. Roosevelt, many in Congress were still reacting negatively and quite strongly to the fact that FDR had been elected four times.

Advocates of the two-term limit wanted to make certain that we would never again have the opportunity to allow one person to govern the country indefinitely. Underlying their concern was the fear that a strong President, not limited to a specific number of years in office, would usurp the powers of government.

In the political climate of those times, Congress overlooked the fact that the men who originally wrote the Constitution trusted the people and our system of checks and balances. The fact is that amending the Constitution at any time is a serious issue. It certainly should only be done after great thought and, most important, after the heat of any issue has died down. Surely one year after Roosevelt's death was not enough time to begin the process of thoughtful evaluation.

Those who passed the Twenty-second Amendment forgot that FDR was elected freely by the people who had the wisdom not to change a leader they believed in during a time of great peril. That trust in the people, built into the Constitution at the birth of our nation, still makes sense today.

Think of it—now, no matter how great the threat, no matter what the people want, the electorate cannot choose to keep someone in office who has a proven record of success.

Some are even urging that the President be limited to just one term. This misguided notion has gone so far that now [1984] we have a commission of prestigious public figures preparing to recommend the idea of a single six-year term.

This is a bad idea because it's based on the concept that for some reason the power or ability of the President to function freely must be further limited. It's one thing to consider lengthening the presidential term, but this should have nothing to do with the freedom of the people to re-elect whom they want for as long as they want.

My argument is that because of the system of checks and balances the President's power is already limited by the Congress and the courts and by the ability of the people to choose whom they want and vote out whom they don't want.

What the Twenty-second Amendment has done is tip the balance of power in favor of Congress and the courts. This is certainly not what the founding fathers intended. They wanted the system of checks and balances to be equal among the three branches of government. The facts are that by limiting, in contradiction to the Constitution, one of the three branches, we have gone against our fundamental principles.

The current imbalance is a threat to the health and future of this great country of ours. Let's re-think what we have done and return the power of our democracy to the people. The best way to do this is to ask your senators and congressmen to act.

Tell them "we the people" want our freedom back.

Should the Twenty-second Amendment Limiting the President to Two Terms Be Repealed?

WILLIAM PROXMIRE

Myth of the Day: Repeal of the Twenty-second Amendment Is a Good Idea

The myth of the day is that repeal of the Twenty-second amendment to the U.S. Constitution—providing for a two-term limitation on the President of the United States—is a good idea.

Here are ten good reasons why repealing the Twenty-second amendment is not in our Nation's best interests.

First. Prohibiting a President to serve a third term allows him to be a more vigorous and forceful leader. Eliminating the third term also increases the President's political independence by freeing him from political considerations attendant on securing his party's renomination. It increases the nonpartisan character and businesslike efficiency of the Executive Office.

Second. A President should not have the extra burden of running a sustained political campaign and governing the nation at the same time. The twenty-second amendment frees the President from pressure of yet again being a candidate and seeking reelection. The possibility of reelection tends to build up a dangerous political machine that interferes with the efficiency of the President as Chief Executive.

Third. Permitting an individual to stay too long in the Presidency stifles the growth of alternative leadership.

Fourth. A third term would endanger democracy and tend to establish a dictatorship by perpetuating one man in office and feeding his ambition for power.

Eight years as President is a sufficient time to effectuate the policy aims which an individual may represent. An additional term would tend to encourage a sense of proprietorship and personal privilege. Personal power rather than public policy would become paramount.

Fifth. A third term violates the tradition and precedent established by such great Presidents as George Washington and Thomas Jefferson.

Sixth. A third term, served by an individual with an exceedingly strong personality, might result in such dependence on his leadership that the people would follow him not with their intellects but with their emotions.

Seventh. No man is indispensable. The American people can be relied upon to produce more than one great leader at a time.

Eighth. The constant infusion of new leadership is the essence of democracy. The doctrine of rotation in office is one of the principal bulwarks of freedom. Proper administration of a democratic government demands that new personnel and fresh viewpoints be injected frequently into the executive branch to prevent the growth of a stagnant bureaucracy.

Ninth. Presidential control of patronage accrues from a long tenure. An excessive length encourages the bureaucratic entrenchment of individuals who are solely dependent upon the President for their position, and who are maintained through adherence to his point of view. Similar abuses might also apply to the judiciary where the President's staunchest supporters, and those of his particular political, social, and economic outlook are rewarded with lifetime judgeships that place them beyond the reach of the electorate.

Tenth. A long Presidential tenure threatens our separation of powers and checks and balances system. A President serving more than two terms could secure a firm control over the enormous and powerful machinery of Federal administration, including the so-called independent agencies, through the political appointments process.

Without the twenty-second amendment, a President could make the legislature a subservient instrument to his will. Even the independence of the judiciary could be influenced indirectly by the appointment of judges whose attitudes are essentially those of the President. The danger of overconcentration of power in the hands of the President for a long period is much more serious now than in the early years of the Nation because of the increased centralization of power in the Federal Government.

Questions for Discussion

1. How has the Twenty-second Amendment affected the power of the president?
2. What conditions would make repeal of the Twenty-second Amendment likely?
3. What effect does the Twenty-second Amendment have on recruiting talented people for top appointive posts in the second term of a presidency?
4. What would be the effect on the U.S. political system of limiting congressional terms to two?
5. How would a single six-year term affect the presidency?

Suggested Readings

Davis, Paul B. "The Future of Presidential Tenure." *Presidential Studies Quarterly*, 10, no. 3 (Summer 1980), 469–475.

————. "The Results and Implications of the Enactment of the Twenty-second Amendment." *Presidential Studies Quarterly*, 9, no. 3 (Summer 1979), 289–303.

Foundation for the Study of Presidential and Congressional Terms. *Presidential and Congressional Term Limitation: The Issue That Stays Alive.* Washington, D.C.: Foundation for the Study of Presidential and Congressional Terms, 1980.

Morgenthau, Tom. "Four More Years?" *Newsweek*, 108, no. 10 (September 8, 1986), 16–17.

Nice, David C. "In Retreat from Excellence: The Single Six-Year Presidential Term." *Congress & the Presidency*, 13, no. 2 (Autumn 1986), 209–220.

Peterson, Dan. "The 22nd Amendment Should Be Repealed." *World & I*, 1, no. 12 (December 1986), 130–133.

Stein, Charles W. *The Third Term Tradition: Its Rise and Collapse in American Politics.* Westport, Conn.: Greenwood Press, 1972.

Sundquist, James L. *Constitutional Reform and Effective Government.* Washington, D.C.: Brookings Institution, 1986.

U.S. Cong., House of Representatives. *One Six-Year Presidential Term.* Hearing before the Subcommittee on Crime of the Committee on the Judiciary, 93rd Cong., 1st Sess., 1973.

U.S. Cong., Senate. *Single Six-Year Term for President.* Hearing before the Subcommittee on Constitutional Amendments of the Committee on the Judiciary, 92nd Cong., 1st Sess., 1971.

Chapter 12

Does Congress Serve the Public Interest?

The phrase "public interest" or "national interest" is often used by government officials to justify their actions. Presidents refer to the national interest when they take military action abroad or call upon U.S. citizens to make sacrifices in accepting reductions in favored domestic programs. Interest groups, too, claim that their goals are in accord with the public interest. Such a claim is often heard when a business group asks for high tariffs to reduce "unfair" competition from foreign countries, or when an environmental organization asks for greater government regulation to prevent air and water pollution, or when a teachers' organization asks for increased expenditures on educational programs.

When the subject of the public interest comes up, Congress also becomes a topic of controversy. Unlike the president who is elected by a national constituency, Congress is composed of officials who are elected in local or state constituencies. Does Congress, consequently, serve the public interest?

Political scientists Clyde Brown and Ryan J. Barilleaux debate the question. Brown argues the affirmative. He contends:

1. The public interest cannot be defined in terms of particular policies that government should follow. It should be defined in terms of procedures that permit a fair and open process and the sum of private interests. In this regard Congress plays a central role.
2. Congress serves the public interest by acting as a check on an all-powerful president and a large bureaucracy and by balancing and accommodating political interests.

Barilleaux takes the negative position. He makes the following case against Congress:

1. Congress is not living up to its chief responsibility to provide representation and deliberation in the public interest.
2. Congress is too parochial in outlook.
3. Congress has inhibited its ability to deliberate on the merits of policy proposals.
4. Congress has "passed the buck" too much to do its job as it should.
5. A number of reasonable reforms are needed.

Does Congress Serve the Public Interest?

CLYDE BROWN

Congress, Politics, and the Public Interest

In this essay I argue that the activity of politics defines the public interest and that Congress promotes the public interest in our political system by checking arbitrary executive rule and by conciliating competing interests. The basic thesis is that self-interested behavior by individuals and groups in a "regulated" political process determines and furthers the public interest of society. In economic thought this has been a central argument in favor of free market economies since Adam Smith, the father of capitalism, wrote *The Wealth of Nations* (1776). By analogy and with some revision, a similar case can be made in the political sphere. To evaluate this argument we will have to examine the concept of public interest, the activity of politics, the role of Congress in our system of government, and how Congress promotes the public interest.

SEARCHING FOR THE PUBLIC INTEREST

Although the common good or the public interest is at the core of what good government is, there is little consensus among philosophers, political scientists, or public officials as to what it is. In this regard political scientists Kay Lehman Schlozman and John F. Tierney classify attempts to define public interest in terms of (1) expressions of value judgments and preferences, (2) procedures that permit a fair and open political process, and (3) the sum of private interests.[1] Let us take a closer look at these three classes of definitions.

Supporters of the first definition claim to know what the public interest is and, as such, feel society should be organized and public decisions made in ways that are consistent with the particular definition. However, such definitions often lack functional utility since they are usually vague and defy consensus. It is little help to define the public interest vaguely in such terms as the "common good" or the "permanent and aggregate interests of the community" if the new words provide no meaningful guidance to public officials. Attempts to get more specific are numerous, but that fact alone indicates that there is no agreement among those advocating such definitions. We are left in the quandary of having to choose. Schlozman and Tierney write, "Although many political analysts believe that the public interest does in fact exist, their elaborations of what it is are diverse indeed."[2] It is incumbent upon those who define the public interest along these lines to be specific and to indicate how their definition is superior to other definitions. Even if that is done, however, there is another fundamental problem. Any such normative definition could be extremely dangerous if it became the inflexible basis for public policy, since the particular definition used by those in power is unlikely to be the definition favored by significant numbers of other people.

Advocates of the second definition emphasize the importance of procedure in securing the public interest. Rather than focusing on any particular output of government as the test of whether the public interest is being served, they contend it is the "process" itself that is of importance. Their prescriptions require a fair hearing for all sides involved and normally include many essential safeguards associated with democratic theory, such as majoritarian rule, separation of powers, checks and balances, the rule of law, public hearings, and conflict resolution through popular elections and political interest group interaction. These safeguards constitute the "rules of the game," a definition of how politics is to be played in the U.S. political system. Just as the economy is regulated to protect the public from false advertising, monopoly pricing, and other unfair practices, so, too, is politics regulated by the provisions of the Constitution, as well as by laws and administrative procedures, to make the process more open and fair to the parties involved. At a fundamental level, I think procedural fairness is essential and absolutely necessary if there is to be a search for the public interest. As Glendon Schubert writes, "Decisions that are the product of a process of full consideration are most likely to be decisions in the public interest."[3]

Those who accept the third definition usually deny the existence of a national or all-encompassing public interest except as it reveals itself during competitive political struggle between individuals and interest groups. Political scientist David Truman, an early proponent of this view, writes, "We do not need to account for a totally inclusive interest, because one does not exist."[4] This perspective holds that public policy reflects the sum total of all the political pressures generated by all political actors concerned about a particular issue. The notion of public interest as defined only by politics is difficult for some to understand and accept. The economic analogy, again, may help; the price of a good and the quantity produced are not predetermined in a free market system, but instead are the result of the autonomous actions of numerous consumers and producers. Likewise, the public interest according to this view is the unintended by-product of individuals and groups seeking their own self-interest. This definition is simply a call for participation in politics to define the public interest through political struggle among competing interests. I think this view makes sense realistically, especially when combined with the procedural safeguards discussed above.

Because of the conceptual difficulties and political dangers associated with normative definitions of the public interest, most political scientists have been reluctant to accept a *priori* notions of what the public interest is. Rather, most have been more comfortable with definitions, such as the last two, which allow politics and the "rules of the game" to determine the public interest. Congress is at the focus of politics over policy in our system when citizens reveal preferences through voting, expressions of public opinion, and organized lobbying. Admittedly, the policies of government are imperfect, but to my way of thinking we could not even approximate the public interest without the activity of politics and an institution such as Congress in which political preferences can be tallied.

AN ADDITIONAL WORD ABOUT POLITICS

Government is a powerful force that affects our lives by sanctioning certain values and activities while punishing others. A few examples: private property can be allowed or banned, interest groups can be permitted to organize or outlawed, religious differences can be tolerated or orthodoxy can be enforced, and abortion can be legal or illegal. People have strong feelings about these issues and countless others. The first task of any government is to keep the political community intact in the face of the many divisions and cleavages that threaten to tear it asunder. Throughout history various solutions have been attempted; unfortunately many have demanded and enforced conformity by coercion if necessary to a particular political ideology or doctrine, tradition, or leader as the means of overcoming these centrifugal forces. The one process which minimizes coercion and seriously entertains the possibility that short-term governmental decisions might be wrong and, therefore, in need of correction is politics.[5] Politics is "the activity by which differing interests . . . are conciliated by giving them a share in power proportional to their importance to the welfare and survival of the whole community."[6] Politics is a messy, inefficient, and frustrating process, but what are the alternatives: iron-fist rule, inflexible ideology, and unyielding habit? Clearly, politics with all its faults is preferred. This point is often difficult to understand and appreciate. A pluralist society requires a means by which competing interests can reach accommodations and compromises that all can live with.

FEARS AND A ROLE FOR CONGRESS

To understand how Congress serves the public interest as a key actor in U.S. politics it is necessary to understand what political problems the Framers were attempting to solve by creating the new government contained in the Constitution. They feared tyranny of the majority in the form of the people and their popularly elected representatives in government, and they feared tyranny in the form of excessive arbitrary authority in the hands of any one individual or branch of government. Let us look briefly at these two problems in turn.

First, the Framers recognized that uncontrolled self-interest had the potential for oppression and destruction of the political community, outcomes certainly not in the public interest. Aggregates of individuals, referred to as factions, could form around any major division in society, such as region, economic or social class, religion, and occupation. The Framers wanted a government with popular elements, but they knew historically that such societies were unstable. Majority factions if they controlled the government might govern in a way "adverse to the rights of other citizens, or to the permanent interests of the community," and preventing this tyranny of the majority required that "the majority . . . be rendered, by their number and local situation, unable to concert and carry into effect schemes of oppression."[7] In this regard they showed their aversion of direct democracy; they wanted a government that would respond to political consensus rather than simple numerical majorities.

Second, they feared concentrated political power in the hands of any single leader or institution because of its potential for tyranny. They were apprehensive about concentration of power anywhere in the political system, but their primary concern was excessive executive authority such as they had experienced under the British Crown. The greater the concentration of political power, the greater the potential for tyranny, they felt. In this respect, the Framers showed their fear of executive rule and hoped to structure a government that would keep the executive in check.

How were these remedies to be implemented? Tyranny of the majority and arbitrary rule were to be obviated by diffusing power widely and by making coordination within government difficult. As James Madison wrote in "Federalist 51":

> In framing a government which is to be administered by men over men, the great difficulty lies in this: you must first enable the government to control the governed; and in the next place oblige it to control itself. A dependence on the people is, no doubt, the primary control of government; but experience has taught mankind the necessity of auxiliary precautions.[8]

The Framers did not believe that good government would be found in human nature; rather it had to be supplied by "contriving the interior structure of the government."[9] The solution was to be supplied by the Constitution.

The Constitution divides political power in several ways: (1) by creating a federal system with two layers of government, the states and the national government; (2) by separating the government into distinct executive, legislative, and judicial parts; and (3) by dividing the legislative branch in two. This partitioning makes coordination within government difficult in and of itself, but cooperation is made more difficult by: (1) establishing a system of checks and balances, especially the counterpoise of presidential and congressional powers; (2) electing officials from different constituencies at different times for different terms of office; and (3) requiring supermajorities for certain actions such as veto overrides, adoption of constitutional amendments, and ratification of treaties. Clearly, the intent is to create a government that has many internal checks to prevent excessive arbitrary authority of any kind.[10]

CONGRESS AND THE PUBLIC INTEREST

With this constitutional background in mind, let us consider how Congress as an institution serves the public interest. Various theories of congressional functions agree that Congress performs many vital functions.[11] Rather than reviewing any particular list, I want to concentrate on two essential functions performed by Congress that grow out of the earlier discussions of politics and the public interest. These functions are critical to the preservation of politics and the prevention of tyranny in the U.S. political system, conditions that must be met if we are to discover the public interest. These two functions are (1) consensus building, and (2) oversight of the executive branch.

With regard to the first function, the institution primarily responsible for conciliation of interests in our political system is Congress. Governing the United States is not easy given our cultural diversity and the numerous competing interests that frequently produce social, economic, and political conflict. Members of Congress, simultaneously representing specific geographic territories and multiple interests, somehow must reach collective agreements on how to attack pressing social problems by enacting legislation. Piecing together majorities in support of legislative proposals involves bargaining and compromise among the lawmakers who represent the relevant interests. The process of combining the demands of constituencies and interests so that each is reasonably satisfied given political realities is what is meant by consensus building. Reaching accommodations that a majority can support without gravely disadvantaging the minority is the height of the legislator's art.

Consensus building is obviously a crucial function that every free society has to perform. It is a precondition in the sense that it is meaningless to speak of the public interest outside of the context of a political community. Additionally, as stated earlier, the Framers crafted a government that responds to political consensus. Consensus building is the very essence of politics in that it adjusts public policy to the strength of competing interests.

Given the legislative process, we should not be surprised when we see occasional instances of "log-rolling" (vote trading), "pork-barrel" projects (spending money on local projects not critically needed), special interest provisions, "pet projects," nongermane amendments, or "Christmas tree" bills (legislation containing many pet projects). It is the price that must be paid if majorities are to be constructed in a political process. We should not judge whether Congress serves the public interest on the basis of any one policy decision but rather by the totality of all public policy enacted by Congress and by the essential functions that Congress performs. Neither should we be surprised if the legislative process is slow and cumbersome on occasion. Social problems at the national level are complex, and such problems are not solved overnight. Interestingly, the Framers took comfort in the inertia of the political institutions they were creating; hasty action might be mistaken action. Politics has the virtue that it permits continued debate, research, and experimentation while policy is being fine tuned. The distinguished political scientist E. E. Schattschneider has suggested that politics in the United States should be studied over generations to clearly see the progress being made.[12] There is no reason to expect consensus building to be quick and easy, but it is crucial to the preservation of the political community.

With respect to the second function, it is a major responsibility of Congress to see that the executive branch is properly implementing laws in compliance with legislative intent. As such, Congress oversees the bureaucracy, and, more important, it is a major check on arbitrary executive rule and is a major protector of the rule of law. As mentioned above, the Constitution provides for the sharing of power between the executive and legislative branches. The president is the chief executive officer of the federal bureaucracy, but Congress has the power to create and to destroy government agencies as well as to determine their funding and to oversee their operation; that is, the president and the bureaucracy cannot frustrate congressional intent by refusing properly to administer laws and programs enacted into law.

Tyrannical executive power is controlled in our political system by the congressional powers mentioned earlier and, ultimately, by the constitutional power granted Congress in Article II to remove the president from office if he is impeached and convicted of "high crimes and misdemeanors." Impeachment involves a congressional determination of whether the president has transgressed against the Constitution. It has been used only in extremely rare instances, but the case of President Richard Nixon gives the process contemporary relevance. In 1974 President Nixon resigned when it became obvious that the House of Representatives would report out impeachment charges on the grounds of obstruction of justice and abuse of presidential powers in connection with the cover-up of White House involvement in the Watergate break-in of the Democratic National Committee's offices in 1972.

The Watergate hearings affirmed the principle that the Constitution applies to all, including presidents. This fundamental premise of our political system is strengthened every time Congress investigates possible wrongdoings by individuals working in the executive branch. In 1987 Congress investigated the involvement of the National Security Council under the direction of Adm. John Poindexter and Lt. Col. Oliver North in the sale of weapons to Iran and the diverting of profits from the sale to support the Contras' guerrilla war in Nicaragua without the apparent awareness of President Ronald Reagan and, possibly, in violation of law prohibiting military support of the Contras. The Iran-Contra hearings are a recent example of how vital it is that Congress check executive power and affirm the rule of law.

Congressional oversight of the bureaucracy and the president is vital because it checks the possibility of executive tyranny. Tyranny, in any form, rules out the possibility of genuine politics, which in turn makes the attainment of the public interest highly improbable. Congress serves the public interest because it limits the power of the executive.

SUMMARY

Congress, as an institution, serves us all by fulfilling vital functions. In an era when we are confronted with "imperial presidents" bent on expanding the power of the office beyond constitutional limits, we need a strong Congress as a counterweight. In an age of the administrative state with a bureaucracy beyond the imagination of the Framers, congressional oversight is essential. In a day marked by popular cynicism about institutions and increased societal complexity, dedicated service to and representation of citizens by elected officials are more crucial than ever to the legitimacy of our government. At a time when the "public interest" is being defined by single-issue interest groups in more and more particularistic terms, the process by which Congress balances and accommodates competing interests is more important than ever to the national welfare.

All of this is not to say that Congress cannot be improved; it can. But the controversy here is not about reform of Congress; to argue that Congress should be a bit more efficient or a little more professional is to miss the point. My defense of Congress is fundamentally the claim that an elected representative legislature is absolutely essential to the discovery and promotion of the public interest. First, Congress contributes to the maintenance of the political community by reconciling the multitude of private interests in the United States. Second, Congress prevents arbitrary executive rule, which is a form of tyranny and which would eliminate the very process of politics essential to the determination of the public interest in a pluralist nation. It seems to me that an institution like Congress is essential to the promotion of the public interest in a free society that utilizes the separation of powers principle as the basis for its government.

NOTES

1. Kay Lehman Schlozman and John T. Tierney, *Organized Interests and American Democracy* (New York: Harper & Row, 1986), p. 27.

2. Ibid., p. 27.

3. Glendon Schubert, *The Public Interest* (Glencoe, Ill.: Free Press, 1960), p. 205.

4. David Truman, *The Governmental Process* (New York: Knopf, 1971), p. 51.

5. See Bernard Crick, *In Defense of Politics* (Baltimore: Penguin Books, 1964).

6. Ibid., p. 21.

7. James Madison, "Federalist 10," in *The Federalist Papers*, ed. Clinton Rossiter (New York: New American Library, 1961), p. 78.

8. James Madison, "Federalist 51," in ibid., p. 322.

9. Ibid., p. 320.

10 See Charles O. Jones, "Historical Perspectives on Congress," in *Congress and Public Policy,* ed. David C. Kozak and John D. Macartney (Chicago: Dorsey Press, 1987), pp. 2–8.

11. See Roger H. Davidson, David M. Kovenok, and Michael K. O'Leary, "Theories of Congress," in ibid., pp. 9–13.

12. E. E. Schattschneider, *Two Hundred Million Americans in Search of a Government* (New York: Holt, Rinehart and Winston, 1969).

☑ *NO*

Does Congress Serve the Public Interest?

RYAN J. BARILLEAUX
Congress and the Public Interest

The government of the United States is distinctive in that it includes an independent and powerful legislature. Indeed, as political scientist Nelson Polsby put it, Congress is "the only competent legislature in the world."[1] In other nations, legislative power is either nonexistent or restrained in deference to the executive. Many dictatorships have legislative bodies, such as the Supreme Soviet, but these assemblies merely rubber-stamp the decisions of the dictators. In parliamentary democracies, the legislature debates the proposals of the executive and sometimes challenges them, but members of the majority party usually accept executive policies in the name of party unity. Few public policy initiatives come from the legislature.

In contrast, the United States Congress constitutes a branch of government unto itself and is the source of many important policy initiatives. Indeed, Congress is the "first branch" of the U.S. government because it is the first branch mentioned in the Constitution and the one given the greatest array of specific governmental powers. Article I of the Constitution establishes a powerful legislative assembly, whose two houses must agree in order for laws to be enacted and money to be spent. The Framers of the Constitution required that agreement precisely because they realized that they were granting Congress such broad and significant authority.

With power comes responsibility, however. Because it is more powerful than any other legislative assembly in the world, Congress has a larger responsibility to act in support of the general public interest. To the extent that U.S. citizens expect their government to "promote the general Welfare," as the Preamble to the Constitution puts it, they expect Congress to contribute to that task as much or more than the other branches. But does it live up to its responsibilities as we might expect? The answer, unfortunately, is that it does not.

No political system or institution is perfect, but even when one judges Congress in light of political reality, it is clear that the national legislature has failed in its task. When the Framers of the Constitution designed the system of separate institutions sharing powers, they fully expected government to involve compromise. Writing about this fact, James Madison, sometimes called the "Father of the Constitution," commented, "If angels were to govern men, no limits on government would be necessary."[2] The point is that Madison, like his contemporaries, expected government to be less than perfect, because human beings are less than perfect. But the Framers also assumed that each branch of government would do its best to promote the overall goals of government, particularly the goal of acting in the public interest.

What is the public interest? Madison defined it as the "permanent and aggregate interests of the community."[3] That is, the public interest is what is good for the whole nation in the long run. Unfortunately, Congress does not service that interest.

As its contribution to promoting the public interest, Congress is to provide for representation and deliberation, two important values that neither the executive nor the judiciary could adequately support. Because members of Congress are elected from districts and states for short terms of office, they are to provide better representation of citizens than a single president can for the nation. Because it is structured to allow, and even encourage, open debate and a thoughtful look at policy proposals, Congress is supposed to deliberate on the benefits, costs, and consequences of those proposals.

There is a gap, however, between what Congress is supposed to provide and what it actually gives to the government. It gives public policy in the United States an emphasis on the parochial needs and demands of congressional districts, little effective deliberation on public issues, and an unwillingness to take responsibility for many hard choices that arise in politics. As a result, Congress will not be able to make its proper contribution to government in the public interest unless several needed reforms are enacted.

Are these charges unfair? They are not, as a closer look at each point will reveal. What follows is a summary of the case against Congress.

1. CONGRESS IS NOT LIVING UP TO ITS CHIEF RESPONSIBILITY TO PROVIDE REPRESENTATION AND DELIBERATION IN THE PUBLIC INTEREST

In order for it to make its contribution to government, Congress was designed as an assembly consisting of two houses: one representing states and the other representing smaller territorial districts. In this way, the national legislature would always be able to keep in touch with the interests and views of people throughout the nation and relate them to the larger public interest. The two chambers of Congress, particularly the Senate, would debate the policy proposals of the day to consider whether those suggestions were in the nation's long-term interest.

The House of Representatives was to be the central institution in the government for popular representation. As Madison explained in *The Federalist Papers*, "The House of Representatives is so constituted as to support in the members an habitual recollection of their dependence on the people."[4] It was to be the duty of the House to ensure that the national government's actions did not overrun the interests of people in the districts.

The Senate was to provide for representation of the states and a view toward the long-term interests of the United States. Its overlapping membership (one-third elected every two years) would provide a "due sense of national character,"[5] that is, a sense of the larger public interest. Moreover, according to the Constitution, the members of the Senate were chosen by state legislatures rather than the people—a practice changed to direct popular election in 1913 with the adoption of the Seventeenth Amendment. Together with the House, the Senate would ensure that the "cool and deliberate sense of the community"[6] would inform the acts of Congress.

If Congress is to live up to the hopes of the Framers, and their hopes are our hopes, then it must be able to contribute effective representation and deliberation in the national interest. When it does not, the overall value of the U.S. government is diminished.

2. CONGRESS IS TOO PAROCHIAL IN OUTLOOK

The value of the constitutional system has been diminished, however, in part because members of Congress have tended to emphasize their role in district and state representation to the point of forgetting the national interest. This parochialism is evident in a number of large and small ways.

Most significantly, the congressional appropriations process is dominated by parochial interests. For decades, the federal treasury has been a "pork barrel" from which Congress extracted money to pay for local demands and interests, often at a very high price. A spending bill approved by Congress in 1987 provides a good example. In an era of mounting budget deficits, Congress allocated $8.5 billion for projects and programs that cannot seriously be defended as in the larger public interest.

- $8 million for North Dakota State University to establish a national center to study weeds
- $750,000 to pay for a program to promote the merits of eating fish
- $5 million to buy land for a wetlands preserve near New Orleans
- $2 million for an international trade center in Iowa
- $10 million for a nutrition research center at Louisiana State University

- an increase in honey subsidies that would benefit twenty beekeepers across the nation.

In defense of the bill, Sen. J. Bennett Johnston of Louisiana claimed, "It is not a perfect bill. If it were, I would have a lot more projects in it."[7] His attitude is typical of many members of Congress.

More than just spending money on these and other "pork-barrel" projects, there is a tendency in Congress to treat all questions of public policy as if they were local matters. For example, each year the federal government spends millions of dollars on construction projects, from post offices to dams, bridges, and roads. Yet it does so on the basis of what districts want, rather than a sense of what the nation needs. Indeed, some members of Congress are so successful at obtaining these sorts of projects that they build their congressional careers on how much money they can bring to their district. One member of the House has been so successful that he was named the "Prince of Pork" by journalists covering Capitol Hill.[8] Moreover, a number of military installations around the nation remain active, despite the fact that the Defense Department wants to close them, because districts do not want to lose the federal money that these bases bring. So the nation continues to operate obsolete bases, even one with a moat around it, in order to satisfy local demands. A debate in 1984 over where to base the battleship *Missouri* centered around local concerns rather than national defense needs.[9]

Local concerns not only dominate spending debates but also permeate every aspect of congressional life. Since reelection is an important consideration for nearly all members of Congress, life on Capitol Hill is structured to increase every member's chances of remaining in office: most business is conducted on a Tuesday–Thursday schedule to allow members frequent trips back to their districts; the congressional franking privilege (i.e., free postage) frequently pays for "reports" to constituents that are thinly disguised campaign literature; members keep large staffs to deal with every constituent request, from help with bureaucratic problems to passes to the White House; and a number of caucuses (informal groups) have appeared in recent years to allow members a chance to demonstrate attention to local interests, from the Congressional Mushroom Caucus to the Senate Wine Caucus and the Northeast-Midwest Coalition.[10] In short, there is little room or time for the national interest to compete with all of these parochial interests.

3. CONGRESS HAS INHIBITED ITS ABILITY TO DELIBERATE ON THE MERITS OF POLICY PROPOSALS

In the 1970s, members of Congress enacted a number of internal reforms designed to "open up" the national legislature: an increase in the number of

subcommittees, a requirement for open meetings of committees and subcommittees, an increase in the staff support for committees and individual members, and changes in the method for selecting leaders. The result of these
changes was to quicken the pace of life on Capitol Hill, increase the workload
of members, multiply the number of bills and policy proposals considered each
year, and distribute decision-making power to a larger number of members
than ever before. In consequence, Congress seriously undermined its own
ability to deliberate on the issues before it.

Political scientist Michael J. Malbin has explained how these changes, particularly the increase in congressional staffs, have interfered with Congress's
ability to deliberate.

> For a process of legislative deliberation to function reasonably well, at
> least three distinct requirements must be satisfied. The members need
> accurate information, they need time to think about that information, and
> they need to talk to each other about the factual, political, and moral
> implications of the policies they are considering. The new use of staff
> undercut each of these.[11]

Larger staffs, more subcommittees, a bigger workload, and a faster pace of
congressional life have left members of Congress with less time to think about
proposals, less time and fewer opportunities to discuss the implications of
proposals with each other, and almost no time to consider the long-term consequences of what they are doing. In short, the reforms of recent years, once
thought to improve Congress's ability to contribute to national government,
have weakened its ability to perform its most important functions.

4. CONGRESS HAS "PASSED THE BUCK" TOO MUCH TO DO ITS JOB AS IT SHOULD

In part because of this weakening, but also because of the desire to protect
members' reelection chances, Congress has failed to exercise its intended role
by refusing to make the hard political choices required of it. Specifically,
members of Congress have "passed the buck" on important political problems
of recent years in order to avoid bearing responsibility for their decisions. Two
examples will bear out this point.

First, many of the so-called abuses of presidential power in recent years have
occurred only because of congressional acquiescence. Unilateral presidential
war making in Vietnam and Korea, regarded by some observers as illegal or
even unconstitutional, occurred with the full knowledge of Congress. Furthermore, for six years the United States observed the nuclear arms limitation
provisions of a proposed Strategic Arms Limitation Treaty of 1979 (SALT II),
despite the absence of Senate approval of the treaty and in apparent violation of

U.S. law.[12] This situation developed because Congress was willing to allow the president to do so. In each of these cases, Congress acquiesced in the expansion of presidential powers because it was politically easier to do so than to restrain the president. If Congress "passes the buck" on foreign policy decisions, then presidents will do as they see fit.

Second, Congress has responded to the problem of mounting budget deficits by once again "passing the buck." In the Balanced Budget Act of 1985 (the Gramm-Rudman-Hollings Act), the legislature enacted a plan for automatic budget cutting rather than take responsibility for deciding what items in the budget ought to be reduced or eliminated. When faced with a 1986 Supreme Court decision voiding parts of the automatic cut plan, Congress did not accept its responsibility but found another automatic plan that would meet the Court's approval. Only after the sharp drop in stock prices in 1987, when the prospect of economic turmoil appeared real to many observers, did Congress agree to deficit reductions by choice rather than by automatic measures.

What is the result? It is that budget cutting will proceed as if the United States has no spending priorities, but regards all expenses as equal. Despite complaints from Democrats in Congress that President Ronald Reagan's budget priorities (defense increases and domestic spending cuts) are wrong, a majority of members in both the House and Senate refused to choose which items need cutting more and which less. In this way, members avoided having to go on record as voting for particular budget cuts and arousing the anger of their constituents or interest groups.

Thus Congress fails to live up to its responsibilities in government. It fails to meet not only the hopes of the Framers, but the expectations of today's citizens. If the situation is to improve, then Congress must be reformed.

5. A NUMBER OF REASONABLE REFORMS ARE NEEDED

In light of the problems described above, some observers of Congress have counseled wholesale changes in the U.S. system of government: the adoption of a parliamentary system, strict limits on the number of terms in office that members can hold, or even powerful party mechanisms in Congress that could discipline members and control campaign funds. Each of these suggestions would, however, distort the deliberative and representative functions of Congress in the name of reform.

The kinds of reforms that Congress needs and the United States deserves are those that enhance the ability of the national legislature to live up to its responsibilities. So, while reforms are essential, only certain kinds of reforms will help: those consistent with the nature and purposes of Congress. Of course, one should not expect Congress instantly to become a body of disinterested philosophers governing the United States according to some abstract notion of a good society, but realistic reforms can contribute to reasonable improvements in Congress's functioning.

First, in order to deal with the problems created by excessive attention to "pork-barrel" spending and local demands, two changes would be beneficial: longer terms for members and an item veto for the president. If members of the House were to have four-year, rather than two-year, terms, they would have a greater opportunity to build records in office on grounds other than just dollars to their districts. This change, coupled with a modification of the president's veto power, would reduce the likelihood of large sums of federal money being appropriated for weed study centers and promoting fish consumption.

How would an item veto help? Under current rules, the president must accept all of a spending bill or veto all of it, so the chief executive is often forced to choose to accept "pork-barrel" spending in order to get money for more essential purposes. In this way, Congress can "pack" money bills with pieces of "pork"; then a member can defend a vote for one district's weed center in order to get honey loan subsidies for his or her district. With an item veto, the president could veto individual items in an appropriations bill, and, if Congress wanted to override the veto, members would have to go on record as voting for each item of the "pork-barrel" spending. An item veto for the president will not balance the budget, but it will help to eliminate the worst aspects of the "pork-barrel" approach to spending. Together with longer terms for members, such a reform could increase Congress's attention to the larger national interest.

In order to increase deliberation, other reforms are necessary. Recall Malbin's analysis of the requirements for effective deliberation: information; time to think about the information; and time for members to talk to each other about the consequences, costs, and benefits of specific policy proposals. How can Congress better meet these requirements? It can reorganize its schedule, its use of staff, and its committee structure to enhance deliberation.

Consider the possibilities. Each year, congressional sessions consist of a continual flow of committee hearings, meetings, floor debates, and conference committees. If the legislative schedule were restructured, so hearings were confined to earlier parts of the legislative year, then there would be time for members to reflect on the information they receive and debate legislation in the later parts of the year. In this way, there would be time for deliberation.

In addition, members are currently pulled between a large number of committee and subcommittee assignments. Even the most dedicated members find themselves with little time for any one aspect of their jobs. A reduction in the number of committees and subcommittees could reduce the demands on members' time.

A reduction in staff resources would also, somewhat ironically, enhance members' ability to deliberate. As Malbin points out, the expansion of congressional staffs has meant an explosion of bills, amendments, proposals, hearings, meetings, and other time demands, with a resulting loss of time to deliberate. A reduction in staff would actually increase the amount of time that members have to think and discuss, especially since staffs now often act as negotiators for their bosses. With smaller staffs, members would be talking to one another more, as well as reflecting on what they are doing.

If Congress were to adopt reforms of this sort, then its members could devote themselves more fully to promoting the public interest and representing the long-term interests of their constituents. In this way, the national legislature could better live up to the hopes of the Framers and the expectations of today's citizens, and do so in the form and spirit of the system of checks and balances.

NOTES

1. Quoted in "Congress, Consensus vs. Chaos," *Christian Science Monitor,* February 6, 1987, p. 19.
2. James Madison, "Federalist 51," in *The Federalist Papers,* ed. Clinton Rossiter (New York: New American Library, 1961), p. 322.
3. Madison, "Federalist 10," in ibid., p. 78.
4. Madison, "Federalist 57," in ibid., p. 352. *The Federalist Papers* is a collection of essays written by Madison, Alexander Hamilton, and John Jay, which appeared in New York newspapers during the period of debate over ratification of the Constitution.
5. Madison, "Federalist 63," in ibid., p. 382.
6 Ibid., p. 384.
7. Quoted in the *New York Times,* May 25, 1987, p. 12.
8. Michael Barone and Grant Ujifusa, eds., *The Almanac of American Politics, 1986* (Washington, D.C.: National Journal, 1986), p. 322. The "Prince of Pork" is Rep. Kenneth J. Gray (D-Ill.).
9. "The MacNeil/Lehrer News Hour," December 6, 1984, transcript 2399, pp. 6–7.
10. Samuel Kernell, *Going Public* (Washington, D.C.: CQ Press, 1986), pp. 28–32.
11. Michael J. Malbin, *Unelected Representatives* (New York: Basic Books, 1980), p. 242.
12. Ryan J. Barilleaux, "Executive Non-Agreements and the Presidential-Congressional Struggle in Foreign Affairs," *World Affairs,* 148, no. 4 (Spring 1986), 217.

Questions for Discussion

1. How does each author define the public interest?
2. How would the reforms of Congress proposed by each author affect the public interest?
3. What responsibility does a member of Congress have in serving the interests of his or her constituency? Why?
4. What responsibility does a member of Congress have in serving an interest broader than his or her constituency? Why?
5. How does Congress's role in national policy making differ from that of the president?

Suggested Readings

Fiorina, Morris. *Congress: Keystone of the Washington Establishment.* New Haven: Yale Univ. Press, 1977.

Fisher, Louis. *The Politics of Shared Power: Congress and the Executive.* 2nd ed. Washington, D.C.: CQ Press, 1987.

Keefe, William J. *Congress and the American People.* 3rd ed. Englewood Cliffs, N.J.: Prentice-Hall, 1988.

Maass, Arthur. *Congress and the Common Good.* New York: Basic Books, 1983.

O'Neill, Tip, with William Novak. *Man of the House: The Life and Political Memoirs of Speaker Tip O'Neill.* New York: Random House, 1987.

Reedy, George E. *The U.S. Senate: Paralysis or a Search for Consensus?* New York: Crown, 1986.

Reid, T. R. *Congressional Odyssey: The Saga of a Senate Bill.* San Francisco: W. H. Freeman, 1980.

Rieselbach, Leroy N. *Congressional Reform.* Washington, D.C.: CQ Press, 1986.

Ripley, Randall B., and Grace A. Franklin. *Congress, the Bureaucracy, and Public Policy.* 4th ed. Chicago: Dorsey Press, 1977.

Sundquist, James L. *The Decline and Resurgence of Congress.* Washington, D.C.: Brookings Institution, 1971.

Vogler, David J., and Sidney F. Waldman. *Congress and Democracy.* Washington, D.C.: CQ Press, 1985.

Chapter 13

Is the Bureaucracy Inefficient, Unnecessary, and Harmful?

When the Constitution was adopted in the late eighteenth century, only a few hundred people were employed by government at the national level. Today, however, there are about 2.9 million civilian federal government employees. Millions of other public employees serve the armed forces and the agencies of state and local governments. About one out of every six employed people in the United States works for government either at the national, state, or local level.

Government has grown remarkably in this century because of its increased activities such as foreign policy, the economy, and welfare. In the late eighteenth century the United States was a small power on the periphery of the world's major powers of Europe. Today it is one of the two strongest military powers, trying to cope with the other superpower, the Soviet Union. In meeting the challenges of the post–World War II period, the United States has adopted a policy of internationalism, rejecting the isolationism of its past history. Today millions of people are employed by the federal government to manage its foreign policy needs. These have required the services of large numbers of people in the armed forces. Government, moreover, has been engaged in dispensing foreign aid, gathering intelligence information, assisting individuals and groups abroad, and helping to promote international trade.

In addition to the growth of foreign policy activities, domestic factors are responsible for government expansion. Business has asked for government assistance to build highways, improve railroads, construct dams, widen waterways, and administer tariffs. It has also requested government support for research in energy, transportation, and military technology. The demands of labor have also increased government involvement in the economy. Labor has asked for government inspection involving safety at work sites, government supervision of minimum wage laws, and government employment of those who cannot find jobs in the market economy. Labor has sought government protection of unions against the strong power of business.

Finally, the emergence of the welfare state has contributed to government growth. Individuals and groups have demanded government help to provide health care, social security, housing, and education. All of these goals require programs that are administered by government, and that administration service is the bureaucracy.

Big government has received its share of criticism. In the election of

1976, for example, Jimmy Carter ran under a campaign theme of reducing the size of the federal government. Ronald Reagan became even more identified than Carter with such a reduction. Both Carter and Reagan failed to achieve their stated purposes, however. The best that Reagan could do was to reduce the rate of growth of the federal government. Although reductions were made in many domestic programs, the Reagan administration greatly increased defense spending in its early years.

Critics of bureaucracy argue that it is inefficient, unnecessary, and harmful. Such is the view taken by Michael Nelson, a former contributing editor of the *Washington Monthly*. Nelson contends:

1. Out where the services of government are delivered, the performance of the bureaucracy constitutes the biggest crisis facing our country today.
2. In the view of many people bureaucratic behavior seems random, arbitrary, and confusing.
3. Congress contributes to the problem of poor bureaucratic performance by writing bad laws.
4. The bureaucracy should be cut down in size in order to minimize the number and complexity of contacts between citizens and government agencies.

The behavior of bureaucracy is defended by Charles T. Goodsell, a professor at the Virginia Polytechnic Institute and State University. He argues:

1. Most direct reports from citizens and public opinion surveys show a generally positive attitude toward the workings of government agencies.
2. Business administration is by no means always superior to public administration.
3. The public bureaucracy of the United States compares most favorably to the public bureaucracies of other nations.

Goodsell is particularly critical of the well-known stereotypes of bureaucrats as bungling and stupid.

Is the Bureaucracy Inefficient, Unnecessary, and Harmful?

MICHAEL NELSON
Bureaucracy: The Biggest Crisis of All

The hallmark of the company town is that it provides its people with not just jobs, but everything else, including entertainment. In Washington, of course, the bureaucracy is the company, and not surprisingly Washingtonians find its foibles to be an endless source of merriment. The *Washington Star* daily runs a "great moments in bureaucratese" feature called Gobbledygook; the *Washington Monthly* has its "Memo of the Month"; and Senator Proxmire grabs headlines with his monthly Golden Fleece Award, uncovering government-funded studies on "the sex life of the fern" and the like.

Washingtonians also seem to assume that if they are laughing at bureaucracy, the whole world must be laughing with them—when it's time for Americans to get serious about politics, they, like their brethren in Washington, surely must drop bureaucracy and start talking about "issues." But to the rest of the country, bureaucracy really isn't the least bit funny. It *is* the issue.

In fact it is not too much to say that out where the services of the government are delivered, the performance of the bureaucracy constitutes the biggest crisis facing our country today. It grows in each of the millions of direct, "routine" contacts that take place every day between citizens and the agencies of their government, many of which are supposed to be helping them. In contrast to Watergate and Vietnam, this crisis is neither readily identified nor easily cured; it is insidious, the more so because it manifests itself in such ordinary ways.

Bureaucracy isn't limited to government, of course, or to the United States. In China, it concerned Chairman Mao more than any other problem, enough so that he plunged his country into near-chaos in an attempt to deal with it. In this country we haven't had a Mao, and with any luck we will never need one, but we do have to recognize that the problem is as serious here as it was in China.

I began to find this out a couple of years ago, after I decided to try to learn what politics and government look like from a citizen's-eye-view—what people think about when they think about the political system. I did so by going to three towns to talk with three classes of people—poor whites in Augusta, Georgia, professionals and businessmen in Towson, Maryland, and blue-collar workers in New Milford, New Jersey. I drew people's names randomly from the phone book, wrote to tell them I was interested in finding out what was on their minds concerning politics, and asked to come visit for a couple of evenings with them and a few of their friends and families. I didn't bring in a long list of questions; instead, when I got to their homes, I repeated my interest in hearing about their concerns, then sat back and listened as they talked, partly to me, but mostly with each other. Unlike a pollster, I was as interested in what people chose to talk about when they talked politics as in the specific opinions they expressed.

As the conversations rambled along, these people began to paint a verbal picture of the political world as they saw it. To my surprise, what loomed largest in that portrait was not presidents or elections or issues or the rest of the stuff we usually think of as "politics." In fact, when people spoke of current affairs and the like (mostly, I suspect, because they thought it would please me), they did so stiffly, with uncomfortable pauses and lags in the conversation. The subject they warmed to with raised-voice, table-thumping intensity was the bureaucracy—not the anonymous, bloated big-B Bureaucracy of Chamber of Commerce after-dinner speeches, but rather the specific agencies of government they felt intruding into their personal lives.

As one might expect, each class of people dealt with somewhat different groups of agencies—the well-off with, for example, the IRS [Internal Revenue Service], the blue-collar families with the unemployment office, the poor with the Social Security Administration. But regardless of their class, almost all saw little connection between political issues and their own lives. They saw a great deal of connection, however, between bureaucracy and their daily concerns— and most of what they saw they didn't like.

Further, they didn't like that intimacy, those intrusions. It meant dealing with organizations that were not only large and impersonal, but whose actions sometimes seemed to defy all reason. For example, Frank, a prosperous middle-aged lawyer, told of trying to find out from the IRS how his purchase of a condominium would bear on his taxes. "I went all the way to the IRS district director before I could get anybody to listen to what I was saying. The district director finally says, 'Well, I can't help you; you have to talk to the agent of the day'—you know, call a number and agent so-and-so answers. So when I finally reach him, he says, 'Does your company subscribe to Prentice-Hall and Commerce Clearinghouse and different tax services?' I said yeah. He says, 'Well, you better look it up there because that's more help than we can give you.' "

Martha, a retired spinster, had been supporting herself with a small social security check. Ordinarily, that would have entitled her to get additional Supplementary Security Income (SSI) benefits. But because she had saved over the years for her burial, she told me, she had accumulated more in the bank than SSI recipients were allowed to have. Thus, the local office turned down her application, though a sympathetic caseworker advised her that if she went out and spent her savings she would be eligible.

Bureaucrats' behavior also seemed random and arbitrary, though for those who were shrewd enough, it could be gotten around. A real estate dealer explained that, "It's very difficult to get the right information out of the government in my business. Trying to get a decent appraisal out of a government official—the VA [Veterans' Administration] or the FHA [Federal Housing Administration]—is unbelievable. The red tape. If he appraised it, that's the last word—that's it. And the only way we could rectify two of the things that came in grossly underappraised was to go to our congressman, who used to be a neighbor. He helped us out."

All too often, though, an inept agency action gave the appearance of being malicious. Curiously, many of the poor whites were certain that the government now discriminated against them, using evidence like Homer and Viola's. "I know a black man who used to work at the truckstop," complained Homer, a young part-time school janitor. "His wife went down there and said him and her was separated and had two young 'uns. And at that time she's been drawing welfare and food stamps for two years and she said they never had so much as come to her house." "And that woman came down here and went through every cabinet I got, that welfare woman," added Viola.

For some, the inherently complicated nature of bureaucratic procedures was a source of anger and confusion. After Willie's husband Fred, a mechanic, broke his arm, she went down to the food stamp office. "I had a note from the doctor saying he'd have to stay out of work for ten months. They told me I could get the stamps but I'd have to wait 30 days. I told her that in 30 days I'd be starving and she could forget about it." Ron, an unemployed landscaper, dreaded going down to the unemployment office. "You have to get on line for this and another line for that, and the people behind the counter—they're busy, I know—but they treat you like you're probably a rip-off artist or something. You know, guilty until proven innocent."

The impersonal nature of agency contacts further incensed people. Diana, a university press editor, complained about "the computerized courtesy" of form letters from the IRS: "We got a letter saying come down to the IRS at such-and-such a time, blah, blah, blah, and bring all your papers—very impersonal.

"So we go down and it turns out that nothing is wrong. Well, Good Lord, I've been paying taxes for 30 years and nothing's ever been wrong. Why do they need to call me now? Just more big brother."

Even worse was having to rely on a large, anonymous, and hence unpredictable organization for basic sustenance. Gene and Ella, who live off his VA disability payments, got very upset when some bureaucrat waited too long to get the checks out. "If a man is depending on that check," said Gene, "he could be sitting out in the street with his family maybe for ten days if his landlord wants his rent on the first. You can get pretty hungry from the first to the tenth waiting for that check, and they should take that into consideration. Some of them wait until the last minute and foul everybody up, and it can be real costly to people."

What is striking about these complaints, and the scores of similar ones I heard, is not that people don't like bureaucracy. After all, who does? I once taught a class of government employees, and even they couldn't muster up a kind word for it.

What is striking is the nature of the complaints. As every scholarly treatise on the subject will tell you, the great advantage bureaucracy is supposed to offer to complex, modern society is efficient, rational, uniform, and courteous treatment for the citizens it deals with. Yet not only did these qualities manage to conceal themselves from the people I talked with, it was their very opposites that seemed more characteristic. People of all classes felt that their treatment had been bungled, not efficient; unpredictable and bizarre, not rational; discriminatory or idiosyncratic, not uniform; and all too often, insensitive or downright insulting rather than courteous. It was as if they had gotten stuck with a new car that not only did not run when they wanted it to, but that periodically started itself up and drove all around their lawn.

Equally curious, the agencies that drew the most fire were, on the whole, those whose business is supposedly providing benefits to people—social security, food stamps, welfare, tax counseling, and so on. It is not surprising, of course, that people grumble when the government exacts taxes and other burdens from them. But when in the process of supposedly doing something for them it makes them hopping mad, then we have a problem.

This last point is underscored in a recent report to Jimmy Carter from Richard Pettigrew, a presidential assistant working on reorganization. Pettigrew sent out a letter to every representative and senator asking them which federal programs their constituents thought were "administered least efficiently," "most confusing," "least successful in achieving their stated objectives," involved the most "excessive paperwork," and, finally, were "most responsive." Though congressmen, who are at the receiving end of almost all citizen complaints about the government, were the logical ones to ask, evidently no one ever had before. More than 200 of them replied, often in great detail. Their answers, interestingly enough, were quite uniform, spanning party and ideological lines. (The author of a call for "less government involvement in the 'daily lives' of individuals and businesses," for example, was George McGovern.)

Two agencies ranked high in all four "bad" categories: the Department of Labor's Office of Workers' Compensation Programs, which administers the black lung program and workmen's compensation for federal employees, and the Social Security Administration. (It is worth remembering here that the agency's old age insurance program seemed to work fine; it was the disability insurance, Medicare, and Aid to Families with Dependent Children that drew all the flak.)

The Veterans' Administration was next on the list; it scored badly in three categories. The IRS, Immigration and Naturalization Service, and Small Business Administration showed up in two. Among the others that were singled out frequently: the Occupational Safety and Health Administration, the Department of Housing and Urban Development, the Civil Service Commission, the Farmers Home Administration, the Postal Service, the Economic Development Administration, and the Employment Retirement Income Security Administration.

Aside from the IRS and, perhaps, OSHA, all of these are, supposedly, benefits agencies. The patterns of complaints Pettigrew found—unnecessary delays in processing cases, agencies' failure to provide people with information, and "outright rudeness"—were very similar to the ones I heard.

Clearly, then, the message Americans are sending—that they feel and resent the weight of government agencies pressing in on their personal lives—is an urgent one; with the benefit of hindsight, it becomes obvious that they have been trying to get it through for some time. It was expressed at Jimmy Carter's town meetings and phone-ins, for example (not to mention his election itself)—in the plea for help from a Cleveland woman who couldn't get her mother's GI Bill benefits straightened out, the complaint of a Lanham, Maryland job-seeker that she had been frozen out of civil service employment, the California man's protests about letters the Post Office takes forever to deliver, and so on. And, most obvious, there is all that congressional mail.

Unfortunately, the message generally has been ignored. Though Carter described his town meetings as "a learning process rather than a teaching process," the White House seemed more excited about the public relations benefits of being seen listening to people than the listening itself. The press was alternately miffed and condescending. *Time,* for example, thought the questions asked at the televised phone-in in Los Angeles were "either soft or silly"; columnist Joseph Kraft said the radio program that started it all was "a set of 'Dear Abby' phone calls to the President."

Similarly, though congressmen respond vigorously to the specific complaints of their constituents, they rarely dig deeper to discover the patterns of agency practice that underlie them. In most congressional offices, the legislative staff almost never tries to learn anything from the casework staff, which handles complaints (in fact, there's a powerful status difference between the two, and snobbery often keeps the high-status legislative assistants from even talking to the lowly caseworkers). Putting out fires as they occur translates into votes; finding out why so many fires take place, though, would be not only long and tedious, but difficult to dramatize to the folks back home as well.

Thus, Pettigrew blandly reports, "even the offices of those senators and congressmen with legislative responsibility for various programs acknowledge the acute need for administrative reform. The office of Senator Harrison Williams, for example, was extremely critical of the Department of Labor's Office of Workers' Compensation Programs, calling the program 'unresponsive, unorganized, and insensitive.' " Representatives John Dent, Phillip Burton, and William Ford were among those equally critical. As all four gentlemen are, and have been for some time, influential members of the congressional committees that are responsible for the OWCP (Williams is chairman of the Senate Labor Committee; Dent, Burton, and Ford are senior Democrats on House Education and Labor), they obviously bear some of the responsibility for the OWCP's shortcomings. Yet, like most of their colleagues, they have found it easier just to slam away at an agency than to do whatever is necessary to improve it.

Congress not only fails to correct a lot of the problems citizens have with government; it creates a good many of them by writing bad laws. Senator

Lawton Chiles' complaint to Pettigrew that many people's SSI payments go down dramatically whenever their VA benefits go up can be traced to a problem in the law, not the agencies. As a VISTA [Volunteers in Service to America] volunteer representing people at social security hearings, I frequently heard vocational experts testify that my clients should be turned down for disability benefits because they were healthy enough to do sit-down jobs like those at a local Borden's plant. The fact that Borden's had had a "no jobs" sign in the window for as long as anyone could remember was irrelevant; the fact that it was irrelevant was due to the way Congress had written the law.

None of this should be taken to mean that agencies are blameless or that there is nothing they could do to make things more pleasant for the people they deal with. For example, the IRS set up a toll-free number that citizens could call for help with their taxes. Fine. But according to Senator William Proxmire, the line is almost always busy during tax season, for 23 consecutive days in one case. Why offer a service and not deliver it? OSHA made it a practice to concentrate its fire on small businesses rather than large ones; where is the sense in that? And what is the justification for outright rudeness in any situation?

Social Security disability hearings again provide an extraordinary case in point. The agency is notorious for having more than half its determinations that applicants are ineligible for disability benefits or SSI overturned if appealed—usually by its own administrative law judges. What is worse, many congressmen reported, in the four to eight months it takes to get a favorable decision, people have lost their homes, spent hundreds of dollars on lawyers, even died. When I asked Michael Naver at Social Security why local bureaucrats made so many wrong determinations in the first place, he pointed out that "the hearing is the first time anyone in the Administration actually sees the applicant—physically sees how he moves, how he talks, how he copes, and so on. Until then, we're just looking at a file." Again, common sense—never mind human decency and courtesy—would seem to cry out for a change in administrative practice here.

As with poor congressional law drafting, obvious deficiencies like these could be remedied with a little more care and concern; for that reason alone they are probably worth reforming. But if bad guys and bad practices were all that there was to the problem, such tinkering with the machinery—the usual activity of reformers—would be all it would take to solve it.

Unfortunately, the problem is far more fundamental than that. It is basic to bureaucracy, built into the relationship between citizens and government in a democratic welfare state. It lies in the simple difference in perspective between agency and citizen, a difference that makes it difficult if not impossible for the two to deal in a mutually satisfactory way. Perhaps it can be best understood by starting with the desk that lies between them.

On one side of the desk is the citizen, a unique individual with a unique set of circumstances. Think of Martha, the woman who, because she had saved for so many years for her burial, had more money in the bank than the SSI law allowed its beneficiaries to have. She is, of course, a whole person, and wanted to be treated as a whole person. Special consideration? Of course. Bend the rules a little? Certainly; I'm different. And she is different, as is every other person who sits on her side of the desk.

Across from her is the bureaucrat. He is there not as a friend or neighbor, but purely as the hired representative of his agency. As much as possible, that agency is supposed to execute the law as written, that is, to function as an efficient machine. It's not supposed to do whatever it—or one of its employees—wants, or feels is right. That means the bureaucrat, sitting as he does at the bottom of the agency ladder, must function as a cog in that machine. He is empowered only to do certain limited things, and only for those clients who are eligible. By definition, he must not look at the whole person, but only at those features that enable him to transform her into a "case," a "file." His first job, then, is to fit this woman before him into a category: eligible or not; if so, for what and on what terms. Once classified, she becomes subject to the same treatment as all others in her category.

So Martha did not get her SSI check. The fact that her savings are for burial purposes, not high living, could not even be considered. If that sounds horrible, consider the alternative: bureaucrats with the discretion to waive the law at their option. One would like to think they would do so for good-hearted purposes, but our experience with government is that agencies that are free to exercise the most discretion in applying the law—the regulatory boards, contracting agencies, even judges sentencing criminals—tend to use that discretion in ways that harm, not help, the average man. As bad as machine bureaucracy is, the obvious alternative is worse.

Even good intentions can't do very much about this fundamental problem of perspective, as I learned from my experience in a legal aid office in Atlanta. Everyone who worked there was zealously dedicated to "serving the people"; their long hours at low pay proved that. We thought of ourselves as the anti-bureaucracy agency, tilting against the local welfare, food stamp, social security, and VA offices on behalf of our clients.

Thus, I was amazed to learn that many poor people regarded us as just another bureaucracy—couldn't they tell the good guys from the bad guys? But they were right. We, too, had our eligibility requirements, kept them waiting in the outer office, got impatient when they didn't keep to our schedules or rambled off the subject. We didn't look at them as whole people any more than our fellow federal employees in the other agencies did.

So what is to be done?

First, although there are limits to what we can do to change bureaucracy, there are ways we can cut it down to size, minimizing the number and complexity of contacts between citizens and agencies. For instance, the vast array of government programs designed to give people sustenance (welfare, disability, social security, unemployment, veterans' pensions, workmen's compensation, food stamps, Medicare, Medicaid) really are addressed only to two simple needs: the need for money to live on, and the need to pay for health care. A guaranteed annual wage (with poverty the only measure of eligibility) and a national health care system would take care of those needs far more simply than the present system, and because of the simplicity, at a reduced cost. Caring for people through outright handouts would also vastly reduce that grating citizen-bureaucrat contact. The advantage of this shines through in the experience of the Social Security Administration. The administration of the old-age pension, whatever you might say about its conception, is simple and popular—I heard almost no complaints about it and neither did the congressmen who reported to Pettigrew. It was the highly complicated SSI, disability, and welfare programs that spawned all sorts of problems.

One reason this kind of simplicity isn't more widespread is that the government's intentions are, in a way, too good—we can't bear to give away money without making sure it's well deserved. Any small-town mayor can tell you that if he wants federal money for some well-deserved project, he has to put up with reams and reams of forms and meetings designed to insure that the construction company doesn't discriminate in its hiring, that the plans are perfectly sound, that the environmental impact of the project won't be adverse, and so on. These are all worthy goals, but they create a lot of bitterness and kill a lot of projects. Sometimes it's better for the government just to take a deep breath and give away the money, trusting its recipient to spend it in reasonable ways and accepting that there will be some who won't.

Of course, any simplification will still leave a lot of bureaucracy standing, so it's important to try to reform what bureaucracy cannot be eliminated. The press can play a large role in this, by giving its audience a running commentary on what parts of the government work, what parts don't, and why, so that we can apply the lessons elsewhere. It certainly doesn't do that now—at the Office of Workers' Compensation Programs, they kept waiting for the flock of reporters to descend when Pettigrew's report came out, but nobody called. Exposing Watergates is fine, but these days lawbreaking is the least of the government's problems.

But most of the burden of dealing with these problems should be shouldered by the government itself. For one thing, we need to teach as well as learn about how bureaucracy works in this country. Our present system of civics education in the public schools, sticking as it does to explications of a constitution that doesn't even mention the bureaucracy, tells people almost nothing about how to make agencies work for them. I would bet that for every thousand people in this country who could list the Bill of Rights and name all nine Supreme Court justices, you would be lucky to find one who could explain his rights against federal agencies and name the members of even one regulatory commission. Because we don't teach these things, we shouldn't be surprised that people feel ignorant and overwhelmed when they have to deal with as many agencies as they do.

Elected officials also need to learn more than they do, and in a democracy learning means listening. Most politicians do this chiefly by taking polls, but pollsters get their answers by asking people questions about the things the pollsters (or more precisely, the people who hire them) think are important. As a result, we end up with reams and reams of data about what grandma thinks about the Panama Canal, assuming she cares enough to have an opinion, and nothing at all about what is on *her* mind. Forums like Jimmy Carter's phone-ins, where the citizens themselves decide what to talk about, would be far more educational for Washingtonians who venture out into the bush than the latest Caddell poll.

Listening, learning, and reading are only the first steps, of course; the government has also to act to make itself work better. Now and then proposals for accomplishing this come forth, usually involving some sort of "ombudsman" agency. But a new spirit is at least as important as a new agency; in fact, the Office of Management and Budget in the executive branch and the General Accounting Office in the legislative could, under their charters, do as much investigating of the government as anyone could want, but they don't. The point is to care enough about the government's grating inefficiencies to attack them with passion.

That passion is mostly absent today because criticism of big government is the exclusive province of the right, which doesn't want social welfare programs in the first place. So proposals to meet the bureaucratic problem head-on usually involve throwing out the baby with the bath—getting rid not only of the bad apparatus but also of the good program it's supposed to implement.

In fact, the bureaucracy crisis is an ideal issue for liberals, who *want* the government to meet the major problems of the nation. As Pettigrew's study showed, popular dissatisfaction with government stems from its failure to deliver on promised services, not from the regulatory ills you see detailed in the Mobil Oil ads. A 1976 survey by Potomac Associates found that Americans—even self-described conservatives—want the government to do more to help the elderly, make college available to young people, reduce air pollution, improve health care, and so on. Liberals need not worry that any concession to critics of bureaucracy is an invitation to reaction—the New Deal has already been ratified.

If anything does set off a wave of right-wing, anti-government fervor, it will be the failure of liberals to see to it that the government Americans want need not be gargantuan or staggeringly complex, and must be delivered efficiently and courteously. Over the years, liberals have responded to popular demands with an impressive set of promises; now they must be willing to deliver on them. It will be a huge effort—Mao, after all, started a "cultural revolution" toward that end, and even that was only partially successful. But if the effort isn't made, the mood of sullen resentment I found in the people I talked with eventually will turn into angry action. And when it does, expect the worst.

Is the Bureaucracy Inefficient, Unnecessary, and Harmful?

CHARLES T. GOODSELL

The Case for the Bureaucracy: A Brief

Our starting point for making the case for bureaucracy is the proposition that its true nature is not outlined in Sunday supplement diatribes, or even in the reasoned argument found in most scholarly writings on the subject. Rather, understanding the quality of American bureaucracy begins with exploring the meaning of actual government agencies for the millions of citizens that experience them every day. The question for these citizens is simply whether the administrative entities encountered do or do not deliver. These "students" of public administration do not approach the subject as a literary or academic plaything but as a set of concrete institutions upon which they depend for obtaining crucial information, providing vital services, alleviating personal problems, and maintaining a safe community. In such "study" the stakes are immediate and the impressions direct and fresh.

Direct reports from citizens on their experiences with bureaucracy—as distinct from generalized conventional wisdom on the subject—indicate that they perceive far more good than bad in their daily interactions with it. Client polls, public opinion surveys, exit interviews, and mailed questionnaires all repeat the basic finding that the majority of encounters are perceived as satisfactory. Bureaucracy is reported as usually providing the services sought and expected. Most of the time it lives up to acceptable standards of efficiency, courtesy, and fairness. Sometimes government agencies perform poorly, of course; innumerable acts of injustice, sloth, and plain rudeness are committed daily in government offices around the country. No one is claiming perfection for bureaucracy. At the same time, the basic conclusion of satisfactory citizen treatment as the *norm* rather than the *exception* flies radically in the face of most literature on the subject. Citizens have an understanding of bureaucracy that those of us who "know" about it professionally seldom seem to attain.

We found, then, that the "water glass" of bureaucracy is perceived by its users as more full than empty. Some critics tend to discount such perceptions as inexact opinions of lay respondents who have been "set up" by the peculiarities of research designs. If so, the citizens were fooled consistently, because different designs revealed the same conclusion. Others say this acceptance reflects the organization's ability to impose an unrecognized ethic of control. The charge is unanswerable since no evidence of mental imprisonment constitutes its "evidence"; but in any case only a few academics are worrying about liberation. Moreover, if direct performance measures can be accepted at face value, several of these measures reveal surprisingly high proportions of success. Unmistakably, the indicators we have say that bureaucracy works most of the time.

Our insights into American bureaucracy are sharpened further when it is studied comparatively rather than as a whole or in isolation. We use the single noun "bureaucracy" but in so doing refer to a vast multitude of enormously varying institutions. The extreme heterogeneity of government agencies is underscored when formally identical or similar pairs of organizations are found, beneath the surface, to differ radically. The bankruptcy of stereotyped thinking about bureaucracy is made even clearer when we discover contrast in aspects of bureaucracy that by reputation are particularly locked into gray uniformity. We noted, for example, that welfare application forms and welfare waiting rooms vary enormously.

Then, too, we find that certain disparaging differentials thought to exist in relation to public bureaucracy disappear under close scrutiny. One of these is the long-standing allegation, made by urban liberals, that municipal bureaucracies deliberately discriminate against the poor and racial minorities. The evidence is overwhelmingly against this proposition. An even older denunciation of bureaucracy, advanced by probusiness conservatives, is that public bureaucracy performs poorly compared to the private sector. Comparison between public and private administration is difficult; but when it is possible to compare, business performance is by no means always shown to be superior to governmental. In fact, government is sometimes favored in measures of efficiency, productivity, and innovation.

Finally, a comparison of American bureaucracy to that of other countries underscores the fact that we in this country have much to be grateful for. Americans usually entertain more favorable perceptions of bureaucratic performance than do citizens of other countries. In the functional area in which every government in the world invests substantial resources—postal service—program statistics rank the United States as a world leader. Doubtless the most caustic critics of American bureaucracy sigh with relief when, after traveling abroad, they return to the relatively efficient public services found in the United States.

A major cause for chronic underestimations of American bureaucratic performance is our tendency to hold unrealistic expectations concerning it. Belonging to a culture used to optimism and problem solving, Americans tend to assume that if announced objectives are not met, something is "wrong." The initial feasibility of the goals tends to remain unconsidered. Belonging also to a business civilization, Americans are used to tangible indicators of achievement, that is, a "bottom line." But in bureaucracy goals tend to be idealistic, diffuse, and vague. They often conflict or even contradict. As a result, observers are easily led to conclude that "failure" has occurred because one or more objectives have not been met. Hence, in a way, public bureaucracy does not "fit" American culture too well, which is one reason why its cultural images are so negative. Although individual citizens have mostly satisfactory concrete experiences with bureaucracy, they too encounter divergence from time to time between personal goals and bureaucratic behavior. Regardless of whether this divergence is justified or not, it is transformed into an objectified symbol of contempt: "red tape."

The reasonably good record of American bureaucratic performance could be even better if more of it were direct in nature. But because of various reasons, U.S. public administration has become marked by extensive use of indirect means of implementation, especially via grants, contracts, and credit mechanisms. This "administration by proxy" operates under several severe handicaps including increased overall complexity and reduced control of resources. Agencies delegating the "proxy" often become little more than application processors and check writers that are held accountable for work they themselves do not perform. For their part, bureaucracies delegated the "proxy" must spend untold resources scurrying for grants, contracts, and loans; on receiving the awards, they must deal with the attached strings and respond to policy desires not necessarily initiated within their own political constituencies. Thus the administrative givers and receivers both end up working under added operational burdens and from an eroded political base.

Bureaucracy is further handicapped by the tendency of Americans to expect more from it than just a good job. Bureaucracy is supposed to manipulate successfully conditions in society so as to remove "problems," that is, things identified by someone as painful or unfortunate. Moreover, because of intervening variables, bureaucracy may do everything possible to correct an external condition without removing it. A manufacturing firm can control the product it produces and is thus in a position to influence the terms on which its work is evaluated. A public bureaucracy, evaluated on the resultant effects of its output, must largely hope for the best.

Bureaucracy is often portrayed as incapable of fostering social change. This is in part also an inflated expectation in that bureaucracies must be recognized as dependent on power and authority external to themselves (even though also possessing both in ample amounts); they cannot be expected to overturn power structures that establish them in the first place. Beyond this limitation, public agencies constantly stimulate and implement changes, although the changes wrought may not always be the particular ones the critics themselves want. Even so, the kinds of substantive change encountered by different public bureaucracies are so manifold in character that somewhere in the society administrative "change agents" operate to please just about everybody, regardless of their position on the political spectrum.

Our misleading stereotypes of bureaucracy extend to the men and women who staff them, the bureaucrats. Yet a sixth of the working population are bureaucrats, broadly speaking. One needs a creative imagination indeed to classify all of these millions as dullards, lazy bums, incompetents, and malicious oppressors. Actually, apart from race and gender considerations, this sector of the population is very similar to the population at large in terms of demographics. Yet, despite the bureaucrats' "ordinariness," the academic model builders have for some forty years entertained the notion of an ominous "bureaucratic mentality." Under empirical examination such an attitudinal syndrome evaporates into thin air. Bureaucrats are no more authoritarian than any citizen, and their attitudes toward clients are a far cry from patronizing or oppressive.

Also, the academicians have labored mightily to portray the bureaucrat as a pathetic victim, subject to repressive controls and deep psychic damage while working under the well-worn nemesis of hierarchy. Certainly Weber's "tight harness" is too restrictive for some, including most of the professors who attack it. But for millions of others, working in bureaucracy is perceived as holding a fairly good job. Empirical studies show that bureaucrats experience no more (and perhaps less) alienation than other individuals, and by various measures, job satisfaction levels are reasonably high. Again, if the "psychic prison" prohibits recognition of deep alienation, only those few outsiders who can miraculously see through the delusion realize its true extent.

Several misconceptions also prevail about bureaucracy's tendencies with respect to organizational size, growth, and aging. Loose talk of giantism—often centering on the huge size of federal budgets and the largest federal agencies—misrepresents the range of bigness versus smallness found in administrative institutions within the public sector. The daily experiences of people with bureaucracy have little to do with gross expenditure totals or the aggregated vastness of the Department of Defense or Postal Service. What counts is the actual offices and institutions where citizens work and obtain services. Most of these entities are surprisingly small, even tiny, in terms of numbers of employees. According to our admittedly imperfect data, the vast majority of federal installations and local governments employ less than twenty-five people.

Moreover, bureaucracies by no means continually or inevitably grow in size. Some get bigger, some remain stable, others actually decline in numbers of employees. Much of the growth that occurs is due to population or work-load expansion rather than Parkinson's Law or similar imperatives, whether jocular or not. Regardless of changes in size, no evidence is available to support contentions that bigness creates "badnesses" of inefficiency and rigidity. In fact, some empirical studies come to the opposite conclusion. Still another misconception is that bureaucracies never die and become ossified and captured with age. All of these venerable notions collapse when confronted by evidence.

Bureaucracy is often regarded as possessing uncontrollable political power and hence engaging in subversion of democracy. Certainly public agencies possess political power, as they must to perform at all. But this power is not unrestrained. Multiple controls exist, and bureaucrats have incentives to follow as well as lead. Bureaucracies check each other, and in the United States external sources of restriction operate in unusual number and with a particularly strong net effect. American bureaucracy may well be the most inhibited on earth.

Bureaucracy is accused of contributing to socioeconomic inequities in society and a sense of policy drift within the polity. The underlying notion here is that administration corrupts politics, a reversal of the causal direction propounded at an earlier time in the field of public administration. Such a view gives far too much credit to bureaucracy's influence. Public administrators may not mount revolutionary barricades or initiate moral crusades, but at the same time they are hardly to blame for the existence of either capitalism or pluralism. In fact, public bureaucracies help considerably to ameliorate the adverse consequences of each.

Questions for Discussion

1. What are the similarities and differences between the government bureaucracy and the private bureaucracy?
2. What demands made on the government bureaucracy weaken efficiency of performance?
3. What criteria should be used to determine the effectiveness of government agencies?
4. What is the relationship between big government and individual liberty?
5. How can waste in government be reduced?

Suggested Readings

Bollier, David, and Joan Claybrook. "Regulations That Work." *Washington Monthly*, 18, no. 3 (April 1986), 47–54.

Fitzgerald, Randall, and Gerald Lipson. *Porkbarrel: The Unexpurgated Grace Commission Story of Congressional Profligacy*. Washington, D.C.: Cato Institute, 1986.

Grace, J. Peter. *Burning Money: The Waste of Your Tax Dollars*. New York: Macmillan, 1984.

Karl, Barry D. "The American Bureaucrat: A History of a Sheep in Wolves' Clothing." *Public Administration Review*, 47, no. 1 (January–February 1987), 26–44.

McKinney, Jerome B., and Michael Johnston, eds. *Fraud, Waste, and Abuse of Government: Causes, Consequences, and Cures*. Philadelphia: Institute for the Study of Human Issues, 1986.

Meier, Kenneth J. *Politics and the Bureaucracy: Policymaking in the Fourth Branch of Government*. 2nd ed. Monterey, Calif.: Brooks/Cole, 1987.

Milward, H. Brinton, and Hal G. Rainey. "Don't Blame the Bureaucracy!" *Journal of Public Policy*, 3, no. 2 (May 1983), 149–168.

Murphy, Cait. "Unfinished Business: Who's Holding Up Grace Commission Reform?" *Policy Review*, no. 38 (Fall 1986), 60–65.

Newitt, Jane. "In Search of the Bloated Bureaucracy." *American Demographics*, 8, no. 3 (March 1986), 26–29, 54–56.

Von Ward, Paul. *Dismantling the Pyramid: Government . . . by the People*. Washington, D.C.: Delphi Press, 1981.

Chapter 14

Should the Supreme Court Be Guided by a Philosophy of Judicial Activism?

Of the three branches of the federal government—president, Congress, and the Supreme Court—the last is the least democratic. Although representative democracy requires periodic elections, the members of the Supreme Court are appointed, never run for office in popular elections, and, once on the Court, usually remain there for life or until they retire. Presidents, senators, and representatives may envy the justices' luxury of not having to run for public office.

The Supreme Court's power of judicial review is—at least on the surface—another undemocratic feature of this arm of government. Judicial review is the power of the Supreme Court to examine state and federal laws and the acts of state and federal public officials to determine whether they are in conflict with the Constitution. If these laws and acts are in conflict, then the Court may declare them invalid. The fact that a majority of nine unelected members of the Court may declare null and void the laws enacted by the representatives of the majority of the people who vote seems to be a limitation on the principle of majority rule. The argument is often made, however, that the specific content of court decisions has strengthened rather than weakened democracy.

Judicial review is not the practice in all representative democracies. The British system of government, for example, permits the courts to interpret the laws but not to declare an act of Parliament void. Judicial review is not specifically mentioned in the Constitution of the United States. Debate surrounds the question of whether the Framers intended the Supreme Court to have this power over the laws of the Federal government. There is general agreement, however, that the Framers understood that judicial review is applicable to acts of state legislatures in conflict with the Constitution. The Supreme Court first declared an act of Congress unconstitutional in *Marbury* v. *Madison* (1803).[1] In this case the court found the Judiciary Act of 1789 to be in conflict with Article III of the Constitution. Today, the Supreme Court's authority to declare a statute unconstitutional is unchallenged.

Over the past century the Supreme Court has exercised its power of judicial review in a variety of cases. Those who have benefited from the Court's decisions have hailed the wisdom of the Court. The "losers" have called for a variety of responses, including limiting the jurisdiction of the Court, amending the Constitution, enlarging the size of the Court, or impeaching the chief justice.

Court decisions have not supported one group of people exclusively. In the early part of the twentieth century, for example, Court decisions were more favorable to property owners, states' rights advocates, and segregationists. Since the days of the Warren Court (for former Chief Justice Earl Warren) in the mid-1950s, however, Court decisions have been more favorable to groups demanding extension of civil rights and civil liberties. The changing character of Supreme Court decisions is a reflection of such factors as the composition of the Court, legal precedents, and the political environment. One other factor that has received much attention, however, is the philosophical outlook of the judges.

Two principal philosophical outlooks have marked the role of the judge: judicial activism and judicial restraint. Those who favor judicial activism contend that judges should exercise individual judgment in declaring statutes unconstitutional. They argue that taking sides politically is inevitable and that there are no neutral principles of law constraining court members but rather a larger concept of justice. Judges, they add, should use their power to achieve goals they consider important for society as a whole.

Those who favor judicial restraint argue that judges should avoid substituting their own policy preferences for those of duly elected public officials. The task of the judges, according to this view, is to apply the law, not assert biases in favor of social reform.

Nonlawyers are often unconcerned with these different philosophies and tend to be more interested in the actual outcomes of Supreme Court decisions than in the attitudes governing the judges in making their decisions. To the layperson, moreover, it is often easier to evaluate the decision of the Supreme Court in liberal-conservative terms than to look at the reasons behind the decisions. These perceptions have led many people to believe that judges have changed their position from liberal to conservative (or vice versa) when in fact the judges have not changed their philosophical outlook.

The case of Felix Frankfurter may be used as an example. Frankfurter was an advocate of judicial restraint. When he was appointed to the Supreme Court during Franklin Roosevelt's second administration, the Supreme Court was declaring New Deal legislation unconstitutional. Frankfurter sided with the liberal Congress over the conservative Court because of his belief in the limited role of the Court.

When in the 1950s Congress was passing conservative laws, Frankfurter often sided with the conservative legislature in upholding laws even when he regarded those laws as undesirable. Frankfurter was then considered a conservative by many people. In fact, Frankfurter did not change. He remained consistent to his principles about what the role of the courts should be.

In practice these two philosophies of the role of the Supreme Court are rarely held in absolute form. More often than not, Supreme Court justices and legal scholars support activism in some cases and restraint in others.

The case for judicial activism is made by Luther M. Swygert, a former senior judge, U.S. Court of Appeals for the Seventh Circuit. He makes the following arguments:

1. Judicial activism is consistent with democratic theory. In this regard, there are checks on the power of the federal courts, and the Constitution contains several provisions that call for non-majoritarian elements in the government.
2. There is evidence that the Framers intended for the courts to have the power to interpret the Constitution and provide the ultimate check on the other branches of government.
3. No other branch of government is so capable of preserving the integrity of the constitutional safeguards of the system as the courts.
4. Decisions that were criticized as being activist in the past were not the result of a judicial usurpation of power but rather of the violations of the constitutional rights of individuals upon which the legislative or executive branches could have acted but failed to do so.

Judicial activism is criticized by Malcolm Richard Wilkey, a former senior judge, U.S. Court of Appeals for the District of Columbia Circuit. He makes the following arguments:

1. Judicial activists have created new procedural mechanisms that expand the class of litigants, causes of action, and available remedies, thus providing a broader base for further judicial activism.
2. The judicial branch has broadened the scope of rights, thus empowering it to act.
3. The courts are unsuited to make policy determinations.
4. Judicial activism produces adverse consequences, such as (a) the imposition of so heavy a burden on the courts that they are unable to fulfill the tasks for which they were originally designed, (b) the opposition of the public to judicial policy making, (c) the diminished reputation of the courts because of their failure to have their decisions accepted by the public, and (d) the emergence of a movement to restrict judicial power.

Wilkey attributes judicial activism to the willingness of individual judges and the abdication of responsibility by the other two branches of the federal government, particularly Congress.

NOTE

1. *Marbury* v. *Madison*, 1 Cranch 137 (1803).

Should the Supreme Court Be Guided by a Philosophy of Judicial Activism?

LUTHER M. SWYGERT
In Defense of Judicial Activism

Judicial activism traditionally uses the principles built into the Constitution and statutory law to foster the ends of social justice. The term connotes a liberal approach so as to read into legal norms the essence of due process and equal protection under the law. Those are the two most fundamental concepts of individual rights embraced by the Constitution. Today judicial activism is under attack.[1]

Recently, the judiciary, especially the federal judiciary, has been criticized for exceeding its powers and invading the province of the legislative and executive branches. In a speech before the Federal Legal Council, the Attorney General of the United States, William French Smith, accused the federal courts of "making unwise intrusions upon the legislative domain." He explained that the policy of the Reagan Administration regarding the federal bench is to discourage judicial activism:

> We believe that the groundswell of conservatism evidenced by the 1980 election makes this an especially appropriate time to urge upon the courts more principled bases [of decisionmaking] that would diminish judicial activism. . . . In recent decades, . . . Federal courts have engaged in a . . . kind of judicial policymaking. In the future, the Justice Department will focus upon the doctrines that have led to the courts' activism. We will attempt to reverse this unhealthy flow of power from state and Federal legislatures to Federal Courts. . . .

Some members of Congress echo the criticism voiced by the Attorney General. Senator Jesse Helms of North Carolina has introduced a bill to deprive the federal courts of jurisdiction to hear cases concerning school prayer. Other bills pending before Congress would restrict federal-court jurisdiction over cases involving abortion and school busing.

The idea that the courts have overstepped the bounds of judicial review and usurped legislative and executive powers is not new. In fact, it has been around since the adoption of the Constitution. Chief Justice Marshall's landmark decision in *Marbury v. Madison,* holding that the Supreme Court had the power to declare acts of Congress unconstitutional, engendered much controversy. Criti-

I am indebted to my law clerk, Barbara E. Rook, for her invaluable assistance in the research and writing of this article.—Author's Note.

cism of the Supreme Court's activism enjoyed a renaissance during the 1920s and 1930s, when the Court struck down much of the economic and business legislation of the day, and again during the years of the Warren Court, which was accused of acting as a "super-legislature," especially in the areas of desegregation, reapportionment, criminal procedure, and prisoners' rights.

Inasmuch as I am, admittedly, one of the so-called "activist" judges, I must respond to these critics, both past and present, by saying that they fail to recognize the basic principles of our constitutional system of government and the structural realities of our political system. It is my contention that judges who have made activist decisions have not done so out of any desire to preempt the powers of other branches of government or to impose their individual political or social philosophies on others. But when other branches of government failed to take action, the courts acted in order to enforce the provisions of the Constitution.

I. DEMOCRATIC THEORY AND THE COURTS

Many commentators have characterized the judicial branch as undemocratic and therefore inconsistent with our form of government. Professor Commager, writing almost thirty years ago, called judicial review "a drag . . . upon democracy," and, more recently, Professor Bickel referred to the Supreme Court as "a deviant institution in the American Democracy." The question often asked is: "Why should a majority of nine Justices appointed for life be permitted to outlaw as unconstitutional the acts of elected officials or of officers controlled by elected officials?"

There are two answers to this criticism. First, there are checks on the power of the federal courts. When the courts are interpreting legislation, their decisions are subject to change by the Congress. Even when a decision is based on the Constitution, it may be altered through the procedure of constitutional amendment. Another political check on the courts is the power of the President to appoint all federal judges and Supreme Court Justices, subject to the approval of the Senate.

There are other informal checks on the power of the federal courts. The Executive Branch may simply refuse to enforce a court order, or lower courts may decline to follow the decision of a higher court. Further, Congress can use its spending power to frustrate enforcement of a judicial mandate. Finally, several commentators have argued persuasively that the power of the courts is subject in the final analysis to the power of the people to accept or reject the principles expounded by their courts. As Professor Bickel stated:

> The Supreme Court's judgments may be put forth as universally prescriptive; but they actually become so only when they gain widespread assent.

They bind of their own force no one but the parties to a litigation. To realize the promise that all others similarly situated will be similarly bound, the Court's judgments need the assent and the cooperation first of the political institutions, and ultimately of the people.

The second answer to the criticism that the courts are undemocratic is that our system of government is not a pure democracy. The dictionary definition of democracy is "government by the people: rule of the majority," but our Constitution contains several provisions that call for nonmajoritarian elements in the government, of which the courts are only one example. The Constitution itself is protected from changes desired by a mere majority by Article V, which requires more than a simple majority to enact amendments.

Our constitutional system embodies the principle of majority rule but limits the power of majorities by guaranteeing certain individual rights which cannot be abridged, even by the majority. Several commentators have concluded that the courts are undemocratic, but properly so. Those who argue that equating democracy with majoritarianism is too simplistic attempt to integrate the courts into their theory by defining "democracy" broadly so as to include the role of the judicial branch. Whether the courts are characterized as consistent or inconsistent with anyone's political definition of democracy is unimportant. What is important is that the Constitution guarantees certain individual rights to those whose interests may not be protected through the traditional democratic processes, and that the courts are the guardians of those rights. As Justice Jackson once noted, "The very purpose of a Bill of Rights was to withdraw certain subjects from the vicissitudes of political controversy, to place them beyond the reach of majorities and officials and to establish them as legal principles to be applied by the courts."

II. THE INTENT OF THE FRAMERS

Some commentators have argued that the Founding Fathers never intended the Supreme Court to be the primary check on abuses of power by the states and other branches of government. They relied in part on the position taken by the Jeffersonian Democrats during the late eighteenth century that the Supreme Court was too powerful and that the legislative branch should predominate. Other scholars have found ample evidence for the conclusion that "the courts were intended from the beginning to have the power that they have exercised." Justice Jackson believed that "[i]t is probable that many, and it is certain that some, members of the Constitutional Convention appreciated that [the clause providing for the judicial power and the supremacy clause] would spell out a power in the Supreme Court to pass on the constitutionality of federal legislation," although he noted that the judicial power was "the least debated of any of the important implications of the instrument."

James Madison, speaking at the congressional debate on the Bill of Rights, stated:

> If [these amendments] are incorporated into the Constitution, indepen-
> dent tribunals of justice will consider themselves in a peculiar manner the
> guardian of those rights; they will be an impenetrable bulwark against
> every assumption of power in the Legislature or the Executive; they will
> be naturally led to resist every encroachment upon rights expressly stipu-
> lated for in the Constitution by the declaration of rights.

This statement shows a recognition by Madison of the powerful role the federal courts would necessarily play in protecting individual rights guaranteed by the Constitution from infringement by the legislative or executive branches. Further evidence that the Founding Fathers intended the courts to have the power to inter- pret the Constitution and provide the ultimate check on the other branches of government may be found in Alexander Hamilton's essay, *The Federalist No. 78:*

> Some perplexity respecting the rights of the courts to pronounce legisla-
> tive acts void, because contrary to the constitution, has arisen from an
> imagination that the doctrine would imply a superiority of the judiciary to
> the legislative power. . . .
> . . . [T]he courts were designed to be an intermediate body between
> the people and the legislature, in order, among other things, to keep the
> latter within the limits assigned to their authority. The interpretation of the
> laws is the proper and peculiar province of the courts. A constitution is, in
> fact, and must be regarded by the judges, as a fundamental law. It there-
> fore belongs to them to ascertain its meaning as well as the meaning of
> any particular act proceeding from the legislative body.

These statements of the framers and the provisions of the Constitution itself demonstrate that the federal courts must have the authority to declare acts of Con- gress, state legislative enactments, and executive actions unconstitutional. The supremacy clause made the Constitution the supreme law of the land, but "main- taining the supremacy of the Constitution [requires] a strong and independent judiciary, possessing the power and the authority to resolve disputes of a constitu- tional nature between the states, between the states and the national govern- ment, and, most importantly, between individuals and governmental institu- tions." Both Madison and Hamilton knew that the rights guaranteed by the Con- stitution would mean little without a federal judiciary to enforce its provisions.

III. THE LEGISLATIVE AND EXECUTIVE BRANCHES

It is certainly true that the legislative and executive branches are as bound by the principles of the Constitution as are the federal courts. Nevertheless, the structure of our system of government makes it imperative that there be an independent judicial branch to ensure that the states and the other two branches of government adhere to the constitutional limitations on their power; no other branch of government is so capable of preserving the integrity of the constitutional safeguards.

A. The Legislative Branch

Legislators are not independent or disinterested; rather, they are politicians who are answerable to the voters who put them into office. They must run on their records and therefore are preoccupied with the possible political consequences of the positions they take on various issues. Legislators are more often subject to significant time pressures; the schedule of a legislative session will be crowded with many bills to be considered, and legislators, in addition to working on legislative business, must participate in political activities and spend time in their home districts.

Legislation is often the product of long, hard-fought negotiation and compromise. Powerful interest groups employ lobbyists to influence legislators' votes on pending bills. Further, legislators must consider the majority of situations to which a law will apply, and potential negative consequences for individuals or minority groups may be outweighed by potential benefits, or even unknown at the time a bill is under consideration.

B. The Executive Branch

An examination of the structure of the executive branch reveals limitations similar to those of the legislature. Executive officials are answerable directly or indirectly to the electorate; therefore, their decisions, like those of legislators, are influenced by what would be politically safe or popular. Executive and administrative officials are also subject to political pressures from constituencies and interest-group lobbyists. Moreover, although executive officials often act on a problem more quickly than legislators, such actions may be in response to a political storm or a public whim.

C. The Judiciary

An independent judiciary is institutionally suited to safeguarding constitutional principles. Federal judges are not answerable to any constituency and are thus insulated from most political pressures. They are therefore in a better position than legislators or executive officials to protect the constitutional rights of individuals, even when that requires a politically unpopular decision.

The other two branches of government and the states may simply refuse to act, but a court, when presented with a concrete case, must make a decision. Many commentators have noted that the courts are most often criticized for activist decisions in cases in which state governments or the other branches of the federal government could have acted to prevent or remedy constitutional violations but failed to do so. Further, with an actual case before it, a court can deal with the possible unforeseen effects of a law on an individual. Finally, the absence of direct political responsibility on judges and the "deliberative, contemplative" nature of the judicial process results in more thoughtful decisions.

IV. "ACTIVIST" DECISIONS OF THE PAST

To support my contention that activist judicial decisions are the result of judges fulfilling their duty to uphold the Constitution and not the result of any judicial usurpation of power, I rely on an examination of some past decisions. These decisions were criticized at the time as examples of the federal courts' overstepping the bounds of judicial review and resolving questions more properly left to the legislative or executive branches. Looking at these decisions with the benefit of hindsight, however, will show that the constitutional rights of individuals had been violated and that the legislative or executive branches could have acted but failed to do so. It was thus left to the federal courts to safeguard the rights guaranteed by the Constitution.

A. Reapportionment

As recently as 1946, the Supreme Court refused to consider a constitutional challenge to a state districting plan. In *Colegrove v. Green*, the plaintiffs alleged that the Illinois legislature had failed to reapportion congressional districts since 1901, and that the great changes in the population distribution in the intervening forty-five years made the 1901 map unfair and unrepresentative. The three-judge district court dismissed the complaint, and the Supreme Court affirmed on the ground that "due regard for the effective working of our Government reveal[s] this issue to be of a peculiarly political nature and therefore not meet for judicial determination."

Justice Frankfurter, writing for the plurality, stated that:

Courts ought not to enter this political thicket. The remedy for unfairness in districting is to secure State legislatures that will apportion properly, or to invoke the ample powers of Congress. . . . The Constitution has left the performance of many duties in our governmental scheme to depend on the fidelity of the executive and legislative action and, ultimately, on the vigilance of the people in exercising their political rights.

Justice Black disagreed:

What is involved here is the right to vote guaranteed by the Federal Constitution. It has always been the rule that where a federally protected right has been invaded the federal courts will provide the remedy to rectify the wrong done. Federal courts have not hesitated to exercise their equity power in cases involving deprivation of property and liberty. . . . There is no reason why they should do so where the case involves the right to choose representatives that make laws affecting liberty and property.

The problems with the remedy for malapportionment suggested by Justice Frankfurter in *Colegrove*—resort to the state legislatures or Congress—are apparent. It is unrealistic to expect legislators to vote to correct malapportionment in the very districts that put them into office. But to allow malapportioned districts to remain in the absence of legislative action would fly in the face of the constitutional guarantee of the right to vote, which would be jeopardized if the voting strength of some persons or groups could be diluted or destroyed by those in power. The inaction of state legislatures and Congress thus made it clear that it was up to the federal judiciary to preserve this constitutional right.

As Professor Auerbach has noted, it is anomalous for critics of judicial activism to suggest that the courts defer to the legislative branch on questions of apportionment. The idea that legislative action or inaction merits deference from the courts is based on the assumption that such action is the product of a vote by the majority of representatives who were elected by a majority of the voters, but malapportionment effectively destroys that assumption.

Access to the legislative process in a truly representative democracy must be open to all citizens. Therefore, the integrity of the political process must be preserved. Because the legislative branch cannot or will not perform this function, it is the responsibility of the courts to ensure that the principle of one-man/one-vote is effectuated in our federal and state electoral systems.

In 1964, in *Reynolds v. Sims* and its companion cases, the Supreme Court recognized its duty to protect the constitutional rights of those citizens whose right to vote had been infringed by malapportionment. In the majority opinion in *Reynolds*, Chief Justice Warren stated:

Since the achieving of fair and effective representation for all citizens is concededly the basic aim of legislative apportionment, we conclude that the Equal Protection Clause guarantees the opportunity for equal participation by all voters in the election of . . . legislators. . . . We are cautioned about the dangers of entering into political thickets and mathematical quagmires. Our answer is this: a denial of constitutionally protected rights demands judicial protection; our oath and our office require no less of us.

The continuing need for federal court action in protecting the constitutional right to vote is evidenced by recent challenges to malapportioned legislative districting plans. This responsibility is one the courts cannot and must not abdicate in deference to the legislative branch of government if the Constitution is to be preserved as the supreme law of the land.

B. Prisoners' Rights

I have witnessed a great change in the development of the law on prisoners' rights during my years on the bench. Originally, courts routinely relied on the "hands-off" doctrine in refusing to review prisoners' complaints charging inhuman treatment and civil rights violations. Even as recently as 1960, a federal district court dismissed a prisoner's complaint alleging that prison officials had failed to provide him proper medical treatment; the court found that "to allow such actions would be prejudicial to the proper maintenance of [prison] discipline."

Courts and commentators offered several justifications for the hands-off doctrine. First, it was said that the administration of federal prisons was entrusted to the discretion of the executive branch and therefore judicial intervention would violate the principle of separation of powers. Second, principles of federalism dictate that federal courts should not interfere in the administration of state prisons. Third, judges lack expertise and experience in prison administration.

The failure of both executive officials and legislators to take action to remedy the shocking conditions that exist in our penal institutions has caused the demise of the hands-off doctrine. As the Supreme Court recognized,

[a] policy of judicial restraint cannot encompass any failure to take cognizance of valid constitutional claims whether arising in a federal or state institution. When a prison regulation or practice offends a fundamental constitutional guarantee, federal courts will discharge their duty to protect constitutional rights.

The inaction on the part of executive officials and legislators is the result of several factors. Prison officials often take no initiative in instituting reform because of "bureaucratic inertia." Further, prison administrators are limited by budgetary constraints beyond their control. Legislators have few incentives to appropriate funds for upgrading prison conditions; prisoners are an unpopular minority whose plight engenders little public support, especially at a time when there is a growing concern about crime. Prisoners themselves are often disenfranchised, and a disproportionately large number of them come from racial and socioeconomic groups that are politically powerless. It is therefore not surprising that inhuman conditions in prisons have persisted despite the power of legislators and administrators to initiate improvements.

Federal judges are not anxious to intervene in the administration of prisons, but they have been forced to do so by the continued action of state and federal executive officials and legislators. For the judges to do otherwise would be an abrogation of their duty to uphold the Constitution.

In 1977, I sat on the panel that heard the case of *Green v. Carlson*. In that case, the plaintiff was the mother of a prisoner who had been incarcerated at the federal penitentiary at Terre Haute, Indiana. The plaintiff alleged that her son had been admitted to the prison hospital suffering from a serious asthma attack, that no physician was on duty and none was called during the eight-hour period the prisoner was in this condition, and that as a result of injections by an unlicensed nurse of a drug inappropriate for the treatment of asthma, the prisoner died. The district court dismissed the complaint on the ground that under state law, the cause of action did not survive the decedent. The Seventh Circuit Court reversed, noting that the anomalous result of that holding would allow recovery for injury but not death. We found that whether or not a federal civil rights action survives must be a question of federal common law because "[t]he liability of federal agents for violation of constitutional rights should not depend upon where the violation occurred." We went on to hold that under the Supreme Court's decision in *Estelle v. Gamble*, the plaintiff's complaint in *Green* stated a claim. In *Estelle*, the Court recognized that "deliberate indifference to serious medical needs of prisons constitutes the 'unnecessary and wanton infliction of pain' . . . proscribed by the Eighth Amendment."

It seems incredible to think that only a few years ago a prisoner in similar circumstances was without a remedy in federal court. Today, it is settled that the deprivation of basic human rights in prison amounts to a constitutional violation that will be remedied by the courts. I believe that whatever improvements have been made in the law concerning prisoners' constitutional rights and in prison conditions have been almost solely due to the decisions of the federal courts. These allegedly interventionist decisions have made it clear that the courts can be relied on to protect the constitutional rights of individuals when the other branches of government do not do so.

C. Desegregation

The desegregation cases decided by the Warren Court during the 1950s and 1960s were particularly controversial. This was an area of the law in which the Constitution, in section 5 of the fourteenth amendment, expressly provided for

Congress to have broad enforcement powers. But, despite this clear authority, Congress refused to exercise its section 5 power to remedy the conditions of racial inequality that existed throughout our nation by the time the Supreme Court decided *Brown v. Board of Education.*

Chief Justice Warren, writing for the Court in *Brown,* found that "education is perhaps the most important function of state and local governments," and concluded that "[s]uch an opportunity, where the state has undertaken to provide it, is a right which must be made available to all on equal terms." In holding that separate but equal educational facilities violated the fourteenth amendment's guarantee of equal protection, the Court relied on the psychological effect of segregation on school children: "To separate them from others of similar age and qualifications solely because of their race generates a feeling of inferiority as to their status in the community that may affect their hearts and minds in a way unlikely ever to be undone."

Much of the criticism of the *Brown* decision is based upon the Court's use of psychological or sociological data. "No court, say the dissatisfied, has the competence or the jurisdiction to weigh evidence which is 'sociological' rather than 'legal' in character. The impact of school segregation upon the psychology of Negro children . . . [is] political . . . not legal . . . , and [is] properly the business of legislators, not judges." To ignore this evidence from the social sciences, however, would have been to ignore the facts. The justices did not hold themselves out as having expertise or training in education or psychology; rather, they relied on the best information available from the experts.

Another criticism of *Brown* and the other desegregation decisions was that the Court was acting "almost entirely without the support of Congress." Although it is certainly correct that the Supreme Court led the way in protecting the constitutional rights of minority groups, the support of Congress was forthcoming, as evidenced by the passage of the Civil Rights Act of 1964 and subsequent equal rights legislation. As Judge J. Skelly Wright has noted, the Court in *Brown* "awakened the nation's conscience" to the problem of racial inequality. Although the principles espoused in the *Brown* decision have been popularly accepted, controversy continues over how best to effectuate those policies.

V. CONCLUSION

Judge Frank M. Johnson of the United States Court of Appeals for the Eleventh Circuit has spoken eloquently on the subject of judicial activism:

> [I]t is my firm belief that the judicial activism which has generated so much criticism is, in most instances, not activism at all. Courts do not relish making such hard decisions and certainly do not encourage litiga-

tion on social or political problems. But . . . the federal judiciary . . . has the paramount and continuing duty to uphold the law. When a "case or controversy" is properly presented, the court may not shirk its sworn responsibility to uphold the Constitution. . . . The courts are bound to take jurisdiction and decide the issues—even though those decisions result in criticism. . . . And, finally, I submit that history has shown, with few exceptions, that decisions of the federal judiciary over a period of time have become accepted and revered as monuments memorializing the strength and stability of this nation.

The responsibility for trends in the development of the law, whether in the direction of activism or judicial restraint, do not belong solely to the members of the federal judiciary. Lawyers play a vital role in shaping this development. The questions presented to judges are framed by lawyers within the context of actual controversies. The decisions of the court are many times influenced by the advocacy of the lawyer; his creativity and persuasiveness often determine whether the law stands still or moves forward.

The responsibility for the growth of the law and for its flexibility in meeting the changing needs of our society has never belonged to the judiciary alone— or even to the legislative or executive branches of government. That responsibility has already been shared by the members of the legal profession. Therefore, the activist trends in judicial decisions could not have come about without support from the bar. Further, although the federal courts may often lead the way in initiating change in some areas of constitutional law, these decisions have become important because they have been accepted by the public and the other branches of government.

Lawyers, judges, members of Congress, executive officials, and state-elected officials share the responsibility for preserving the independence of the judiciary. The judicial branch must continue to be insulated from political pressures in order to function properly; if the independence of the judiciary is destroyed by the "court curbing" bills now pending in Congress or by increased political answerability to the electorate or to members of Congress, the only effective safeguard against the infringement of constitutional rights will be lost.

NOTE

1. As it has come to be used today, the word "activism" connotes a liberal and expanding judicial approach to legal problems. This usage, however, perverts the true meaning of the word. A politically conservative judge may be just as active in narrowing the application of a statute or in cutting back individual rights as a liberal judge may be in the pursuit of what he regards as desirable social or political ends. . . .

Should the Supreme Court Be Guided by a Philosophy of Judicial Activism?

MALCOLM RICHARD WILKEY

Judicial Activism, Congressional Abdication, and the Need for Constitutional Reform

After a long hot summer in Philadelphia, on September 17, 1787, delegates to the Constitutional Convention signed the document described by Prime Minister Gladstone as "the most wonderful work ever struck off at a given time by the brain and purpose of man." On September 17, 1987, America will celebrate the bicentennial of the first of the modern written constitutions, and one of the most influential single documents in history. This great instrument, which has served as a model for other constitutions around the globe, has survived with comparatively scant textual changes.

Although the letter of the Constitution may endure, the nature and spirit of that document have never been more obscure. Great structural and philosophical changes have been smuggled into the relatively static text by the very authority charged with guarding the Constitution's original design. There is an increasingly widespread perception that the Judiciary has created this problem by making law instead of performing its ordained role of discovery and interpretation. Proposals for judicial reform have proliferated.

After serving in the Judiciary for fifteen years, I have an increasing perception of vices in my own branch and of a need for reform. While change in the Judiciary is crucial, the ultimate source of judicial vice is broader and more deeply rooted. A simple solution, confined to that one branch of the Federal Government, would not suffice to restore the Constitution's true character. The causes of judicial waywardness derive from and have produced related problems in the other two branches, indeed a distortion of our whole fabric of constitutional government. In order to restore true constitutional government, we must look not only to judicial activism, but to those related problems in the Executive and Legislature.

Congress is paralyzed. This is due in large part to its constant attention to the need for reelection—a need on which powerful special interest groups play. It no longer performs the role set for it in the Constitution to make the fundamen-

This article is based upon a speech delivered before the Harvard Society for Law & Public Policy on April 3, 1984, at the Harvard Law School. The author wishes to acknowledge the use in sections I and II of material from his monograph, Activism by the Branch of Last Resort: Of the Seizure of Abandoned Swords and Purses *(1984), published by the National Legal Center for the Public Interest in Washington, D.C.*

tal policy choices for the nation. Consequently, the federal courts now make many of those choices. Judges, because they need not stand for reelection (and perhaps because making fundamental policy choices is interesting work), are willing to make and administer difficult policy decisions. Courts, however, are ill-suited to be the policy-makers in a democratic society: They are not privy to the sort of information needed to make policy decisions, and, more to the point, allowing them to play that role injects a fundamentally anti-majoritarian element into what should be a democratic process. A policy-making judiciary is directly contrary to the role of the courts contemplated in the Constitution.

Given that a great part of the problem is Congress's inability to function, two related solutions may be pursued. First, reform Congress so that it can perform its proper policy-making role. Second, shift some of Congress's policy-making power to other decision-making bodies, but choose decision-making bodies that are more appropriate than the federal courts. The following discussion is designed for both heuristic and practical purposes—to cast more light on the need for and difficulty of reform, and to provide a few practical proposals for restoring the Constitution's original design. We have been fortunate that amendments have been few, for most of the proposals would have done violence to the original design. Indeed, at the very birth of the constitution James Madison counseled prudence in ever exercising the great power of the people to alter its form of government. It is thus with all due deference, indeed reverence and trepidation, that anyone should approach the subject of additions to or revisions in the Constitution. I offer these in the belief that restoration, revitalization, and modernization will do no harm, and much good, if faithful to and consistent with the Framers' design.

I. THE JUDICIARY AS BRANCH OF LAST RESORT

The Judiciary has become the branch of last resort. In spite of Alexander Hamilton's assurance that "[t]he judiciary . . . has no influence over either the sword or the purse," the judicial activist is all too often seen distributing the contents of the legislator's purse or wielding the executive's sword. All this he does while, of course, dissembling obeisance to the theory of the separation of powers by keeping on his robe. While Hamilton quoted Montesquieu to the effect that the Judiciary is "next to nothing" and argued that it would "always be the least dangerous" branch, the American Judiciary, even in 1787, was far more powerful than the judiciary of Montesquieu. Judicial review and other powers hitherto accorded only to the Monarch and the House of Lords had been granted to the new federal bench. Also, like monarchs and lords the new federal Constitution's judges had life tenure. This life tenure, however, was a device designed to insulate judges from politics, and to foster judicial objectivity. Indeed, Publius could only sell the notion of life tenure to post-Revolutionary America by arguing that the judicial function would be to exercise "neither Force nor Will, but merely judgment."

Judicial intervention to right a wrong left unrighted by the responsible branch ignores the condition upon which the rather singular powers of the American judiciary were conferred. While the judiciary in all civilized countries has a considerable degree of independence, no other nation has coupled a life term with the power of judicial review unchecked by any other branch. The justification for judicial review itself hangs on the objective and limited nature of its exercise, as we see in John Marshall's seminal exposition of this doctrine in *Marbury v. Madison.*

Current judicial activism takes many forms, with its strands spread throughout the fabric of our society, but in all areas one consequence is clear: The original constitutional understanding that the Judiciary, in recognition of its independence and unreviewable power, would play a limited and objective non–policy-making role has been violated. Procedurally, courts have created new mechanisms which expand their power. Substantively, the courts have arrogated to themselves the authority to make policy decisions that should be made by Congress or by other responsible institutions.

A. Procedural Devices

Judicial activists have created new procedural mechanisms that expand the class of litigants, causes of action, and available remedies. These mechanisms have, in turn, provided a base for further judicial action. Article III of the Constitution limits the jurisdiction of the federal courts to "cases or controversies," that is, it requires that actions be justiciable. Justiciability generally involves four criteria: standing, ripeness, lack of mootness, and the absence of a political question. The application of these criteria limits the possibility of judicial encroachment on the Executive and Legislative Branches and on state governments. The relaxation of justiciability standards has, consequently, permitted litigants to assert broad claims concerning the inadequacy of decision-making by the other branches or by the States.

A few examples of such an expansion of the judicial sphere are illustrative. In *COPPAR v. Rizzo,* a district court held that individuals, simply because of *fear* of possible harassment, had standing to bring a suit that, in effect, invited the court to manage the entire Philadelphia police system. In *Metropolitan Housing Development Corporation v. Village of Arlington Heights,* the circuit court permitted individuals to challenge zoning laws simply because they *might attempt* to buy houses in the zoned areas. Under traditional doctrines the individuals in these lawsuits had no standing. There was no judicially cognizable injury, and therefore no case or controversy, but the plaintiffs were permitted to fabricate one. While the Supreme Court ultimately rejected the claims of the plaintiffs in both these cases, only a few of the lower court cases that grossly expand the doctrine of standing ever make it to the Supreme Court. Justice Powell has spelled out the danger: "Relaxation of standing requirements is directly related to the expansion of judicial power."

The greater willingness of judges to utilize certain procedural devices expands first their power to try suits and then their power to grant remedies. This expansive combination is best illustrated by broad class actions followed by sweeping managerial injunctions. In these institutional reform actions there is no single legal issue joined between two parties; rather, there are a host of parties, many of whom purport to represent different groups with the same general interests, and one definite overall issue—"to reform" or "not to reform." Nothing could be more clearly a policy judgment meant for legislators. The problem is thus far deeper than ill-adapted judicial procedures followed by clumsy remedies. The problem is that judges have substituted their values for those of the popularly elected legislature.

B. Substantive Expansion of Judicial Power

In addition to utilizing purely procedural devices, the Judiciary has also expanded its power by proliferating the underlying "rights" that empower it to act, often relying upon "creative" procedural means by which to do so. On a statutory plane, for example, courts have been increasingly eager to confer on private individuals a right to sue for damages or to secure an injunction to enforce a statute even when the statute is silent on the question. In his dissent in *Cannon v. University of Chicago*, Justice Powell cited twenty circuit-court decisions in four years that had found implied private rights of action where Congress had conferred none. The creation of these new rights presents another example of substantive judicial policy-making through procedural innovation. Moreover, these new rights of action often provide further occasion for judicial expansion of vague statutory norms—as, for example, in section 10(b) of the Securities Act and in the Commodities Exchange Act.

On a higher plane, by an expansive interpretation of the Constitution, particularly the Eighth and Fourteenth Amendments, the courts have undertaken the management of unwieldy, delicate, and complex institutions. The cases are legion. For example, school desegregation suits can take courts not only into ordering remedies such as busing, but also into redrawing school attendance lines, reallocating teachers, instructing school boards on how much to spend on each school or on different programs, and where and when to build new school buildings. These suits are nearly interminable, ending up as ongoing management instead of circumscribed injunctions. Similarly, with reference to public housing systems, the court has sometimes selected housing sites and the method for assigning tenants. Eighth Amendment cases have involved courts in prison management—in how many prisoners are to be placed in a cell, in how many guards are to be used, in food service, in fire hazards, and in medical and mental health care. The Eighth and Fourteenth Amendments have also been used to justify judicial management of mental institutions. In one case, the judge filled thirteen double-column pages of the *Federal Reporter* with mandates covering subjects from linen service to personal housing.

Undoubtedly, reforms and improvements are desperately needed in many instances, but the philosophical and constitutional issues that these decisions raise cannot be ignored. The basic question is, which part of the government should make these reforms? In many cases of judicial overreaching we have arguably worthwhile ends, but nonetheless questionable means to reach these ends. Our confusion over ends and means obscures other issues. Is it really so clear, given the high cost involved and the limited nature of society's resources, that all of these ends are ends for which society, given an informed opinion, would choose to pay? Is the public given the opportunity to understand the cost of what it is compelled to buy? Are some of the goals of judicial activism as misguided (and anti-democratic) as the means used? Does the activism of many judges, basking in the glow of academic and media approval, mask a contempt for the democratic process? More generally, whence cometh the power of these Platonic guardians? Was the role of the robed figure on the bench ever envisaged thus by the Framers? And if ever so thought of, *Quis ipsos custodes custodiet?*

Not only have some judges felt spurred to assume normal executive prerogatives, but Congress has also encouraged judicial decisions trenching on the decision-making responsibilities of the Executive or the States. Such encouragement of judicial activism has often been accomplished through broadly written legislation. In the field of employment discrimination, for example, Title VII has been interpreted to give the courts the power to step in and make managerial decisions about promotional systems, pay scales, and assignments of tasks to workers on the grounds that all these *could* be discriminatory and therefore may be controlled by the managerial decisions of judges.

The energy field epitomizes the distortion in the judicial role caused by broadly written congressional enactments. Were it not for the Supreme Court decisions in *Vermont Yankee* and *PANE* [People Against Nuclear Energy], the complete shape of our policy on nuclear power might have been designed in the courts through extensive litigation under the broadly drawn nuclear power statutes and related environmental and safety laws. In *PANE,* the court of appeals held up reopening the Three Mile Island reactor until the Nuclear Regulatory Commission considered, as an "environmental impact" under NEPA [National Environmental Policy Act] the fears of local residents. Sensing the deleterious ramifications of the decision, the Supreme Court admonished the lower court for authorizing litigants to present "claims that are grounded solely in disagreement with a democratically adopted policy." In *Vermont Yankee* the Court added, "Resolution of these fundamental policy questions lies . . . with Congress and the agencies to which Congress has delegated authority."

Other choices of energy sources, such as the extent to which the United States will rely on coal, have been and will be made by court decisions under loosely drafted environmental and safety laws. Americans' access to the oil of the Alaskan North Slope was delayed four years by litigation in the District of Columbia federal courts. The cost to the American people of the delay by reason of the increased cost of construction and dependence on foreign oil is incalculable.

Energy policy issues are difficult and complex, far beyond the technical capacity of most judges. Yet at the same time the issues are important and the judges feel an obligation to scrutinize them with care. The problem is that judges, lacking the expertise necessary for an informed review, and yet fearful of an easy acquiescence in an agency's decision, find it natural to remand cases for further proceedings so as to ensure that all relevant factors have been taken into account. The temptation to do so, especially for a judge predisposed against nuclear power, is almost irresistible. Yet that temptation must be resisted if courts are not to usurp, or to allow the shirking of, prerogatives and responsibilities reserved for the other branches of government.

The problem with judge-made energy policy has been simply put: "Even if . . . every judicial seat could be filled with a Renaissance man, no court has the tools necessary to deal with the energy problems in a coordinated and comprehensive fashion. While courts cannot develop broad national policies, they can frustrate them through their decisions on narrow, discrete issues, the 'cases' and 'controversies' of which judges are so fond. . . ." The courts and Congress should take note of the costs of judicial activism in the energy field and apply the lessons learned to other policy areas.

The preceding is only a brief glance at some areas of current judicial activism. The complete record follows similar lines and reveals the totality of the Judiciary's assumption of functions delegated to the other branches and the States, an arrogation that is impossible to square with the separation of powers.

C. Unsuitability of Policy Determinations by Courts

In addition to the constitutional objections to judicial policy-making, there are other practical reasons why the courts are unsuitable for the determination of these policy choices. First, unlike Congress, courts have no facilities for holding public hearings to gather expert information and facts on which important policy decisions should be based. Harry Wellington, former dean of Yale Law School, once observed that the use of "consequentialist or policy justifications in constitutional law . . . seems acceptable enough if the evidence on which the policy is based is clear." But, he continued, "When it is not, when judges rely on intuition but do not know, and social scientists . . . cannot tell them very much about the consequences of legal rules, should not policy be the domain of the legislatures . . . ?"

Second, courts have no administrative staff to follow up and police their edicts, or to study their effects in order to determine the ultimate wisdom of the policies they impose. Even in the unlikely event that more personnel were to become available, courts would probably still find it difficult to perform this follow-up function. Judges are notoriously poor administrators and to improve their administrative capacity may be to diminish the quality of those peculiarly judicial virtues needed to decide cases justly as well as efficiently. Justice cannot always be done according to the principles of sound administrative science.

Third, most judges are not adequately trained to make policy decisions on political, social, and economic matters. Experience in legal analysis is not a sufficient credential for making comprehensive policy decisions. Political decision-making requires practical political experience, which most judges do not have. Further, as his years on the bench increase a judge often becomes even more isolated from the forms of knowledge and experience essential to wise policy-making.

Finally, judges are unacceptable as ultimate policy-makers because in a de-mocracy political and moral choices of society's goals (the allocation of scarce resources, for example) should be made by the people, as expressed through their elected representatives. The evident truth of this proposition may be illus-trated by examining one problem posed by recent court activism. Judicial reme-dies designed to make up for taxpayer neglect (as in the case of decaying prisons) mandate public expenditures. These public expenditures must be supported by taxation, and taxation is quintessentially the province of the popularly elected legislature. Courts do not have the power to tax, an incapacity derived from their unrepresentative nature. Yet, for all intents and purposes, courts exercise this power when they order costly institutional reforms.

The Judiciary serves best when it performs its constitutionally defined role. When judges involve themselves in policy controversies they become the rulers of the people. The ancient Israelites grew tired of being ruled by judges and, searching for relief, turned to a king. How ironic it would be if the fruits of 1776 and 1787 should come to that in America.

D. Consequences of Judicial Activism

The immediate consequences of judicial activism are easily seen; however, the full implication of these consequences is not always appreciated. It will thus be helpful to review a few of these consequences and the results to which they could lead.

Leaving aside for the moment the impact on citizens by judicial policy-making, what of the impact on the courts themselves? Judicial activism puts an inordinate burden on the courts, preventing them from performing the tasks for which they were originally designed. This may ultimately alter the nature of the judiciary. As Judge Robert Bork has noted, the courts may be converted "from deliberative institutions to processing institutions, from a judicial model to a bureaucratic model. . . . Assembly line processes cannot sustain those virtues for which we have always prized federal courts: scholarship, a generalist view of the law, wisdom, mature and dispassionate reflection, and . . . careful and reasoned explanation of their decisions."

The public rebels when lifetime judges make policy decisions in the guise of unprecedented remedies for constitutional violations, decisions that neither the voters nor Congress can change. A Supreme Court decision is overturned only rarely by anything other than another Supreme Court decision. The difficult constitutional amendment process was never meant to overturn court decisions, and judicial review was never intended to be the most accessible path to broad social reform.

Even though the courts' decisions may be insulated from the public, their standing may not be so protected. The ability of the courts to gain acceptance of and support for their legitimate tough decisions is impaired by judicial activism. When courts enter the arena of economic and social policy—the domain of partisan politics—they lose credibility as impartial, unbiased interpreters of the Constitution and the laws. Once people thoroughly accept the idea that the Judiciary, like the Legislature and Executive, is engaged in politics instead of an objective and impartial interpretive exercise, the demand may be irresistible that judges, as the third policy-making branch, be less independent, and even popularly elected.

Short of the complete politicization of the Judiciary, there may be lesser but still serious ramifications for the structural authority of the courts. Increased judicial activism leads to the rise of movements to take jurisdiction away from the courts on controversial issues such as abortion, busing, and school prayer. Sharpshooting specific substantive issues by changing appellate jurisdiction is a remedy for the disease of judicial activism the side effects of which may be as pernicious as the disorder itself. Yet, the frustrations of millions of citizens, who find that the fruits of judicial activism are bitter, seek—and ultimately will find—an outlet. The targets of the people's frustrations are symptoms, not sources, of the disease; treating the symptoms will not cure the malady. Only by carefully discerning the causes of judicial activism, and treating them, can we banish both the irritating symptoms and the devastating causes.

II. CAUSES OF JUDICIAL ACTIVISM AND OTHER DISTORTIONS OF THE CONSTITUTIONAL FABRIC

Departures from the accepted and planned role of the judiciary—to interpret the Constitution, statutes, and precedents as justly and prudently as possible in any real controversy—can be laid to two general causes: the willfulness of individual judges and the abdication of responsibility by the other two branches of the federal government, particularly Congress.

A. Willfulness of the Judiciary

"The disposition of mankind . . . to impose [its] own opinions and inclinations as a rule of conduct on others is so energetically supported by some of the best and by some of the worst feelings incident to human nature, that it is hardly ever kept under restraint by anything but want of power." The truth of John Stuart Mill's observation was fundamental for the Constitution's Framers. The separation and division of powers provide precisely for "restraint" through "want of power."

Yet, some decisions of the Judiciary can be characterized as nothing less than sheer usurpation achieved by ignoring constitutional bounds. By stretching the concept of justiciability almost to the point of meaninglessness, courts permit themselves to hear those cases that they want to hear. In the hands of some judges, the fabric of justice is a stretch fabric. The general trend is disquieting. Over the past thirty years the courts have steadily and dramatically expanded their authority to oppose legislative judgment. They have banned prayers in schools. They have entered into moral and scientific controversies over pregnancy and have transformed relations between parents and children on delicate questions of contraception and abortion. Indeed, the constitutional aspects of reproduction have exerted a particular fascination for courts. Further, they have reapportioned legislatures, all but abolished the death penalty, and hampered the investigation and prosecution of crime.

Throughout our history the Supreme Court has had a limited policy role to play, but it has been limited, not merely by the Constitution, but by the usually careful judgment of the Justices. Moreover, what the High Court can—and sometimes, perhaps, should—do in its position at the peak of the pyramid, where accountability and responsibility are easily fixed, is no model for the inferior courts. Seven hundred federal judges and many thousand state judges simply cannot wander all over the jurisprudential map in deciding what the law should be or in performing managerial tasks for which they are unsuited. In lieu of a clear line between correct and incorrect constitutional interpretation, it is often necessary to rely upon the cautious restraint and informed circumspection of individual judges. The traditions of such restraint, however, have been eroded.

B. Abdication of Responsibility by Congress

While sheer willfulness has clearly led to judicial intervention on political and social issues, the abdication of responsibility by Congress is an even greater cause of judicial activism. Congressional shirking of responsibility manifests itself in several forms—legislative overaction, nonaction, and, above all, evasive congressional decision-making.

Aside from the numerically few truly constitutional law and diversity cases, every action in the federal courts rests on some law passed by Congress; paralleling an expansion in federal law there has been an explosion of federal litigation in the past two decades. This country prides itself on the rule of law, but clearly it is possible to get too much of a good thing. Legislation and adjudication are essential in moderate quantities, but beyond this, they add not one bit to the enjoyment of life. Harvard President Derek Bok has observed that "[e]ngineers make the pie grow larger; lawyers only decide how to carve it up. . . . Not only does the law absorb many more young people in America than in any other industrialized nation; it attracts an unusually large proportion of the exceptionally gifted. . . . The net result of these trends is a massive diversion of exceptional talent into pursuits that often add little to the growth of the economy, the pursuit of culture, or the enhancement of the human spirit."

While legislation and adjudication have always been necessary functions in an organized society, the greater the volume, the greater the indication that the society has failed to organize itself. Just as the presence of a large number of uniformed police and machine pistol-toting paramilitary forces signals the weakness, not strength, of a political community, so volume after volume of detailed legislation and regulation reveal the governors' lack of confidence in the governed to regulate their own affairs. This may lead, in turn, to a gradual vitiation of the people's ability to govern themselves. Correspondingly, the greater a society's resort to a formal judicial system for the adjustment of differences among its citizenry or between its citizenry and government, the less cohesive and more fragmented is that society. As Grant Gilmore put it, "The better the society, the less law there will be. In Heaven there will be no law, and the lion will lay down with the lamb. . . . The worse the society, the more law there will be. In Hell there will be nothing but law, and due process will be meticulously observed."

In spite of the ingenuity of judicial activists in finding new rights and remedies, the cause of action that the lawyer pleads has usually been created by some act of Congress. If Congress could develop a greater capacity to say no, then it could do what it really needs to do much better and do much less of what the country can do without. Many legislative acts, for instance, only confer benefits on those hired to administer them. One hears much about judicial restraint, but in many instances there would be no need to invoke judicial restraint if there had first been legislative restraint. Congressional overaction demands a response from the courts; this response is inevitably forthcoming. Judicial action piled on top of legislative action results in a curtailment, not enhancement, of individual liberty. Viewed in this perspective, judicial activism is part of a greater pernicious phenomenon.

Not only does Congress do too much, but what it does it could do with considerably more care and thought. Ill-conceived mandatory language is a variant of congressional abdication that has an adverse impact on the judiciary. Few laymen realize that the Bail Reform Act of 1966 mandates the release of the accused, irrespective of the likelihood of additional criminal activity, if the bail set plus other factors are sufficient to ensure his presence at trial. Judicial obedience to this statute appears to the public as dangerous judicial whimsy when a vicious criminal is released on bail pending trial—released with the possibility that he may commit another crime before being tried for the first.

The excessive authority of judges is not due merely to an excess of laws, or even to the willfulness of some judges. The most significant factor of all has been congressional abdication on vital and controversial issues. From the point of view of both a court and the public, congressional abdication of responsibility for difficult decisions is far worse than congressional hyperactivity. At least in the latter case the court can point to a statute to justify its decision, while in the absence of congressional action it sometimes feels compelled to act on nothing but a generalized constitutional clause.

The two best known instances of Supreme Court intervention in the absence of legislative action are *Brown v. Board of Education* and *Baker v. Carr*. These decisions, involving respectively school desegregation and legislative reapportionment, were rendered under Fourteenth Amendment provisions that Congress failed to implement. The controversy swirling about them has obscured the fact that in many other instances, almost on a routine basis, courts have been provoked by congressional surrender of legislative authority into making policy decisions.

Similar problems arise when Congress enacts a statute but leaves unsettled crucial policy issues within the statutory scheme. A typical example is the actual cash value of food stamps. The Senate could not agree on this issue so it deliberately drafted vague statutory language to satisfy both Senators Taft and McGovern, whose positions on the optimal value of food stamps were poles apart. The value of food stamps, a transfer payment from the taxpayer to the welfare recipient, is the epitome of a political decision that should be made by elected officials. Yet, the elected representatives could not decide, so they simply left this policy choice to the courts.

The effective date of clean-air restrictions is another example of congressional abdication. The statute was put together just prior to the congressional recess in the summer of 1977 as a compromise between the chambers. The two bills of the House and the Senate contained separate dates months apart for compliance with the Clean Air Act restrictions on pollution. For industry, the chosen date made a difference of millions of dollars. The compromise statute contained both irreconcilable dates, and after a full month of work trying to agree on one date, both chambers gave up and said they would "leave it to the courts." The issue left to the courts was one impossible for them to answer given the legislative history: What *is* the will of the Congress? How can the courts determine that when confronted by two directly contradictory provisions deriving from the two co-equal Houses?

The instances in which congressional legislation is deliberately left to the courts could be listed endlessly. The Congress's solution for all difficult drafting or decision-making dilemmas, "leave it to the courts," has become instinctive, habitual, chronic, and endemic. Consider the remarkable dialogue between two Senators on May 26, 1983 at a hearing on the Equal Rights Amendment before the Constitution Subcommittee of the Senate Judiciary Committee. The Senator testifying as principal co-sponsor of the ERA [Equal Rights Amendment] was asked several specific questions as to its meaning, because in some instances the Amendment's supporters had given directly contradictory interpretations of the language. For example, would veterans' hiring preference still exist? Would the ERA impact upon federal, state, and local limitations on public funding of abortions? Would the ERA prohibit any aid to private educational institutions that are "men only" or "women only," or outlaw single-sex public schools and universities? Would the ERA deny tax exemption to churches that deny various privileges to women in the exercise of their religious doctrine? Would the ERA jeopardize labor seniority systems? Would the ERA ban male-only draft registration? To each of some fifteen questions of this nature the Senator testifying responded, "We have what is called the Supreme Court, which is in the position to resolve those particular matters"; "that is a matter which is going to be decided in the courts"; "that issue would be resolved in the courts"; "they would go to the courts and have it resolved"; or with some other variation on the theme of "the courts will decide." In fact, the principal sponsor testifying specifically declined to offer an amendment curing recognized ambiguities.

Commentator George Will's conclusion was that "[the Senator] is content to have courts make policy. . . . [His] testimony exemplified the complacent abdication of responsibility by legislators." The conclusion of the Senator presiding was apt: "I think we ought to determine some of these things in the Congress of the United States, because we are elected to determine them, not unelected judges who are not. . . . [T]he courts determine unanticipated conflicts. That is the purpose of the courts. But we are discussing fully anticipated conflicts."

This legislative abdication of the authority to deal with pressing public issues does more than simply place the courts in the position to resolve the issues according to their own notions; it gradually saps the willingness and ability of the people to govern themselves through their elected representatives. No one has pointed out more fully the dangers of such an assumption of authority by the courts, even by default, than did Theodore Roosevelt:

[F]or the courts to arrogate to themselves functions which properly belong to the legislative bodies is all wrong, and in the end works mischief. The people should not be permitted to pardon evil and slipshod legislation on the theory that the court will set it right; they should be taught that the right way to get rid of a bad law is to have the legislature repeal it, and not to have the courts by ingenious hair-splitting nullify it. A law may be unwise and improper; but it should not for these reasons be declared unconstitutional by a strained interpretation, for the result of such action is to take away from the people at large their sense of responsibility and ultimately to destroy their capacity for orderly self restraint and self government. Under such a popular government as ours, founded on the theory that in the long run the will of the people is supreme, the ultimate safeguard of the Nation can only rest in training and guiding the people so that what they will shall be right, and not in devising means to defeat their will by the technicalities of strained construction.

C. Fundamental Problems in Representative Democracy (U.S. Style)

The reason for continual congressional abdication is readily apparent. In it one can see not only the principal cause of judicial activism, but also the fundamental problem of representative democracy: the inability of elected officials to make a desperately needed decision for the long-term public good if short-term consequences may endanger their reelection.

This problem must be analyzed with understanding and sympathy. It takes a certain kind of courage to make a judicial decision that the judge knows will be highly unpopular. It takes a different and probably greater measure of courage to make a decision that the elected official knows is not only going to subject him to the slings and arrows of outraged constituents, but also might well cost him his job in a matter of months. Nevertheless, congressional abdication to the courts is an evil that must be not only understood but also addressed. If not acted upon, congressional abdication and subsequent judicial legislation may spread even further.

For example, energy policy—surely one of the greater economic problems of the last decade—is still a potential source of judicial legislation despite the *PANE* and *Vermont Yankee* decisions. Neither the Executive nor Congress has come up with any semblance of a long-term, overall solution to our energy problems. Why? Every viable long-term solution involves the short-term discomfort of the American public, and the people's representatives are terribly afraid that the discomfort might be reflected in the next election. Given the likelihood of continued congressional impotence, the courts may find themselves drawn deeper into the energy debate.

Free trade is another area in which legislative solutions to problems are almost sure to be fudged. Whatever Congress comes up with in this area has a great potential for ending up in the courts for final resolution. The scheme for compensation to workers laid off because of "unfair" foreign competition has already resulted in litigation.

Social Security reforms present yet another possibility for a judicial excursion into the abandoned legislative realm. The actuarial and revenue problems of Social Security are well defined and so are their solutions. All of these solutions are unacceptable to Congress because they involve some voters getting less than they anticipated—either by reduction in the amounts paid to them or by an increase in the amount of taxes taken from them. Every attempt to face up to this reality has been howled down, so Congress has passed the buck for reform to a commission and adopted its recommendations. Those points left unde- cided and those problems left unsolved by the commission are eventually going to be handled by the courts.

Success achieved by assigning difficult problems, such as Social Security revision, MX missile siting, and Central America, to an outside commission has engendered suggestions that the same process be tried with the equally intracta- ble problem of the budget. Reductions in spending, higher taxes, and larger deficits appear abhorrent to elected officials. To the extent that an escape can be found in an acceptably balanced group of outside consultants, anguish at both ends of Pennsylvania Avenue will be eased. Nevertheless, whether the outside consultants are members of a commission or members of the federal bench, and whether they succeed in finding a solution or not, a constitutional problem remains. Is this government as was constitutionally designed?

The powers of taxation and expenditure were carefully reposed in our elected representatives. The Framers contemplated something more than a mere congressional ratification of policy choices made by unelected and unrep- resentative bodies. If budget-making by referee consultants is realized, this will epitomize the paralysis of elected representative assemblies that has created in such a great degree the excuse or necessity for judicial activism. In an editorial last year, the *Wall Street Journal* summarized all this with a headline recom- mending, "Decommission Congress."

Our constitutional system must provide those in each branch of government with an opportunity for reflection and independent decision-making. This is as great a need in the legislature as it is in the judiciary. Perhaps the duties of the people's representatives were summed up best by Edmund Burke:

> Your representative owes you, not his industry only, but his judgment; and he betrays, instead of serving you, if he sacrifices it to your opin- ion. . . . Parliament is not a *congress* of ambassadors from different and hostile interests; . . . but parliament is a *deliberative* assembly of one nation with *one* interest, that of the whole; . . . You chuse a member indeed; but when you have chosen him, he is not a member of Bristol, but he is a member of *parliament*.

The paralysis evident in the Executive Branch is also derived from an inability to exercise judgment in the face of hostile opinion. The Executive is almost as disinclined as Congress to sponsor unpopular measures, and where the President is willing to make difficult decisions, his measures are likely to be blocked by Congress. Today, no branch of the government possesses the level of judgment and independence necessary to provide effective leadership. The Judiciary's independence and its ability to judge objectively and well—its ability to protect constitutional government by making a difficult decision—has diminished with increased politicization and a mounting workload.

Are the short-term benefits of judicial activism worth the long-term costs—the atrophying of citizenship, the encouragement of legislative paralysis, and the perversion of the judicial process? The same Constitution that established the three separate branches of government has placed economic and social policy-making in the political branches, whose members must face periodic election. This power has not been and should not be granted to a rather aged and isolated group of seven hundred life appointees. To grant legislative powers to the judiciary is not to save popular government from the shame of inaction in the face of injustice, but to admit that popular government is not possible—that America's experiment has failed.

No matter how meritorious the desired political and social ends, manipulating the judiciary as a means to achieve those ends is bad constitutional practice. In contrast to other political and philosophical systems, American theory has never accepted the rationale that the end justifies the means. This point must be remembered if viable solutions to our social and economic problems are to be found.

Questions for Discussion

1. What difference has judicial review made to the course of U.S. political history?
2. How should the Supreme Court decide cases where moral issues are in conflict with the law?
3. What are the appropriate questions that should be asked by the Senate of presidential nominees to the Supreme Court?
4. How should the Supreme Court be guided by the Framers of the Constitution in evaluating contemporary cases?
5. How can judicial review be reconciled with democratic theory?

Suggested Readings

Abraham, Henry J. "The 'Least Dangerous Branch' Revisited: Reflections on a Half-Truth Two Centuries Later." *Teaching Political Science*, 14, no. 1 (Fall 1986), 28–37.

Bennett, Robert W. "Judicial Activism and the Concept of Original Intent." *Judicature*, 64, no. 4 (December 1985–January 1986), 219–223.

Bork, Robert H. "Judicial Review and Democracy." *Society*, 24, no. 1 (November–December 1986), 5–8.

Clinton, Robert M. "Judges Must Make Law: A Realistic Appraisal of the Judicial Function in a Democratic Society." *Iowa Law Review*, 67, no. 3 (March 1982), 711–741.

Meese, Edwin, III. "The Battle for the Constitution: The Attorney General Replies to His Critics." *Policy Review*, no. 35 (Winter 1986), 32–35.

O'Brien, David M. *Storm Center: The Supreme Court in American Politics.* New York: Norton, 1986.

Posner, Richard A. "The Meaning of Judicial Self-Restraint." *Indiana Law Journal*, 59, no. 1 (1983–1984), 1–24.

Rabkin, Jeremy. "Constitutional Roulette." *American Spectator*, 19, no. 5 (May 1986), 14–15.

Rakove, Jack N. "Mr. Meese, Meet Mr. Madison." *Atlantic*, 258, no. 6 (December 1986), 77–86.

Taylor, Stuart, Jr. "Meese v. Brennan." *New Republic*, 194, nos. 1–2 (January 6–13, 1986), 17–21.

Wasby, Stephen L. "Arrogation of Power or Accountability: 'Judicial Imperialism' Revisited." *Judicature*, 65, no. 4 (October 1981), 208–219.

Wolfe, Christopher. *The Rise of Modern Judicial Review: From Constitutional Interpretation to Judge-Made Law.* New York: Basic Books, 1986.

Part IV

Public Policy

15. *Should the Government Be Asked to Solve the Social and Economic Problems of Minorities?*

16. *Should the Death Penalty Be Abolished?*

17. *Should the Media Be Regulated in Reporting Acts of Terrorism?*

18. *Should the United States Engage in Arms Control Negotiations with the Soviet Union?*

19. *Should U.S. Troops Withdraw from Europe?*

20. *Is It Wise for the United States to Use Economic Sanctions against South Africa?*

olitical democracy involves a contest over public policy. An element of that contest includes convincing individuals, private groups, and political leaders that particular policies are wise and just. An underlying theme of democratic rule is that conflicts should be resolved peacefully through discussion, freedom of association, and agreed-upon procedures for determining policy outcomes.

People who choose sides on different issues of public policy do so for many reasons. Sometimes, the choice is based on self-interest, as when a manufacturer or trade union favors protectionism so as to reduce competition from abroad. At other times, the choice is based on a perception of justice, as in issues relating to the elimination of racism or the protection of the environment. Often, choices derive from a combination of self-interested and altruistic impulses.

This chapter deals with some contemporary issues in domestic and foreign policy matters of concern to the people of the United States. Specifically, the debate questions concern government responsibility for solving social and economic problems, the constitutionality and morality of the death penalty, the responsibility of the media in reporting acts of terrorism, the value of arms control negotiations with the Soviet Union, the consequences of withdrawing U.S. troops from Europe, and the wisdom of economic sanctions against South Africa.

Should the Government Be Asked to Solve the Social and Economic Problems of Minorities?

The initial focus of political concern for blacks was to achieve civil and political rights. And so efforts were made to end segregation, discrimination, and denial of the vote on the basis of race. The political battleground became the courts, Congress, and the executive branch of government at the national level, and the political institutions of state and local governments as well. Peaceful protests led by such people as Martin Luther King, Jr., in alliance with labor, religious, and other groups sought to gain approval for these changes.

The civil rights movement succeeded in ending segregation and in ensuring civil and political rights for blacks. The major laws were the Civil Rights Act of 1964 and the Voting Rights Act of 1965. The federal government, particularly, enforced those rights.

Once having achieved civil and political rights, many leaders in the civil rights movement turned their attention to economic equality. They allied with liberals who believed that government should play a positive role in bringing about racial equality in such areas as housing, education, economic development, welfare, and social services generally. They sought to open opportunities for blacks by supporting programs of affirmative action and set-asides.

Although there is no universally accepted definition of "affirmative action," it means at the minimum that government and many private organizations should make special efforts to recruit minority members and others from groups that had previously experienced discrimination. Critics of affirmative action argue that such efforts result in quotas requiring the employment of specific percentages of minority members and others from affirmative action categories. Supporters of affirmative action contend that they favor goals and targets, and not quotas.

"Set-asides" are programs in which only minority firms may bid for government contracts. The purpose of such programs is to open economic opportunities to minority businesses. Such programs began during the administration of Lyndon Johnson and were also supported by presidents Richard Nixon, Gerald Ford, and Jimmy Carter. Black groups achieved many successes during this time, although they often remained critical of the extent of the federal commitment to improving the plight of black people.

The Reagan administration, however, fought against many of the programs on the agenda of black civil rights groups. It sought to reduce federal expenditures on social programs that often benefited black people, opposed affirmative action in general, and tried to have the courts weaken affirmative action practices of previous administrations.

The Reagan administration argued that blacks would benefit more from general economic health than from government programs. Its thesis in this regard was that everyone benefits when the U.S. economy is strong— a rising tide lifts all boats. And the U.S. economy will be strong, the administration argued, only if government plays a minimal role in the economy and allows the private sector to flourish. In its first year in office the administration achieved a tax cut that reduced the flow of revenues to federal government coffers. In principle the tax reduction was supposed to stimulate economic growth to such an extent that federal government revenues would increase dramatically. Although there was an economic recovery during the Reagan years, the extent of the recovery was not so great as the Reagan administration had hoped. As the federal government produced ever larger deficits, increasing pressure was exerted to reduce expenditures in social programs.

If the prospects for expanding social programs have been dimmed by a decline in federal government economic resources, they have also been hurt by challenges to the effectiveness of those programs. Critics argue that many of the social programs designed to help minorities and the poor have, in fact, harmed these groups. They contend that government social programs diminish work incentives, weaken the family, increase the number of households with single parents, aid middle- and upper-class people rather than the poor, produce slums, make crime more likely, and promote waste and inefficiency.

Should the government be asked to solve the social and economic problems of minorities? That is a question considered in the selections by John E. Jacob, president of the National Urban League, and Glenn C. Loury, a political scientist at Harvard University.

Jacob, who heads one of the major civil rights organizations, argues:

1. Federal government policies have historically promoted economic and social mobility.
2. Federal policies have led to significant black advances.
3. Current government policies have intensified the problems facing black and poor people.

Jacob concludes by calling for a national effort to promote jobs, strengthen education, and improve social welfare policies.

Glenn C. Loury contends that the emphasis of black groups should be on self-help rather than government programs. He argues:

1. Many of the problems of the black community lie outside the reach of effective government action.

2. Too much attention has been directed to "the enemy without"—that is, those practices that have promoted racism and discrimination—rather than to "the enemy within"—that is, those practices that promote family instability and individual irresponsibility.

Neither Jacob nor Loury is an absolutist on the role of government. Jacob accepts the idea of self-help, but the emphasis of his selection is on government programs. Loury accepts the idea of government programs, but the emphasis of his selection is on self-help.

☑ YES

Should the Government Be Asked to Solve the Social and Economic Problems of Minorities?

JOHN E. JACOB
The Government and Social Problems

America today is in the midst of a national debate on the proper role of government in dealing with social problems—chief among them the disproportionate poverty and social disorganization afflicting the black community.

During much of the post-war era that debate centered on how our institutional structures could secure civil rights for black citizens and help minorities enter the mainstream of American life.

In recent years, the terms of the debate have changed. Under the leadership of an Administration that labels government itself as "the enemy," the debate centers more and more on how government can effect a strategic withdrawal from social policy.

Today's great river of debate is being fed by many streams of thought.

They range from the belief that government has an inescapable duty to implement positive social policies, to the view that anything government does is likely to worsen existing problems and create new ones. Some also suggest black problems are rooted in behavior and values beyond the reach of public policy.

To place the current debate in context, I would like to suggest several propositions:

1. that federal policies have historically promoted economic and social mobility.
2. that federal policies have led to significant black advances.
3. that current government policies have intensified the problems facing black and poor people.

American history shows the extent to which government policies shaped opportunities. From the institution of free public education to free land to subsidized railways, Washington's policies always served social ends.

Some of today's critics of social policies were educated under the GI Bill, bought houses with FHA [Federal Housing Administration] loans, own businesses started with SBA [Small Business Administration] loans, are treated in VA hospitals, drive to work on federally subsidized highways, educate their children with federally guaranteed loans, and look forward to retirement income from Social Security.

Government bailed out Chrysler. It publicly states that it will not allow large banks to fail. It subsidizes farm interests. Even rugged individualists from the oil patch run to Washington for welfare.

Given that record, the argument that government has no role to play in social policy rings hollow. Government policies created a large middle class and preserve the wealth of the affluent. Government should play an equally decisive role in providing opportunities for the poor.

When the federal government did intervene to protect black rights and to reduce poverty, its efforts were by and large successful.

They helped millions out of poverty, secured civil rights for black citizens, and, despite the Reagan counter-revolution, continue to provide opportunities.

Contrary to today's myths, affirmative action and social programs worked.

Affirmative action increased black employment opportunities. A Labor Department study found that federal contractors under affirmative action mandates increased minority employment and promotions at a far higher rate than other employers.

Poverty was sharply reduced in the late 1960s, with about half of the decline directly due to government transfer payments. In those years too, the income gap between black and white families narrowed.

In the 1960s, hunger was a serious national problem. Thanks to food stamps, it virtually disappeared from the national agenda until recently.

Federal education aid helped raise black childrens' performance on basic skills tests. Head Start resulted in higher school achievement and better social adjustment. Student aid programs were instrumental in the fivefold increase in black college attendance.

The Job Corps and other programs targeted to the disadvantaged opened employment opportunities for many. Black infant mortality rates were almost halved thanks to Medicaid and nutrition programs.

At a time when cutting such programs is becoming an article of faith among some who consider themselves "conservatives," we should recall that conservative columnist George Will wrote: "It is cheaper to feed the child than jail the man. Persons who do not understand this are not conservatives, just dim."

It is also dim to brand such programs as taxwasters. Evidence suggests they pay for themselves.

For example, successful job training programs typically return 3–4 dollars for every dollar spent in training costs. A Congressional study recently estimated that the WIC [Special Supplemental Food Program for Women, Infants, and Children] saves $3 for every $1 spent by reducing future hospitalization costs. Cost-benefit ratios for other programs were found to range from 1½-1, to 10-1.

The Reagan era has seen a reversal of federal policy—a shift away from intervention to neglect. The result has been to worsen the conditions of poor and black Americans.

Between 1979 and 1984 real dollar income for the poorest fifth of families with children declined by 24 percent, and the income gap between whites and blacks grew.

Overall, poverty rates rose by a third. More than a third of all black people—over 9 million—are poor today, 2 million more than in 1978.

But federal programs were severely cut. Between 1981 and 1984—years of deep recession and slow recovery— 4 million people lost welfare, Medicaid, SSI [Supplemental Security Income] and food stamps. Benefits were reduced for millions more.

The deepest cuts came in programs that invest in education and employment skills, such as job training, which was cut by more than half.

There is a distinction among welfare programs between universal programs affecting everyone and means-tested programs designed for the poor. Universal programs like Social Security have not been touched for political reasons. Blacks are less likely to reap the benefits of such programs because they die too young or earn too little to fully share in the payoff.

But blacks typically account for 30 to 40 percent of participants in means-tested programs. And the cuts in those programs reduced the income of poor families by 7.5 percent and drove 2 million people into poverty.

The Congressional Budget Office reports a massive transfer of wealth from low income families to the affluent. The tax and budget changes reduced incomes of low and moderate income families by $20 billion between 1983–85, while *increasing* the after-tax incomes of the wealthiest two percent by $35 billion.

Those who believe that government can and should devise policies that reduce inequality and poverty can point to some considerable past successes.

Those who believe that government cannot and should not implement such policies must defend the results of current policies that have dramatically increased inequality and poverty.

Their only recourse is to say that market forces, unimpeded by government interference, will create wealth and jobs.

That view has only a tenuous relationship to reality. It ignores the persistence of discrimination and its effects. It embodies a fantasy of the blacks and whites lining up at the starting line as equals, when black people run the race of life carrying heavy historical and present burdens on their shoulders.

Everything we know about race and poverty in America suggests that unless the poor are given some extra help—in the form of social policies that enlarge their opportunities—they will not compete on equal terms with the affluent.

The results of the current economic recovery bear that out. We are in the longest sustained economic recovery in memory, and the results are barely perceptible in poverty communities.

Unemployment and poverty are far higher than they were before the recession. Jobless rates for every group, including white men of prime working age, are higher than they were in 1979.

Black unemployment, which was 6.7 percent in 1970, is stuck at fifteen percent—more than double the white rate. Black unemployment has been in the double digits since the mid-1970s—a 13-year depression with no end in sight.

An April survey of business leaders found that while they expect the boom to continue, 70 percent predict their employment rolls will either decline or be unchanged this year.

Economic growth alone cannot create sufficient employment opportunities for the poor and the unskilled.

Some argue that even with supportive government policies, many will remain poor because they have neither the skills nor the attitudes to allow them to escape poverty.

That view has become an article of faith among the neo-conservatives and the neo-liberals who dominate the current debate.

While there is a grain of truth to the argument, it totally neglects the way people adapt to extreme situations such as poverty in the midst of affluence. And it leads us into the blind alley of refusing to do anything about the root cause of poverty—the lack of opportunity.

The scars borne by those who have been brutalized by poverty and discrimination are deep. But skills can be acquired and attitudes changed.

The primary factor is *opportunity*. People respond to opportunities.

Studies show that children whose parents work do better in school—they see a real-world link between their studies and employment. Dropout rates are lower where students are promised jobs or college admission upon graduation. Other programs demonstrate the eagerness of welfare mothers to obtain skills and jobs.

So you can't write off 35 million people who happen to be poor. In all essentials other than income they are not appreciably different from the rest of us.

That is important to remember at a time when the policy debate increasingly centers on the black family.

Half of all black families are headed by single women and over two-thirds of poor black children live in those families.

The rise in female-headed households is blamed for the rise in black poverty. It is further asserted that there has been a breakdown in moral values leading to family instability and welfare dependency.

Those assumptions are wrong.

The central cause of black poverty and black family instability is the lack of economic opportunity.

The rise in female headed families is directly linked to the decline in black male employment.

In 1960 almost three-fourths of black families were intact and almost three-fourths of black men had jobs. In 1985 only half of black families are intact and only about half of black men have jobs.

Even as the economy successfully absorbed a massive influx of white females into the labor force, it failed to provide jobs for the black unemployed, with terrible results for black family stability.

The breakdown in economic opportunities cuts across racial lines. Teenage pregnancy, out-of-wedlock births, and female-headed households are typical to poor white communities as well as black ones.

The web of behavior patterns labelled by some as "pathological" and by others as "dysfunctional" is driven by abject poverty and hopelessness.

So while it is convenient to argue that family instability causes poverty, it is more accurate to say that *poverty causes family instability.*

The dependency issue is largely a sham. Some people may settle into long-term dependence on welfare, but most move in and out of the welfare system depending on circumstances.

Nor is there proof that welfare encourages formation of single-parent households. Since 1970 inflation cut welfare benefits by one-third, and there was a drastic increase in the percentage of children in female-headed households. But the percentage of children in families on welfare remained stable.

So I see no evidence that welfare contributes to family instability, but I see plenty of evidence that the welfare system is not reaching enough of the poor with enough assistance.

Welfare reaches only about three-fourths of eligible families—excluding over two million poor people, mostly children—and benefits do not even begin to approach the artificially low poverty line.

Over a third of the poor aged do not receive SSI benefits. Most eligible women, infants and children who qualify for the federal nutrition programs do not get aid. About ten million people eligible for food stamps don't get them. Less than a quarter of eligible households are in the low income energy assistance program. Head Start reaches less than a fifth of eligible children. And federal training programs reach only a small fraction of those eligible.

Social welfare policies in America are not characterized by wide participation and generosity but by very low participation and meanness.

Poverty existed in the past—and as I have pointed out, poverty rates were significantly higher than they were after the Great Society programs.

But America was different then. Most Americans had low and moderate incomes but there was an abundance of jobs for unskilled laborers. Men might not earn much, but they had jobs, salaries, and self-respect. They were able to assume traditional family roles.

Over the past two decades however, we have seen the systematic destruction of unskilled jobs, including high-paying jobs in auto factories and steel plants.

Today, blacks are concentrated in industries most affected by job losses and by competition from imports. They live in cities where low-wage manufacturing jobs were replaced by office and skilled service jobs.

Blacks didn't leave jobs—jobs left blacks.

So the real issue in public policy is not whether federal social programs encourage dependency, but whether they offer opportunities—opportunities to survive the ravages of extreme poverty and opportunities to participate in the economy.

That does not exclude internal community efforts we often call "self-help." Blacks have been picking themselves up by their bootstraps ever since we've been here—even when we didn't have boots.

Today, that tradition continues. In literally hundreds of communities we see creative programs initiated and run by black community-based civil rights agencies and neighborhood groups, ranging from economic development to housing management to food banks.

There is a growing myth today that civil rights organizations are busy fighting yesterday's battles and neglecting today's.

Nothing could be further from the truth. I know of no major civil rights group that says civil rights strategies are the only way to improve the black condition.

But because discrimination remains a stubborn factor in our society, it is a necessary part of our activities. Despite their diversity, civil rights leadership has been consistent in saying that while racism is still a problem, we can't let it become an excuse.

At the same time, those agencies are busy fighting for social policies that would advance the interests of the black poor and of the white poor who vastly outnumber them.

And they are deeply involved in efforts to cut the teenage pregnancy rate, to raise educational expectations and achievements, and to constructively deal with a host of community problems.

The Urban League is intensively involved in the two-front war—working to change national social policies while at the same time working within the black community to expand opportunities.

We targeted key black family issues such as teenage pregnancy and female-headed households as priority concerns long before national television discovered them.

This year we will launch a major five-year effort to mobilize the black community to improve our schools—a program designed to raise black student performance, with measurable goals and timetables.

So blacks do not need any lectures about self-help. We *are* helping ourselves. And it is instructive that the people most deeply involved in those self-help efforts are often the same people who demand more positive national social policies.

Precisely because we are the poorest and most vulnerable part of our society, we know there is no substitute for policies that provide employment and training opportunities and create the conditions that make self-help efforts feasible. We know that *black poverty cannot be significantly altered without changes in social policies.*

Yes, there is much that black people can do—and are doing—for themselves, but the place of blacks in our society will ultimately be determined by national policies that provide opportunities and make full use of all of America's human resources.

I believe that such policies will eventually be adopted because they are in the national interest.

Changing demographics mean that a third of new entrants into the labor force are non-white. A severe labor shortage is predicted before the end of the century.

Unless we equip our neglected minorities with the education and the skills to fully participate in a post-industrial economy, America can expect second class economic status, a weakened world position, and deep unrest at home.

Rather than commit suicide for the sake of antigovernment ideology, I believe America will return to a more activist social policy.

We have only limited time today, so I can only sketch the outlines of a policy aimed at reducing poverty and inequality and increasing opportunities.

I would suggest that those goals can be met by a targeted, sustained, three-part national effort. It would include:

1. A Universal Employment and Training System that ensures jobs and training for all. It would include private and voluntary sector participation and provide skills training for jobs that will be in short supply along with support services to reach and motivate participants.
2. Education reforms that equalize opportunities for children in poor families, offer quality pre-school learning experiences, and ensure that students are equipped with employable skills and with the services to help them move from the world of school to the world of work.
3. Social welfare policies that stress human development and ensure decent living standards for all of the needy, while providing child care and support services that encourage work.

I believe such a national effort would go far to end poverty and dependency in America, secure social justice and launch our economy into the twenty-first century.

The halting steps taken in the social programs of the 1960s and 1970s should be seen as extensive research and development into what works and what doesn't.

Today, we are well placed to frame effective programs that avoid past mistakes—including the mistake of untargeted, underfunded and underutilized programs that promised more than they could deliver.

Public policy today is at an impasse. It is dominated by an ideology that rejects government involvement, an ideology bankrupted by tolerating gross human suffering and by its inability to meet the demands of global economic reality.

In its more humane form, it offers a futile belief in self-help efforts that are not fully adequate to the needs of 35 million poor people living in an affluent, post-industrial society.

Absent an activist government social policy we are left with what I call the "if only" alternative:

- "If only poor people acted like middle class people . . ."
- "If only poor people didn't have so many children . . ."
- "If only blacks would stop complaining . . ."

The "if only" school of thinking is an exercise in racial fantasy. It avoids social problems instead of confronting them. And it feeds the false assumption that nothing can be done about our problems.

There is an air of desperation about some of the "if only" beliefs—a hunger for quick fixes like supply side economics or doing away with minimum wage and occupational health and safety laws or preaching to kids not to engage in sex.

But the real desperation today is in the poverty-stricken streets of urban black neighborhoods. It is in the eyes of hungry children, overburdened women and hopeless men.

It's a desperation that can—and must—be countered by national policies that replace bitterness with hope, failure with accomplishment, and hunger with food, training and jobs.

President Franklin D. Roosevelt said: "The test of our progress is not whether we add more to the abundance of those who have much; it is whether we provide enough for those who have too little."

Fifty years later, those words remain as public policy guides that recognize government's responsibility to create opportunity for all.

Should the Government Be Asked to Solve the Social and Economic Problems of Minorities?

GLENN C. LOURY

*Internally Directed Action
for Black Community Development:
The Next Frontier for "The Movement"*

The primary argument set forth in this essay is that there is today both the possibility and the necessity to expand the range of activities undertaken by blacks ourselves, aimed directly at mitigating the worst conditions of lower-class black life. A long tradition of philanthropy and internally directed action aimed at self-improvement exists among black Americans, pre-dating the emancipation. One of the major civil rights organizations today, the National Urban League, was founded early in this century to assist new black migrants from the rural South in adjusting to life in the cities of the North. Black fraternal and professional organizations, through a wide array of programs and activities, have been "giving something back to the community" for decades. But the nature of problems facing the black community today, the significant recent expansion of opportunities for blacks in American society, and the changing political environment in which black leaders now operate, all dictate that greater stress should be placed upon strategies that might appropriately be called "self-help."

This noble tradition of mutual concern notwithstanding, the dominant theme among those who speak publicly on behalf of black interests today emphasizes the responsibility of government to deal with the problems of blacks. Policies of the local, state, and federal governments have significant impact on the welfare of black Americans who, therefore, have the right and responsibility to enter the political arena and participate in shaping those policies. But it is now virtually beyond dispute that many of the problems of contemporary Afro-American life lie outside the reach of effective government action, and require for their successful resolution actions that can only be undertaken by the black community itself. These problems involve at their core the values, attitudes, and behaviors of individual blacks. They are exemplified by the staggering statistics on early unwed pregnancies among black women, and criminal participation and incarceration among black men. These problems are part cause, part effect of the economic hardship readily observed in the ghettos of America, but in their complexity defy simplistic explanations. These problems will not go away with the return of economic prosperity, with the election of a liberal

Democrat to the presidency, or with the doubling in size of the Congressional Black Caucus.

I will not pretend here that there exist any easy solutions for these difficulties. My only contentions are that: (1) any effective response will necessarily require the intimate involvement of black institutions, politicians, educators, and other concerned individuals; and (2) the nature and extent of the problem is such as to demand greater attention than is now received from these quarters. My concern is that too much of the political energy, talent, and imagination abundant in the emerging black middle class is being channelled into struggle against the "enemy without," while the "enemy within" goes relatively unchecked.

FAULT VERSUS RESPONSIBILITY

At this point many readers may be saying to themselves, "But these problems of family instability and crime, of which you speak, are themselves but the worst manifestations of oppression and denial of opportunity due to the racist behavior of the 'enemy without.' To expand upon internally directed action aimed at the behavior of blacks is but to treat the symptoms of oppression, and not its causes. If more jobs were provided for those seeking work, these internal problems would surely take care of themselves." I believe this argument to be seriously mistaken, and under circumstances not unlikely to prevail in the United States, possibly quite dangerous. For this line of argument invariably ends by placing the *responsibility* for the maintenance of personal values and social norms compatible with stable community life among blacks on the shoulders of those who do not have an abiding interest in such matters.

It is important to understand that the invalidity of this argument, in the sense that I assert it to be mistaken, is not a matter of the social scientific truth of its premises. I am not questioning the existence of a causal nexus between behavioral difficulties readily observed among blacks on the one hand, and the effects of racism on the other. To the extent, for example, that the fraction of black children raised in single-family homes is greater by virtue of the fact that black men are differentially denied access to employment opportunities, one could correctly conclude that the problem has been caused by the racist denial of opportunity. For instance, there exists a large body of research linking the incidence of various indices of social decay—alcoholism, child abuse, divorce, crime—to the level of unemployment in a given community. The existence of this evidence permits us to assign blame or *fault* to racist whites, to the extent that their racism has caused certain difficulties among blacks. What makes the foregoing argument invalid in my view is the equation of this presumed *fault* with a concomitant *responsibility* to resolve the difficulties that have emerged. As Orlando Patterson has argued in the brilliant essay, "The

Moral Crisis of the Black American,"[1] "fault" and "responsibility" should not be presumed to go hand in hand.

The reason that it is so important for blacks to distinguish between the fault which may be attributed to racism as the cause of the black condition, and the responsibility for dealing with that condition, may be simply stated: No people can be genuinely free so long as they look upon others as responsible for their deliverance. The pride and self-respect universally valued by aspiring peoples throughout the world cannot be the gift of outsiders—they must derive from the thoughts and deeds of the peoples themselves. Neither the guilt nor the pity of one's oppressors is a sufficient basis upon which to construct one's own sense of worth. When faced with the ravages of black-on-black crime, the depressing nature of social life in many low-income black communities, the increasing incidence of early, unwed pregnancy among black teenagers, or the growing dependency of our people on transfers from an increasingly hostile polity, it is simply insufficient to respond by saying, "This is the fault of racist America. These problems will be solved when America finally does right by its black folk." Such a response begs entirely the issue of responsibility, both at the level of individual behavior (the criminal perpetrator being responsible for his act), and at the level of the group (the black community being responsible for the values embraced by its people).

As an illustration of the point I am trying to make here consider the recent public statements that black leaders have been making on the problems of the black family. In the publication *A Policy Framework for Racial Justice*, issued by the Joint Center for Political Studies, a group of 30 prominent black leaders and intellectuals stated:

> No strategy designed to improve the status of black Americans can ignore the central position of the black family as the natural transmitter of the care, *values*, and *opportunities* necessary for black men, women and children to reach their full potential as individuals.[2]

There is thus the clear recognition that values and opportunities available only within families, and insufficiently available to too many blacks, play a crucial role in determining individual achievement. But in the very next sentence, responsibility for this state of affairs is laid at the feet of American society:

> The present black family crisis, characterized chiefly by the precipitous growth of poor female-headed households, can be traced almost directly to American racism. . . . As large numbers of blacks migrated to large cities from rural areas, black males have often been unable to find work, and government policies and other social forces further sapped family strength. These trends proceed apace today, aided by the widespread failure even to recognize the pressures on the black family as central to other problems and by the failure to devise both preventive and healing strategies.

The "failure" being discussed is clearly that of "racist American society," not of the political, intellectual, and religious leadership of the black community itself, which might more appropriately be regarded as responsible for the normative health of the group. My point here is not that one cannot trace some of these family difficulties to American racism. What is crucial is that, having recognized that these difficulties have to do with the behavior of black youngsters, we begin to confront directly the question of how that behavior may be changed. Whatever *fault* may be placed upon "racist American society," the *responsibility* for the behavior of black youngsters lies squarely on the shoulders of the black community itself.

There is a great potential danger in ignoring this responsibility. The risk is that those who are legitimately held at fault for the black condition may nonetheless fail to act to improve that condition. It is becoming increasingly obvious that the spirit which animated the Great Society era, in which government took seriously the responsibility to help solve the problems of the black poor, is on the wane. Those now [1984] proclaiming the enormous stake the black community has in preventing the re-election of Ronald Reagan must confront the possibility not only that he may win the coming election, but that his sense of the extent of government obligation to the black poor may be shared by a durable majority of American voters. Recently John Jacob, president of the National Urban League, stated the problem quite clearly when he said of the problems of the black family:

> We see the problems facing black families as being problems facing our nation. But the nation is not addressing those problems. The administration and the Congress have cut lifeline programs that help all poor people and especially poor black families. They have drastically cut programs that help poor children survive—including nutrition and health programs.
>
> Given that failure to act, we feel that the network of black institutions must play a greater role both in advocacy on behalf of the black family, and *in concrete programmatic ways that provide aid to black families*— assistance to help two-parent families stay intact, resources to help single-parent families survive, and programs that help our children to take their rightful place in our society.
>
> We are confident that the black community has the institutional and voluntary resources to be effective in this great task. . . . For every element of our society must deal with that aspect of the problem for which it is best suited. . . . That means government must be supportive, black institutions must marshal volunteer resources, and *individual black people must accept responsibility for themselves* and for preserving the family values that helped us to survive.[3]

Jacob is keenly aware of the dangers of inaction in an indifferent, if not actually hostile, political environment. By stressing his confidence in the ability of blacks to grapple with these profoundly difficult problems, he by no means absolves the larger society of its obligations. He recognizes however that ultimately it is the leaders of the black community like himself who are responsible for addressing these problems should, for whatever reasons, the government fail to meet its obligations.

A NEW FRONTIER?

This early effort of organizations such as the National Urban League to come to grips with these internal difficulties is suggestive of a new direction in which the institutional and intellectual resources of the black community might be channelled in the struggle for equality still before us. It is now two decades since the enactment of the Civil Rights Act of 1964, and some 30 years since the landmark *Brown* decision was rendered by the Supreme Court. These and the other monumental achievements of the civil rights movement are, for the current generation of American youth, the stuff of history books. Today's young people have no recollection of the struggles from which they emerged. These crowning achievements of the civil rights era dwarf in significance anything likely to issue from the litigation and lobbying efforts of today's advocates. In other words, the civil rights strategy—seeking black advancement through the use of the legal system to force America to live by its espoused creed—has reached the point of "diminishing returns." It is no exaggeration to say that we now live in the "post–civil rights" era.

Yet, if one were to poll that community of activists, lawyers, politicians, and concerned citizens whose effort made "the movement" a reality, a sizable majority would, I believe, say that the work they began remains seriously incomplete. They would point to the significant economic inequality that remains between the races in the United States: A growing fraction of black children are living below the poverty line. The prisons of the country are disproportionately populated by black men. Black families are more often dependent on public assistance than the population as a whole. Residential segregation by race is commonplace in our central cities, as is the racial segregation of public schools that so often accompanies it. Moreover, it would be observed that overt expressions of racism have not yet vanished from the American scene. Thus, it would be argued, much on the civil rights front remains to be done.

It is clear, however, that in the last few years the civil rights leadership and organizations have entered a critical period. The social and political landscape has been dramatically and irrevocably altered since the height of the movement. With the expansion of voting rights has come a new and growing cadre of elected officials providing direct representation for blacks at all levels of government. With the opening of educational opportunities at the elite universities and professional schools, a new class of young black men and women has emerged, with positions of responsibility and influence in the leading institutions of this society. Blacks are thus no longer solely dependent upon the "protest" route for a voice in American affairs. Much of what is accomplished by blacks today no longer issues from current lobbying and litigating activities of the traditional civil rights organizations. It is becoming increasingly obvious (and not only to external critics) that, in order to continue making a contribution to the improvement of the black condition, these organizations must broaden the conception of their mission.

Thus, while many veterans of the struggle would point to the great social disparity between blacks and whites as evidence that the work of the civil rights movement remains unfinished, it is much easier to assert that something must be done than it is to set out an agenda for action. Many veterans of the movement find themselves today in the position of sensing how crucial it is that action be taken, and yet not quite knowing what to do. I want to suggest that the next frontier for the movement should be sought through a concerted effort to grapple directly with the difficult *internal* problems that lower-class blacks now face. That is, I am advancing the notion that the energy and imagination of those individuals and organizations that achieved prominence during the past decades in the struggle for civil rights may be most useful in the post–civil rights era if employed in efforts to directly confront those serious internal difficulties that beset our low-income black communities.

Again, it is important to avoid misunderstanding. I do not suggest that black advocates abandon our traditional concern with the issues of desegregation, equal employment opportunity, or voting rights. There is important work to be done in these areas, even if it is mainly defending past gains against encroachment. But a realistic assessment of the current prospects of the poorest black Americans strongly suggests that their lives may not be profoundly altered by these historically important civil rights strategies. In central-city ghettoes across America, where far too many young black mothers (themselves not yet beyond adolescence) struggle alone to raise the next generation of black youth, it is difficult to see the potential for fundamental change via these traditional methods. Even the election of black candidates to the highest municipal offices has so far failed to affect such change. Yet to the extent that institutions within the black community can be created that are dedicated to the encouragement of responsible male involvement in parenting, the prevention of unplanned pregnancies, and the support of young unwed mothers in their efforts to return to school and become self-supporting, important changes in the lives of this most vulnerable segment of the black population can be made.

Thus, these ought not be seen as mutually exclusive strategies. Internally directed action of the sort just described can be aided by financial and other support from government, and will certainly be more effective, the more complete is the elimination of those historical forms of discrimination against which the civil rights struggle has been waged. Moreover, the traditional civil rights institutions, because of their strong network of affiliated local organizations throughout the country, their reputations for service to the black community, the respectful regard in which they continue to be held by many in the philanthropic institutions, and their ability to call upon the most talented and accomplished individuals within the black community for assistance, are especially well situated to undertake these internally directed efforts.

DISCOURSE TRUNCATION AND THE NEED FOR MORAL LEADERSHIP

The undertaking which I advocate here—an expansion of internally directed action in the black community aimed at improving the life conditions of poor blacks by reducing the incidence of problematic behaviors among them—will necessarily involve a discussion of values, social norms, and personal attitudes. This is always a difficult matter, and especially so in recent years for black Americans. Black leaders and intellectuals have, on the whole, sought to avoid public discussion of the role that such normative factors might play in the perpetuation of poverty within the group. This is both understandable and unfortunate. It is unfortunate because there really is no other manner in which such matters can enter the public discussion effectively. For government to attempt as a matter of public policy to mandate, or even to discuss, what the values and beliefs of any segment of the society should be, is to embark on a course fraught with political, constitutional, and moral pitfalls. Moreover, concerned external observers of the black community are in no position to raise such issues if they desire to maintain their credibility as "liberals." Only blacks can talk about what other blacks "should" do, think, value, etc., and expect to be sympathetically heard. That is, *only* blacks can effectively provide moral leadership for their people. To the extent that such leadership is required, therefore, it must come from within.

And yet, it must be acknowledged that such leadership has been in relatively short supply. While black communities and their residents have been dramatically, and negatively, affected by "black-on-black" crime (of such a magnitude that many inner-city merchants now offer their goods from behind bullet-proof partitions, and black ghetto-dwelling women face a risk of rape higher by several magnitudes than that faced by whites), the principal topic of black congressmen concerned with criminal justice issues has been "police brutality." Police behavior is obviously an issue of legitimate concern to blacks, but the damage done to us by the criminal element within our own communities might plausibly be regarded as an even greater concern. As the gap in academic achievement between black and white youngsters persists at intolerably high levels, very little can be heard from our leadership (with a few, noteworthy exceptions) regarding the extent to which this performance gap is the result of the behavior and values of black children and their parents. As black women struggle without appropriate financial support from their men to provide for themselves and their children, discussion of male irresponsibility has been largely confined to the writings of black feminists.

This is a curious situation. For individual, middle-class blacks and their families have long placed great emphasis upon the kind of positive values and norms entirely inconsistent with the behavior just described. The problematic behaviors of which I have been speaking are thus not only inconsistent with success in American society, but as well with the ethos of much of the black community itself. The current and future spokespersons and leaders of the black community are drawn almost exclusively from this social stratum. These people, having achieved considerable professional success, appear not to recognize their accomplishments as an indication of those personal qualities, exemplified in their own lives, which enable one to best take advantage of such opportunities for blacks as exist in American society. As a result, the possibility that their lives might stand as examples of what can be done, and as models for the lower class of the black community on how it is to be done, goes relatively unexploited.

However, a moment's reflection on the history of black Americans provides some hints as to why the discussion of values and norms has been such a limited part of the group's struggle for social advance. Of fundamental importance in this regard is the atmosphere of racist ideology within which blacks have had to function. From the early days of slavery and the need to fashion some justification for its practice in a democratic Christian society, but continuing into recent times, blacks have had, in various ways, to defend their basic claim to an equal humanity before the general American public. The presumed inferiority of the African was the primary rationalization of his enslavement. The social Darwinists of the last century and this one had, by finding the explanation of blacks' poverty in black culture or genes, posed basic challenges to the integrity and self-respect of the group. The "retrogressionists," who well into this century argued that the black population was, after emancipation, doomed to slip back into its natural state of depravity without the civilizing influence of paternalistic masters, created an environment for thoughtful blacks virtually unique among American ethnic groups.

Among the major consequences of this ideological environment has been the stifling effect that the need to refute these racist beliefs has had on the internal intellectual life and critical discourse of the black community itself. Objective assessment and discussion of the condition of the community has been made difficult for blacks because any critical discussion within the group (about problems of early unwed pregnancy or low academic performance, for example) must be guarded by conscious concern for how such discussion might be appropriated by external critics, all too happy to find black spokesmen willing to provide support for their base hypotheses.

It is hard to overstate the significance of this constraint on discourse among blacks. Its consequences have not gone unnoticed by outside observers. One finds Daniel Patrick Moynihan writing in 1973 regarding his earlier study of the Negro family:

> It is now about a decade since my policy paper and its analysis. As forecasting goes, it would seem to have held up. . . . This has been accompanied by a psychological reaction which I did not foresee, and for which I may in part be to blame. . . . I did not know I would prove to be so correct. Had I known, I might have said nothing, realizing that the subject would become unbearable and rational discussion close to impossible. I accept that in the social sciences some things are better not said.[4]

Moynihan, of course, had argued that the growth of single-parent families posed an emerging and fundamental problem for blacks, which would impede the ability of some to advance in the post–civil rights era. The supercilious arrogance of the above-quoted statement notwithstanding, it is quite evident that he had been right. The problem he identified nearly 20 years ago is today twice as severe, with no solution in sight. And yet, when he released his study he was savagely attacked for "blaming the victim" and for failing to see the inner strengths of these families whose form represented a necessary adaptation in the face of American racism.

A similar scenario could be offered to describe reaction from some black leaders to discussions of racial differences in arrest and incarceration rates for various criminal offenses. The NAACP [National Association for the Advancement of Colored People] views this disparity as further evidence of inequality of opportunity:

> Blacks make up only 12 percent of the nation's total population . . . but an incredible 50 percent of the total prison population. With half of all the prisoners in the United States being black, the fact that only 4 percent of the nation's law-enforcement personnel is black is a sad commentary on equality of opportunity. . . . Why are so many blacks in prison? And why are so few blacks in law enforcement? One inescapable answer applies to both questions: racism. Superficially, it would appear that blacks commit more crimes than anyone else. . . . [However the] only explanation for this . . . discrepancy is conscious choices of key decision makers to focus on crimes committed more frequently by blacks.[5]

The intellectual perspective offered in these remarks is clearly incompatible with serious discussion by blacks of the problem of criminal behavior among a very few young men, which occasions such great costs for the majority of the black poor. It is incredible, in light of the obviously harmful consequences for those who must live in the crime-ridden neighborhoods of our central cities, that organizations dedicated to improving the welfare of blacks are so reticent to state clearly their principled opposition to this behavior. There are worse things than running the risk of "blaming the victim." I submit that "blaming the system" can also be highly dysfunctional for blacks, to the extent that it prevents us from accurately conceptualizing the nature of our circumstance and formulating appropriate responses.

Examples of this sort could also be produced illustrating a similar reaction from black leaders to discussions in the social science community of racial differences in performance on intelligence tests. These problems—family instability, criminal behavior, academic performance—have in common the features that: (1) they are critically important to an accurate characterization of the condition of the black population; (2) their resolution is fundamental to the progress of blacks; but (3) they are used by those outside the black community who subscribe to racist propositions about black inferiority as evidence in support of their views. As a result, many blacks have imposed on themselves a kind of censorship, wherein they agree not to discuss these matters frankly in public, and to ostracize those blacks who do.

One can generalize about the source of this difficulty. Political discourse within a community such as ours requires trust. The nature of the external threat is such that members of the community must always be "on guard." There are individuals who would prove our inferiority, rationalize our predicament and their indifference to it, and roll back our progress. These forces may have supporters, witting or not, even among us. When a politically relevant sentence is uttered by one of our own then, it must be understood in light of these possibilities. We cannot know with certainty where the speaker is "coming from," but the opinions expressed by the speaker give us a signal about his underlying posture. Someone who speaks on behalf of the "free market," or who intimates that there are deep structural problems within black communities having to do with values and attitudes, courts trouble because of the known enemies of the group who have made similar claims. In such an environment it is likely that individuals within the community will tacitly agree not to enunciate certain conceptions, at least not publicly. A *truncation of their political discourse* then ensues.

Moreover, this can be a stable situation because suspicion of those who violate the implicit accord can become a rational act, in a self-fulfilling way. Only someone who places relatively slight weight on social acceptance within the community—someone who, therefore, is objectively less likely to share a group's prevailing conception of its interests—would be willing to breach the implicit contract of silence. In such a situation it is possible that the limitation on the group's discourse might live on after most individuals within the group have recognized that something is wrong. It is a situation aptly captured by the children's tale "The Emperor Has No Clothes."

This line of reasoning suggests that when the barriers to discussion of certain issues finally break down, as they must—no group can tolerate an indefinite period during which objective and subjective so widely diverge—the change will be both rapid and complete. Institutions such as the black churches, fraternal and sororal organizations, and the nationally based civil rights organizations are particularly well suited, because of their unimpeachable integrity and commitment to the community, to initiate the internal task of broadening the discourse on these matters of vital concern to the welfare of black Americans. While the behavioral problems described here are by no means unique to blacks, our ability to openly analyze them and to develop methods for their resolution is limited by this truncation of critical discourse within the group.

CLASS SCHISM, POLITICAL CAPITAL, AND INTRA-GROUP EXPLOITATION

The fact that values, social norms, and personal behaviors often observed among the poorest members of the black community are quite distinct from those characteristics of the black middle class is indicative of a growing divergence in the social and economic experiences of Afro-Americans. The extent and importance of this divergence is the subject of often acrimonious debate, but its existence is beyond serious dispute. The simple fact is that the opening of opportunities occasioned by the legal and political successes of the civil rights movement has led to a dramatic increase in the numbers of blacks attending elite colleges and universities, entering the professions, and engaging in successful business enterprise, relative to a generation ago. Yet the ghetto-dwelling residents of central Harlem, of Watts, of the west side of Chicago, or the east side of Detroit are not often found among this new cadre of aspiring young blacks. Nor is the prospect that their children will enter this social stratum nearly as great as that of black children not subject to the debilitating effects of life in these communities. There are thus genuine differences among blacks in their social circumstances, differences that suggest the much abused sociological concept of "class."

   I submit that these differences in social circumstance, together with the realities of political advocacy on behalf of blacks in contemporary American life, provide a strong *moral* argument for the expansion of internal actions aimed directly at improving the circumstances of the black poor. The main point is that better-off blacks benefit, through the political system, from the conditions under which the poorest blacks must live. This implies a concomitant obligation to contribute to the mitigation of those conditions, although there is no incentive to do so.

   The methods by which blacks wield influence on the formulation of public policy in this country are several. There is, of course, the effect of the ballot. Many are the southern politicians who have learned to "sing a different tune" by virtue of their recognition that election without black support has become impossible. In major urban areas throughout the country black candidates now successfully compete for the highest offices, significantly affecting the conduct of local governments. The [1984] presidential campaign of Jesse Jackson suggests ways in which even greater influence on policy formulation can be had via the black vote.

In addition to raw political muscle, however, there is also this fact: Blacks enjoy the benefit of the widely (though, obviously, not universally) held perception that our demands on the political system are a test of its justice and fairness. The extent to which a political administration is perceived as "sensitive" to the claims of blacks is a measure of its compassion, or a sign of its callousness. Many Americans accept the notion that the government should, in some way, deal with the problems of blacks because that is the proper and decent thing to do, in light of the historical culpability of American society implied by its past racist practices. The existence of "liberal guilt" has been instrumental in sustaining political support for initiatives of substantial benefit to blacks.

There are, I suggest, few things more valuable in the struggle among competing claimants for government largess than the clearly perceived status of victim. Blacks "enjoy" that status by brunt of the many years of systematic exclusion from a just place in American life. Thus, a substantial source of black influence derives from the fact that blacks are perceived as having been unjustly wronged and thus worthy of consideration. The single most important symbol of this injustice is the large inner-city ghetto, with its population of poor blacks. These masses and their miserable condition sustain the political capital that all blacks enjoy because of their historical status as victims.

The growing black "underclass" has become a constant reminder to many Americans of a historic debt owed to the black community. Were it not for this continued presence among us of those worst-off of all Americans, blacks' ability to sustain public support for affirmative action, minority business set-asides, and the like would be vastly reduced. (Even women's groups, by citing in support of their political objectives the "feminization of poverty"—a phenomenon substantially influenced by the increasing number of black families headed by women with low incomes—derive benefit from this source.) That is, the suffering of the poorest blacks creates, if you will, a fund of political capital upon which all members of the group can draw in the pressing of racially based claims.

It is thus not surprising to find that whenever any black leader argues for special assistance to some members of his community, whether that assistance flows directly to the poorest blacks or not, one can hear invoked the black teenage unemployment rate or the increasing percentage of blacks living below the poverty line. The fact that the median black family income has not increased much relative to white family income over the period 1960–1980 has been frequently cited by black spokesmen and others to support the general claim that "nothing has changed." No major government purchasing effort at the local, state, or federal level can proceed now without the question being raised, "What is in this for minority business?" Inevitably the low economic status of the black poor will be referred to as justification for the claim.

I would like to clearly state that nothing is being implied here about the motives of black leaders, businessmen, or professionals. I intend only to observe that, in the nature of the case, their advocacy for policies of benefit to blacks who are not necessarily poor is most effective when couched in terms that remind the American polity of its historic debt, and this is most readily done by reference to the condition of the poorest blacks.

The question should be raised though as to how the black poor are to be benefited by the policy actions extracted from the system in their name? The evidence of which I am aware suggests that for many of the most hotly contested public policies advocated by black spokesmen, not much of the benefit "trickles down" to the black poor. There is no study of which I am aware supporting the claim that set-asides for minority business have led to a significant increase in the level of employment among lower class blacks. It is clear from extensive empirical research on the effect of affirmative action standards for federal contractors, that the positive impact on blacks that this program has had accrues mainly to those in the higher occupations. If one examines the figures on relative earnings of young black and white men by educational class, by far the greater progress has been made among those blacks with the most education. Looking at relative earnings of black and white workers by occupation, one finds that the most dramatic earnings gains for blacks have taken place in the professional, technical, and managerial occupations, while the least significant gains have come in the lowest occupations, like laborer and service worker. Thus, a broad array of evidence suggests, at least to this observer, that better placed blacks have simply been able to take better advantage of the opportunities created in the last 20 years than have those mired in the underclass.

The Marxian notion of exploitation refers to a circumstance in which workers receive less from the process of production than their labor has contributed. It seems evident that poor blacks today gain less from the political process than their votes and misery contribute to the effectiveness of black advocacy. Sadly, this circumstance may continue for some time.

Again, I should not be understood as suggesting the presence of any malice or bad faith on the part of those middle-class blacks who are able to extract concrete gains from the system. Like Marx's capitalists, these individuals need have no consciousness of how their behavior, along with that of many others within a given social system, leads to a situation in which exploitation occurs. It seems to be a feature of the contemporary American political economy that the kind of benefits most readily generated for blacks are those appropriable more easily by blacks already not too badly off. It is a simple matter to see that the prime contractor on a large municipal construction project uses a certain percentage of black subcontractors, and much harder to assure that the fatherless child of a poverty-stricken mother avoids the hazards everywhere about our ghettoes. We can demand that a consumer franchise company give dealerships to black entreprenuers, but not that the high school valedictorian be black.

This circumstance provides, to my mind, a compelling moral argument for the position that ways must be sought in which those blacks who have achieved a modicum of security and success can be enlisted in the decades-long task of eradicating the worst aspects of black poverty. The nature of the problems besetting inner-city communities, the character of political advocacy by blacks in the post-civil rights era, and the ominous drift of politics in contemporary America seem to require that any morally defensible and factually based program of action for the black community must have primary among its objectives that of improving the personal efficacy of members of the black "underclass." It seems certain that the federal government can play a critical role in this process. Yet it is equally clear that the black business, academic, and political elites have the obligation to press for improvement in their own peoples' lives, through constructive internal institution-building, whether government participates or not.

NOTES

1. *The Public Interest,* summer 1973, pp 43–69.
2. *A Policy Framework for Racial Justice.* (Washington, D.C.: Joint Center for Political Studies, 1983), p. 9 (emphasis added).
3. *The Urban League News,* April 1984, p. 2 (emphasis added).
4. *The Public Interest,* spring 1973, p. 7.
5. *The Crisis,* April 1982, p. 13.

Questions for Discussion

1. Advocates of a market economy argue that "a rising tide lifts all boats." In other words, if the U.S. economy overall experiences boom times, then *all* groups in the country benefit. The prescription of these advocates for improving the condition of black people is to allow market forces to operate rather than to rely on government assistance programs. What criteria would you use to evaluate this prescription?
2. Is the prescription mentioned in Question 1 valid? Why or why not?
3. What effect does welfare have on the formation of single-parent households?
4. What role can the government play in strengthening the black family?
5. To what extent should the responsibility for the behavior of black youngsters lie "squarely on the shoulders of the black community itself"?
6. What role, if any, should nonblacks play in solving problems of blacks? Why?

Suggested Readings

Beverly, Creigs C., and Howard J. Stanback. "The Black Underclass: Theory and Reality." *Black Scholar*, 17, no. 5 (September–October 1986), 24–32.

Gilder, George. *Wealth and Poverty*. New York: Bantam, 1981.

Gilliam, Franklin D., Jr. "Black America: Divided by Class?" *Public Opinion*, 9, no. 1 (February–March 1986), 53–60.

Kaus, Mickey. "Up from Altruism: The Case against Compassion." *New Republic*, 195, no. 24 (December 15, 1986), 17–18.

Kuttner, Robert. "A Great American Tradition: Government Opening Opportunity." *Challenge*, 29, no. 1 (March–April 1986), 18–25.

Levitan, Sar A. "How the Welfare System Promotes Economic Security." *Political Science Quarterly*, 100, no. 3 (Fall 1985), 447–449.

Murray, Charles A. *Losing Ground: American Social Policy, 1950–1980*. New York: Basic Books, 1984.

Rustin, Bayard. "The King to Come." *New Republic*, 196, no. 10 (March 9, 1987), 19–21.

U.S. Cong., House of Representatives. *Poverty, Hunger, and the Welfare System*. Hearing before the Select Committee on Hunger, 99th Cong., 2nd Sess., 1986.

U.S. Cong., *War on Poverty: Victory or Defeat?* Hearing before the Joint Economic Committee, 99th Cong., 1st Sess., 1985.

"What Does the Government Owe the Poor?" [forum with Charles Murray and Jesse Jackson]. *Harper's*, 272, no. 1631 (April 1986), 35–39, 42–47.

Wilson, William Julius. "Cycles of Deprivation and the Underclass Debate." *Social Service Review*, 59, no. 4 (December 1985), 541–559.

See also Suggested Readings for Chapter 4.

Chapter 16

Should the Death Penalty Be Abolished?

The Eighth Amendment to the Constitution forbids "cruel and unusual punishments" but does not specify what makes a punishment cruel or unusual. When the Bill of Rights was adopted, the dominant view accepted the legitimacy of the death penalty, or "capital punishment" as it is called. But particularly since the nineteenth century, there has been continuing controversy about the morality of capital punishment, not only in the United States but throughout the world. The global trend has been away from capital punishment. Today the United States is one of the three advanced industrial societies that allow the death penalty. South Africa and the Soviet Union are the other two.

The death penalty has been brought before the Supreme Court on a number of occasions. In 1972, the Supreme Court decided in *Furman* v. *Georgia* to bar the death penalty as it was imposed under statutes at the time. The Court objected to the randomness of the procedures governing the death penalty.[1] As a result of the decision, most state legislatures enacted new laws complying with the decision in *Furman* so that capital punishment could still be legal as a punishment in major violent crimes.

The Supreme Court again considered capital punishment in 1976 in the case of *Gregg* v. *Georgia.* In that case and in four related cases it accepted the constitutionality of the death penalty under certain conditions.[2] Execution, which had not been implemented in the United States since 1967, was resumed in 1977.

The death penalty is under continuous legal challenge. One issue the Supreme Court considered was the subject of racism in death penalty sentences. In 1987 the Court rejected a challenge that capital punishment was more likely to be inflicted on black defendants than whites and therefore violated the Equal Protection Clause of the Fourteenth Amendment.[3] The death penalty is also under continuous consideration in the legislative branch. Bills to abolish the death penalty have been introduced but not enacted into law. Some members of Congress, representing the opposite view, have sought to apply the death penalty to acts of treason and drug trafficking instead of only for the most extreme cases of murder.

Should the death penalty be abolished? The Committee on Civil Rights of the Association of the Bar of the City of New York contends that it should. It argues:

1. Mistakes are inevitable in the application of the death penalty.
2. Capital punishment is cruel, barbaric, and adversely affects the administration of justice.
3. It is discriminatorily applied against the poor minorities.
4. It is inconsistent with our self-respect as civilized people.
5. It is not working in accordance with required constitutional principles.

An opposing viewpoint is taken by Edward I. Koch, the mayor of New York City. He argues:

1. The death penalty is not barbaric.
2. The fact that other democracies have outlawed capital punishment is irrelevant. The United States has a high murder rate, and, consequently, the death penalty is appropriate in this country.
3. The argument that errors can be committed in putting to death an innocent person falsely convicted of a heinous offense is irrelevant. If government functioned only when the possibility of error did not exist, government would not function at all.
4. The death penalty strengthens the value of human life.
5. The assertion of racial discrimination is not a valid argument for ending the death penalty but rather for extending such a punishment.
6. Biblical sources and leading philosophers throughout history have supported the death penalty.
7. The execution of a lawfully condemned killer is no more an act of murder than is legal imprisonment an act of kidnapping.

NOTES

1. *Furman* v. *Georgia*, 408 U.S. 238 (1972).
2. *Gregg* v. *Georgia*, 428 U.S. 153 (1976).
3. *McCleskey* v. *Kemp*, Supreme Court docket no. 84-6811 (April 22, 1987).

Should the Death Penalty Be Abolished?

COMMITTEE ON CIVIL RIGHTS
OF THE ASSOCIATION OF THE BAR
OF THE CITY OF NEW YORK
The Death Penalty

I. INTRODUCTION

Seven years ago this Committee issued a report urging the abolition of the death penalty. At that time a ten-year moratorium on executions had come to an end. This Committee felt then, as it feels even more strongly now, that the death penalty has no place in the American criminal justice system.

Today executions have begun proceeding apace. Since Gary Gilmore was killed by a Utah firing squad in 1977, at least 18 more people have been electrocuted, gassed or killed by lethal injection. At present 38 states have death penalties and approximately 1,300 people await execution on death rows in 33 states. One person is under sentence of death in New York, and his appeal is now before the Court of Appeals. Unless capital punishment is eliminated, as death cases wend their way through the courts and inmates exhaust their remedies, the frequency and number of executions will no doubt increase almost exponentially.

We continue to urge abolition of the death penalty for the same reasons set forth in our 1977 Report: "because mistakes are inevitable in its application, because it is cruel and barbaric and adversely affects the administration of justice, and because it has been, and in our view will continue to be, discriminatorily applied against the poor and racial minorities." And as we also noted in our prior Report, "[A]bove all, we oppose the death penalty because we believe it to be inconsistent with our self-respect as civilized people."

But more importantly, at this time we renew our call for abolition because of what has occurred since our 1977 Report. All available evidence leads to the conclusion that the death penalty is not working in accordance with the standards constitutionally required by the Supreme Court.

If the country must continue with capital punishment, the courts and the bar must continue to recognize the unique nature of the punishment and afford capital defendants adequate representation from indictment to execution. In this regard, the courts or the legislatures should recognize a right to counsel in state and federal post-conviction capital *habeas corpus* proceedings, a right not now extended. Until such a right is recognized, the bar must volunteer its efforts to ensure that no defendant is executed without at least having had full and adequate representation in all proceedings, including crucial post-conviction proceedings. Finally, courts should refrain from unfair criticism directed at counsel in capital cases such as that recently made by Chief Justice Burger and others.

II. THE DEATH PENALTY IS NOT WORKING IN ACCORDANCE WITH REQUIRED CONSTITUTIONAL PRINCIPLES

In 1972, *Furman v. Georgia* and its companion cases struck down as unconstitutional all then-existing state death statutes because of their arbitrariness and their potential or actual discriminatory application. Since that time state legislators have grappled with *Furman* and its progeny in attempts to draft statutes that are neither arbitrary nor discriminatory. Sadly, these attempts are futile, mainly because they ignore the uniqueness and finality of the death penalty.

Nonetheless, in 1976, the Supreme Court, in *Gregg v. Georgia* and its companion cases, resurrected the death penalty by upholding the constitutionality of capital punishment under the Eighth Amendment. At the same time, the Court noted that the death penalty is permissible only under "a carefully drafted statute that ensures that the sentencing authority is given adequate information and guidance." In a series of contemporaneous and subsequent decisions, the Court, having upheld the constitutionality of death as punishment, sought to "fine tune" the penalty in an attempt to maintain it within constitutional bounds. Understandably, the lower courts have also struggled with the many problems inherent in capital cases.

Although the various lower courts have attempted to see that death sentences are carried out in accord with constitutional principles, we believe that the fundamental requirements of *Furman*—that the punishment not be arbitrarily or discriminatorily applied—are not being met; nor do we believe that, as a practical matter, they can ever be.

Our analysis proceeds from the assumption, accepted by the plurality in *Gregg v. Georgia,* that the definition of cruel and unusual punishment is not a "static concept" and is always open to review. Between 1972, when *Furman* was decided, and 1981 there were over 204,000 murders committed in the United States. During approximately the same period 2,400 people convicted of such crimes were sentenced to death, and to date 18 of these were executed. Thus, there is still a disturbing randomness to the imposition of the death penalty.

There is, of course, a randomness to many circumstances in life, and many of those are within the discretion of the government but not necessarily constitutionally interdicted. But whatever confusion may have been created by the numerous opinions in *Furman*, that case does make it clear that the Eighth and

Fourteenth Amendments prohibit imposition of the death penalty in an arbitrary, capricious or discriminatory manner. The very randomness with which the penalty has been imposed in the twelve years since *Furman* points to nothing more than an unfair lottery in which the poor, disadvantaged and underrepresented are most clearly the losers.

Demographics of the nation's growing death row populace indicate that these inmates are disproportionately members of minority groups. Available facts and studies also indicate that death row inmates are generally uneducated, illiterate and poor. In addition, although all of the figures have not been marshalled, it appears that the greatest single determinant of chances of a defendant receiving the death penalty is the race of the victim; people who kill whites are much more likely to be sentenced to death than people who kill blacks or other minorities.

We need look no further than the very first involuntary execution since *Furman* for evidence that the death penalty is still being administered arbitrarily and capriciously. John Spenkellink, an unemployed drifter with a history of alcoholism, was executed in Florida in 1979 for the murder of another unemployed drifter with whom he had been travelling. There was substantial evidence that the homicide was committed in self defense or, at worst, in circumstances that would justify a lesser than capital conviction. In addition, a number of extraneous factors such as the defendant's foreign and strange sounding surname, his poverty and his lack of family or roots in the area where the case was tried may have led to the death sentence being imposed. In any event, there are persons who have committed more repugnant crimes with fewer mitigating circumstances and who have escaped execution, no doubt for a number of reasons not fairly related to the decision of whether or not to impose the sentence.

In *Pulley v. Harris,* the Supreme Court recently held that a "comparative proportionality review," which would determine whether the death sentence in a particular case was proportionate to sentences imposed on others convicted of similar crimes, is permissible but not constitutionally required. But we believe that this lack of "proportionality," while generally inherent to some extent in the criminal justice system, creates incurable flaws of arbitrariness and discrimination in all death sentencing schemes, flaws pointed up by Spenkellink's execution.

A related problem leading to arbitrary and capricious infliction of the death penalty is created by the many situations in which a prosecutor is unable to obtain a conviction without the testimony of an accomplice who may well be as culpable as, or even more culpable than, the defendant who actually is sentenced to death. In the Texas case of Charles Brooks, the prosecutor never proved who fired the fatal bullet, but Brooks was executed while the accomplice was able to plea-bargain a 40-year term. And in the case of Robert Sullivan, the accomplice who testified against him received, as a result, a lesser sentence, and was free on parole on the day Sullivan died in Florida's electric chair.

Thus, the ten year experience in capital sentencing has shown that the procedures have been neither nonarbitrary nor nondiscriminatory. The nation's death rows are populated by those who are there largely by virtue of the unfortunate circumstances of their lives and their distinctively low place in society, combined with the unfortuitous manner in which their cases were prosecuted and defended. Factors equally irrelevant to whether these people should be the ones to die, such as the location of the crime or the trial, the defendant's name, the victim's race or adverse pre-trial publicity, all exert influence.

In sum, the case against the death penalty is overwhelming. It is simply intolerable that a system of justice predicated upon equal protection of the law can countenance the ultimate penalty of death when it has been so amply demonstrated that the penalty is still being applied arbitrarily and discriminatorily.

In view of the untenable manner in which it is being applied, we fail to perceive any compelling justification for the death penalty. Concurring in *Gregg v. Georgia,* in which evidence of the deterrent effect of capital punishment was presented, Justice Stewart noted that such evidence was inconclusive at best. Since that time the statistics, if anything, make out a case against deterrence. The highest murder rates exist in states with capital sentencing schemes and large death row populations. Indeed, while the nation's 1983 murder capitals were Odessa, Texas and Miami, Florida, Florida and Texas have the country's largest death row populations. Although some may argue than these states have high death row populations because of their high murder rates, the existence of the Florida and Texas death statutes certainly does not appear to be diminishing the murder rates there.

In fact, there is compelling evidence that executions may increase murder rates. Some postulate that death penalties encourage murder, either because they lend legitimacy to the act of killing or because certain self-destructive persons commit capital crimes in the hope that they will be executed. In any event, we perceive no forceful evidence to the effect that the existence, imposition or carrying out of the death penalty does anything more than to assure that the person executed will not kill again; and we believe that this end can be largely achieved by less drastic, constitutionally acceptable means such as mandatory life sentences.

"Retribution" is the other most often posited rationale for capital punishment; proponents, including the plurality in *Gregg v. Georgia,* contend that for certain heinous crimes "the only adequate response may be the penalty of death." As this Committee noted in its 1977 Report:

[W]e no longer tolerate as morally acceptable punishment by rack, screw or wheel even though some people may feel such punishment is deserved for gruesome crimes. For the same reasons that we reject those punishments today, the deliberate killing by the state of a human being should be rejected by our society.

The notion that the death penalty is an adequate response to killing or represents a societal entitlement to vengeance or retribution must be rejected as a rationale for society committing that same act. Although there is no doubt that the practice has been endorsed by many societies over the centuries, at this time we find it illogical, if not immoral, for society to kill people who kill people in order to demonstrate that killing is wrong. No other country among the western democracies actively engages in killing its criminals. By returning to capital punishment the United States joins the ranks of nations such as the Soviet Union, South Africa, Saudi Arabia and Iran, as one commentator has noted, "a rogues' gallery of the most repressive and backward-looking regimes in the world."

In sum, we continue to believe that the case against the death penalty is overwhelming, the case for it weak and inconclusive at best. In these circumstances we continue to urge its abolition.

☑ NO

Should the Death Penalty Be Abolished?

EDWARD I. KOCH
Death and Justice

Last December a man named Robert Lee Willie, who had been convicted of raping and murdering an 18-year-old woman, was executed in the Louisiana state prison. In a statement issued several minutes before his death, Mr. Willie said: "Killing people is wrong. . . . It makes no difference whether it's citizens, countries, or governments. Killing is wrong." Two weeks later in South Carolina, an admitted killer named Joseph Carl Shaw was put to death for murdering two teenagers. In an appeal to the governor for clemency, Mr. Shaw wrote: "Killing is wrong when I did it. Killing is wrong when you do it. I hope you have the courage and moral strength to stop the killing."

It is a curiosity of modern life that we find ourselves being lectured on morality by cold-blooded killers. Mr. Willie previously had been convicted of aggravated rape, aggravated kidnapping, and the murders of a Louisiana deputy and a man from Missouri. Mr. Shaw committed another murder a week before the two for which he was executed, and admitted mutilating the body of the 14-year-old girl he killed. I can't help wondering what prompted these murderers to speak out against killing as they entered the death-house door. Did their newfound reverence for life stem from the realization that they were about to lose their own?

Life is indeed precious, and I believe the death penalty helps to affirm this fact. Had the death penalty been a real possibility in the minds of these murderers, they might well have stayed their hand. They might have shown moral awareness before their victims died, and not after. Consider the tragic death of Rosa Velez, who happened to be home when a man named Luis Vera burglarized her apartment in Brooklyn. "Yeah, I shot her," Vera admitted. "She knew me, and I knew I wouldn't go to the chair."

During my 22 years in public service, I have heard the pros and cons of capital punishment expressed with special intensity. As a district leader, councilman, congressman, and mayor, I have represented constituencies generally thought of as liberal. Because I support the death penalty for heinous crimes of murder, I have sometimes been the subject of emotional and outraged attacks by voters who find my position reprehensible or worse. I have listened to their ideas. I have weighed their objections carefully. I still support the death penalty. The reasons I maintain my position can be best understood by examining the arguments most frequently heard in opposition.

1. THE DEATH PENALTY IS "BARBARIC"

Sometimes opponents of capital punishment horrify with tales of lingering death on the gallows, of faulty electric chairs, or of agony in the gas chamber. Partly in response to such protests, several states such as North Carolina and Texas switched to execution by lethal injection. The condemned person is put to death painlessly, without ropes, voltage, bullets, or gas. Did this answer the objections of death penalty opponents? Of course not. On June 22, 1984, the *New York Times* published an editorial that sarcastically attacked the new "hygienic" method of death by injection, and stated that "execution can never be made humane through science." So it's not the method that really troubles opponents. It's the death itself they consider barbaric.

Admittedly, capital punishment is not a pleasant topic. However, one does not have to like the death penalty in order to support it any more than one must like radical surgery, radiation, or chemotherapy in order to find necessary these attempts at curing cancer. Ultimately we may learn how to cure cancer with a simple pill. Unfortunately, that day has not yet arrived. Today we are faced with the choice of letting the cancer spread or trying to cure it with the methods available, methods that one day will almost certainly be considered barbaric. But to give up and do nothing would be far more barbaric and would certainly delay the discovery of an eventual cure. The analogy between cancer and murder is imperfect, because murder is not the "disease" we are trying to cure. The disease is injustice. We may not like the death penalty, but it must be available to punish crimes of cold-blooded murder, cases in which any other form of punishment would be inadequate and, therefore, unjust. If we create a

society in which injustice is not tolerated, incidents of murder—the most fla-
grant form of injustice—will diminish.

2. NO OTHER MAJOR DEMOCRACY USES THE DEATH PENALTY

No other major democracy—in fact, few other countries of any description—
are plagued by a murder rate such as that in the United States. Fewer and fewer
Americans can remember the days when unlocked doors were the norm and
murder was a rare and terrible offense. In America the murder rate climed 122
percent between 1963 and 1980. During that same period, the murder rate in
New York City increased by almost 400 percent, and the statistics are even
worse in many other cities. A study at MIT [Massachusetts Institute of Technol-
ogy] showed that based on 1970 homicide rates a person who lived in a large
American city ran a greater risk of being murdered than an American soldier in
World War II ran of being killed in combat. It is not surprising that the laws of
each country differ according to differing conditions and traditions. If other
countries had our murder problem, the cry for capital punishment would be
just as loud as it is here. And I daresay that any other major democracy where
75 percent of the people supported the death penalty would soon enact it into
law.

3. AN INNOCENT PERSON MIGHT BE EXECUTED BY MISTAKE

Consider the work of Adam Bedau, one of the most implacable foes of capital
punishment in this country. According to Mr. Bedau, it is "false sentimentality
to argue that the death penalty should be abolished because of the abstract
possibility that an innocent person might be executed." He cites a study of the
7,000 executions in this country from 1893 to 1971, and concludes that the
record fails to show that such cases occur. The main point, however, is this. If
government functioned only when the possibility of error didn't exist, government wouldn't function at all. Human life deserves special protection, and one
of the best ways to guarantee that protection is to assure that convicted murderers do not kill again. Only the death penalty can accomplish this end. In a
recent case in New Jersey, a man named Richard Biegenwald was freed from
prison after serving 18 years for murder; since his release he has been convicted of committing four murders. A prisoner named Lemuel Smith, who,
while serving four life sentences for murder (plus two life sentences for kidnap-
ing and robbery) in New York's Green Haven Prison, lured a woman correc-

tions officer into the chaplain's office and strangled her. He then mutilated and dismembered her body. An additional life sentence for Smith is meaningless. Because New York has no death penalty statute, Smith has effectively been given a license to kill.

But the problem of multiple murder is not confined to the nation's penitentiaries. In 1981, 91 police officers were killed in the line of duty in this country. Seven percent of those arrested in the cases that have been solved had a previous arrest for murder. In New York City in 1976 and 1977, 85 persons arrested for homicide had a previous arrest for murder. Six of these individuals had two previous arrests for murder, and one had four previous murder arrests. During those two years the New York police were arresting for murder persons with a previous arrest for murder on the average of one every 8.5 days. This is not surprising when we learn that in 1975, for example, the median time served in Massachusetts for homicide was less than two-and-a-half years. In 1976 a study sponsored by the Twentieth Century Fund found that the average time served in the United States for first-degree murder is ten years. The median time served may be considerably lower.

4. CAPITAL PUNISHMENT CHEAPENS THE VALUE OF HUMAN LIFE

On the contrary, it can be easily demonstrated that the death penalty strengthens the value of human life. If the penalty for rape were lowered, clearly it would signal a lessened regard for the victims' suffering, humiliation, and personal integrity. It would cheapen their horrible experience, and expose them to an increased danger of recurrence. When we lower the penalty for murder, it signals a lessened regard for the value of the victim's life. Some critics of capital punishment, such as columnist Jimmy Breslin, have suggested that a life sentence is actually a harsher penalty for murder than death. This is sophistic nonsense. A few killers may decide not to appeal a death sentence, but the overwhelming majority make every effort to stay alive. It is by exacting the highest penalty for the taking of human life that we affirm the highest value of human life.

5. THE DEATH PENALTY IS APPLIED IN A DISCRIMINATORY MANNER

This factor no longer seems to be the problem it once was. The appeals process for a condemned prisoner is lengthy and painstaking. Every effort is made to see that the verdict and sentence were fairly arrived at. However, assertions of discrimination are not an argument for ending the death penalty but for extending it. It is not justice to exclude everyone from the penalty of the law if a few are found to be so favored. Justice requires that the law be applied equally to all.

6. THOU SHALT NOT KILL

The Bible is our greatest source of moral inspiration. Opponents of the death penalty frequently cite the sixth of the Ten Commandments in an attempt to prove that capital punishment is divinely proscribed. In the original Hebrew, however, the Sixth Commandment reads, "Thou Shalt Not Commit Murder," and the Torah specifies capital punishment for a variety of offenses. The biblical viewpoint has been upheld by philosophers throughout history. The greatest thinkers of the 19th century—Kant, Locke, Hobbes, Rousseau, Montesquieu, and Mill—agreed that natural law properly authorizes the sovereign to take life in order to vindicate justice. Only Jeremy Bentham was ambivalent. Washington, Jefferson, and Franklin endorsed it. Abraham Lincoln authorized executions for deserters in wartime. Alexis de Tocqueville, who expressed profound respect for American institutions, believed that the death penalty was indispensable to the support of social order. The United States Constitution, widely admired as one of the seminal achievements in the history of humanity, condemns cruel and inhuman punishment, but does not condemn capital punishment.

7. THE DEATH PENALTY IS STATE-SANCTIONED MURDER

This is the defense with which Messrs. Willie and Shaw hoped to soften the resolve of those who sentenced them to death. By saying in effect, "You're no better than I am," the murderer seeks to bring his accusers down to his own level. It is also a popular argument among opponents of capital punishment, but a transparently false one. Simply put, the state has rights that the private individual does not. In a democracy, those rights are given to the state by the electorate. The execution of a lawfully condemned killer is no more an act of murder than is legal imprisonment an act of kidnapping. If an individual forces a neighbor to pay him money under threat of punishment, it's called extortion. If the state does it, it's called taxation. Rights and responsibilities surrendered by the individual are what give the state its power to govern. This contract is the foundation of civilization itself.

Everyone wants his or her rights, and will defend them jealously. Not everyone, however, wants responsibilities, especially the painful responsibilities that come with law enforcement. Twenty-one years ago a woman named Kitty Genovese was assaulted and murdered on a street in New York. Dozens of neighbors heard her cries for help but did nothing to assist her. They didn't even call the police. In such a climate the criminal understandably grows bolder. In the presence of moral cowardice, he lectures us on our supposed failings and tries to equate his crimes with our quest for justice.

The death of anyone—even a convicted killer—diminishes us all. But we are diminished even more by a justice system that fails to function. It is an illusion to let ourselves believe that doing away with capital punishment removes the murderer's deed from our conscience. The rights of society are paramount. When we protect guilty lives, we give up innocent lives in exchange. When opponents of capital punishment say to the state: "I will not let you kill in my name," they are also saying to murderers: "You can kill in your *own* name as long as I have an excuse for not getting involved."

It is hard to imagine anything worse than being murdered while neighbors do nothing. But something worse exists. When those same neighbors shrink back from justly punishing the murderer, the victim dies twice.

Questions for Discussion

1. How would you determine whether the death penalty is an instrument of racial oppression?
2. What role should family members of a murdered victim play in influencing a sentence involving the death penalty?
3. If the death penalty is acceptable, in what kinds of cases should it be applied?
4. What effect would public executions have on violent crimes?
5. What role does arbitrariness of the people subjected to capital punishment play in your evaluation of this issue?

Suggested Readings

Amsterdam, Anthony G. In Favorem Mortis: The Supreme Court and Capital Punishment." *Human Rights*, 14, no. 1 (Winter 1987), 14–17, 49–60.

Bedau, Hugo Adam. *Death Is Different: Studies in the Morality, Law, and Politics of Capital Punishment*. Boston: Northeastern Univ. Press, 1987.

Berger, Raoul. *Death Penalties: The Supreme Court's Obstacle Course*. Cambridge, Mass.: Harvard Univ. Press, 1982.

Berns, Walter. *For Capital Punishment: Crime and the Morality of the Death Penalty*. New York: Basic Books, 1979.

Black, Charles L., Jr. *Capital Punishment: The Inevitability of Caprice and Mistake.* 2nd ed. New York: Norton, 1981.

DeParle, Jason. "Executions Aren't News: Why They Should Be." *Washington Monthly,* 18, no. 2 (March 1986), 12–21.

Nakell, Barry, and Kenneth A. Hardy. *The Arbitrariness of the Death Penalty.* Philadelphia: Temple Univ. Press, 1987.

U.S. Cong., Senate. *Capital Punishment.* Hearings before the Committee on the Judiciary, 97th Cong., 1st Sess., 1981.

———. *Death Penalty Legislation.* Hearing before the Judiciary Committee, 99th Cong., 1st Sess., 1985.

White, Welsh S. *The Death Penalty in the Eighties: An Examination of the Modern System of Capital Punishment.* Ann Arbor: Univ. of Michigan Press, 1987.

Zimring, Franklin E., and Gordon Hawkins. *Capital Punishment and the American Agenda.* Cambridge, England: Cambridge Univ. Press, 1986.

Chapter 17

Should the Media Be Regulated in Reporting Acts of Terrorism?

Terrorism may be defined as the use of violence by substate actors against civilian and political targets for the purpose of dramatizing a political cause. Substate actors are small groups that are not countries, or states as they are called in international politics. It is often the case, however, that terrorist acts, although carried out by substate actors, have the backing of states so that it is difficult to be precise about what kinds of actions may properly be defined as acts of terrorism.

In the past, the term *terrorism* has been applied to the actions of states, and it originated, in fact, in the more radical phase of the French Revolution. Earlier in the twentieth century it was used to describe the behavior of totalitarian dictators, such as Adolf Hitler and Joseph Stalin.

Today some of the major organizations identified as terrorist by their adversaries include the Irish Republican Army (IRA), the Palestine Liberation Organization (PLO), Basque Nationalists, and the Red Brigades.

Terrorists often see themselves, however, as "freedom fighters," and it has been pointed out that one person's terrorist is another person's freedom fighter. Some observers argue that if PLO activists are terrorists, then so, too, were George Washington and Thomas Jefferson. Critics of such a view argue that George Washington and Thomas Jefferson did not advocate the willful killing of civilians to make a political point.

Terrorists rely on spectacular events, such as political assassination, hijacking of aircraft, the use of explosives on civilian targets, and kidnapping or hostage taking. Some recent examples are the murdering of Israeli athletes in Munich during the Olympic Games of 1972, the hijacking of a TWA aircraft to Beirut in 1985 with the killing of one passenger and the taking of civilian hostages, and the hijacking of the Italian ship *Achille Lauro* in 1985.

Because they rely on surprise, terrorists have achieved tactical successes, but for the most part they have not been able to secure their overall political objectives. Still, their actions have had profound consequences in many countries, requiring at times emergency measures by governments in attempts to deal with clandestine terrorist organizations.

One of the major objectives of terrorists is to get attention for their actions, and in this they rely upon the media, particularly television. The TWA hijacking was especially dramatic, and television cameras covered every aspect of that event. Viewers in the United States were stunned by pictures of a terrorist pointing a gun at the head of the TWA pilot while the pilot was talking before television cameras. Media people sought interviews with various members of terrorist organizations, thus giving publicity to the terrorists' goals.

People in the United States are also made aware of terrorist activities through videotapes of hostages made and released by terrorists. From time to time during the 1979–1981 captivity of members of the U.S. diplomatic corps in Teheran, videotaped statements by the hostages were televised with dramatic effect. Such statements served to remind the nation of the inability of the Carter administration to remedy the situation. Similarly, televised videotapes of U.S. hostages held in Lebanon in the 1980s called attention to the fact that the Reagan administration was unable to remedy that situation either.

Do telecasts and other media coverage of terrorist activities make it more likely that the terrorists will achieve their goals? Should the media therefore be regulated in reporting acts of terrorism? Edward Jay Epstein, author of works on the media and on national security, argues that they should. He contends:

1. The purpose of terrorism is to get media attention.
2. The media should not provide the means by which terrorists can achieve this goal.
3. The curtailment of coverage of terrorist events is not an abridgment of the public's right to the truth.
4. When terrorist organizations find that they cannot get media attention, they will largely abandon their terrorist activities.

Ben H. Bagdikian, dean of the Graduate School of Journalism at the University of California at Berkeley, makes the case against regulation of the media in covering terrorist events. He argues:

1. Controlled reporting, whether done voluntarily or not, is likely to produce more rather than less political violence.
2. Controlled news under those circumstances will create more public hysteria and irrational behavior than does the present competitive coverage with all its flaws.

Should the Media Be Regulated in Reporting Acts of Terrorism?

EDWARD JAY EPSTEIN
Terrorism: What Should We Do?

International terrorism may productively be defined as the staging of a violent drama in a neutral setting to draw public attention to an otherwise lost or faltering cause. The victims are almost always innocent bystanders, chosen at random, either because of their symbolic importance (as in the case of the Israeli athletes in Munich) or their availability (as in a hijacking). The terrorists act throughout the drama as representatives of a clandestine group or faction, which characteristically takes credit for the entire production. The proximate objective is not to change the balance of power, or even win a tactical military victory: it is, get a message on the media.

There is little point in confusing this kind of pathological stagecraft with statecraft—especially in seeking remedies. It is a very different phenomenon from a state using military force to suppress or destroy dissidence—as, for example, is being done by Russia in Afghanistan, Vietnam in Laos and Cambodia, Iraq in Kurdistan, Indonesia in East Timor and India in Assam. In that case, the perpetrator is a sovereign state that can be ostracized, embargoed or punished militarily—if such action is deemed worth the cost. Nor can international terrorism be equated with guerrilla warfare, insurrection against a military occupation, or a civil war. The issue here will turn on which side has the moral right, power, will, and international support to prevail. To be sure, at times, sovereign states covertly use terrorist groups—or even create fictive ones—to hide their own interventions. Since the purpose of this masquerade is to avoid the international consequences, it can be remedied by exposing the surreptitious principal, which is an intelligence problem. Once the mask is penetrated, the offending nations are inhibited diplomatically, economically, or militarily. Of course, as in any other geopolitical calculus, the cost of imposing penalties might outweigh benefits and the offending nation not be publicly exposed.

The real problem proceeds from international terrorism which is not traceable back to a sovereign state. The most recent examples include the hijacking of the TWA airliner to Beirut by a Shiite faction, bombs planted in Indian and Japanese airliners by a Sikh faction and attacks on a U.S. air base in Germany by a radical German underground group (in collaboration with a French group). None of these crimes had a military or economic motive. The demands in each case were entirely nominal (the Shiites, for instance, knew that Israel had already announced it was releasing the Shiites it had been holding captive). Nor were they planned, as far as can be determined, by a sovereign state.

315

All these actions were designed by freelance groups solely to get international publicity for their cause. The media, albeit unwitting, supplied in each case the means by which this objective was accomplished.

In this case, the most effective remedy for international terrorism would be to deny its prime objective: unrestricted access to the media. For hijackings, the restrictions would not necessarily be any more stringent than they are for the coverage of a criminal trial in Great Britain and other European countries. The press simply should not be allowed during the event itself to interview the terrorists or hostages, just as it cannot interview participants at a trial. (There is also the pragmatic consideration that journalists themselves, if available, could be seized to prolong a crisis.) The list of demands would also be kept secret on security grounds—as are notes in ransom and other extortion cases.

While journalists might object to these restrictions as an abridgment of their right to earn a living, as they do to courtroom restrictions, there is no reason to believe that it is an abridgment of the public's right to the truth. To the contrary, the story related by hostages is almost by definition given under duress and coercion, a fact which is not always visible during the interview; as such, it may as likely further a false picture as the truth.

In the case of bombings, terrorist organizations can be denied the fruit of their atrocities by delaying the press and broadcasters from revealing notes and tapes they receive from them until the police investigation is completed. These messages characteristically take credit for the bombings, issue demands and explain organizational goals. Yet, even though they are sent to the media, they are evidence in a crime, and could be prohibited from publication—just as is other evidence. Eventually, after a reasonable time delay, these messages, as well as the other evidence, would be released—so that the public would not be denied the truth. The net effect of the delay would be to deprive the terrorist organization of the immediate benefit of being associated with a highly-visible event (presumably, months later, it would be well out of the headlines).

When terrorist organizations find that kidnappings, hijackings, and bombings do not achieve their objective of immediate and unrestricted access to the media, they will, I submit, largely abandon these repugnant techniques.

Should the Media Be Regulated in Reporting Acts of Terrorism?

BEN H. BAGDIKIAN
Terrorism and the Media

I will confine my statement to two main points, namely that I believe that controlled reporting, whether done voluntarily or not, is likely to produce more rather than less political violence; and that controlled news under those circumstances will, according to past experience and research, create more public hysteria and irrational behavior than does the present competitive coverage with all its flaws.

I recognize the reasons given in favor of altered news coverage of events like the Beirut kidnapping and murder. Much of the coverage was excessive for strictly self-serving, competitive reasons and in the process it obliterated other important news. It favored physical drama to the exclusion of vital background that would make the drama more understandable. And the resulting publicity undoubtedly produced some measure of satisfaction among the groups committing political violence and may well have increased difficulties of behind-the-scenes negotiations. I acknowledge the disadvantages of the present uninhibited, competitive coverage.

In the fear, anger, and humiliation of events like the TWA hijacking, the desire for revenge, for preventing repetitions, and the disapproval of some news media behavior make it easy to overlook the lasting disadvantages of voluntary or mandatory central control of news in general but also in precisely this kind of frightening episode.

Adjusting news coverage in order to deny satisfaction to the source of the news is just as bad as adjusting the news to satisfy the source. Both result in flawed news. Unfortunately, important news is not always made by the good guys. And filtering news in order to produce some pre-determined result is called propaganda and has no place in responsible reporting in a democracy.

But aside from that general observation, I would like to make two main points.

First, it has been suggested that massive coverage by the news media may produce repetition in the future among groups who desire world attention for themselves and their causes. It is said that if such criminals are denied this kind of vivid exposure on television and the country's front pages it will remove or induce the stimulus for others who may try the same kind of violence.

I think it is inevitable that the worldwide publicity did provide some satisfaction to the perpetrators at Beirut. The idea of being on television display in a momentary position of power must appeal to many groups around the world.

But I believe that the arbitrary control of news coverage will not reduce political violence and has at least an equal chance of increasing it.

We are dealing here not with a businesslike public relations agency. We are dealing with people who are willing to kill and be killed for their cause. Furthermore, only the most isolated psychopathic individuals commit this violence solely or mainly in order to get publicity. Most such groups, including those who hijacked the TWA plane, are interested in wide exposure but they also have quite specific political demands. In fact, except for clearly psychotic individuals without political aims, the publicity is a way of creating pressure for concessions on political goals. Because political violence is their method and publicity about the violence increases the pressure for concessions, it is tempting to deny them the publicity in the hope that it will reduce or cancel the demand for political concessions. But I think it will not. Most such groups will simply escalate the violence to a level that is no longer possible to conceal or to keep subdued in the news.

When politically motivated people are willing to die for their cause, the simple act of denying them public exposure will not frustrate them. There is enough explosive power readily available in the world and the nature of modern commerce is so vulnerable that such groups can find ever more frightening ways to break through filters of silence in the news.

Permit me to give one generalized example and one specific one. Even in the Soviet Union where there is total control of press and television, and where anti- and even non-governmental public acts are among the most hated by the authorities, individuals and groups who feel strongly enough about their cause also escalate their physical acts until they must be acknowledged.

The specific example comes from the TWA hijacking. According to news reports, the original hijackers demanded that the more moderate Amal militia join in controlling the hostages. At first the Amal militia declined. As a result, the hijackers beat and killed an American and pushed his body out of the plane. At that point, the Amal militia agreed to take over. The implication was clear that until there was serious consideration of their demands, body after body would be thrown out of the plane. It is this escalating process that I think would be stimulated by controlled or artificially subdued news.

Let me conclude with the effect that controlled news would have on audiences in the United States and elsewhere. Scholars of propaganda, rumor and public hysteria, like the late Gordon Allport, discovered that two concurrent events maximize the possibility of irrational public responses. One begins when the public becomes intensely interested or anxious about a subject. In the case of violence against fellow Americans as at the Beirut airport and other similar acts, it is inevitable that the public will learn about the existence of the crisis and will become angry and anxious.

The other element that makes for irrational public response, once the public interest is aroused, is if there is only limited information or the public does not believe the information it is given. Under those circumstances the odds of wild or irrational behavior go up sharply. I believe that as this happens, the odds also increase for unwise or irrational official responses.

It is precisely during times of crisis and anxiety that the public needs not only as much information as possible but has to believe that it is being told everything that is available. In the recent hijacking we often saw more than we needed to know. But that is far better than not being told enough or believing that we are not being told enough, leading to rumor and hysteria.

I will not dwell on what others will testify to at length, so I will do so only in passing. First, the massive and overheated coverage by the news media did not present a simple message that glorified the hijackers. Whatever else it did, it also dramatized the horror that the hijackers inflicted on their victims. I doubt that the result was sympathy for the hijackers or their cause.

Secondly, the history of attempts to control news of dramatic, anxiety-producing events is one of failure and futility. It simply does not work. The problems it creates are generally more socially and politically troublesome than any created by uncontrolled news. The unpleasantness of excessive coverage is, for all the flaws, less dangerous than the tensions in the public and among officials when there is an attempt to control news of what is essentially an uncontrolled scene.

But my main points are that quite aside from that, even if the controls worked, they would probably increase political violence rather than decrease it and it would produce more irrational public behavior than all the anger and humiliation aroused by seeing uninhibited and sometimes thoughtless coverage.

Questions for Discussion

1. What is a terrorist?
2. What is the purpose of terrorist acts?
3. What effect do you think denial of media coverage would have on acts of terrorism?
4. How should a responsible media organization handle a terrorist event?
5. If the media are to be regulated in covering terrorist events, who should be the regulator?

Suggested Readings

Clawson, Patrick. "Why We Need More but Better Coverage of Terrorism." Orbis, 30, no. 4 (Winter 1987), 701–710.

Dowling, Ralph E. "Terrorism and the Media." *Journal of Communication,* 36, no. 1 (Winter 1986), 12–24.

Greer, Herb. "Terrorism and the Media: Myths, Illusion, Abstractions." *Encounter* (London), 59, no. 2 (August 1982), 67–74.

Hitchens, Christopher. "Wanton Acts of Usage." *Harper's,* 273, no. 1636 (September 1986), 66–70.

Joyce, Edward M. "Reporting Hostage Crises: Who's in Charge of Television?" *SAIS Review,* 6, no. 1 (Winter–Spring 1986), 169–176.

Martin, L. John. "The Media's Role in International Terrorism." *Terrorism,* 8, no. 2 (1985), 127–146.

Netanyahu, Benjamin, ed. *Terrorism: How the West Can Win.* New York: Farrar, Straus & Giroux, 1986.

Pfaff, William. "Terrorists Are Now in Charge—Thanks to the Press." *Los Angeles Times,* September 19, 1986, sec. II, p. 5.

Sick, Gary G. "Terrorism: Its Political Uses and Abuses." *SAIS Review,* 7, no. 1 (Winter–Spring 1987), 11–26.

U.S. Cong., House of Representatives. *The Media, Diplomacy, and Terrorism in the Middle East.* Hearing before the Subcommittee on Europe and the Middle East of the Committee on Foreign Affairs, 99th Cong., 1st Sess., 1985.

Walzer, Michael. "Follow That Network." *New Republic,* 194, no. 22 (June 2, 1986), 8.

Should the United States Engage in Arms Control Negotiations with the Soviet Union?

Since the end of World War II, the United States and the Soviet Union have been adversaries. The war had left these countries as the strongest military powers in the world. Although they were allies in World War II, bickering and confrontation have marked the relations between the two countries with varying degrees of tension from 1945 to the present.

The sources of the conflict are diverse. Part of the problem stems from the global position of two mighty military powers. Security concerns are certainly one of the reasons for the conflict. Ideological concerns are another. The Soviet Union professes a philosophy of Marxism-Leninism that calls for the destruction of the capitalist system and the establishment of communism throughout the world. The United States professes a philosophy of political democracy and capitalism, and many people in the country see in the Soviet Union as a country and in Marxism-Leninism as an ideology a threat to their way of life.

Mutual hostility has led to the establishment of military alliances by both countries. Most important for the United States was the formation of the North Atlantic Treaty Organization (NATO) in 1949, in which the United States allied with eleven countries. The Soviet Union formed the Warsaw Pact in 1955, joining with its Eastern European communist allies.

At times, the relations between the two countries have had the appearance of breaking down into military confrontations. In the 1940s and 1950s Berlin became a major issue of contention. In 1962 the United States threatened the use of nuclear weapons against the Soviet Union if the Soviets did not remove nuclear weapons from Cuba. Both the United States and the Soviet Union compete, moreover, for influence, particularly in Africa, Asia, South America, and Central America. The Soviet Union provides assistance to countries such as Afghanistan and Cuba; and the United States supports its friends, such as Israel and South Korea.

Despite this hostility, both powers recognize the need to coexist in a nuclear age. At various times since the 1950s, both superpowers have made efforts to reduce tensions and resolve differences. The most notable example was during the administrations of Presidents Richard Nixon and Gerald Ford, when *détente*, that is, the relaxation of tensions, was the approved policy. In the minds of its advocates détente was based on the belief that arms control and improved trade ties between the United States and the Soviet Union would lead to peaceful relations between the two nations. Détente came under attack by conservatives in the United

States because they thought that the Soviet Union was using the illusion of peaceful relations to cloak its expansionistic impulses.

Whatever their attitudes toward the Soviet Union, all presidents since Dwight Eisenhower have met with Soviet political leaders to continue a dialogue and find areas of mutual agreement. One such area is arms control. The movement toward arms control is partially based on the fact that both the Soviet Union and the United States possess enough nuclear weapons to destroy each other many times over. The accidental explosion of a nuclear reactor at Chernobyl in the Soviet Union in 1986 demonstrated that death, permanent injury, and environmental contamination need not await a nuclear weapon detonation but may occur with the escape of radioactive elements on a grand scale. Whatever fundamental differences exist between the Soviet Union and the United States, all leaders have sought to prevent a nuclear war.

At the same time, both the Soviet Union and the United States have at times threatened the use of nuclear weapons and have tried to build sufficient forces so that, in the event of a surprise attack by the other, enough of a nuclear arsenal would remain to allow a devastating counterstrike. The strategic principle has been "deterrence"—the notion that an adversary will be prevented from attacking for fear of the consequences.

And so, both sides have deployed strategic forces composed of long-range bombers, intercontinental ballistic missiles, and nuclear submarines. Both superpowers, moreover, have built tactical and medium-range nuclear arsenals that have shorter delivery ranges and lower yields than strategic weapons.

Most observers agree that there is no defense against an all-out nuclear attack at the current level of technology. In 1983, however, President Ronald Reagan made a speech advocating a Strategic Defense Initiative (SDI) that would provide a shield against nuclear weapons. Scientists had made breakthroughs in a technology that, at least in theory, makes it possible to construct such a shield, and, in fact, the Soviets were already working on the same kind of technology. Although some scientists doubted it would be possible to build an effective shield, others have been more enthusiastic about the prospects of success—if not for protection of population centers then at least for protection of strategic forces.

For their part, the Soviets have expressed fear that if the United States were to build a shield, then it could launch a sneak attack against the Soviet Union without fear of retaliation. President Reagan has promised to give the information about SDI to the Soviets once the United States has put its system in place—a promise that the Soviet leaders regard as ludicrous. All observers agree that, even if a shield can be developed, it could not be put in place until the 1990s or even into the next century.

In the meantime, arms control remains a policy goal of both superpowers. The major agreements on nuclear weapons have involved regulation based on geographic regions, testing, nuclear proliferation, strategic and other forces, and communications. Those involving geographic regions have ruled out the deployment, use, or testing of nuclear weapons in some regions. The Antarctic Treaty of 1961 was one such treaty. Testing was the specific focus of the Partial Test Ban Treaty (PTBT), concluded in 1963. It prohibits nuclear tests or any other nuclear explosions in the atmosphere, in outer space, and under water.

Nuclear nonproliferation has also been a mutual goal of the superpowers. The Nonproliferation Treaty of 1968 provides that the nations that do not have nuclear weapons agree not to build nuclear weapons provided that the states that have nuclear weapons make efforts to reduce their nuclear arsenals.

Agreements involving strategic forces have sought to put limits on particular long-range nuclear weapons. The Strategic Arms Limitation Treaties of 1972 and 1979, known respectively as SALT I and SALT II, are cases in point. (The United States ratified SALT I but did not ratify SALT II. President Carter abided by the terms of SALT II nonetheless, and until 1986 President Reagan followed the Carter policy, breaking it technically that year in a limited way.) In late 1987, the United States and the Soviet Union signed the Intermediate-range Nuclear Force (INF) Treaty that would eliminate intermediate-range nuclear missiles from Europe. Both countries were considering the ratification of the INF Treaty in 1988.

Finally, both the United States and the Soviet Union have sought to improve communications so as to prevent war from breaking out because of misunderstanding, unauthorized use of nuclear weapons, or accidents. A "hot line" links Moscow and Washington, D.C., to allow for instant communication in a crisis.

Do arms control agreements work? Should the United States engage in arms control negotiations with the Soviet Union? Michael MccGwire, a senior fellow in the Foreign Policy Studies program at the Brookings Institution, argues that the Soviets are serious about arms control, and the United States should be, too. He contends:

1. Since 1967–1968, the Soviets have believed that limiting strategic arms would contribute significantly to Soviet-U.S. relations and hence reduce the likelihood of war.
2. The United States has been ambivalent toward arms control.

National security analyst Colin S. Gray argues that arms control has ill served U.S. security interests. He cites six myths of arms control:

1. Arms control reduces the size of superpower nuclear arsenals and creates stability.
2. The Anti-Ballistic Missile Treaty saves money and contributes to stability.

3. Verification and compliance are virtually synonymous.
4. Arms control violations do not affect our national security.
5. Strategic defense poses a threat to arms control.
6. The arms race is futile, and arms control is the only rational approach.

☑ *Y E S*

Should the United States Engage in Arms Control Negotiations with the Soviet Union?

MICHAEL MCCGWIRE

Why the Soviets Are Serious about Arms Control

Arms control is a value-laden term, dependent for its meaning not only on a definition of the words but on the viewpoint with which one looks at the process. Most Americans assume that the West has sought the mutual limitation of strategic nuclear weapons while the Soviets have obstructed negotiations. The record of the last two decades argues otherwise.

In truth, Americans have always been ambivalent about the value of arms control. Many believe that it works against U.S. interests. Until the late 1960s, the Soviets shared this ambivalence, believing that world war would inevitably be nuclear and that arms control agreements would impair their ability to survive such a war. Then in 1966 they concluded that nuclear war—and the devastation of Russia—might possibly be avoided. Under that assumption, arms control agreements would not only help avoid war but also promote Soviet military objectives in the event that war could not be avoided. Since then the Soviets have actively sought to limit and reduce strategic nuclear arms. They have even been willing to make unilateral concessions to achieve agreement.

The assumption that the Soviets are eager to seize any chance, however slight, to destroy the United States, coupled with the focus on our own interests and vulnerabilities, has blinded most of us to the tangible evidence of the Soviets' interest in arms control. That evidence is apparent in their strategic missile programs—and the cuts they imposed on those programs. Moreover, the Soviet readiness to negotiate is documented in the memoirs of several U.S. officials. Most recently [1984], in his account of his time as secretary of state, Alexander Haig writes that from the earliest days of the Reagan administration, the Soviets indicated their eagerness to enter into arms control talks on almost any basis.

American misperceptions about Soviet motivations have almost certainly resulted in missed opportunities for meaningful arms control agreements. A continued misreading of Soviet interests and aims could lead the United States to adopt policies whose results are the opposite of what it desires. The Strategic Defense Initiative is a case in point. This article explains the logic of the Soviet policy on arms control and sets out concrete evidence of the changed approach. It then examines the roots of U.S. arms control policy and the reasons for our misperceptions. Finally it considers what this combination portends for arms control in the wake of the Reagan-Gorbachev meeting in Reykjavik last October [1986].

THE POSSIBILITY OF AVOIDING DEVASTATION

Since the 1950s Soviet doctrine had held that a world war—a war they absolutely want to avoid but cannot afford to lose—would inevitably be nuclear and just as inevitably entail massive strikes on Russia. In such a fight to the finish, where defeat would be synonymous with extinction, the twin Soviet objectives were to preserve the socialist system and destroy the capitalist one. The latter objective required nuclear attacks on the United States and its allies, and to the extent these attacks could disarm the West's ability to retaliate, they would help preserve the socialist system. Soviet strategy was therefore predicated on successful nuclear preemption.

The Soviet belief that a world war would inevitably be nuclear reflected the declared Western policy of relying on "massive retaliation" and NATO's [North Atlantic Treaty Organization] stated readiness to resort immediately to nuclear weapons in the event of war in Europe, policies that went back to the mid-1950s. The West began to move away from those policies in 1961 when the Kennedy administration introduced the concept of "flexible response," proposing to check a Soviet offensive in Europe for several days using conventional forces only. Initially the Soviets misread this concept as an attempt to improve NATO's ability to wage nuclear war, in part because its introduction coincided with the deployment of new U.S. nuclear weapons in Europe. By 1964, however, the Soviets were coming to recognize that flexible response implied that a war in Europe might start with a conventional phase, although they continued to assume that nuclear escalation was inevitable.

It was only in the second half of 1966, probably as the result of a reevaluation following France's withdrawal from NATO, that the Soviets appear to have reached two conclusions. One was that a war in Europe would not inevitably lead to massive strikes on Russia, except in retaliation for an attack on North America. The other was that the size and diversity of the U.S. strategic arsenal meant that a preemptive strike on the United States would do little to limit the devastation of Russia. During this period the strategic opportunity presented by the NATO doctrine of "flexible response" became clear to the Soviets. If, during this initial conventional phase of a war in Europe, the Soviets could neutralize NATO's theater nuclear forces, they could remove the first rung of escalation. If they could knock NATO out of the war using nonnuclear forces, the question of intercontinental escalation might become moot.

These new considerations led the Soviets to conclude in December 1966 that a world war would not necessarily be nuclear and, even if it were, it would not necessarily include massive strikes on Russia. Under this new doctrine, it became logically possible for the Soviets to adopt the objective of avoiding the nuclear devastation of Russia.

As a corollary, the Soviets had to forgo the wartime objective of destroying the capitalist system because that could be achieved only by launching nuclear strikes on the United States, which would invite retaliatory attacks on Russia. Instead, the Soviets had to adopt a lesser objective, such as gravely weakening the capitalist system, and accept that North America would be left undamaged. Leaving the United States untouched meant that the U.S. military-industrial base would remain intact, and it therefore became essential to deny America a bridgehead in Europe from which to mount an attack on Russia.

The strategic requirements were clear. There remained the problem of how to defeat NATO in Europe in the event of war without precipitating a nuclear attack on Russia. In 1967–68 the Soviets set out to restructure their forces to provide the capability, using conventional means only, to disable NATO's nuclear delivery systems and to mount a blitzkrieg offensive into Western Europe. Even if the Soviets were not fully successful, NATO's nuclear capability would be greatly reduced and the escalatory momentum lessened. This new Soviet capability was largely in place by the second half of the 1970s, when it was supplemented by a political campaign to persuade NATO to adopt a policy of "no first use" of nuclear weapons in the theater and to persuade the United States that the resort to nuclear weapons in Europe would inevitably lead to strikes on North America.

The Soviets also had to deal with the danger that the United States, when faced by the impending defeat of NATO in Europe, would launch a full-scale nuclear strike on Russia. No defense against such an attack existed. The only means of preventing it was deterrence: the threat of nuclear retaliation on North America.

The need to reverse Soviet policy on preemption made it harder for the Soviets to ensure the credibility of this deterrent. Preemption had been a cornerstone of the 1960s strategy. The new 1970s hierarchy of objectives required the Soviets to forgo any suggestion of first use that might precipitate a NATO decision to resort to nuclear weapons or a U.S. decision to strike at Russia. The evidence now suggests that the Soviets will wait to launch their strategic forces until they have warning of a U.S. attack. In other words, they are braced for NATO and the United States to launch first in the course of a war.

LESS IS BETTER

It took the Soviets the best part of 10 years to restructure their ground and air forces sufficiently to allow them to adopt the 1970s hierarchy of objectives; the restructuring of naval forces is taking even longer. During this transition they could not afford to cut back their forces in central Europe, which was why they did not begin to negotiate seriously on mutual and balanced force reductions until 1979. The converse pertained in the case of strategic systems. The logic of the 1970s objectives required the curtailment of existing programs and active negotiations to limit strategic weapons.

While arms control agreements can serve important economic purposes, at the core of Soviet arms control policy are two objectives: the political objective of avoiding world war; and the military objective, should war prove inescapable, of not losing. Before 1967–68 the Soviet Union had a limited interest in arms control. Because it lagged so far behind the United States in most aspects of military capability, its primary aim was to draw level and, if possible, to move ahead, a goal that an arms control agreement might well prevent. Nor was there strong evidence that arms control agreements made war less likely.

During 1967–68 the Soviets came to realize that constructive negotiations on limiting strategic arms could contribute significantly to improved Soviet-American relations and hence reduce the likelihood of war. Meanwhile the logic of the 1970s hierarchy of military objectives argued strongly for limits on the size of the superpowers' nuclear arsenals. Combining the two levels of objectives changed the cost-benefit calculus of arms control from negative to positive. More was no longer better.

OFFENSIVE STRATEGIC SYSTEMS

Under the 1970s hierarchy, the primary mission of Soviet intercontinental ballistic missiles (ICBMs) was no longer strategic preemption but wartime deterrence—to deter the United States from striking at Russia even when faced with the defeat of U.S. forces in Europe. The effectiveness of this deterrence did not depend on the size of the ICBM force. Indeed, the Soviets could reason that if a U.S. president was not deterred from striking at Russia by a Soviet threat to destroy 5 or 10 of America's largest cities, then he was unlikely to be stopped by a threat to 50 or 100 cities. Should the Soviet wartime deterrent prove ineffective, however, the smaller the size of the U.S. intercontinental missile inventory, the less extensive the nuclear devastation of Russia. Under this logic, less was better. And the only way to reduce the size of the U.S. nuclear inventory was through mutual agreement on arms limitations.

This downward pressure on Soviet ICBM levels was, however, constrained by the need to match the U.S. inventory. An equivalent Soviet capability provided the leverage required to negotiate reductions in U.S. strategic forces and at the same time denied Washington the advantage of conducting its foreign policy "from a position of strength." And despite their emerging doctrine that no one can win a nuclear war, the Soviets were not prepared to allow the United States an advantage in weapons that might allow it to dictate the outcome, should such a war occur.

DEFENSIVE SYSTEMS

A comparable change took place in the calculus of advantage for defensive systems. Under the 1960s hierarchy, defensive weapons would help preserve the socialist system in the event of intercontinental nuclear exchange. Furthermore, military doctrine stressed the interrelatedness of offense and defense.

The 1970s objective of avoiding the nuclear devastation of Russia introduced a new consideration. If nuclear attacks on Russia could not be physically prevented, only deterred, and if the credibility of deterrence depended on the certainty that Soviet ICBMs, if launched, would strike home on North America, then an effective U.S. anti-ballistic missile (ABM) system would threaten that credibility. Assuming that it might not be possible to launch Soviet strategic forces on warning, such a U.S. defense became a live possibility because a Soviet retaliatory strike would only be a fraction of the original ICBM force. It was now more important to halt the development of U.S. ballistic missile defense systems than to deploy a marginally effective Soviet ABM system.

EVIDENCE OF THE CHANGE

The Soviets pressed for the maximum limitations on ABM systems from the start of the strategic arms limitation talks (SALT) in November 1969. They were even willing to consider a complete ban, which would have involved dismantling the existing ABM sites around Moscow. And when difficulties emerged in reaching agreement on limits for offensive weapons, the Soviets sought to defer discussion of those weapons until after the conclusion of an ABM treaty.

This volte-face in Soviet policy was evidence of the shift in wartime objectives. It was accompanied by equally significant changes in Soviet modernization plans for strategic missiles. In the first half of 1970, when the first strategic arms limitation talks had been in progress for a few months, the Soviets abandoned the construction of more than 70 newly started ICBM silos, including 18 for the "heavy" SS-9 missile that was of particular concern to the United States. Further evidence came with the signing of SALT II in 1979, when the Soviets aborted the conversion of about 100 ICBM silos from third to fourth generation systems. Underlying both these outward indications were even more fundamental changes in the Soviet ICBM program.

The United States made no comparable concessions. Neither SALT agreement had any effect on existing U.S. plans for modernizing its strategic forces. SALT I did not touch U.S. plans to MIRV [multiple independently targetable re-entry vehicles] Minuteman, that is, to fit the missile with multiple, independently targeted warheads. Weapons limits in SALT II did not include ground- and sea-launched cruise missiles. The SALT weapons limits did not really bite until late 1985, when the U.S. Navy had to dismantle a 20-year-old, 16-tube Poseidon submarine to bring a 24-tube Trident on line.

Soviet interest in arms control as an ongoing process leading to weapons limitation was again demonstrated at the strategic arms reduction talks (START) in 1982–83, when Soviet negotiators were presented with a proposal that Haig later described as "non-negotiable" and "two-faced." The package would have left U.S. plans unaffected but required the Soviets to reduce the number of existing warheads by 60 percent and dismantle about 75 percent of their modern MIRVed missiles. Instead of breaking off the negotiations as pointless, the Soviets responded by proposing further reductions in the SALT II limits. These new ceilings would have required them to cut their MIRVed ICBM force by 138 launchers but would have accommodated the additional 100 MX [missile experimental] mobile launchers projected in the 1982 U.S. defense budget as well as the 18 Trident submarines allowed under SALT II.

AMERICAN AMBIVALENCE

Given the striking evidence of Soviet interest in arms control, how does one account for the widespread perception that the Soviet Union has to be pressured into negotiations? Part of the explanation lies with the Soviets themselves. They see arms control as an incremental process and, until recently, have responded negatively to radical new initiatives. Once embarked on negotiations, the Soviets aggressively pursue relative advantage, seeking to cap Western capabilities and fence off dangerous new developments whenever possible, while protecting their own programs and possibilities for future development. At the same time, their fear of disclosing key military objectives accentuates their natural secretiveness.

The misreading is also a function of U.S. domestic politics. To gain support for arms control from the conservative right, successive administrations have funded new weapons programs, explaining that they were necessary to bring the Soviets to the negotiating table. But the main reason for misperception lies in our mistaken assumption that Soviet arms control policy continues to mirror the ambivalence of the U.S. policy.

The United States acquired strategic superiority in World War II and has been understandably reluctant to give it up. U.S. policymakers have used arms control negotiations to limit and, if possible, reduce Soviet inventories in areas where the Soviets were catching up or moving ahead. U.S. negotiators have rejected limits in areas where asymmetries in force structure or advanced technology give the United States an edge. The Strategic Defense Initiative (SDI) is the latest variation on this theme.

During the 1960s and 1970s the emerging concepts of parity, equivalence, and sufficiency ran into tenacious resistance in the United States. In the 1980s the Reagan administration sought explicitly to restore some measure of superiority, while denigrating existing arms control agreements. The SDI reflects this logic. Defense Secretary Caspar W. Weinberger explained to the Senate Armed Services Committee on February 1, 1984, that the SDI offered the prospect of returning to the situation of the immediate post-World War II years when the United States was "the only nation with nuclear weapons and did not threaten others with [them]."

However, the difference in the two sides' approaches extends beyond the level of their interest in arms control to the theoretical underpinnings of the term. For the Soviet Union arms control implies limiting and reducing the size of nuclear arsenals. For the United States it has more to do with crisis stability, a concept that derives from nuclear deterrence theory and its offshoot, reassurance theory. Deterrence theory, which emerged in the early 1950s and reflected the lessons of Munich and World War II, held that Soviet aggression in Europe could only be prevented by the threat of dire punishment and that the credibility of that deterrence depended on the certainty of the U.S. response. The means of retaliation, therefore, had to be held totally secure, a requirement that gave full rein to a new form of worst-case analysis as imaginative theorists sought to discover possible chinks in the armor of assured response.

In the second half of the 1950s, as the Soviets began to acquire the capability to strike at North America, other theorists focused on a danger that stemmed from the nature of nuclear weapons and did not depend on either side's having aggressive intentions. In a confrontational situation, the advantage of disarming the other side by getting in the first blow was so great that a prudent national leader might be prompted to launch a nuclear strike on the mere suspicion that the other side was contemplating war. This pressure to preempt in a crisis introduced a new concern for the "stability" of deterrence. It became necessary to find ways of reassuring the Soviets in a crisis that the United States would not initiate preemptive war.

U.S. arms control theory had its intellectual origins in this recognition of the need for mutual reassurance, which was to be achieved by both sides having an assured "second strike" (or more properly, strike second) capability. Deterrence theory requires that the United States be able to launch its whole force under attack. Reassurance theory is more demanding and requires that each side should have enough weapons to survive a first strike and still be able to devastate the opponent's homeland. The theory, which underlies the concept of mutual assured destruction, also assumes that both sides would avoid weapon systems that might deprive the other of such a capability. Failing that, reassurance theory becomes a recipe for arms racing, as each side seeks to ensure that it can absorb a first strike and still retaliate.

In any case, there is a world of difference between the theory of arms control as developed in the United States and arms control policy as pursued by successive U.S. administrations. American policy is a shifting amalgam of the viewpoints of the reassurers, the deterrers, and those who seek to retain military superiority. The reassurers' requirement to be able to ride out an attack links the two opponents in an upwards spiral, and concern for the credibility of deterrence provides arguments for more, different, or better offensive weapons. Both theories can be manipulated to require de facto U.S. superiority. Nor does an assured response have to depend on arms control; it can be pursued unilaterally through new weapons programs and innovative basing modes.

The American ambivalence toward arms control explains why the United States could more than triple its warheads in the years immediately surrounding the signing of SALT I. Between 1970 and 1975, the number of U.S. warheads shot up from 1,775 to 6,800. During the same period, Soviet warheads increased from 1,700 to 2,700. It explains why SALT II allowed the United States to add 3,360 air-launched cruise missiles to the strategic inventory (trading in gravity bombs and short-range standoff weapons), and why the United States refused to accept any limits on the ground- and sea-launched versions of these strategic systems. By 1979 the United States had authorized production of both versions and, besides the 464 cruise missiles already earmarked for Europe, it plans to deploy about 750 nuclear cruise missiles aboard some 80 surface ships and about 100 attack submarines. The Soviets are following suit.

There is also a fundamental difference in how the two sides view the danger of war. Deterrence theory fosters the idea that war can only come about through a premeditated Soviet attack or some other initiative that the West must counter. Reassurance theory worries about the pressure to preempt in a crisis. Both theories focus on the danger of sudden attack, and both seek to prevent war by the threat of certain punishment. The Soviets are not primarily concerned about a bolt from the blue, and by 1959 they had largely discounted the possibility of a premeditated U.S. attack. They also see little relevance in the "pressure to preempt" that underlies the American concern for crisis stability, having themselves discarded as counterproductive the concept of intercontinental nuclear preemption. The Soviets believe war is most likely to arise from a chain of events that cannot be deterred by some threat of punishment. The first requirement is, therefore, to reduce the causes of East-West tension, amongst which arms racing ranks high in Soviet, if not American, eyes.

BEYOND REYKJAVIK

No one should have been surprised that the negotiations in Reykjavik last October [1986] foundered on the SDI. The Soviets immediately objected to placing weapons in space when Reagan first broached the idea in 1983. They reasserted those objections at the Geneva summit in 1985, and they implicitly conditioned a summit in Washington on progress in preventing the extension of the arms race into space.

The Soviets repeatedly noted the lack of such progress in the months preceding Reykjavik, but the Reagan administration dismissed these objections as a negotiating ploy. Officials acknowledged that the SDI would cause the Soviets the expense of matching or outflanking a U.S. ballistic missile defense system, but were unable to grasp the more fundamental nature of the Soviet objections.

The SDI requires the United States to scuttle the only strategic arms limitation treaty it has ratified. Abrogation of the ABM treaty will reverse the arms control process, depriving the Soviets of their only means of effecting reductions in the U.S. nuclear arsenal, and will open up a new arena for arms racing. The SDI also makes conflict in space almost inevitable. The Soviet Union cannot afford to let the United States build a space-based weapon system that could neutralize the Soviets' wartime deterrent and spell the demise of the Soviet state. A multilayered missile defense, even if less than perfect, would have some chance of absorbing a Soviet retaliatory attack in the wake of a U.S. disarming strike. If the United States refuses to be bound by treaties banning space weapons, the Soviets will have to consider whether to prevent the assembly of the SDI components in space. . . .

The Soviets must also be prepared to defeat a space-based defense system by saturating it with more warheads than it can handle. They cannot therefore afford to reduce their ICBM inventory unless the ABM treaty is strengthened to exclude permissive interpretations and unless they are convinced that the United States will abide by it. But even if these major obstacles were removed, the two sides still have quite different interests in limiting strategic nuclear weapons.

The primary mission of the Soviet force is to deter a U.S. nuclear attack on Russia in wartime. If America has no strategic nuclear weapons, Russia needs none. If nuclear weapons remain, the smaller the two sides' arsenals, the better for the Soviets. U.S. nuclear forces are intended to deter all forms of Soviet aggression, a requirement that would persist in the absence of Soviet nuclear weapons. Furthermore, even moderates in the United States consider that some 6,000 warheads are necessary to ensure that the Soviet Union is "deterred" in all circumstances.

The difference in requirements extends to nuclear delivery systems. This fact was demonstrated in the wake of Reykjavik, when the United States wanted to limit the proposed ban on nuclear weapons to ballistic missiles, whereas the

Soviets were prepared to accept a ban across the board. The United States has always had a technological lead in bombers and long-range cruise missiles, as well as in defense against them, which is helped by America's geographical isolation. It refused to allow bombers to be counted in SALT I and excluded ground- and sea-launched cruise missiles from SALT II. The Soviets, therefore, cannot afford to give away their ICBMs—one of the few negotiating levers they retain—without securing concessions in bombers and cruise missiles, where the United States has a significant advantage.

Theater systems are a separate issue. The Soviets believe that the elimination of nuclear weapons in Europe is to their operational advantage and will also reduce the likelihood that conflict will escalate to nuclear strikes on Russia. However, they have had to balance their interest in banning theater systems against the possibility that the prospect of such agreement can be used as leverage to bring the United States to the table on the SDI. I suspect that the Soviets' overall negotiating position could be improved by concluding an agreement on theater nuclear forces, even if there is no progress on the SDI. With its recent proposal to negotiate separately on theater forces, it may be that Moscow now sees the situation the same way.

The ironies surrounding the present impasse are inescapable. Since 1969 the Soviets have sought to reduce the size of nuclear arsenals but have been unwilling to divulge that aim lest it weaken their negotiating position. They have been willing to make unequal concessions, but these have not been recognized as such by a United States preoccupied with its own vulnerabilities. If we had pressed ahead within the negotiating framework agreed upon at the Vladivostock summit in 1974, we might have halted the Soviet buildup at a significantly lower level and then gone on to achieve reductions in strategic forces. Instead arms control became hostage to U.S. domestic politics. Successive administrations have embarked on new weapons systems as a way of securing the political acceptance of those agreements that have been negotiated. The Reagan administration, skeptical of any kind of arms control, now offers the implausible argument that the SDI will force the Soviets to cut back on their strategic missile force.

A second irony is that it is left to the Soviet Union, the "evil empire" berated by the United States for its aggressive behavior, to draw attention to the portentous consequences of putting weapons in space. The Soviets believe that such a step is at least comparable to the introduction of atomic weapons in 1945. There is some discussion in the United States of the SDI's implications for crisis stability but no significant debate on the advisability of opening the Pandora's box of "weaponizing" space.

A third irony is that a president untutored in Western arms control theory, leading a fractious administration that is largely unsympathetic to arms control and holds outdated assumptions about Soviet doctrine, should have engendered a situation that is peculiarly favorable to reaching an agreement on major reductions in nuclear weapons. This turn of events has occurred partly because the

Soviets are prepared to make major concessions to keep weapons out of space and partly because Reagan is still uniquely qualified to deliver the Senate votes to ratify such a revolutionary treaty. But it is also attributable to a new readiness in the United States to question the theories of deterrence and reassurance.

Having been ridiculed from the right for basing America's defense on the threat of mutual suicide and challenged from the left on the morality of threatening nuclear devastation, the arms control community must now assimilate the proposals for sweeping reductions in nuclear weapons that were agreed on in principle at Reykjavik, proposals that evoked widespread popular support. There may now be a new willingness to recognize that the West's oversophisticated theory of arms control has resulted in ridiculously high levels of armaments on both sides and to examine the merits of a less complicated approach—one that assumes that deterrence can work at a low level of threat and that concentrates on reducing the size of the two sides' nuclear arsenals. That this also happens to be the Soviet approach is no reason to reject it.

 NO

Should the United States Engage in Arms Control Negotiations with the Soviet Union?

COLIN S. GRAY
Nuclear Delusions

The enormous criticism heaped on President Reagan for his decision that the United States will no longer feel obliged to abide by the constraints of SALT [Strategic Arms Limitation Treaty] II shows the extent to which arms control mythology pervades American culture and American elites. It is not that Americans are naive about the nature of the Soviet Union. Surveys show a quite sensible appreciation by the American public of the threat this country faces from the Soviet Union. Yet Americans have been seduced by the arms control narcotic. They have been led to believe that the very fact of arms control, or the "arms control process" as it is often loftily termed, is an automatic protection against the risk of war.

The U.S. commitment to the arms control process today may be likened to what Dr. Samuel Johnson had to say about second marriages—it is a triumph of hope over experience. A proper respect for experience should be a principal source of guidance for debate over U.S. arms control policy. It so happens that we have a very great deal of historical experience, both of the negotiation of arms control agreements with totalitarian powers and of the ways in which those powers behave and misbehave when nominally constrained by treaty.

What is described here is a record of actual arms control performance. People are at liberty to dream of ways in which the United States might seek the control and reduction of arms far more effectively in the future than has been the case to date.

But if those dreams are to be offered as responsible advice for possible adoption as policy, they must meet some tests of reality. Much too often, there is a missing first sentence to some bold new vision from the heartland of the arms control community, which should read: "First, let us imagine a quite different Soviet Union."

Assuming the Soviet Union as it exists, and assuming arms control as we have had it and as we continue to perceive it, the record shows that arms control has ill served our national security. In particular, it has generated myths that continue to thrive, uninhibited by experience and evidence. These myths have the effect of averting our gaze from the real threats we must face if we want to preserve our freedom and security.

MYTH 1. ARMS CONTROL REDUCES THE SIZE OF SUPERPOWER NUCLEAR ARSENALS AND CREATES STABILITY

Despite what its name implies, arms control has clearly not stopped the growth of superpower arsenals. One of the most damning indictments of the SALT era is that it has licensed, or at least been compatible with, a truly massive growth in both the U.S. and Soviet strategic arsenals. According to studies by John Collins for the Congressional Research Service of the Library of Congress, and by the International Institute for Strategic Studies, the number of strategic nuclear weapons deployed by the Soviet Union between 1970 and 1985 increased by 533 percent, from 1,876 to 9,987. The increase registered by the United States was 275 percent, from 4,000 to 10,174. This brings to mind Richard Pipes's ironic comment, "If this is arms control, it might be interesting to experiment for a while with an honest arms race."

Arms control advocates argue that while the arms control period has seen these rapid buildups, nevertheless arms control has controlled the rate of growth of strategic arsenals, which would otherwise be even higher. The reason for this, they say, is that each side builds weapons in response to, and in anticipation of, what the other side builds; therefore, a certain knowledge of the outer bounds of what the adversary will do should serve to dampen the engine of competition. By channeling arms growth into "stable"channels, where neither side can hope to launch a successful first strike against the other, arms control diminishes appetites for aggression and reduces the risk of war.

This is the theory. It is not entirely without merit. Arms control probably has curtailed the rate of growth of superpower arsenals, which might have been higher without it. But the real issue is the relative strength of those arsenals. If arms control has restrained the U.S. arsenal in such a way that the restrained Soviet arsenal is still in a position to destroy it, that would defeat the very purpose of arms control, which is to achieve stability and diminish the threat of war. The Soviet Union, using only a fraction of its total ICBM force, is in a position to destroy the vast majority of land-based U.S. silos in a first strike. Moreover, American bombers would have a difficult time penetrating Soviet air defenses, the best in the world. Even our nuclear submarines may be vulnerable as detection techniques become more sophisticated; in any case, military analysts have long been opposed to allowing national security to hinge on a single "leg" of our deterrent triad. What could be more "unstable" than this?

All the evidence suggests that the Soviet Union builds its missiles in response to its perceived military necessities, not in congruence with agreements signed with the West. Indeed the Soviet Union only signs treaties that do not inhibit its weapons-building plans; when those plans are threatened by treaty, the Soviet Union has not been shy to violate treaties to which it has affixed its name.

According to recently declassified British intelligence documents from the late 1930s, the British admiralty used the argument that the Anglo-German Naval Agreement of 1935 was worth abiding by because otherwise the situation would be even worse. Actually, it's difficult to see how. The Germans may have built more ships, but the British could have as well. As it was, the Germans violated the agreement flagrantly, building, for example, 45 percent larger cruisers than permitted.

Americans have the false impression that we are successfully preventing the growth of Soviet missiles and warheads. In fact, we are not. SALT II places limits on weapon launchers or silos. The reason for this is that silos are holes in the ground and consequently easy to count; missiles and warheads are much more difficult to tabulate. Arms control places no direct constraints on numbers of missiles and warheads, or on quantity of missile "throw weight." It is these that are significant in conflict, not the holes they come from. In this respect, the fundamental premise of arms control is misguided.

MYTH 2. THE ABM TREATY SAVES MONEY AND CONTRIBUTES TO STABILITY

The Anti-ballistic Missile (ABM) Treaty of 1972 has been described as the "jewel in the crown" of arms control. A founding father of modern arms control theory, Thomas Schelling, claimed recently in *Foreign Affairs*, "I consider [the ABM Treaty] the culmination of 15 years of progress, not merely the high point but the end point of successful arms control."

Arms controllers believed that the ABM Treaty, by preventing the United States and the Soviet Union from deploying missile defenses, would put a brake on the offensive-defensive spiral of the arms race. Specifically, it was felt that both countries would react to the other side's missile defenses by trying to bolster their offensive arsenals in order to be able to penetrate and overwhelm the defense. Outlawing defenses would eliminate the incentive for this offensive proliferation, arms control advocates insisted. Further, they believed that mutual offensive reductions could be more easily negotiated in an atmosphere that was not complicated by missile defense. Essentially, ABM advocates felt that the treaty expressed a notion of strategic stability held by both the United States and the Soviet Union, that it would curtail offensive nuclear competition, and that it would save money on defensive and offensive weapons that would not need to be built.

The United States signed the ABM Treaty on the clear understanding that its utility depended on its ability to restrain the Soviet offensive arsenal. Today experts with roughly equal access to the technical data can disagree on whether it would have been possible for the United States to build a technologically viable missile defense in 1972. There is no disagreement, however, on the fact that Soviet defensive and (more importantly) offensive nuclear efforts have proceeded in massive disregard for both the spirit of arms control and nuclear restraint, and of the letter of arms control law.

During the 1970s, the United States did very little about missile defenses. Indeed it even dismantled the one missile defense site permitted by the ABM Treaty—the site at Grand Forks Air Force Base in North Dakota. Nor did the United States build nuclear missiles designed to be maximally lethal against Soviet missiles in hard silos. This country imposed on itself a unilateral "nuclear freeze." All this was aimed at generating reciprocal restraint from the Soviet Union. And it did save the country money on weapons that were not built.

But at what cost? During the mid- and late 1970s, the Soviet Union spent an astonishing sum on strategic offensive and defensive measures. In his *Annual Report* for fiscal 1987, Caspar Weinberger shows the Soviet Union outspending the United States by $80 billion on strategic defense procurement from 1970 to 1985. In the same period, the United States was outspent by $390 billion in the field of nuclear offense procurement.

Why did the Soviet Union build all these weapons? There can only be one reason. It does not share the theory of strategic stability so lucidly outlined by arms control advocates in this country. However bewildered arms controllers were by the escalating Soviet arsenal, we must assume that it did not bewilder Soviet leaders, since they consciously directed the increase and backed it up with huge amounts of scarce resources. Soviet military journals, moreover, expressed open contempt and derision for the assumptions that underpinned the ABM Treaty. Anyone reading the Soviet literature and taking it seriously would not be surprised when our theory that the Soviet Union was merely trying to "catch up" and would stop building weapons after that, was rudely refuted by the historical evidence.

So what the ABM Treaty essentially permitted was the development of a plausible Soviet theory of military victory. The Soviet Union might be able to maneuver itself into a position where it could threaten the destruction of the majority of U.S. nuclear forces, and absorb much of our retaliatory strike through strategic defensive measures of all kinds. This would be a very dangerous situation indeed. Knowledge of this possibility has led President Reagan to direct initiation of our own strategic defense efforts, plus nuclear modernization to make our missiles less vulnerable to Soviet attack. Unfortunately, after a decade of relative neglect, such a belated effort to restore equilibrium has proved and is proving very expensive. So the ABM Treaty turns out not to have saved money in the long run; what we didn't spend in the 1970s we now have to spend on missile modernization, Midgetman, strategic defense research, and other measures designed to frustrate Soviet plans for military victory.

MYTH 3. VERIFICATION AND COMPLIANCE ARE VIRTUALLY SYNONYMOUS

The organized arms control lobby (the Arms Control Association, Federation of American Scientists, Union of Concerned Scientists, Center for Defense Information, and so on) argues that the Soviet Union basically is complying with its legal obligations under arms control agreements and treaties. It is argued, further, that such violations as there may be, are minor in scale and importance and that there are established diplomatic procedures for coping with compliance problems. In particular, the ABM Treaty established a Standing Consultative Commission that is said to have worked well in the past.

Until quite recently, at least, the U.S. defense community behaved and spoke as though verification and compliance were fully interchangeable concepts. In the 1960s and 1970s, it was orthodox wisdom among conservatives as well as liberals, that the Soviet Union would be deterred from non-compliance by the fear of being discovered. Generally it was believed that an arms control agreement would be self-enforcing. It was argued that since states only sign an arms control agreement that serves their interests, they would not imperil the benefits by violating its provisions and risking discovery and retribution in pursuit of marginal illicit gain. Arms control non-compliance was considered highly improbable, given modern tools of verification and the pressures to conform.

Again, history proved the theory wrong. Soviet violations have been important and persistent; indeed it is difficult to think of an arms control treaty, with the possible exception of the nuclear non-proliferation treaty, that the Soviet Union has not violated. It would take too long to catalogue Soviet violations in literally dozens of categories. Here are a few:

- Flight testing and deploying a second new type of ICBM (the SS-25): a violation of SALT II.

- Encrypting missile testing telemetry, thereby impeding verification: a violation of SALT II.
- Deploying more strategic nuclear delivery vehicles than are permitted: a violation of SALT II.
- Backfire bombers have been deployed to the far north, thereby violating the Soviet commitment not to give Backfire an intercontinental capability: a violation of SALT II
- Deploying a large phased array radar at Krasnoyarsk that is neither on the periphery of the U.S.S.R. nor oriented outwards: in violation of the ABM Treaty.
- Concurrent testing of ABM and SAM system components: in violation of the ABM Treaty.
- Using former SS-7 ICBM facilities in support of ICBMs: in violation of SALT I Interim Agreement.
- Conducting underground nuclear tests that vent radioactive debris beyond the Soviet borders: in violation of the Limited Nuclear Test Ban Treaty of 1963.
- Conducting nuclear tests of greater than 150 kiloton yield: in violation of the Threshold Test Ban Treaty of 1974.
- Maintaining an offensive biological warfare program and capability: in violation of the Biological and Toxic Weapons Convention of 1972.

In sum, Soviet non-compliance and circumvention has meant that the treaties and agreements at issue have failed to accomplish the habits of obedience and control of the Soviet arsenal that they were designed, on our side, to achieve. Nonetheless, the U.S. military disadvantages that have flowed from "the expanding pattern of Soviet violations," as Weinberger calls them, are really smaller in significance than the lack of nuclear modernization that the United States, affected by arms control treaties and what may be termed the arms control temperament, failed to pursue during the late 1970s.

MYTH 4. ARMS CONTROL VIOLATIONS DO NOT AFFECT OUR NATIONAL SECURITY

Congressman Les Aspin (D-WI) reflects the view of the arms control community when he says:

> The violations [of SALT by the Soviet Union] are politically harmful because they undermine American support for arms control and because they cry out for an American response, but in military terms they don't amount to a hill of beans.

Arms control advocates like Aspin seem to think that the main problem with arms control violations is that silly Americans get all worked up about them, operating on the principle that mutual agreements should be rigorously kept and other such bourgeois assumptions. In fact, the Aspin point of view only reflects the arms control narcotic at work. Many advocates have such a quasi-mystical view of arms control that they see it as an end in itself—they refuse to consider the significance of treaty violations or to hold the arms control process accountable or hostage to such violations.

This is also the historical reality. Western democracies have tended to place so much value on arms control that they do not want to hazard its termination by insisting on strict compliance. The idea seems to be that if the door is kept locked too tightly, the burglar may be tempted to shoot his way in.

Japanese, German, and Italian treaty violations before World War II were just about as militarily significant as Soviet violations in recent decades. For example, in a recent study of arms control, Robin Ranger writes that in its battleship and cruiser building program, Japan violated the terms of the 1922 Washington Naval Treaty by 70 to 100 percent on all 10 of its ships with reference to the 3,000-ton modernization allowance, while four ships also exceeded the 35,000-ton displacement limit. Germany demonstrated its regard for arms control and the Anglo-German Naval Agreement of 1935 by constructing its two *Bismarck* class battleships with 42,000-ton displacements, considerably above the 35,000 tons permitted.

These violations were politically harmful not merely because they reduced public support in England for the arms control process, as Les Aspin would have it. They were politically harmful because they convinced Germany and Japan that the Allies were weak, that they could not enforce their treaties, that they were not even bold enough to insist on compliance, that there was constant hand-wringing and rationalization for hostile behavior. Thus arms control demonstrated weakness that could only have increased the confidence of Germany and Japan that increasing the military pressure would bring political capitulation from the Western democracies.

On the military front, military power is most effective when it does not have to be used. Stable deterrence is not a function of a large arsenal of weapons alone; such an arsenal deters only if a possible enemy believes he should respect the contingent threats. U.S. decisions not to undercut a SALT regime that the President claims the Soviet Union is violating, and indeed to pursue new agreements, invite and merit a Soviet disrespect that is dangerous for peace. Les Aspin is right that the political implications of Soviet treaty violations are most important, but it is for this reason, not the one he gives.

Aspin is wrong [in stating] that violations are unimportant in military terms: pause to consider why they are taking place. Obviously Germany in 1935, and the Soviet Union in recent years, both felt that they were benefiting from going beyond the bounds of the agreements; otherwise they would not have violated them. In the case of the Soviet Union, one simply has to look at the treaty violations listed earlier to see that they are by no means trivial in military terms.

It should be obvious that bolstering the engine of Soviet strategic power, its long-range ICBMs, brings military advantages; defending its military targets and top leadership through illicit defense fulfills the goal of protecting the lives that the Soviets value most.

MYTH 5. STRATEGIC DEFENSE POSES A THREAT TO ARMS CONTROL

In a *Foreign Affairs* article published in the winter of 1984–85, McGeorge Bundy, George Kennan, Robert McNamara, and Gerard Smith asserted that the United States has reached a fork in the policy road—"The President's Choice: Star Wars or Arms Control?" It is their view, indeed it is the leading item in the Athanasian Creed of the arms control lobby, that defensive deployments, actual or in prospect, *must* stimulate countervailing offensive deployments. Therefore, the President cannot have both the strategic defense initiative (SDI) and arms control. The arms control lobby claims that what they like to call "Star Wars" would stand an outside chance of fulfulling some of its strategic promise only in the context of supportive arms control agreements to reduce the quantity, and perhaps quality, of offensive firepower and, even more important, to help protect vulnerable space-based assets. The elementary logic of this position is that the inevitable effect of SDI upon the arms competition will preclude the possibility of its being a strategic success.

The technological and tactical feasibility and cost-effectiveness of strategic missile defenses remain to be demonstrated. It should not be forgotten that strategic defenses, functionally speaking, would be a form of arms control. Frequently in public debate, opponents of SDI will concede the probability that defenses could be 50, 60, or 70 percent effective, for the purpose of highlighting the size of the likely "leakage" of warheads. (Speaking off the record, Soviet officials have conceded the likelihood of an even higher range of effectiveness than this.) Strategic defenses that were, say, 50 percent effective, in practical terms would reduce the size of the Soviet missile force by a like amount. What is more, such a level of effective defense would achieve a practical scale of reduction in Soviet offensive arms that goes far beyond any arms control program that is likely to be negotiated.

When facing a United States utterly bereft of strategic defenses (with air defense capability reduced to the status of a peacetime Coast Guard), the Soviet Union has chosen to effect a more than fivefold increase in its strategic force loadings. Plainly, it cannot have been the plausible anticipation of U.S. missile defenses that stimulated the buildup in the Soviet strategic arsenal. We have over a decade of experience with a zero level of U.S. BMD (ballistic missile defense) deployment. This should have been ample time for the concept of strategic stability focused upon assuredly vulnerable homelands to show its mettle as a generator of arms control agreements.

To note the fact that the ABM Treaty of 1972 has failed miserably to choke off the Soviet will to bid for a combat advantage with strategic offensive and defensive programs is not, of course, to demonstrate that strategic defense will automatically function as a catalyst for arms control worthy of the name. But the beginning of wisdom for an arms competition management strategy has to be frank recognition that a U.S. strategic defense program has been shown by the historical record not to be the critical stimulus to Soviet competitive effort. It can hardly be a coincidence that the first Soviet proposals for a radical scale of reduction in strategic offensive arms were presented late in 1985, in the context of their campaign to discourage the United States from proceeding with SDI. It would appear to be the case that SDI has brought the Soviets back to Geneva with some of the trappings, at least, of an attractive position.

U.S. strategic missile defenses of the kind under investigation by the SDI office should threaten the military integrity of Soviet strategic war plans, though not—for several decades at least—the Soviet ability to retaliate massively. There is no need to invent a fictitiously cooperative Soviet Union in order to anticipate the strong probability that Soviet leaders are very likely indeed to grow very interested in quite radical arms control measures. Soviet leaders would need to believe that it makes no strategic sense to amass more and more offensive arms that can have little if any military utility. Furthermore, if they believe that the United States might implement a strategic defensive addition which would place the Soviet Union in a condition of growing military disadvantage, then the quality of Soviet cooperation in the arms control process would be truly amazing to behold.

The world already is very familiar with a future from which strategic defenses are effectively precluded: it is a world at risk to a competition in offensive nuclear armaments that is "regulated" by the fraying bandage of very permissive and violated SALT agreements. Determined pursuit of defensive capabilities by the United States—we can rely on the Soviets to behave responsibly in their pursuit of homeland defense—may, indeed is likely, to lead to a competition dominantly of a defense-defense character. This will not be real peace, but it should be a far safer and more stable environment than that provided by its offensive alternative.

Only in a situation where strategic defenses were deployed very heavily could the superpowers reduce their offensive nuclear arsenals down to a very small scale. Because of the practical impossibility of the United States knowing *exactly* how many nuclear weapons and delivery vehicles the Soviet Union has produced, absolute confidence in verification is a pipe dream. Adequate security against Soviet cheating can be provided only by active defense. Fortunately for the prospects of cooperation in disarmament, suspicious Soviet officials may be relied upon to agree with the logic of defense as a practical guarantee of self-help against foreign perfidy.

MYTH 6. THE UNITED STATES AND THE SOVIET UNION CAN DESTROY THE WORLD SEVERAL TIMES OVER, SO THE ARMS RACE IS FUTILE AND ARMS CONTROL IS THE ONLY RATIONAL APPROACH

The "overkill" thesis holds that the superpowers already have sufficient nuclear weapons in their arsenals to make the rubble bounce at least several times. Holding to an apocalyptic view of nuclear strategy, critics of perceived "overkill" allege that the superpowers simply are adding redundancy upon redundancy as they augment their nuclear arsenals.

The "overkill" assertion against further rounds of competitive armament may look fine on a bumper sticker, but it bears no relation to the facts of strategic policy, here or in the Soviet Union, or to the probable consequences of very large-scale nuclear use. "Destroying the world" is of no policy interest as threat, let alone as action, to anybody. Nuclear weapons are weapons, in the traditional sense of the word—they can be used to disarm an enemy, politically through coercion or physically through the damage and disruption they could cause. Against the kind of offensive and defensive strategic weapons arsenal that the Soviet Union is acquiring, the kind of minimum city-busting deterrent that propagators of this myth recommend, would, in all likelihood, be no deterrent at all.

The popularity in debate of the morally repugnant, as well as strategic, idea of "overkill" points to the unfortunate fact that the U.S. government has performed very poorly over 40 years in explaining its strategic policy to the American people. The size of the U.S. strategic nuclear arsenal—approximately 10,000 weapons—naturally appears extravagant, even obscene, to those who believe both that a weapon in the arsenal is the same as a weapon on a target, and that the targets are cities. After all, how many cities are there in the Soviet Union?

The public should be able to understand that 10,000 nuclear weapons in the peacetime arsenal might be reduced to, say, 3,000 by a Soviet surprise attack. Those hypothetical 3,000 surviving weapons would be targeted against the assets of the Soviet state, not Soviet society. As a target structure, the Soviet state comprises literally thousands of more and less important military, political-control, and defense-economic assets. Furthermore, our 3,000 weapons would be opposed by Soviet air and missile defenses. The purpose of our arms buildup is to be able to develop a force that, even depleted by a Soviet first strike, and even impaired by Soviet anti-aircraft missiles and missile defense, will still be able to wreak massive damage upon the Soviet state—this knowledge, we hope, will deter the Soviet Union from attacking in the first place. But without the capacity to threaten such retaliation, not in the abstract but in the actual circumstances of war, the United States cannot rely on deterrence to protect its people.

There is enough dynamite in the world to blow us all up numerous times, and enough water in the oceans to drown us all countless times. But the real issue is under what circumstances can we expect lethal devices and materials to be used and what the precise goals are of the weapons we build. The same may be said of the overkill slogan.

There is only one way in which arms control agreements of a kind beneficial to stability might be secured, and that is if the Soviet Union anticipates suffering important military, and hence political disadvantage, if competition is not legally constrained. The road to an arms control agreement of which a U.S. administration could be justly proud, lies—alas—only through competitive armament of a kind and on a scale that scores high marks for the creation of healthy anxiety in Moscow. It is not a question of choosing to compete or to cooperate; the terms for success cited here simply reflect the way of the world.

LESSONS OF HISTORY

It follows from the discussion in the main body of this article, and from the caveats cited above, that arms control is very unlikely to be important as an instrument for the alleviation, let alone solution, of U.S. security problems. But it follows also that arms control continues to remain a magnet for the attraction of a pervasive mythology that reduces significantly the ability of Western publics to think in suitable terms about the choices they face in national security policy. In his Third Philippic of 341 B.C., Demosthenes wrote:

> But in heaven's name, is there any intelligent man who could let words rather than deeds decide the question of who is at war with him? . . . For he [Philip] says that he is not at war, but for my part, so far from admitting that in acting thus he is observing the peace with you, I assert that when he lays hands on Megara, sets up tyrannies in Thrace, hatches plots in the Peloponnese, and carries out all these operations with his armed force, he is breaking the peace and making war upon you—unless you are prepared to say that the men who bring up the siege-engines are keeping the peace until they actually bring them to bear on the walls.

Questions for Discussion

1. What are the domestic pressures in the United States that promote arms control?
2. How do the domestic pressures for arms control in the United States compare to corresponding domestic pressures in the Soviet Union?

3. What criteria should be used in evaluating the wisdom of an arms control proposal?
4. What is the significance of verification to arms control agreements?
5. How do you account for the fact that neither the United States nor the Soviet Union has used nuclear weapons, though each power has possessed these weapons for decades? What lessons can be drawn from your answer?

Suggested Readings

Blacker, Coit D., and Gloria Duffy, eds. *International Arms Control: Issues and Agreements*. Stanford: Stanford Univ. Press, 1984.

Carlton, David, and Herbert M. Levine, eds. *The Cold War Debated*. New York: McGraw-Hill, 1988.

Gervasi, Tom. *The Myth of Soviet Military Supremacy*. New York: Harper & Row, 1986.

Howard, Michael. "Is Arms Control Really Necessary?" *Harper's*, 272, no. 1632 (May 1986), 13–16.

Kruzel, Joseph. "From Rush-Bagot to START." *Orbis*, 30, no. 1 (Spring 1986), 193–216.

Laird, Robbin F. *The Soviet Union, the West, and the Nuclear Arms Race*. New York: New York Univ. Press, 1986.

Panofsky, Wolfgang K. H. "Arms Control: Necessary Process." *Bulletin of the Atomic Scientists*, 42, no. 3 (March 1986), 35–38.

Salter, Stephen H. "Stopping the Arms Race: A Modest Proposal." *Issues in Science and Technology*, 2, no. 2 (Winter 1986), 74–82.

Schwartz, William A., and Charles Derber. "Arms Control: Misplaced Focus." *Bulletin of the Atomic Scientists*, 42, no. 3 (March 1986), 39–44.

Vigor, P. H. *The Soviet View of Disarmament*. New York: St. Martin's Press, 1986.

Chapter 19

Should U.S. Troops Withdraw from Europe?

In April 1949, the United States joined with Belgium, Canada, Denmark, France, Iceland, Italy, Luxembourg, the Netherlands, Norway, Portugal, and the United Kingdom in a peacetime alliance whose purpose was to strengthen the security interests of individual member nations. The alliance, called the North Atlantic Treaty Organization (NATO), has since added four countries—Greece, the Federal Republic of Germany, Spain, and Turkey—so that today it has sixteen members. NATO, in the late 1980s, remains what it was at the time of its creation—a symbol of western security.

The key provision of NATO is Article Five, which states that an armed attack on any member will be considered as an attack on all of them. Since the formation of NATO, no member has been attacked by the Soviet Union, and the alliance continues although it suffers from the strain of differing interests and perceptions of NATO members.

The guiding spirit of NATO has been that the existence of NATO serves as a deterrent to war. In this regard the Soviet Union would see that NATO members were creating a formidable military force and, consequently, would not attack Western Europe for fear that Moscow would lose. If war did occur, however, existing NATO conventional forces would slow down a Soviet attack and serve as a "trip-wire" in which the United States could then use its nuclear weapons.

The conditions under which NATO was formed have changed over the last four decades in at least three fundamental ways. First, when NATO was created, the United States had nuclear weapons and the Soviet Union did not. Second, the Soviet Union was considered by most western leaders as an expansionist power that might use military force to gain influence. Third, the economies of Western Europe were in shambles because of the devastation of World War II.

Today, these conditions are no longer the same. First, the Soviet Union built its own nuclear force and gradually achieved a status of nuclear parity with the United States. Second, the Soviet Union appeared to be less menacing over time, and many leaders in the West began to lower their fears of Soviet military interventionism in Western Europe. Third, the economies of Western Europe recovered from the war and grew stronger with respect to the economy of the United States.

Because of these developments, the relationship between the United States and its alliance partners has changed, and has led to a rethinking of fundamental policies by NATO members. One policy which is currently receiving attention is the deployment of U.S. troops in Western Europe.

Some U.S. troops had remained in Europe at the conclusion of World War II. The event which had a dramatic impact on the level of U.S. troops in Europe, however, was the invasion of South Korea by North Korea in 1950. After the invasion, U.S. forces were increased in other areas of the world for fear that fighting outside of Korea might occur.

U.S. conventional forces in Europe were also increased because of growing Soviet power in nuclear weapons. In effect, the deployment of large numbers of U.S. troops to Europe meant that if the Soviet Union engaged in military action against Western Europe, the United States would become involved. Otherwise, NATO's European members might doubt that the United States would be willing to sacrifice its own security for that of its NATO allies.

The number of U.S. troops in Western Europe has varied since 1950 when it was 145,000. Today, 352,000 U.S. troops are stationed there. As early as the 1960s, Senator Mike Mansfield introduced resolutions calling for substantial troop withdrawals from Europe. Other members of Congress have called for linking the number of U.S. troops in Europe to the willingness of NATO allies to make a greater contribution to their own defense.

In the following debate, economist Melvyn Krauss argues that the United States should withdraw its forces from Europe. He contends:

1. The cost of maintaining the troops is high.
2. There is no causal relationship between the existence of U.S. troops in Europe and peace between the Soviet Union and NATO members.
3. Because U.S. troops are in Europe, NATO's European members have had no incentive to spend more on defense.
4. Because the Europeans have been unwilling to spend more on conventional forces, the use of nuclear weapons becomes more likely in the event of war.
5. If the Soviet Union attacks Western Europe, it is unlikely that the United States will use nuclear weapons against targets in the Soviet Union.
6. Anti-Americanism has been encouraged in Western Europe by the presence of U.S. forces there.
7. The withdrawal of U.S. troops would not lead to isolationism in the United States, neutralism in Western Europe, or an unwillingness by Europeans to defend themselves.

Foreign policy writer Josef Joffe argues for retaining U.S. troops in Europe. He contends:

1. The nuclear threat posed by the United States against the Soviet Union is more credible because a significant number of U.S. troops are in Europe.
2. To withdraw U.S. troops at a time when entire categories of nuclear weapons are being eliminated from Europe because of arms control agreements would be sending the wrong signal to the Soviet Union.
3. Europeans will not make greater defense efforts to compensate for the reduction or elimination of U.S. troops.
4. If U.S. troops withdraw, Europeans would be encouraged to accept a policy of appeasement of, and accommodation with, the Soviet Union.
5. The decision to withdraw cannot be easily reversed.

Should U.S. Troops Withdraw from Europe?

MELVYN KRAUSS
The U.S. and NATO: Should the Troops Stay?

After World War II, the devastated and demoralized Western Europe felt vulnerable to a Soviet invasion. To pacify European anxieties and deter a potential aggressor, the United States agreed to station the equivalent of six infantry divisions in Europe. According to President Dwight D. Eisenhower, first supreme commander of the allied forces in Europe, U.S. troops were to remain in Europe for a limited time only. When the economies of the European allies recovered, it was envisaged that the U.S. troops would be brought home.

"When I went back to Europe in 1951 to command the forces of NATO [North Atlantic Treaty Organization]," wrote President Eisenhower in 1963, "the United States agreed to supply the equivalent of six infantry divisions, which were to be regarded as an emergency reinforcement of Europe while our hard hit allies were rebuilding their economies and capabilities for supporting their own defense. Now, twelve years later, these forces, somewhat reinforced, are still there."

Indeed, today, some thirty-six years after President Eisenhower took up his NATO command, more than 340,000 U.S. troops remain in Europe, despite the fact that aggregate European gross national product now equals that of the United States.

The cost of these troops to the U.S. taxpayer is enormous. It is estimated that the U.S. government spends between $130 and $160 billion per year to support NATO. If the U.S. were to withdraw from Europe, a significant portion of this money could be saved and used for other purposes. For example, as a result of the savings derived from the U.S. troop withdrawal, taxes could be cut, or the federal deficit reduced, or an anti-missile system, such as SDI [Strategic Defense Initiative], financed. Such savings, of course, would be foolhardy if sufficient benefits to this country from our gargantuan expenditures on NATO could be proved, that is, if the benefits from NATO could be shown to be greater than their costs.

NATO supporters claim that the most significant benefit from U.S. troops in Europe is that they have kept the peace for some forty years, a dubious argument that makes the elementary error of confusing correlation with cause and effect. True, there has been peace in Europe for forty years, and just as true, the U.S. troops have been in Europe for nearly that same period of time. But just because one of them correlates with another in no way implies a casual relationship between the two.

For example, President Eisenhower wrote, in 1963, "I believe the time has now come when we should start withdrawing some of the U.S. troops. One American division in Europe can now show the flag as definitely as can several."

Do NATO defenders, such as David Abshire, Richard Burt, and Lawrence Eagleberger, really mean to imply that, had the U.S. followed the advice of this most preeminent NATO expert and removed the five infantry divisions from Europe, war would have broken out in Europe? NATO supporters also claim that the alliance has strengthened our European allies. The truth, however, is the opposite. By providing Europe with a defense guarantee symbolized by the troops in Europe, the U.S. has robbed its allies of the incentive to defend themselves. In 1983, for example, the U.S. spent 6.6 percent of its gross national product [GNP] on defense, while non-U.S. NATO spent only 3.6 percent of its GNP.

It should come as no surprise, then, that of all our Western European allies, France, which is least dependent on the United States for its defense, is the least accommodationist toward the Soviet Union, while West Germany, which is most dependent on the United States for its defense, is the most accommodationist. Not only has NATO created weak allies when it is supposed to create strong ones, but to a large extent, it is responsible for the world living on the nuclear precipice.

Feeling safe because of U.S. nuclear guarantees, the Europeans neglected to build up their conventional defenses as their economies recovered from the devastation of World War II. At the same time, the Soviet Union built up its conventional forces to the point where it currently enjoys a three to one edge in tanks, a five to one edge in infantry fighting vehicles, a five to one edge in artillery, better than parity in attack aircraft, a monopoly on automated tactical fire control, a one and a half to one edge in manpower, a huge edge in chemical weapons, a virtual monopoly in 50- to 500-mile range ballistic missiles.

Indeed, because the present balance of conventional forces so strongly favors the Soviet Union, if Moscow were to launch a conventional attack on Western Europe, according to the [former] NATO Supreme Commander Bernard Rogers, NATO could fight for only days, not weeks, before facing the doomsday decision of surrender or launching a nuclear first strike. This is the so-called problem of the nuclear threshold.

The only way the nuclear threshold can be increased would be for Europe to spend more on its conventional forces. But Europe has been unwilling to do this, so long as U.S. troops remain on European soil and the symbol of [a] U.S. defense guarantee persists.

The low nuclear threshold puts the lie to the often heard claim by NATO supporters that the U.S. troops in Europe provide this country with forward defense. This forward defense argument, "Beggar thy neighbor in the extreme," is that, in case of a Warsaw Pact conventional attack, it is better that the fighting take place on our allies' soil than our own. This argument is false.

Because of the conventional imbalance, a prolonged conventional exchange is not very likely. Conventional fighting could be expected to escalate rapidly to nuclear weapons. The sad truth is that, thanks to NATO, the West has little, if any, conventional deterrent in Europe. This does not mean they do not have conventional forces, but that they are not a deterrent.

What deterrent is there, then, to prevent a Soviet invasion? The centerpiece of NATO, of course, has been the U.S. nuclear umbrella. But as the Soviet Union has approached, and perhaps surpassed, nuclear parity with the United States, the credibility of the U.S. nuclear guarantee has been called into question. Would the destruction of American troops by invading Soviet forces serve as a tripwire to bring on American nuclear strikes against Moscow? I think not.

Plus, the American troops in Europe today promise the Europeans something the U.S. has no intention of delivering. The troops, however, do serve an important function as a political symbol. They give European politicians the excuse they are looking for to justify their unwillingness to cut into their welfare states and spend on defense. In the meanwhile, these same leaders bribe the Soviets with economic and political favors to give Moscow a vested interest in preserving the status quo in Europe.

Not only have the U.S. troops in Europe created weak allies who are more apt to appease than confront an enemy, they have fanned the flames of anti-Americanism abroad. This is particularly true in West Germany. Now some West Germans view the U.S. troops as protectors. Others, still traumatized by their defeat in World War II, see the troops as a continuing army of occupation. Rather than making the Germans feel more a part of the Western team opposing Soviet imperialism, American troops make them feel disengaged and resentful. Were the U.S. to withdraw its troops in Germany, on the other hand, the Germans would feel less like spectators and more like players in the East-West struggle.

If the United States troops in Europe serve this country's interests so poorly, why, then, is there such resistance in the country to calls for their withdrawal? Perhaps because of the association in the public's mind of troop withdrawal with isolation. But this association clearly is mistaken. Isolationists typically argue that America needs no allies. Yet, advocates of U.S. troop withdrawal from Europe, like Tom Bethel, Angelo Codevilla, Gregory Fossedal, Irving Kristol, and myself, recognize that the U.S. needs strong allies and are concerned that NATO has made our allies weak. Ironically, pulling the troops out of Europe is not an isolationist argument; today, it is an internationalist one.

A more likely explanation of the resistance to withdrawal is simply that the Europeans are vehemently against it. The State Department, for example, typically seeks to please U.S. allies, even when such an attitude is less than appropriate. To justify their compliant posture, State Department officials argue that a U.S. troop withdrawal would split or decouple Europe from America, which, we are told, is precisely what the Soviets want.

However, the Soviets have made no concerted effort to get the U.S. troops out of Europe, comparable, for example, to their effort to get the Pershing missiles out of Europe, or shortcircuiting President Reagan's Strategic Defense Initiative. This should come as no surprise. The NATO link between the U.S. and Europe has very much worked to the Soviet's advantage.

Without doubt, since the late 1960s, the Europeans have been the foremost lobby to convince the United States not to defend itself seriously. When Americans try to decide whether or not to build neutron bombs, whether to rely on missiles or treaties, whether to oppose Soviet conquest in some corner of the world, or whether to build an anti-defense missile defense, we can count on the Europeans to weigh in to our political process with this message: "If you do this thing that you naively believe will add to your strength and security, you will lose us." No one who reads communist literature can fail to notice that the Soviet Union's main message to its followers in Europe is not to decouple from the United States, but to use that coupling to Soviet advantage.

Finally, resistance to U.S. troop withdrawal also comes from that I call "*Commentary* Conservatives." Named after *Commentary* Magazine, they are people like Norman Podhoretz, Midge Decter, Steve Munson, and Alvin Bernstein, who fear that Europe would collapse if America pulled its troops out, as if the only thing standing between Europe and total Finlandization was the political symbolism provided by U.S. troops. The implicit assumption of this argument is that Europe's values have deteriorated so badly that Europe could not or would not stand on its own feet to oppose the Soviets. The evidence, however, does not support this view.

Europe's values today appear as sound as our own. For example, the recent severe decline of the influence and popularity of the Communist Party in several West European countries, France and Italy in particular, is evidence that Western values have strengthened, not declined, in Europe. The defeat of domestic terrorists in Italy and West Germany through legal means is evidence that Western values of due process and democracy are alive and well in these countries.

The British proved their values meant more to them than many had expected when, in 1982, they fought a war with Argentina to recover the Falkland Islands. By this action, the British showed they were willing to fight and die to keep the Falklands British. Would they dare do less for Britain itself?

In all their lamentations about failed American resolve and the expansion of Soviet power, "*Commentary* Conservatives" fall into the Soviet trap by their apparent willingness to concede substantial amounts of political influence within the Atlantic Alliance to forces that serve Soviet interests, that is the Europeans. The myth that Europe would collapse if the U.S. withdrew its troops is a powerful lever. Europeans and their spokesmen in this country use it to shape U.S. foreign policy and military policy, for the troops in Europe are the symbol that keeps NATO and the doctrine of allied unity alive, a doctrine that the Soviets can and do use to influence American foreign policy to their own advantage.

If NATO and allied unity did not exist, an important avenue of influence over U.S. foreign policy would be closed to the Soviets.

☑ NO

Should U.S. Troops Withdraw from Europe?

JOSEF JOFFE
The U.S. and NATO: Should the Troops Stay?

Let me begin with a little anecdote, which is actually true and can be read in Barbara Tuchman's book, *The Guns of August*. In 1911, if I recall correctly, the British Marshal Wilson came over to France to have talks with his counterpart, Marshal Foch, and he asked him, "Listen, in the Alliance, we're talking about how many British soldiers do you need on French soil to make you believe that we will be involved in a war against Germany?" And with his Gallic logic, Foch replied, "We only need one British soldier and we'll make sure that he gets killed in the first hour of the war."

Now the logic of that is self-evident. But the question is, could we transfer that logic to the current case? Would one GI who gets killed be enough to embroil the United States in a kind of credible execution of its commitment to West European security?

Well, first of all, I do not think that one soldier was enough in 1911 or 1914, because great powers always have been forced to ignore nationals killed by enemies. Even then, one soldier would not have been enough. But we are now living in a nuclear age and that, as Kennedy used to say, has changed all the answers and all the questions. Certainly, one or even many hostages do not, would not automatically embroil the United States because the risks of being embroiled are now so gigantic. They have risen so exponentially that it takes a much greater provocation to make sure that the United States is actually credibly involved.

For a hostage position today to be really credible, the *value* that hostage force represents has to be big enough to approach somewhere in the vicinity of the risks that you have to incur if you really get involved. The assets that you put in a hostage position have to be valuable enough to make credible [the] resorting to the ultimate weapon. That is the difference between a conventional and nuclear situation.

Let me put this thought in a different way. It is an ancient article of faith in Europe, certainly, and probably here too, that the nuclear threat posed by the United States has been slowly devalued in a parity situation with the Soviet Union, because the U.S. will not sacrifice Chicago for Hamburg or Milan. So the dilemma is how do you make commitments credible in a nuclear age? The United States will not sacrifice Chicago for Milan, but the threat does grow a great deal more credible, I would submit, if you are wielding that threat not just on behalf of European cities, but on behalf of city-sized contingents of your own nationals, who happen to be situated on foreign soil. . . . [T]he credibility of the U.S. commitment does depend on numbers. It cannot just be a trip wire, not in the nuclear age. Trip wires, just pure trip wires, will not work. The value that has to be threatened has to approach the risks that you might face if you execute your commitment. But the question is how many soldiers do you need to make that commitment credible?

. . . I do not have an answer, but let me go back to the great sage of international politics, namely, to Henry Kissinger, some 20 years ago, when we had the first wave of a troop withdrawal campaign, also known as Mansfieldism, named after the then Senator, later the Ambassador to Japan. In the 1960s, Mike Mansfield introduced his annual resolution in the Senate calling for substantial troop withdrawals from Europe. And so when Henry Kissinger was asked, "Well, how many troops do you really need for credibility," he said, to paraphrase him, "in the nuclear age . . . the price of credibility may have risen to six divisions." How did he know that? Well, he did not, but what he meant was that six divisions have been the status quo since the decision was taken to beef up the two divisions left after the war to six. And what he meant was, if you take out a substantial number, as Mansfield was then asking, and if you do so in the absence of compensating events in the system, such as the draw-down of Soviet troops, if you change the status quo unilaterally, you signal something. You send a message to friends and foes alike, "Listen, you guys, friends and foes, I no longer care as much as I once did about my position in Europe and the security of my allies."

Why is commitment such an important thing? If you give a guarantee to your allies, to your weaker allies, there have to be two conditions. I would call those the *clarity* of commitment and the *certainty* of commitment. Now clarity means that you say, under such and such clarified circumstances, I will help you, no matter what. That is clear commitment. But that, unfortunately, is not a sufficient condition. To really make the guarantee tight, you have to have certainty.

Why certainty? The French and the British gave a very clear commitment to the Poles in 1939: "If you're attacked by Germany, we're going to declare war on them." But that did not quite work to deter the Germans; they attacked anyway, because the commitment was not certain. The commitment was not certain because, in the end, the French and British did not live up to their commitment, at least not for a long time.

And so the criterion of certainty that I am invoking means that you create a situation that, no matter what you would like to do in the moment of truth as a guarantor, you cannot just bug out. You have to be at the front line, as the French and the British were not, and you have to be in a position where you are embroiled, no matter whether you want to be or not. And you have to do so with enough numbers, which somehow compresses the irreducible gap of geography and sovereignty, because, after all, it is not your country that you are defending; you are defending somebody else. And you have to force the enemy to threaten values of yours, which somewhere aproach the importance of core values, of the nation's integrity, the nation's border, the nation's population, and so on.

Now the question is still—what about 100,000, what about 200,000 troops? Is it not enough if you put them on the front line? Is not *that* enough to underline both the clarity and the certainty of the commitment? And I have my grave doubts here. Let me give you a number of reasons why.

The first arises from the fact that we may withdraw entire categories of nuclear weapons from Europe. If you pull out conventional troops at a time when they necessarily become more important because of the draw-down on nuclear weapons, then you are sending a very grave signal. . . . [L]ook at the military situation . . . [and] at the central front. There are really only two armies worth talking about on the ground, and those are the American and the German armies. Why? Well, first of all, the German Army is the largest. It is half a million people, and the second largest is, of course, the American contingent. And then what else do we have? Well, we have the British Army on the Rhine, good people, well-trained force, as they showed in the Falklands. But as the name says, it is the British Army on the Rhine. They are way back, far away from the potential confrontation. This cuts into your certainty principle.

Then we have the French with 30,000 people; well-armed, nuclear armed, tough fighters. But look at where they are. They are tucked away in the southwest corner of West Germany, because that is the French occupation zone. But let me also suggest that the historical fluke has a nice payoff because they do not get automatically embroiled if a war breaks out.

And then there are the Belgians and the Dutch, who are supposed to take their place in the "layer cake" defense along the Iron Curtain. But it so happens that the Belgian and Dutch are not there either. They are supposed to go there by rail, for instance, from their garrisons at home. And I suggest that, given the nature of modern warfare, they are not going to get there when they have to get there.

And the Danes—nothing against the Danes, but I think that the Danes are going to detract from the central front, rather than add to it, because the Germans will have to go up there and defend the Danish.

So who is going to defend the old Fulda Gap there? Well, some American critics of NATO [North Atlantic Treaty Organization] say let those Germans, French, Danes, and Belgians make up for the gap left by the Americans who can be withdrawn. But I suggest that we all know in our hearts they will not, contrary to what Mr. Melvyn Krauss says. And there are lots of reasons.

First, there are the demographics. Those Europeans do not breed enough any more. People in the Germany Army are going around traumatized, asking what are we going to do in the 1990s, when we will not have enough recruits in the pool of 18-year-olds to maintain present peacetime strengths? And there is that old welfare state, which, if you look at the long-term numbers in the key European countries, has not been all that bad. It is true that, as their gross national product expanded, defense spending expanded as well. But defense spending has not expanded as fast as the welfare budget. In absolute terms, defense spending has risen steadily, risen much more steadily than in this country, mind you, but it has not risen as much, proportionately, as the welfare state. And then look at the third factor, which is the disappearance of anti-Sovietism or anti-communism as a kind of legitimizing, mobilizing value system.

But how will this troop withdrawal really work? How do you make others do more for their defense when you—I mean the United States—by your own actions, namely withdrawing, are signaling that conventional power is not important any more? Has anybody ever tried to work this logic on kids, saying do not do what I do—do what I say? It does not work with kids, and it does not work with nations. You cannot say, "I am going to draw down my conventional presence here, which means the threat is not big enough any more for me to stay here. But on the other hand, I want you to increase your contribution because the threat is looming quite dramatically." You cannot say both of these things at the same time. It does not work.

Let me suggest some more analytical reasons why it does not. The basic logic of the troop withdrawals in this country is [that] if we kick them hard enough in the butt, they will get off the same. If we really pull out, if we finally do what we have threatened to do, they will have no other choice but to fend for themselves. They have to. If they care about their security, they are going to have to do what we have provided for them all these decades gratis. They have the money. Let them get the guns and the men, too.

Now I am not sure at all whether that theory is correct. I think it is bad psychology, bad politics, and even bad economics. And I suggest to any economist who makes economic arguments in favor of troop withdrawal to study *The Logic of Collective Action* by Mancur Olson. The message of this book is that certain collective goods, like defense, parks, or roads, are provided only if there is one partner in the group who is so big and so committed that he produces most of the collective goods himself. In this respect, the history of the Atlantic Alliance confirms very nicely the model of *The Logic of Collective Action*. It is quite doubtful whether the Alliance would have got off the ground without the United States' willingness to invest in organizing it.

What is more likely, or at least as likely an outcome of the "kick them in the butt so they'll get off it" school of thought, is that, instead of producing more of the collective good, none of these little Europeans, rich as they are, will produce the collective good, but something else, which is they will make their own side deals.

And the side view in terms of international politics would go like this in the European context: here is a bunch of small nations, faced with an objective loss or objective reduction in the supply of security. Instead of making up that supply by generating more of it, they will likely reduce their demand for security. They will want to make sure that their common enemy has fewer and fewer reasons to threaten and to attack. That is called the policy of accommodation or propitiation, or even nastier, appeasement. And that common enemy happens to be the Soviet Union.

And I suggest that part of the logic of *Ostpolitik*, which was a policy of accommodation between West Germany and the Soviet Union in the early 1970s, was driven precisely by Mansfieldism. In an age when the clarity and certainty of the American commitment suddenly began to wobble, the Europeans wanted to make sure that, as the supply of security went down, the demand for security went down, too. And, therefore, you get into a policy of accommodation with your common enemy.

Let me get to my conclusion. The whole troop withdrawal debate comes down to a bet. And the question is whether the United States is likely to win that bet. My answer is no. You want to make a bet on the basis of a hidden premise. If the Europeans are going to do what you expect them to do—and I outlined the logic why this may not happen—and if you still want to go ahead and make that bet, then you must accept the fact that Europe no longer matters as much as it once did. And if you scratch any of those new isolationists, such as the Pacific Firsters, you find a resentment against Europe and a sense that Europe does not matter so much any more.

There is another hidden premise behind the bet. Even those who believe that Europe still matters can say, "Well, you know, if the bet goes wrong, we can always reverse it." We have reversed this bet twice already. After not going into Europe soon enough in 1917, we left Europe after World War I was over, making that bet again on isolationism, but then having to go back in 1941, or at least declare war in 1941. So you can say, "Well, you know, we reversed the bad bet twice in the past. Why can't we reverse it again?"

I would come back in conclusion to where I began, which is that the nuclear age has changed all the answers. It is one thing to go in against Kaiser Bill, another thing to go back in 1944 against the conventional and weakened enemy, and it is another thing to go back into a Europe dominated by an intact, large, nuclear-armed superpower, and to go back in the shadow of the apocalypse, in the shadow of nuclear weapons. I do not think a third wrong bet can be reversed.

And so I suggest that the whole issue really boils down to the crucial philosophical question, which is, how important is Europe in the global rivalry between the two great superpowers?

. . . [T]he Soviet Union has never believed that Europe no longer matters. Quite the contrary. It is easy to forget how important Europe is here. The Soviets have never forgotten that the real stakes, the real competition, are not in Korea but in Europe.

Questions for Discussion

1. How would U.S. troop withdrawal affect the foreign and defense policies of West European members of NATO?
2. Would withdrawal affect the likelihood of nuclear war between the United States and the Soviet Union?
3. How have the changes in Soviet military power since 1950 affected the issue of U.S. troop withdrawal from NATO?
4. What leverage does the United States have to encourage other NATO members to make a greater contribution to their own defense?
5. How important is West Europe to the security of the United States? What are the reasons for your answer?
6. If Soviet conventional forces seem to be succeeding in an invasion of West Europe, how should the United States respond?

Suggested Readings

Bender, Peter. "The Superpower Squeeze." *Foreign Policy*, no. 65 (Winter 1986/87), 98–113.
Bethlen, Steven, and Ivan Volgyes, eds. *Europe and the Superpowers: Political, Economic, and Military Policies in the 1980s*. Boulder: Westview Press, 1985.

Cohen, Eliot A. "Do We Still Need Europe?" *Commentary*, 81, no. 1 (January 1986), 28–35.

Dean, Jonathan. *Watershed in Europe: Dismantling the East-West Military Confrontation.* Lexington, Mass.: Lexington Books, 1987.

Flanagan, Stephen J., and Fen Osler Hampson, eds. *Securing Europe's Future.* London: Croom Helm, 1986.

Krauss, Melvyn. *How NATO Weakens the West.* New York: Simon and Schuster, 1986.

Layne, Christopher. "Atlanticism without NATO." *Foreign Policy*, no. 67 (Summer 1987), 22–45.

Rogers, Bernard W. "Why NATO Continues to Need American Troops." *Wall Street Journal*, (July 8, 1987), 19.

Safire, William. "The European Pillar." *New York Times*, (April 7, 1988), A27.

Williams, Phil. *The Senate and U.S. Troops in Europe.* New York: St. Martin's Press, 1985.

Chapter 20

Is It Wise for the United States to Use Economic Sanctions against South Africa?

The South African government stands defiant against the world in its efforts to maintain white control of a country in which only one out of five people is white. It is a government condemned by most countries in the world for its racism, as exemplifed by its system of *apartheid* (separateness), which enforces separation of the races and treats black people as inferior to whites. Massive demonstrations by blacks in South Africa in the past several years have drawn the world's attention, and violence has become common.

Because of its racist policies, South Africa has become an important issue in U.S. foreign policy. The Reagan administration adopted a policy of "constructive engagement," through which it sought to convince the South African government to liberalize its society. U.S. officials argued that U.S. influence in improving conditions for blacks in South Africa is strengthened if the United States maintains a presence in the country.

Although the South African government has decreased the harshness of apartheid, human rights advocates regard these changes as too weak. They have argued that imposing economic sanctions might force the South African government to abandon apartheid. In addition, these advocates have put pressure on U.S. corporations to stop doing business in South Africa. Some universities as well as state and city governments agreed to divest themselves of stocks of companies that conduct business in South Africa.

Some major U.S. corporations with branches in South Africa had been complying with the Sullivan Principles. Named for Rev. Leon H. Sullivan, pastor of Zion Baptist Church in Philadelphia, these principles call upon U.S. corporations to provide greater opportunities in South Africa for blacks. The Sullivan Principles, however, were undermined as the clamor for economic sanctions and divestiture grew louder. In June 1987 Rev. Sullivan himself gave up on his own code of conduct for companies operating in South Africa and called for the United States to break diplomatic relations and impose a total economic embargo on South Africa until that country abandons apartheid. As of June 1987, nearly two hundred U.S. firms operated in South Africa, but more than one hundred firms had withdrawn from the country within the previous eighteen months.[1] Many U.S. companies doing business in South Africa indicated that they would not pull out, but would continue to abide by Sullivan Principles.

359

Sullivan's call for breaking diplomatic relations came after legislative actions on sanctions. In 1985 Congress imposed some limited economic sanctions against South Africa. In 1986 Congress considered expanding economic sanctions to include prohibiting the import of articles produced by South African government-owned or government-controlled organizations, barring U.S. bank loans to the South African government or any entity under its control, forbidding U.S. companies from making any new investments in South Africa, and revoking U.S. landing rights for all South African airliners. These sanctions were passed.

In debates in the Senate, Christopher J. Dodd, a Democrat from Connecticut, supported the sanctions, and Malcolm Wallop, a Republican from Wyoming, opposed them.

Dodd argues:

1. The time has passed to wait for the South African government to act on its own initiative.
2. Limited sanctions imposed by the United States in 1985 did produce results: pass laws were abolished; funding for black education was increased; and some restrictions of private life were lifted. It can be expected that more severe sanctions will produce even better results.

Wallop contends:

1. It is hypocritical to single out South Africa for punishment when other countries with worse records on human rights are granted most-favored-nation trade status.
2. South Africa is already in the process of dismantling some of the worst features of apartheid.
3. Blacks will be hurt the most by economic sanctions.

NOTE

1. Stuart Auerbach, "Sullivan Abandons South African Code," *Washington Post*, June 4, 1987, p. E4.

Is It Wise for the United States to Use Economic Sanctions against South Africa?

CHRISTOPHER J. DODD
The Case for Sanctions

I think we are all aware of the fact that there is a worsening national emergency in South Africa. No one would question that or doubt that. Recently expanded security laws have granted the South African police and military sweeping powers to use force against groups and individuals. Since the current state of emergency was imposed, some 160 people have been killed and over 4,000 detained. During preceding months, the earlier state of emergency brought some 900 deaths and 8,000 arrests before it ended. There is a level of violence, pain, and death in South Africa today which is intolerable, and it is the violence, pain, and death of the apartheid system.

Apartheid is the highest expression of bigotry and of man's capacity to be indifferent to the fate of his fellow man. Under the apartheid system, blacks are stripped of fundamental civil and political liberties. Under the apartheid regime, blacks are told where they may live, where they may work, and with whom they may associate. And, under the law of apartheid, blacks are denied the right to own land or to hold citizenship in their country of birth. Mr. President, our contribution—no matter how indirect—to the maintenance of this repugnant system must come to an end. That is the principle upon which we must act here today, and that must be our goal.

Yet, even at this late date, the President's recent statements remind us that there are those who say that the blacks in South Africa can wait; that justice will come in its own time; that our strategic and geopolitical interests in the southern African region outweigh moral imperatives and political values; and that we in the United States ought to advise those who have been abused, exploited, and exiled to have faith in their oppressors' good intentions.

I reject such advice and counsel. I reject it because in good conscience we cannot ask the blacks of South Africa to wait any longer. I reject it because we know the South African Government is determined to perpetuate its system of racial injustice and to feed off the suffering and misery that system imposes on the black majority of that country. Further, Mr. President, I reject it because we have something better to offer the people of South Africa than our investment dollars and our technological know-how.

With an historical record such as ours, Mr. President, replete with visionaries, revolutionaries, and radical reformers, I am frankly puzzled by the advice of these Americans who would place the United States among the patient and wishful, among the quiet and the passive who can only slow, but not stop, the march of progress in South Africa. Their thinking will no more benefit the blacks of South Africa than it would have benefited the blacks in this country, and those who marched in Selma and elsewhere at the head of the great civil rights movement that swept this country in the 1960's.

Recalling the events of that time, I would like to share with my colleagues the words of Dr. Martin Luther King, who during that particular period of strife penned a letter from his prison cell, which I think is particularly poignant in the debate we are sharing today. Dr. King wrote from that prison cell these words:

> Actually time is itself neutral. It can be used either destructively or constructively. More and more I feel that the people of ill-will have used time much more effectively than have the people of good will. We will have to repent in this generation not merely for the hateful words and actions of the bad people, but for the appalling silence of the good people.

Mr. President, we have a choice here today, and I think Dr. King frames that choice quite properly. It is a choice between looking the South African Government in the eye and saying "We will do everything in our power to impel you to accept the judgment of your own people and of the people in the world;" or embracing an insidious silence—a silence we know as the policy of "constructive engagement."

Let there be no doubts as to what such silence means. It means continuing to pump dollars, energy, and expertise into a racist, elitist economic system. It means continuing to finance an apparatus of repression and state violence. And it means placing our faith in Pretoria's dubious promises when our own history tells us radical change does not happen without the compelling force of those who will no longer tolerate their condition. And it is regrettable that the administration does not recognize its guilt in maintaining that silence, a silence which can only ally itself with the people of ill-will; which can only be the friend of exploitation, abuse, and inhumanity.

Mr. President, the administration does not begin its understanding of the South African tragedy with a recognition of the struggle of the oppressed against the oppressor. Rather, with an unbelievable turn of illogic, the administration has come to treat the South African Government and the policy of apartheid as separate entities—one as a trusted friend, the other as a manageable foe. And it is from such a judgment that emerges a policy both ineffective against apartheid and frankly, "nauseating" to many of that system's victims.

It is a policy not based on the moral outrage of the human compassion which should determine U.S. posture. Rather, it compares the benefits of order with the costs of disorder. It weights the profit of commerce against the price of change. And most disturbingly, it equates the fears of whites who stand to lose valuable property with the fears of blacks who face continuing generations of oppression, deprivation, and disenfranchisement.

It is a policy which is both immoral and unacceptable. The American people, the overwhelming majority of the American people, and our own consciences would have us do more today for the people of South Africa, and the measure before us is the way to do it. Keep in mind that the sanctions imposed by the President during the last year had meaningful impact. They had an impact on the pass laws, which have been abolished; on funding for black education, which has increased sevenfold in the last year; and on restrictions on private life such as the intermarriage laws, which now have been lifted, I would argue, because the President imposed sanctions a year ago.

I would like to believe, as I believe most of us would, that the South African Government made those changes because they thought it was right. But frankly, Mr. President, I do not believe that any more than any one else in this Chamber or in this country. The Pretoria regime made those changes because the President of the United States imposed a number of economic sanctions and that message got through.

Mr. President, it is time for another message, a stronger message that breaks and rejects that inexcusable silence the administration would have us maintain. That message is in the bill before us. This bill both incorporates the sanctions of the President's Executive order and extends their scope even further. But, it is important to note, it emphasizes specifically and meticulously those sanctions most detrimental to the white regime, not the overall South African economy. Thus, the bill prohibits the importation of articles produced by South African Government-owned or controlled organizations. It bars U.S. bank loans to the Pretoria government or any entity under its control. It forbids American companies from making any new investments in South Africa. And, Mr. President, it revokes United States landing rights of all South African airliners.

This bill, however, was nurtured not on hostility or hate but on hope. It sets goals for the South African Government which, if achieved, could earn back our trust and our respect. It requires among other things a lifting of the current state of emergency, the release of ANC [African National Congress] leader Nelson Mandela, and concrete steps toward the dismantling of the system of apartheid.

I sincerely hope these goals will be reached and reached soon. They would represent important steps in the right direction and signal the South African Government's willingness to change course and pursue the path toward reform.

But until that happens, Mr. President, it is incumbent upon us to pursue the course charted by the legislation before us. I urge my colleagues to give it their overwhelming support, and to impose strong sanctions on the Government of South Africa.

Is It Wise for the United States to Use Economic Sanctions against South Africa?

MALCOLM WALLOP
The Case against Sanctions

I wish that I could think that this was an exercise in anything but domestic racial politics. I have searched around for grounds on which I can justify the selective application of morality by those who support this legislation and ignore problems in the world far worse, looking for a compass that I think perhaps Congress can use in a desire to place its moral indignation on track.

If South Africa were a Communist nation, we would be granting it most favored nation trading status.

It is more than a little amusing—in fact, it is repugnant—to read the debate in the House of Representatives by those who voted for South African sanctions and see how they treat that repressive, repugnant country of Romania. A Communist country receives capitalist inducements to change its ways. Listen to Mr. Rostenkowski:

> The annual most favored nation renewal process has proved to be a highly effective lever in achieving the goals of increased emigration and has strengthened our hand in improving the human rights conditions for those thousands of Rumanians.

Curious that not sanctions but blessings flow on a Communist country that has a human rights record far more disgusting and repugnant than that of the regime we are looking at now.

I suggest . . . that what we are looking at is middle-class, comfortable white Senators playing up to the black population of America and the liberal population of America.

You can come to no other conclusion than that this is a racist proposition. It finds repugnance in the moral behavior of a white regime and so do I. It finds repugnance in apartheid and so do I. It finds repugnance in pass laws and discrimination on the basis of race, and so do I.

But it is silent on its repugnance to human rights violations far in excess of those which occur in South Africa. It seeks to go no further than one nation.

So the only conclusion that you can come to, this merry band of white legislators sitting here, is that if a white man does evil things to a black man, that is repugnant. And so it is. But if a white man does it to a white man, or a yellow man to a yellow man, or a black man to another black man, what else can you expect? Is that really what this Senate stands for? Apparently so, if you take a look at the vote that we exercised last year.

I asked this body last year to consider while it was seeking to impose sanctions on South Africa what it was we were doing. And to answer our own consciences as to whether what we were doing we really believed to be the right thing. There was then a lot of talk about standing up for human rights and for our principles, and the need to do something for the poor oppressed blacks of South Africa.

I asked the Senate, I asked all of us, to answer in our own consciences whether we had thought through whether sanctions against South Africa would in fact help anybody deserving of our help, and whether our imposing them would be a responsible assertion of the belief upon which our own political life is founded, that "all men are created equal."

Specifically, I asked if we were so outraged at the South African white suppression of blacks as to declare economic war upon them with the purpose of encouraging the overthrow of the regime, why do we then not declare economic war to seek to overthrow regimes that are by all responsible measures far worse than that of South Africa? Lest there be some doubt as to just where South Africa ranks among the modern world offenders against our principles that all men are created equal I mentioned that according to the State Department's Human Rights Bureau on the African continent only Botswana is a lesser violator. Only Botswana is a lesser violator and yet where are we postured?—on the backs of a regime that has a court that found its country in violation of its own laws and sought to change it. Peculiar how simple our arrogance becomes.

Anyone willing to challenge that would have to argue that Ethiopia's international starvation of millions of its own is preferable to South Africa or that Egypt's persecution of its Coptic Christians is preferable to South Africa or that Nigeria's hungry found the solution to the Biafran problem preferable to South Africa, or that Zimbabwe's North Korean trained and led killer battalions let loose on Matabeleland is preferable to South Africa, or that Tanzania's forced collectivization farming that has cost untold lives is preferable to South Africa, or that Mozambique's human rights practices are preferable to South Africa, and that black Africa's most enlightened leaders have treated the East Indian minorities better than those terrible white South Africans have.

Indeed, I asked any of my colleagues that care to argue that black Africa's most enlightened rulers, not to speak of their worst, have treated nonruling black tribes, tribes that are not their own, better than those terrible South African whites have treated all blacks.

I asked earnestly if anyone cared to make such arguments and no one would. Perhaps some of my colleagues who have shown stern and impassioned faces to the cameras on South Africa will care to make any of the arguments that I just mentioned. But I doubt that they are any more ready today than they were last year, even with television in the Senate. Any such argument this year or last would have to confront a question that just about every American understands. If South Africa is so much worse than the other countries of Africa, so bad as to justify economic war meant to make it like those other countries, why then are hundreds of thousands of blacks walking hundreds and even thousands of miles just to get into that terrible land?

Why is there no mass migration of blacks out of South Africa and into the likes of black-ruled Africa? Be careful, my colleagues. Be careful. Do not denigrate these peoples' yearning for the basics of life. They want safety. They want work. They want shelter. They want freedom from oppressors, for oppression is made no lighter by their dark skins.

If you denigrate these basic concerns, our constituents, who remember their immigrant fathers and grandmothers, will know us as liberals who hid an inhuman social agenda behind fancy words. Last year no one was able to take up this challenge, or willing. Is anyone willing this afternoon, this morning, or before we are done? Apparently not. The argument embarrasses.

Last year I asked those burning with moral furor against South Africa why they did not place on their list of countries marked for economic war and international auspices not just South Africa, but also every country whose human record is equal to or worse than South Africa's, or that commit terrorism against Americans. The biggest and worst offender against human rights, of course, is the Soviet Union. Without doubt, the Soviet Union is also doing its very best to make the lives of every American poor and more precarious. And without doubt is it not curious that we sit here and impose economic sanctions on South Africa and ask them to release Nelson Mandela, yet remain silent about Dr. Sakharov, and subsidize shipments of grain to the Soviet Union? Where is the compass that points with moral passion against human rights? Where is it? Or is this, in fact, domestic racial politics at its worst?

It is inconceivable that South Africa could ever threaten us as the Soviet Union does. Why then spend our moral frenzy to try to bring down the lesser offender that does not threaten us? We smile at Mr. Gorbachev, and facilitate his acquisition of U.S. technology. We subsidize his American grain and offer him Western capital at rates below that which westerners can borrow money. You ask us to bargain our future with Mr. Gorbachev's tyrannical world, yet say to us that South Africa's strategic location and South Africa's strategic minerals can be comfortably foresworn to the Soviet bloc.

Questions for Discussion

1. How effective are economic sanctions against South Africa?
2. What would happen in South Africa if the current government would relin-

quish its power and the new political system were based on the principle of one person, one vote?
3. What criteria should determine whether the United States should use economic sanctions against another country?
4. How does the Soviet role in southern Africa affect your thinking about the use of U.S. economic sanctions in South Africa?
5. What role should the United States play in the internal affairs of other countries?

Suggested Readings

Becker, Charles M. "Economic Sanctions against South Africa." *World Politics*, 39, no. 2 (January 1987), 147–173.
Gosiger, Mary C. "Strategies for Divestment from United States Companies and Financial Institutions Doing Business with or in South Africa." *Human Rights Quarterly*, 8, no. 3 (August 1986), 517–539.
Karis, Thomas G. "South African Liberation: The Communist Factor." *Foreign Affairs*, 65, no. 2 (Winter 1986–1987), 267–287.
Laitin, David D. "South Africa: Violence, Myths, and Democratic Reform." *World Politics*, 39, no. 2 (January 1987), 258–279.
Massing, Michael. "The Business of Fighting Apartheid." *Atlantic*, 259, no. 2 (February 1987), 26–32.
Relly, Gavin. "The Costs of Disinvestment." *Foreign Policy*, no. 63 (Summer 1986), 131–146.
U.S. Cong., House of Representatives. *Anti-Apartheid Act of 1986.* Hearing before the Subcommittee on Financial Institutions Supervision, Regulation and Insurance of the Committee on Banking, Finance and Urban Affairs, 99th Cong., 2nd Sess., 1986.
U.S. Cong., Senate. *The Anti-Apartheid Act of 1986.* Hearing before the Subcommittee on International Finance and Monetary Policy of the Committee on Banking, Housing, and Urban Affairs, 99th Cong., 2nd Sess., 1986.
———. *Situation in South Africa.* Hearings before the Committee on Foreign Relations, 99th Cong., 2nd Sess., 1986.
Waldorf, Lars. "After the Pullout." *New Republic*, 195, no. 26 (December 29, 1986), 14–16.
Williams, Oliver F. *The Apartheid Crisis: How We Can Do Justice in a Land of Violence.* New York: Harper & Row, 1986.

Contributors

HERBERT M. LEVINE taught political science at the University of Southwestern Louisiana for twenty years. He has written and edited several political science textbooks, including Political Issues Debated *(1987) and* World Politics Debated *(1989). He is currently a writer who lives in Chevy Chase, Maryland.*

BEN H. BAGDIKIAN is Dean, Graduate School of Journalism, University of California at Berkeley.

RYAN J. BARILLEAUX is an assistant professor of political science at Miami University, Ohio. He is the author of *The Post-Modern Presidency* (1988) and *The President and Foreign Affairs: Evaluation, Performance and Power* (1985).

CLYDE BROWN is assistant professor of political science at Miami University, Ohio. He managed congressional campaigns and worked as a staff member in the U.S. House of Representatives.

COMMITTEE ON CIVIL RIGHTS OF THE ASSOCIATION OF THE BAR OF THE CITY OF NEW YORK is a professional group of attorneys.

COMMITTEE ON THE CONSTITUTIONAL SYSTEM is a nonpartisan, nonprofit organization devoted to the study and analysis of the U.S. constitutional system.

WILLIAM CROTTY is professor of political science at Northwestern University.

CHRISTOPHER J. DODD, a Democrat, is a U.S. senator from Connecticut.

DINESH D'SOUZA is senior domestic policy analyst at the White House. He has also been managing editor of *Policy Review,* a publication of the Heritage Foundation.

EDWARD JAY EPSTEIN is the author of *News from Nowhere: Television and the News* (1974) and *Between Fact and Fiction: The Problem of Journalism* (1975).

JOSEPH J. FANELLI is president of the Business-Industry Political Action Committee.

DANIEL P. FRANKLIN is an assistant professor at Colgate University. He is currently doing research and writing on the legislative veto and the limits of presidential prerogative.

CHARLES T. GOODSELL is professor of public administration and policy at Virginia Polytechnic Institute and State University.

COLIN S. GRAY is president of the National Institute for Public Policy. He is author of numerous books on military strategy, including *Nuclear Strategy and National Style* (1986).

MARK GREEN is president of the Democracy Project on Campaign Reform. He was head of Congress Watch, a consumer lobby, in the 1970s. He is the author of *Who Runs Congress?* (1984).

ROBERT B. HAWKINS, JR., is the chair of the Advisory Commission on Intergovernmental Relations. He is president and chief executive officer of the Institute for Contemporary Studies in San Francisco.

JOHN E. JACOB is president of the National Urban League.

JOSEF JOFFE is foreign editor and columnist of the *Suddeutsche Zeitung* in Munich.

XANDRA KAYDEN is a member of the Campaign Finance Study Group at the Institute of Politics, Harvard University. She is the author of *Campaign Organization* (1978).

EDWARD I. KOCH is the mayor of New York City.

MELVYN KRAUSS is professor of economics at New York University and a senior fellow at the Hoover Institution.

SUSAN S. LEDERMAN is associate professor of political science at Kean College.

GLENN C. LOURY is professor of political economy at the Kennedy School of Government, Harvard University.

THURGOOD MARSHALL is an associate justice of the U.S. Supreme Court.

MICHAEL MASSING is a writer in New York. He is a contributing editor of the *Columbia Journalism Review* and a past executive editor of that publication.

EDDIE MAYE, JR., a former deputy chair of the Republican National Committee, is a political consultant.

MICHAEL MCCGWIRE is a senior fellow in the Foreign Policy Studies program at the Brookings Institution.

MICHAEL NELSON is associate professor of political science at Vanderbilt University. He is a former contributing editor of the *Washington Monthly*.

PHILIP PERLMUTTER is a writer living in Newton, Massachusetts. His articles have appeared in the *Boston Globe, Christian Science Monitor, Commentary*, and *Christian Century*.

GERALD M. POMPER is professor of political science and director of the Eagleton Institute's Center on Political Parties at Rutgers University.

ROBERT PREVIDI has held different posts in the banking industry, including senior vice-president–marketing at the European-American Bank.

WILLIAM PROXMIRE, a Democrat, served as a U.S. Senator from Wisconsin from 1957 until 1988.

HOWARD L. REITER is associate professor of political science at the University of Connecticut.

WILLIAM BRADFORD REYNOLDS served as counselor to the attorney general and assistant attorney general in the Civil Rights Division of the Justice Department in the Reagan administration.

JOSEPH P. RILEY, JR., is mayor of Charleston, South Carolina, and has served as a member of the Advisory Commission on Intergovernmental Relations.

RICHARD A. SNYDER, a former state senator of Pennsylvania, is of counsel to Barley, Snyder, Cooper & Barber, in Lancaster, Pennsylvania.

LUTHER M. SWYGERT, who died in 1988, was senior judge, U.S. Court of appeals for the Seventh Circuit.

MALCOLM WALLOP, a Republican, is a U.S. senator from Wyoming.

DOROTHY WICKENDEN is managing editor of the *New Republic*.

MALCOLM RICHARD WILKEY is U.S. ambassador to Uruguay. He served as a judge, U.S. Court of Appeals for the District of Columbia, from 1970 to 1985.

JUAN WILLIAMS is national correspondent for the *Washington Post*. He is the author of *Eyes on the Prize: America's Civil Rights Years, 1954–1965* (1987).

JAMES Q. WILSON is Collins Professor of Management at the University of California at Los Angeles. He is the author of numerous books, including *Thinking about Crime* (1975).

Acknowledgments (continued from page iv)

"Does the Separation of Powers Still Work?" by James Q. Wilson. *Public Interest*, no. 86 (Winter 1987), 36–52. Reprinted by permission of the copyright holder, James Q. Wilson.

"Turnbacks: A Promising Approach," by Robert B. Hawkins, Jr. *Intergovernmental Perspective*, 12, no. 3 (September 1986), 10–13. Sidebar has been omitted.

"Turnbacks: A Misguided Effort," by Joseph P. Riley, Jr. *Intergovernmental Perspective*, 12, no. 3 (September 1986), 14–16.

"Closed Doors: Benign Racism in America," by Juan Williams. *New Republic*, 195, no. 19 (November 10, 1986), 22, 24, 25. Reprinted by permission of the *New Republic*, © 1986, The New Republic, Inc.

"Fallacies of Evaluation," by Philip Perlmutter. *Lincoln Review*, 5, no. 3 (Winter 1985), 41–44. Reprinted by permission of The Lincoln Institute.

"The New Feminist Revolt," by Dinesh D'Souza. *Policy Review*, no. 35 (Winter 1986), 46–52. *Policy Review* is the flagship publication of The Heritage Foundation, 214 Massachusetts Ave., NE, Washington, D.C. 20002.

"What NOW? The Women's Movement Looks beyond 'Equality'," by Dorothy Wickenden. *New Republic*, 194, no. 18 (May 5, 1986), 19–21, 24–25. Reprinted by permission of the *New Republic*, © 1986, The New Republic, Inc.

"Elections and Democratic Politics," by Gerald M. Pomper and Susan S. Lederman. Reprinted by permission of the authors from Gerald M. Pomper with Susan S. Lederman, *Elections in America: Control and Influence in Democratic Politics*, 2nd ed. (New York: Longman, 1980), pp. 210–227. Tables have been renumbered.

"The Fallacy of Voting," by Howard L. Reiter. *Parties and Elections in Corporate America* (New York: St. Martin's Press, 1987), pp. 1–9. Notes have been renumbered. Copyright © 1987 by St. Martin's Press, Inc., and used with permission.

"The Case against Political Action Committees," by Mark Green. Prepared statement in U.S. Cong., Senate, *Proposed Amendments to the Federal Election Campaign Act of 1971*, Hearings before the Committee on Rules and Administration, 99th Cong., 2nd Sess., 1986, pp. 190–193.

"The Case for Political Action Committees," by Joseph J. Fanelli. Prepared statement in U.S. Cong., Senate, *Proposed Amendments to the Federal Election Campaign Act of 1971*, Hearings before the Committee on Rules and Administration, 99th Cong., 2nd Sess., 1986, pp. 304–308.

"A Concluding Note on Political Parties and the Future," by William Crotty. *American Parties in Decline*, 2nd ed. (Boston: Little, Brown, 1984), pp. 275–283. Copyright © 1984 by William Crotty. Reprinted by permission of Scott, Foresman/Little, Brown College Division.

"The Case for Resurgence," by Xandra Kayden and Eddie Maye, Jr. *The Party Goes On: The Persistence of the Two-Party System in the United States* (New York: Basic Books, 1985), pp. 87–93. Notes have been renumbered. Copyright © 1985 by Xandra Kayden and Eddie Maye, Jr. Reprinted by permission of Basic Books, Inc., Publishers.

"Can We Trust the Big Media?" by Richard A. Snyder. "Can We Trust the Big Media? Is Our News Free of Bias?" speech to the Hershey Rotary Club, Hershey, Pennsylvania, November 5, 1984, printed in *Vital Speeches of the Day*, 51, no. 6 (January 1, 1985), 171–175. Reprinted by permission of the author, former State Senator Richard A. Snyder.

"A Liberal Media Elite?" by Michael Massing. Statement in *A Liberal Media Elite?* ed. Nick Thimmesch (Washington, D.C.: American Enterprise Institute for Public Policy Research, 1985), 17–20. Reprinted with permission.

"Is the President Too Powerful in Foreign Affairs?" by Daniel P. Franklin. Copyright © 1988 by Daniel P. Franklin. Printed by permission of the author. This article has been specially written for *Point-Counterpoint*.

"Seeing Presidential Power Clearly," by Ryan J. Barilleaux. Copyright © 1988 by Ryan J. Barilleaux. Printed by permission of the author. This article has been specially written for *Point-Counterpoint*.

"Rejoinder," by Daniel P. Franklin. Copyright © 1988 by Daniel P. Franklin. Printed by permission of the author. This rejoinder has been specially written for *Point-Counterpoint*.

"Rejoinder," by Ryan J. Barilleaux. Copyright © 1988 by Ryan J. Barilleaux. Printed by permission of the author. This rejoinder has been specially written for *Point-Counterpoint*.

"Why Do We Limit the Democratic Process Only When It Comes to the Presidency?" by Robert Previdi. *Presidential Studies Quarterly*, 14, no. 1 (Winter 1984), 132–133.

Permission is granted by the Center for the Study of the Presidency, publisher of *Presidential Studies Quarterly*.

"Myth of the Day: Repeal of the Twenty-Second Amendment Is a Good Idea," by William Proxmire. *Congressional Record*, 132, no. 33 (October 1, 1986), S14371–S14372.

"Congress, Politics, and the Public Interest," by Clyde Brown. Copyright © 1988 by Clyde Brown. Printed by permission of the author. This article has been specially written for *Point-Counterpoint*.

"Congress and the Public Interest," by Ryan J. Barilleaux. Copyright © 1988 by Ryan J. Barilleaux. Printed by permission of the author. This article has been specially written for *Point-Counterpoint*.

"Bureaucracy: The Biggest Crisis of All," by Michael Nelson. *Washington Monthly*, 9, no. 11 (January 1978), 51–59. Reprinted with permission from the *Washington Monthly*. Copyright by the Washington Monthly Co., 1711 Connecticut Avenue, NW, Washington, D.C. 20009. (202) 462-0128.

"The Case for Bureaucracy: A Brief," by Charles T. Goodsell. *The Case for Bureaucracy: A Public Administration Polemic*, 2nd ed. (Chatham, N.J.: Chatham House, 1985), pp. 139–143. Reprinted with permission.

"In Defense of Judicial Activism," by Luther W. Swygert. *Valparaiso Univ. Law Review*, 16, no. 3 (Spring 1982), 439–458. All notes have been omitted, except note one. Reprinted with permission of *Valparaiso University Law Review*. Copyright © 1982 by *Valparaiso University Law Review*. All rights reserved.

"Judicial Activism, Congressional Abdication, and the Need for Constitutional Reform," by Malcolm Richard Wilkey. *Harvard Journal of Law and Public Policy*, 8, no. 3 (Summer 1985), 503–524. Notes have been omitted.

"The Government and Social Problems," by John E. Jacob. "The Government and Social Problems: Hope, Accomplishment, Food, Training and Jobs," speech at the Sixth Annual Oliver C. Cox Lecture Series, John F. Kennedy School of Government, Harvard University, Cambridge, Massachusetts, May 1, 1986, printed in *Vital Speeches of the Day*, 52, no. 18 (June 15, 1986), 540–544. Reprinted by permission of the author.

"Internally Directed Action for Black Community Development: The Next Frontier for 'The Movement'," by Glenn C. Loury. *Review of Black Political Economy*, 13, nos. 1–2 (Summer–Fall 1984), 31–46. Reprinted by permission of Transaction, Inc. Copyright © 1984 by Transaction, Inc.

"The Death Penalty," by the Committee on Civil Rights of the Association of the Bar of the City of New York. *Record of the Association of the Bar of the City of New York*, 39, no. 5 (October 1984), 419–425. Notes have been omitted. Reprinted with permission.

"Death and Justice," by Edward I. Koch. "Death and Justice: How Capital Punishment Affirms Life," *New Republic*, 192, no. 15 (April 15, 1985), 12–15. Reprinted by permission of the *New Republic*, © 1986, The New Republic, Inc.

"Terrorism: What Should We Do?" by Edward Jay Epstein. *This World*, no. 12 (Fall 1985), 43–44. Copyright © 1985 by The Rockford Institute. Reprinted with permission.

"Terrorism and the Media," by Ben H. Bagdikian. Prepared statement in U.S. Cong., House of Representatives, *The Media, Diplomacy, and Terrorism in the Middle East*, Hearing before the Subcommittee on Europe and the Middle East of the Committee on Foreign Affairs, 99th Cong., 1st Sess., 1985, pp. 20–21.

"Why the Soviets Are Serious about Arms Control," by Michael MccGwire. *Brookings Review*, 5, no. 2 (Spring 1987), 10–19. Sidebars have been omitted.

"Nuclear Delusions," by Colin S. Gray. "Nuclear Delusions: Six Arms Control Fallacies," *Policy Review*, no. 37 (Summer 1986), 48–53. *Policy Review* is the flagship publication of The Heritage Foundation, 214 Massachusetts Ave., NE, Washington, D.C. 20002.

"The U.S. and NATO: Should the Troops Stay?" by Melvyn Krauss. Speech during "The Heritage Lectures," reprinted in "The U.S. and NATO: Should the Troops Stay?" ed. W. Bruce Weinrod, *The Heritage Lectures*, no. 118 (1987), 2–5. The Heritage Foundation, 214 Massachusetts Ave., NE, Washington, D.C. 20002.

"The U.S. and NATO: Should the Troops Stay?" by Josef Joffe. Speech during "The Heritage Lectures," reprinted in "The U.S. and NATO: Should the Troops Stay?" ed. W. Bruce Weinrod, *The Heritage Lectures*, no. 118 (1987), 23–28. The Heritage Foundation, 214 Massachusetts Ave., NE, Washington, D.C. 20002.

"The Case for Sanctions," by Christopher J. Dodd. Speech to the Senate, printed in the *Congressional Record*, 132, no. 113 (August 14, 1986), S11649–S11650.

"The Case Against Sanctions," by Malcolm Wallop. Speech to the Senate, printed in the *Congressional Record*, 132, no. 113 (August 14, 1986), S11636–S11637.